*Gratitude

KOYOHARU GOTOUGE

Hello! I'm Gotouge. Here's volume 14! It's an honor to see a *Demon Slayer* anime, figures and other merch coming out. It's entirely thanks to everyone who supports me. I get feedback from a variety of people, but when they tell me something is wonderful or impressive, I think their attitudes and sensibilities are incredible. I'm grateful from the bottom of my heart that such people pick up my book.

DEMON SLAYER:
KIMETSU NO YAIBA
VOLUME 14
Shonen Jump Edition

Story and Art by
KOYOHARU GOTOUGE

TRANSLATION John Werry
ENGLISH ADAPTATION Stan!
TOUCH-UP ART & LETTERING John Hunt
DESIGN Jimmy Presler
EDITOR Mike Montesa

Printed in the U.S.A

Published by VIZ Media, LLC
P.O. Box 77010
San Francisco, CA 94107

10 9 8 7 6 5 4 3 2 1
First printing, July 2020

RATED T TEEN
ratings.viz.com

PARENTAL ADVISORY
DEMON SLAYER: KIMETSU NO YAIBA is rated T for Teen and recommended for ages 13 and up. This volume contains realistic and fantasy violence.

VIZ MEDIA
viz.com

SHONEN JUMP
shonenjump.com

DEMON SLAYER
KIMETSU NO YAIBA

14

THE MU OF MUICHIRO

KOYOHARU
GOTOUGE

CHARACTERS

TANJIRO KAMADO

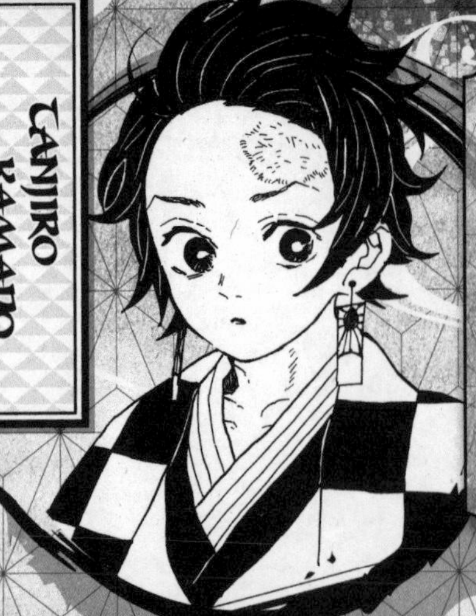

A kind boy who saved his sister and now aims to avenge his family. He can smell the scent of demons and an opponent's weakness.

NEZUKO KAMADO

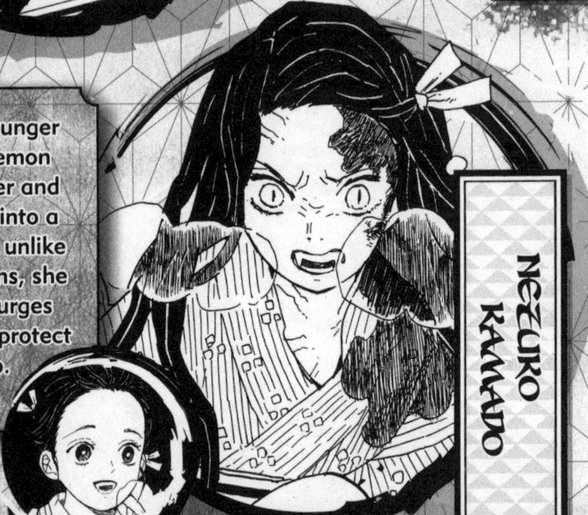

Tanjiro's younger sister. A demon attacked her and turned her into a demon. But unlike other demons, she fights her urges and tries to protect Tanjiro.

STORY

In Taisho-era Japan, young Tanjiro makes a living selling charcoal. One day, demons kill his family and turn his younger sister Nezuko into a demon. Tanjiro and Nezuko set out to find a way to return Nezuko to human form and defeat Kibutsuji, the demon who killed their family!

After joining the Demon Slayer Corps, Tanjiro meets Tamayo and Yushiro—demons who oppose Kibutsuji—who provide a clue to how Nezuko may regain her humanity. In search of a new katana, Tanjiro visits a hidden village of swordsmiths. But the upper-rank demons Hantengu and Gyokko infiltrate and attack the village. Together with Genya (who is also visiting the village), the Love Hashira Kanroji and the Mist Hashira Tokito, Tanjiro fights the demons, but the upper-rank demons are very strong!

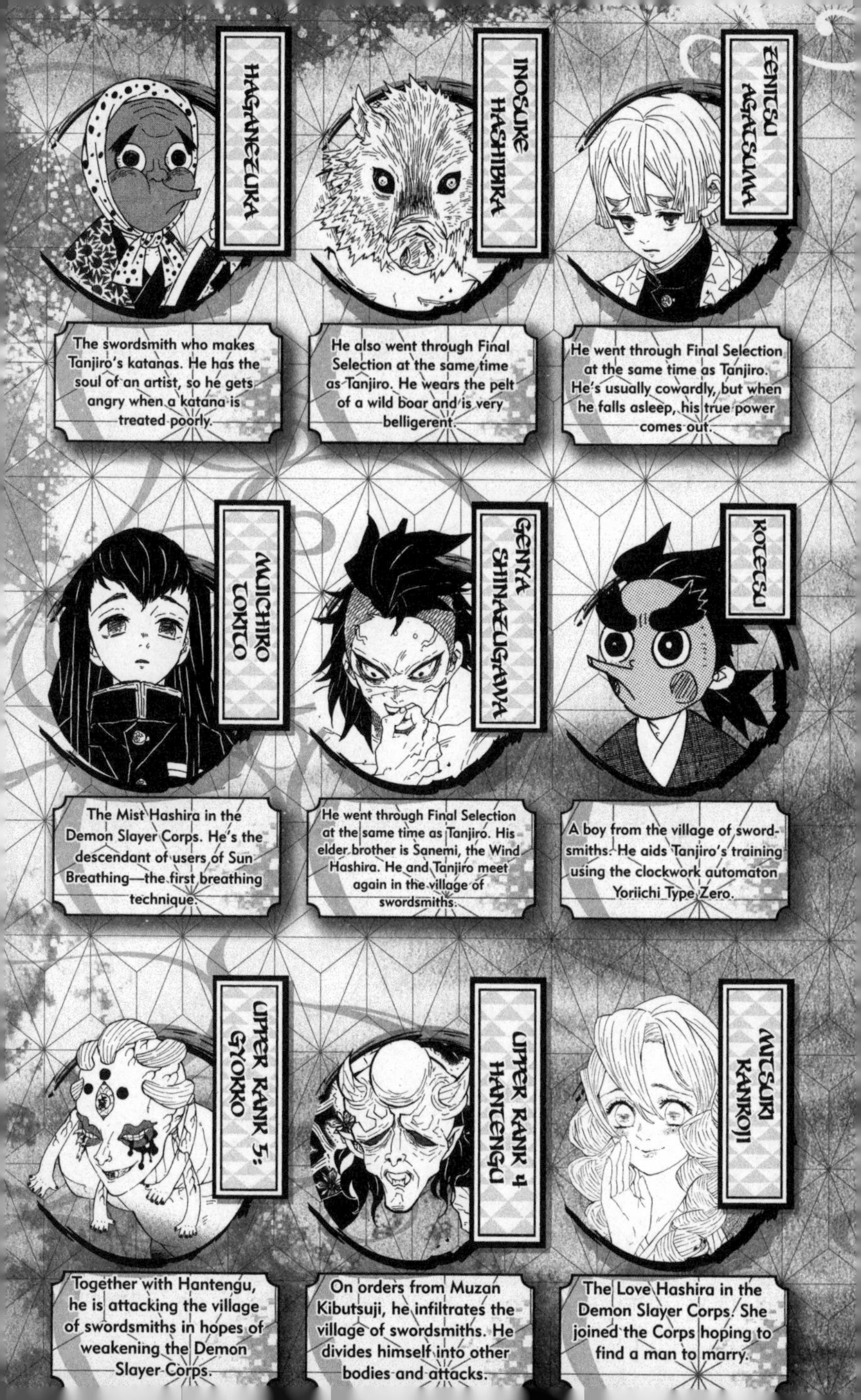
ZENITSU AGATSUMA
He went through Final Selection at the same time as Tanjiro. He's usually cowardly, but when he falls asleep, his true power comes out.
INOSUKE HASHIBIRA
He also went through Final Selection at the same time as Tanjiro. He wears the pelt of a wild boar and is very belligerent.
HAGANEZUKA
The swordsmith who makes Tanjiro's katanas. He has the soul of an artist, so he gets angry when a katana is treated poorly.
KOTETSU
A boy from the village of swordsmiths. He aids Tanjiro's training using the clockwork automaton Yoriichi Type Zero.
GENYA SHINAZUGAWA
He went through Final Selection at the same time as Tanjiro. His elder brother is Sanemi, the Wind Hashira. He and Tanjiro meet again in the village of swordsmiths.
MUICHIRO TOKITO
The Mist Hashira in the Demon Slayer Corps. He's the descendant of users of Sun Breathing—the first breathing technique.
MITSURI KANROJI
The Love Hashira in the Demon Slayer Corps. She joined the Corps hoping to find a man to marry.
UPPER RANK 4 HANTENGU
On orders from Muzan Kibutsuji, he infiltrates the village of swordsmiths. He divides himself into other bodies and attacks.
UPPER RANK 5: GYOKKO
Together with Hantengu, he is attacking the village of swordsmiths in hopes of weakening the Demon Slayer Corps.

CONTENTS

DEMON SLAYER

KIMETSU NO YAIBA

14

THE MU OF MUICHIRO

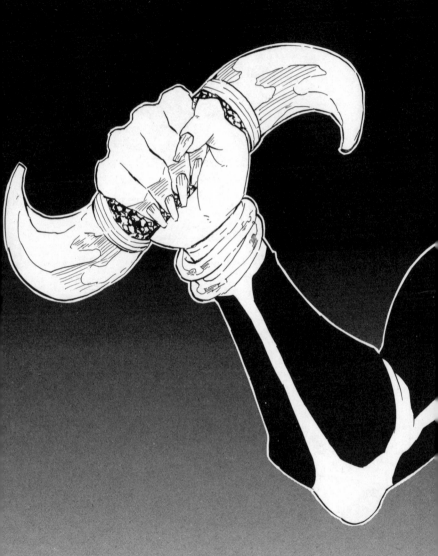

CHAPTER 116:
AWFUL VILLAIN

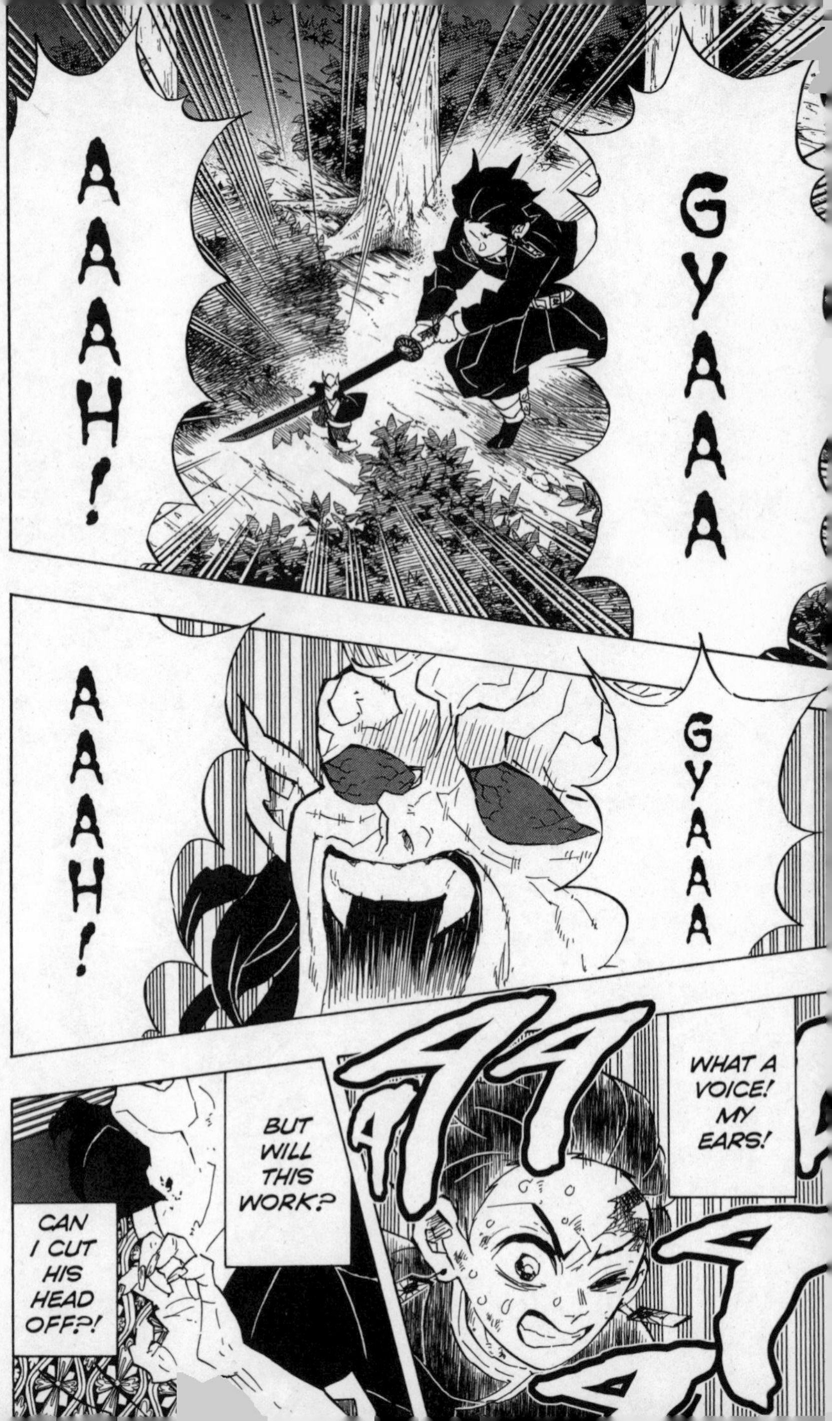
GYAAAA
AAAH!
GYAAA
AAAH!
WHAT A VOICE! MY EARS!
BUT WILL THIS WORK?
CAN I CUT HIS HEAD OFF?!

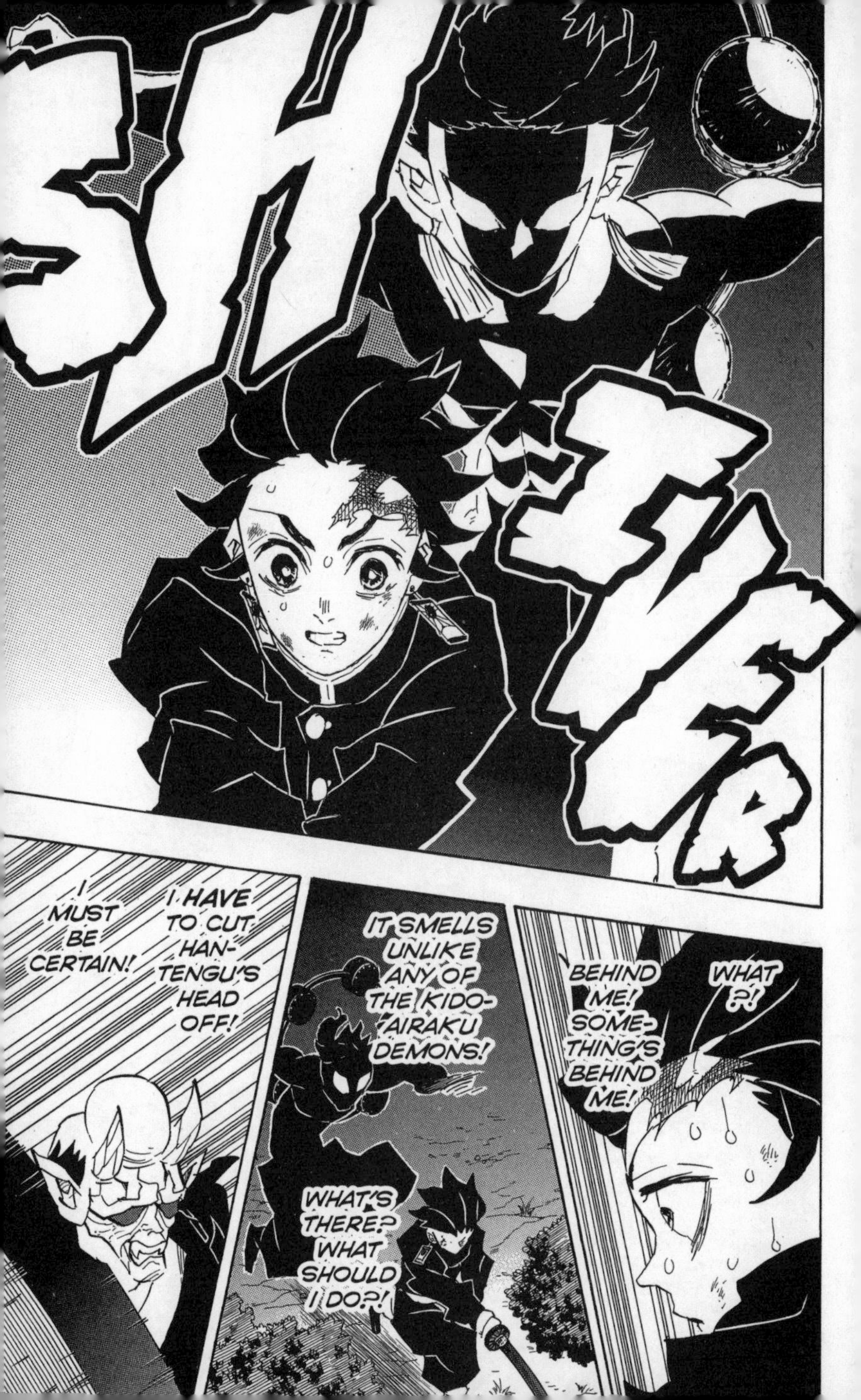
WHAT?!
BEHIND ME! SOMETHING'S BEHIND ME!
IT SMELLS UNLIKE ANY OF THE KIDO-AIRAKU DEMONS!
WHAT'S THERE? WHAT SHOULD I DO?!
I HAVE TO CUT HAN-TENGU'S HEAD OFF!
I MUST BE CERTAIN!

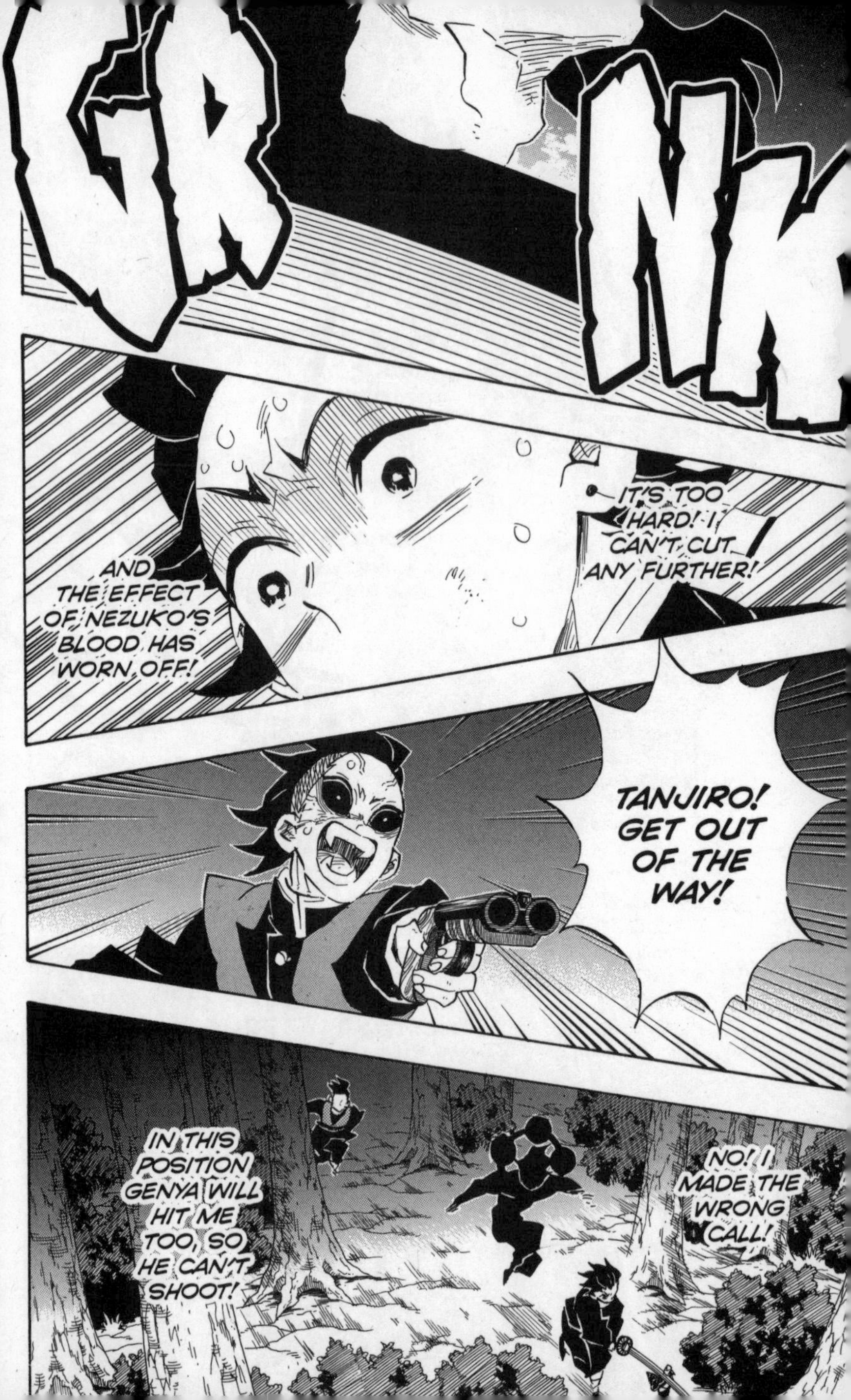
GRNK
IT'S TOO HARD! I CAN'T CUT ANY FURTHER!
AND THE EFFECT OF NEZUKO'S BLOOD HAS WORN OFF!
TANJIRO! GET OUT OF THE WAY!
NO! I MADE THE WRONG CALL!
IN THIS POSITION GENYA WILL HIT ME TOO, SO HE CAN'T SHOOT!

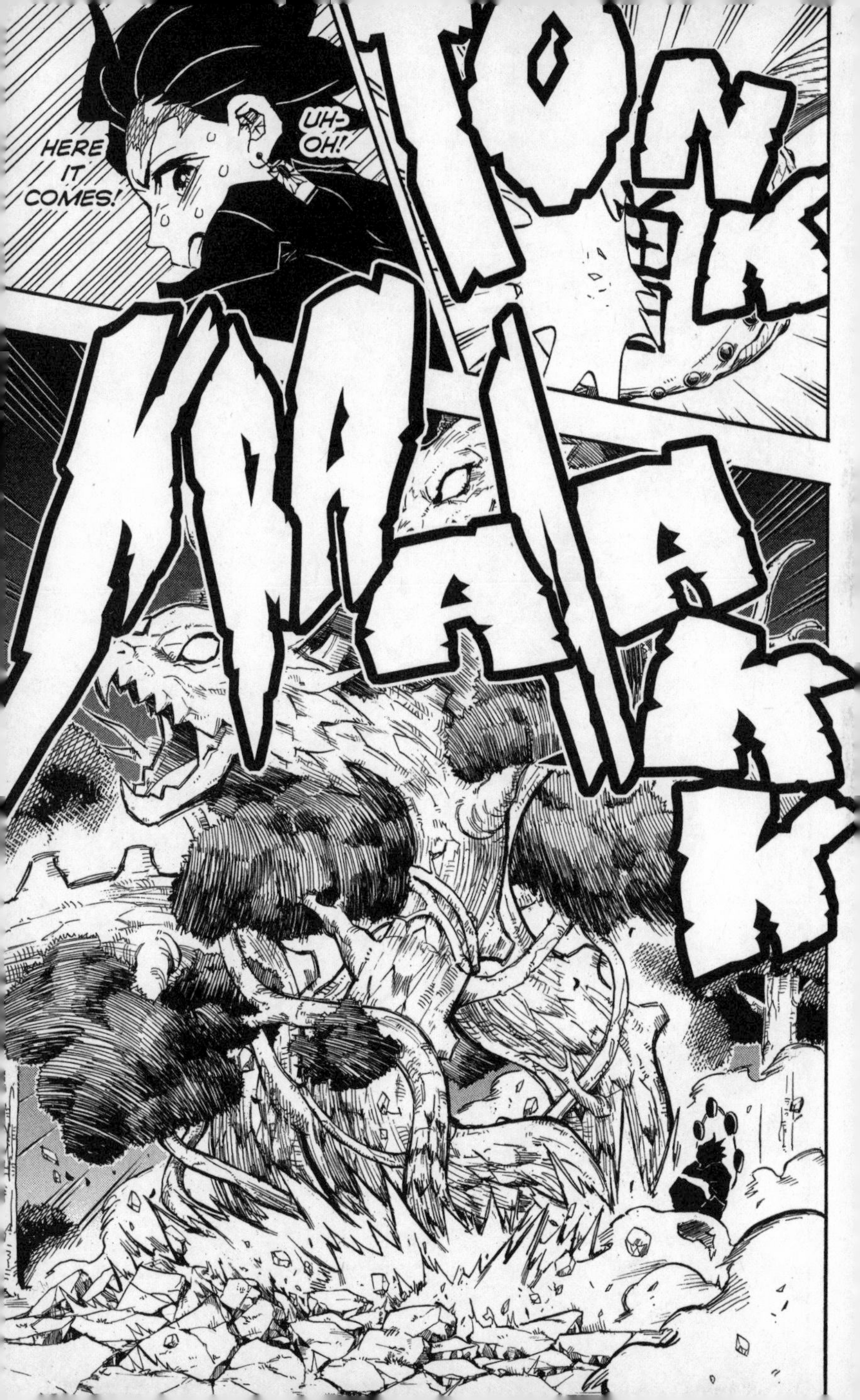
UH-OH!
HERE IT COMES!

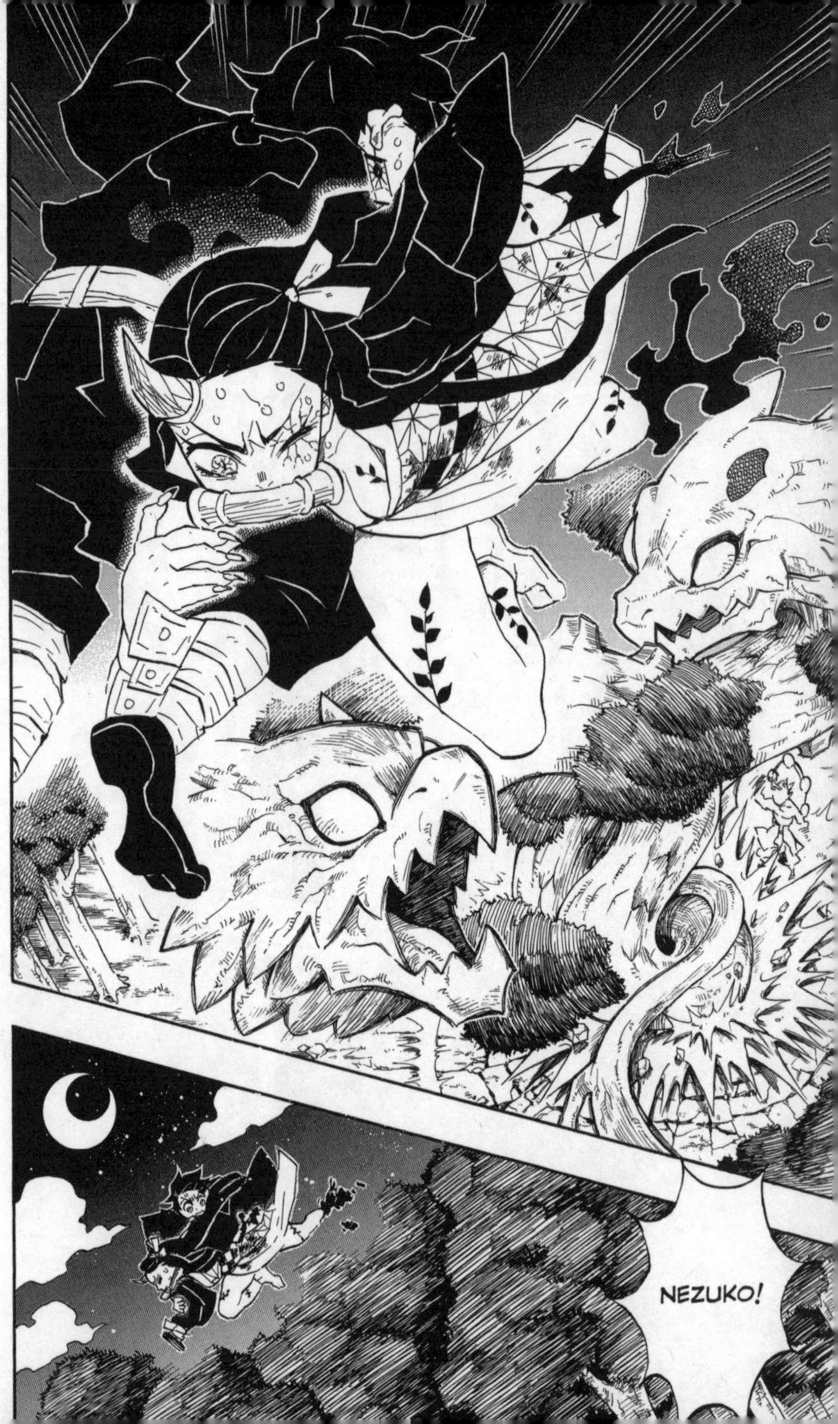
NEZUKO!

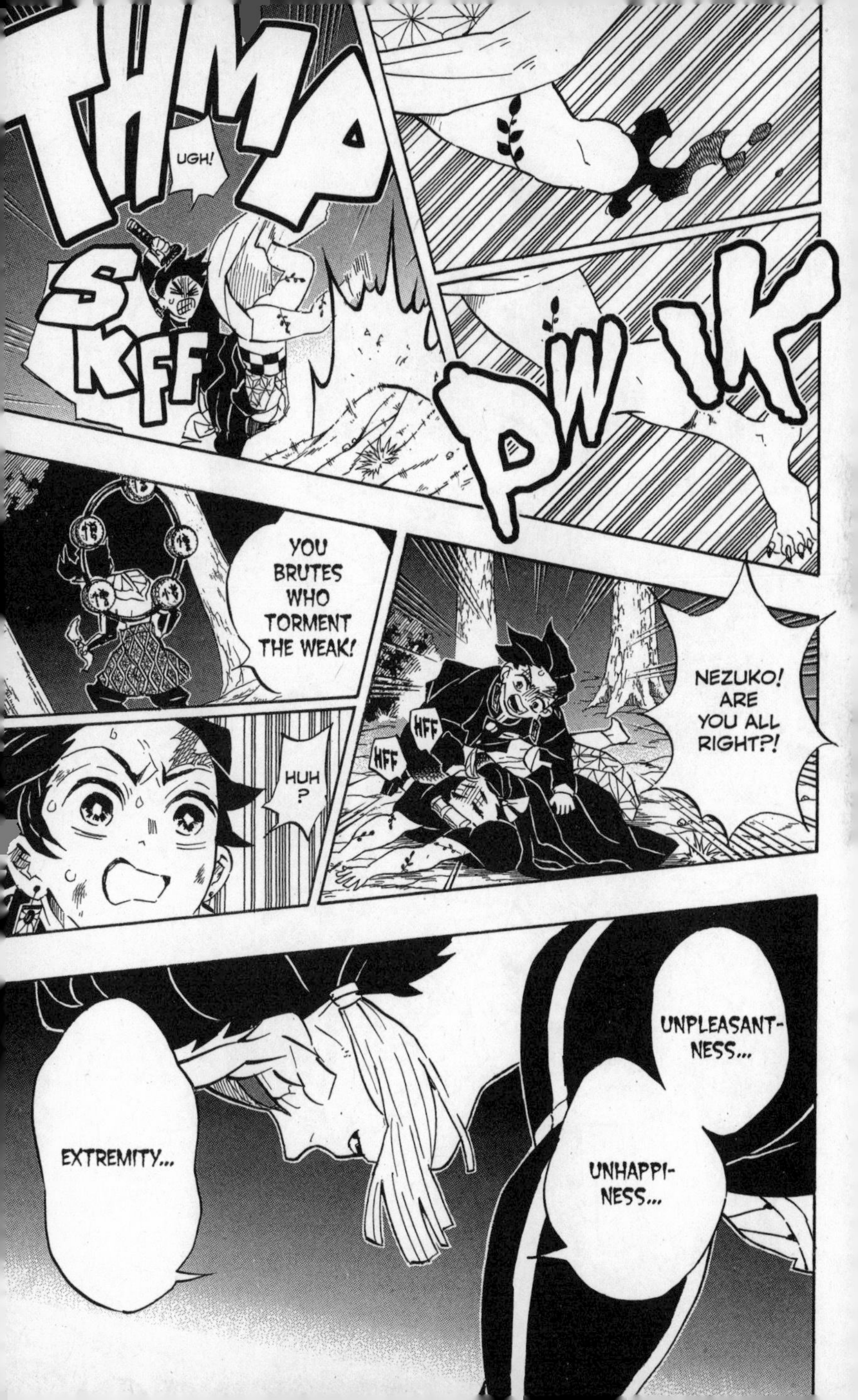
PWIK
THMP
UGH!
SKFF
NEZUKO! ARE YOU ALL RIGHT?!
HFF
HFF
YOU BRUTES WHO TORMENT THE WEAK!
HUH?
UNPLEASANT-NESS...
UNHAPPI-NESS...
EXTREMITY...

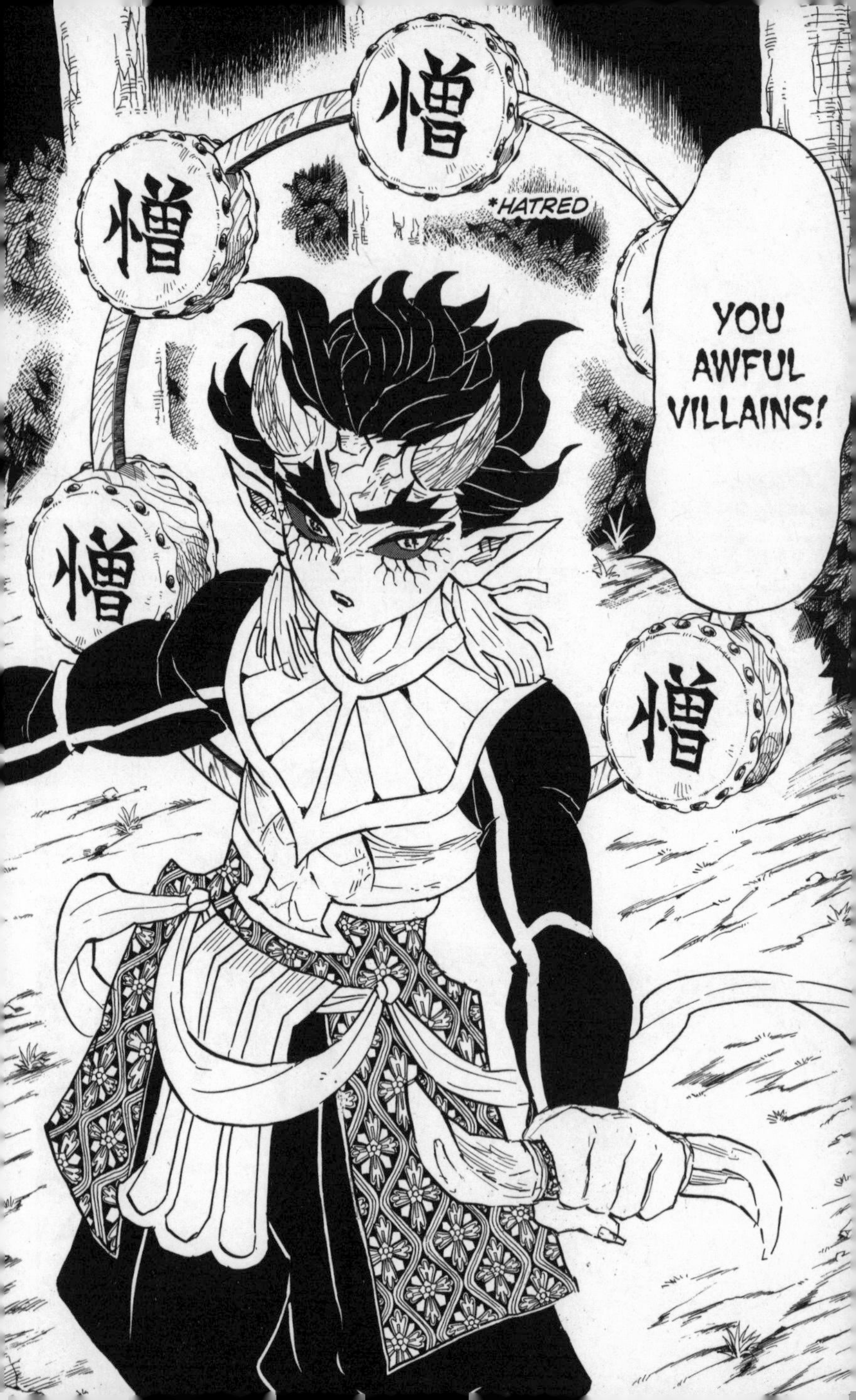
YOU AWFUL VILLAINS!
憎
*HATRED
憎
憎
憎

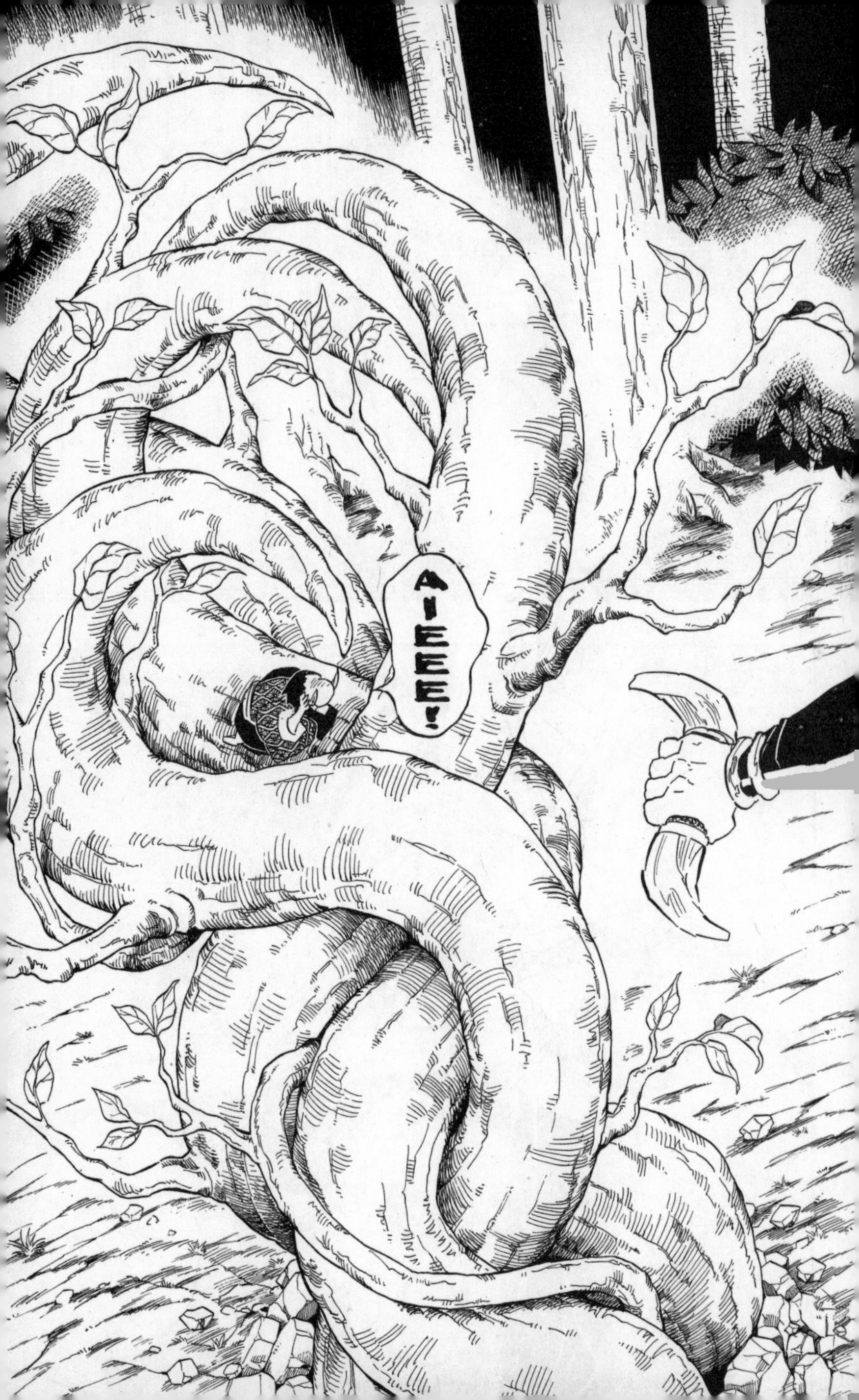
AIEEE!

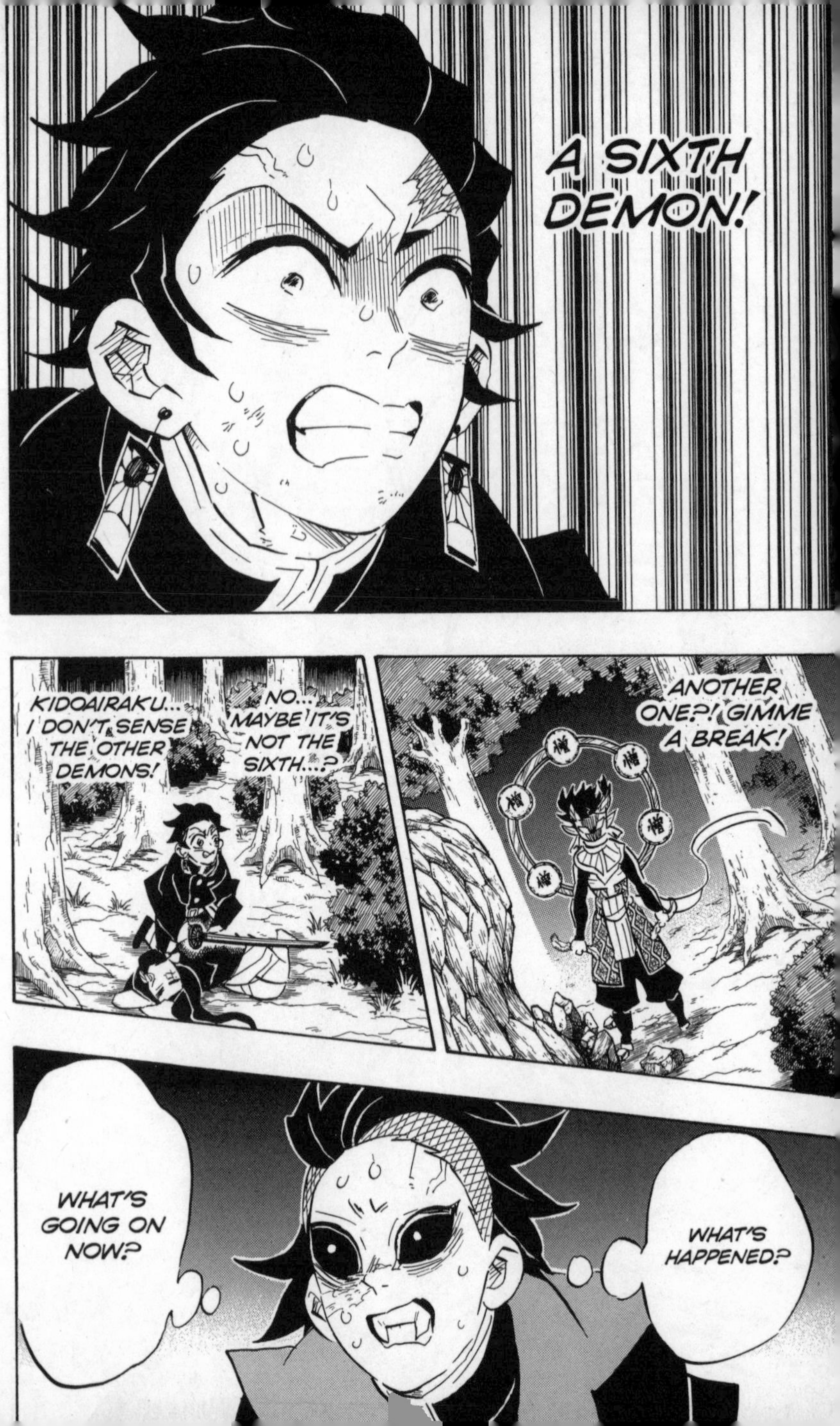
A SIXTH DEMON!
ANOTHER ONE?! GIMME A BREAK!
NO... MAYBE IT'S NOT THE SIXTH...?
KIDOAIRAKU... I DON'T SENSE THE OTHER DEMONS!
WHAT'S HAPPENED?
WHAT'S GOING ON NOW?

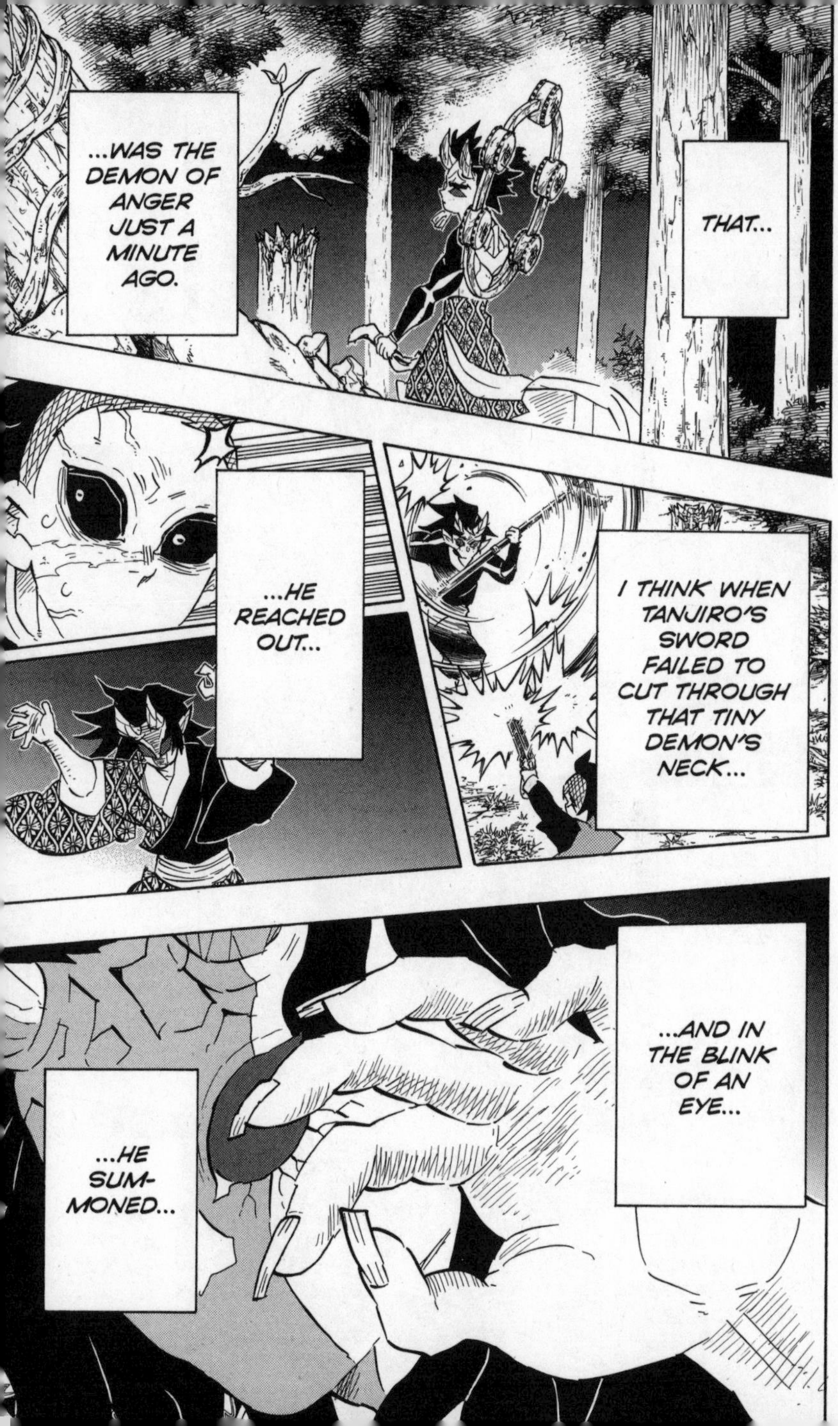
THAT...
...WAS THE DEMON OF ANGER JUST A MINUTE AGO.
I THINK WHEN TANJIRO'S SWORD FAILED TO CUT THROUGH THAT TINY DEMON'S NECK...
...HE REACHED OUT...
...AND IN THE BLINK OF AN EYE...
...HE SUMMONED...

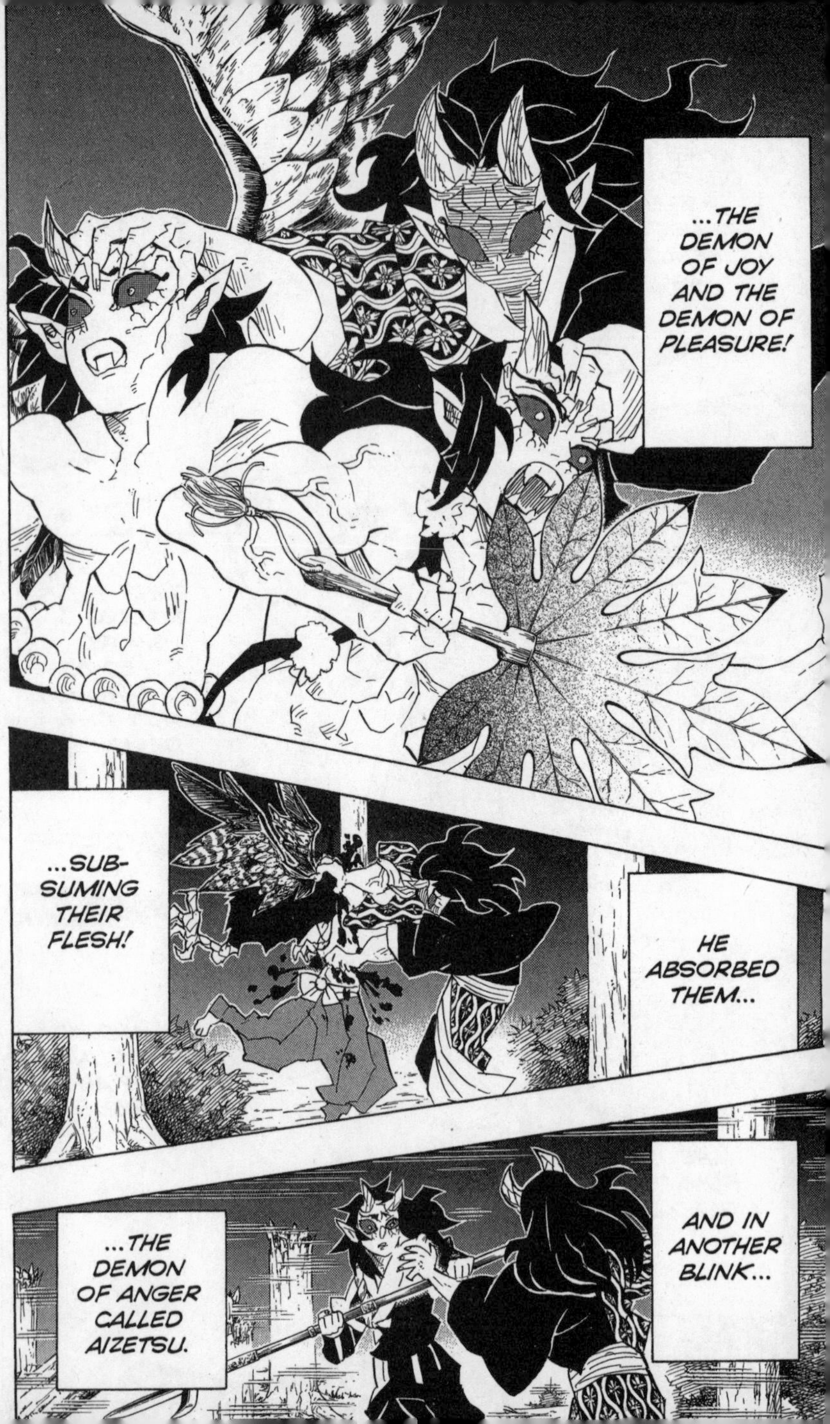
...THE DEMON OF JOY AND THE DEMON OF PLEASURE!
HE ABSORBED THEM...
...SUB-SUMING THEIR FLESH!
AND IN ANOTHER BLINK...
...THE DEMON OF ANGER CALLED AIZETSU.

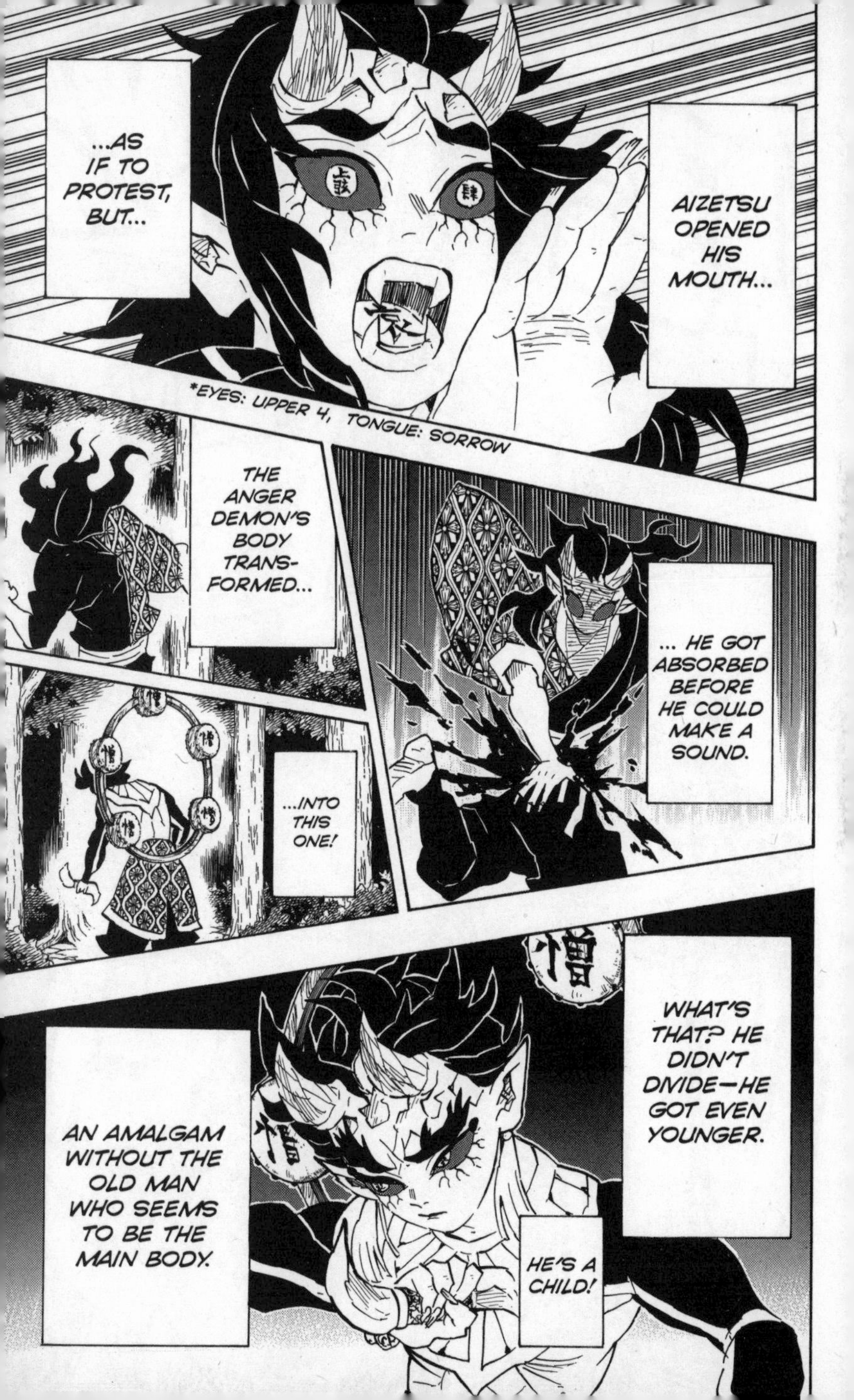
AIZETSU OPENED HIS MOUTH...
...AS IF TO PROTEST, BUT...
*EYES: UPPER 4, TONGUE: SORROW
... HE GOT ABSORBED BEFORE HE COULD MAKE A SOUND.
THE ANGER DEMON'S BODY TRANS-FORMED...
...INTO THIS ONE!
WHAT'S THAT? HE DIDN'T DIVIDE—HE GOT EVEN YOUNGER.
HE'S A CHILD!
AN AMALGAM WITHOUT THE OLD MAN WHO SEEMS TO BE THE MAIN BODY.

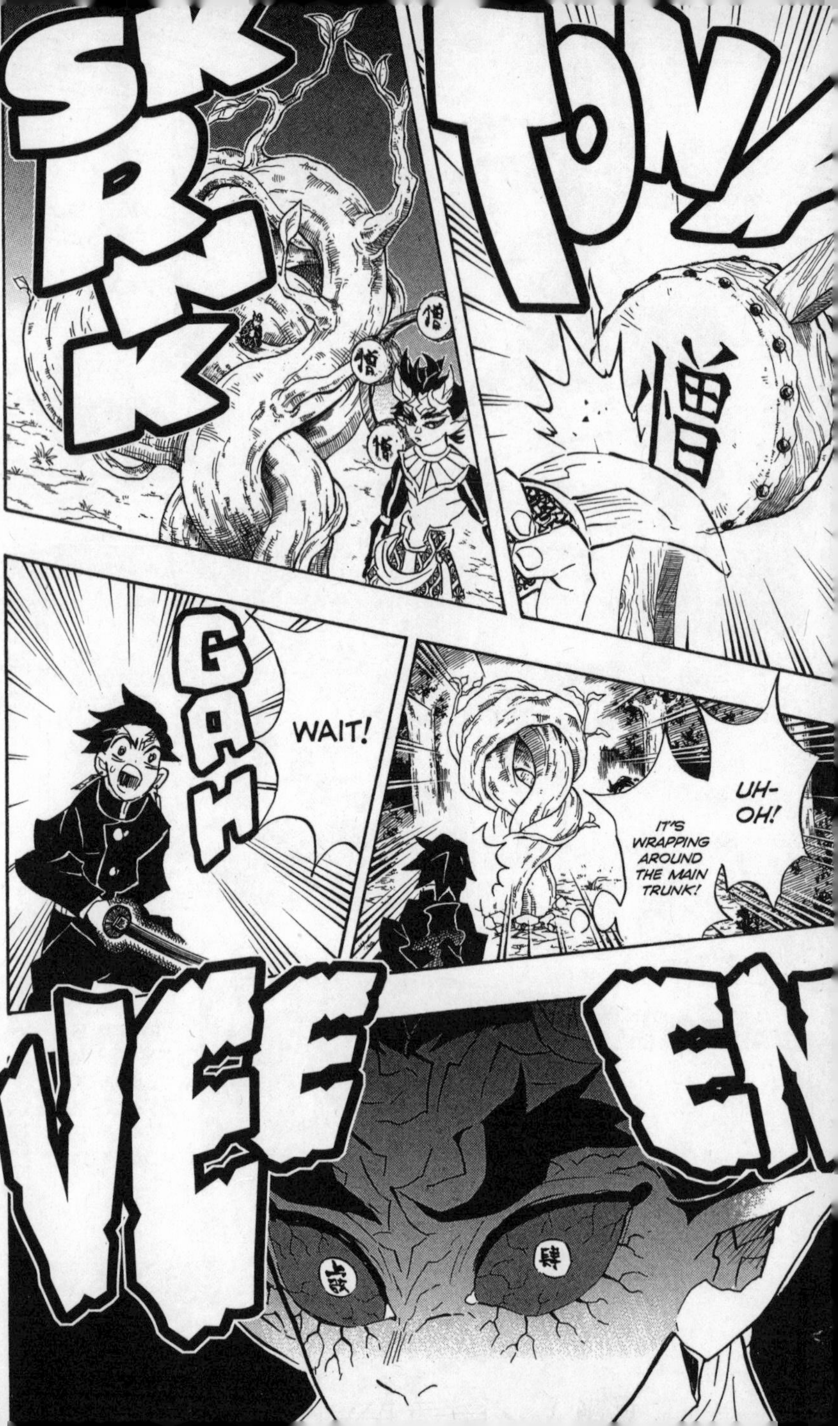
憎
UH-OH!
IT'S WRAPPING AROUND THE MAIN TRUNK!
WAIT!
GAH

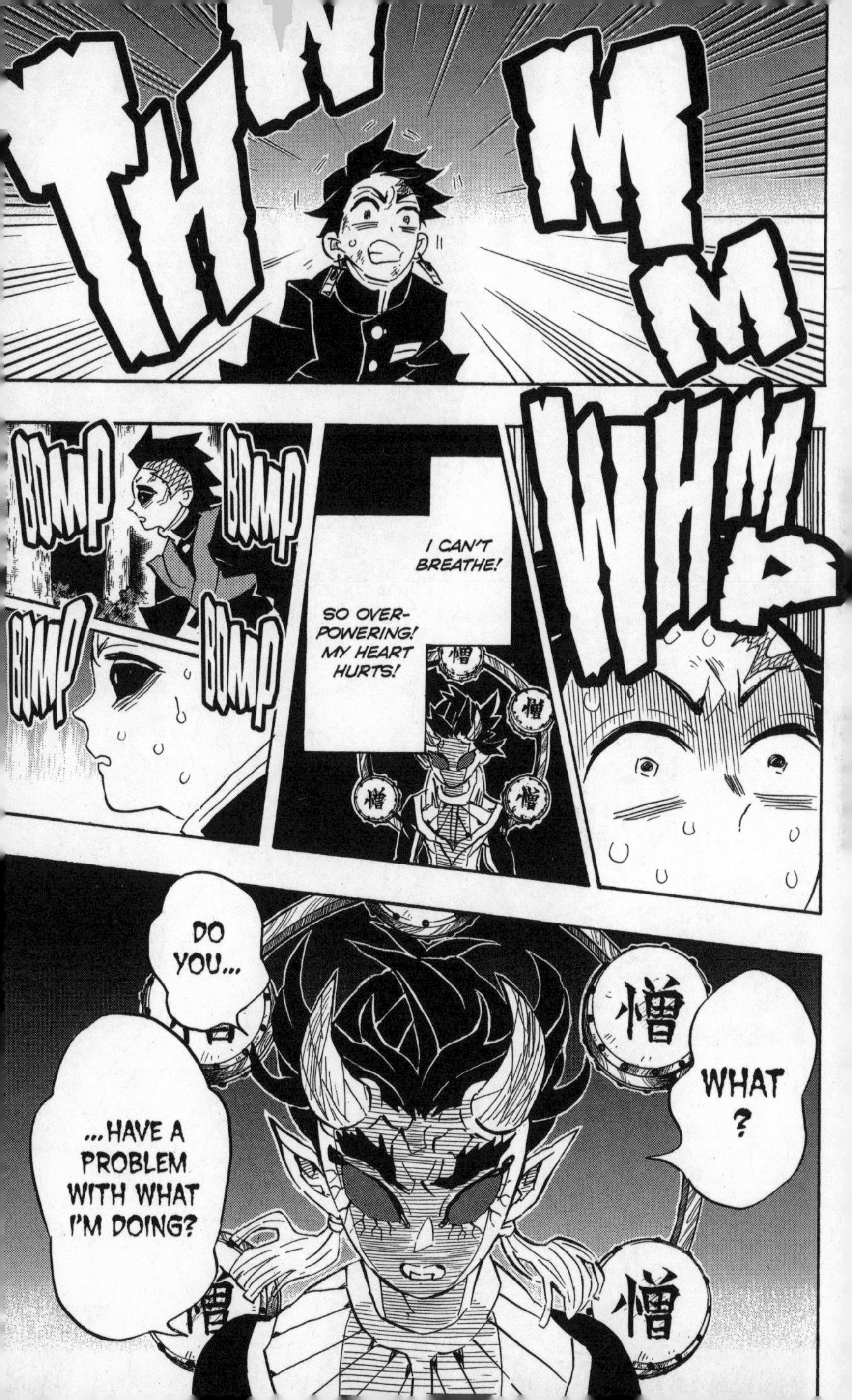
TH
MM
WHMP
I CAN'T BREATHE!
SO OVER-POWERING! MY HEART HURTS!
BOMP
BOMP
BOMP
BOMP
DO YOU...
WHAT?
...HAVE A PROBLEM WITH WHAT I'M DOING?

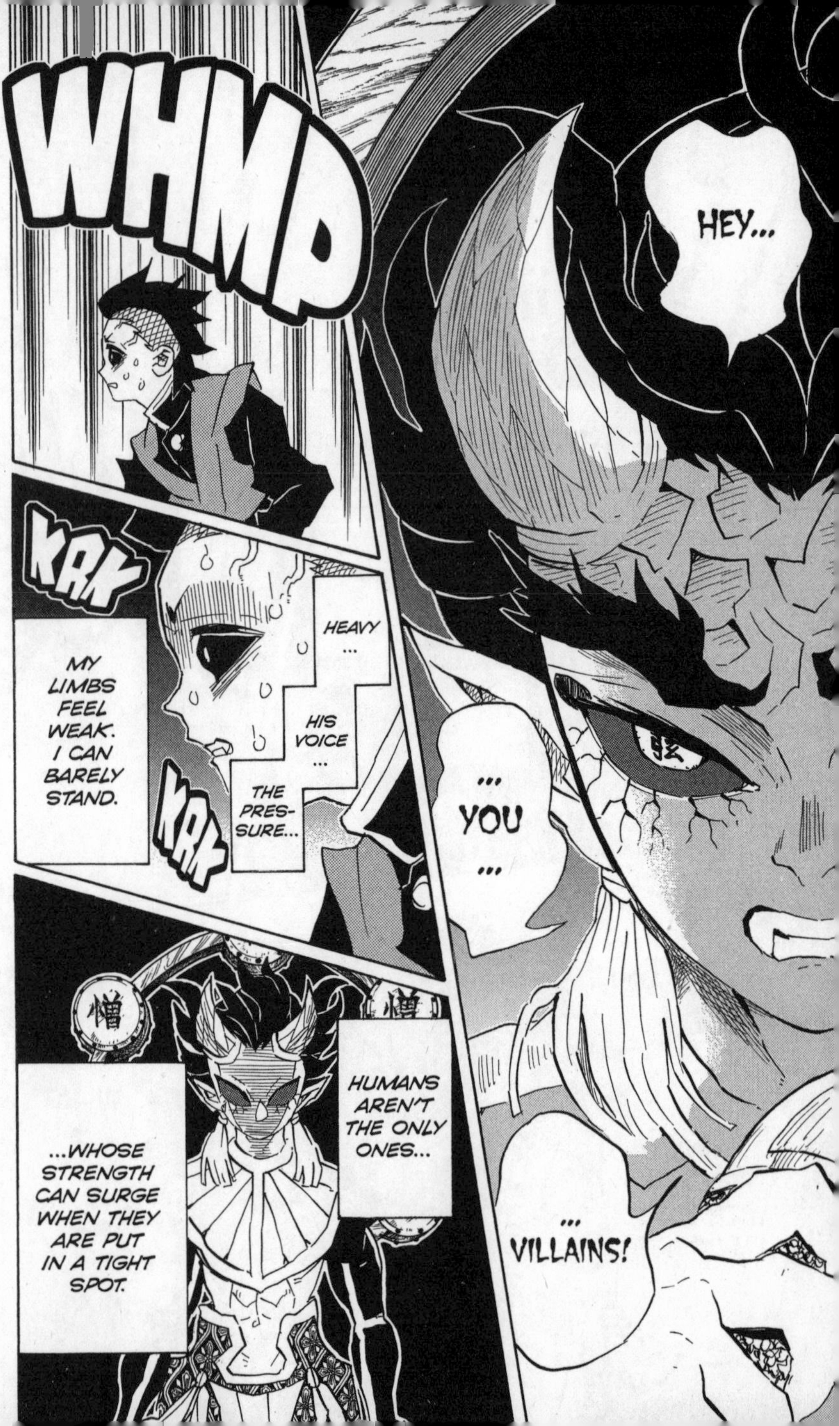
HEY...
... YOU ...
... VILLAINS!
WHMD
KRK
HEAVY ...
HIS VOICE ...
THE PRES-SURE...
KRK
MY LIMBS FEEL WEAK. I CAN BARELY STAND.
HUMANS AREN'T THE ONLY ONES...
...WHOSE STRENGTH CAN SURGE WHEN THEY ARE PUT IN A TIGHT SPOT.

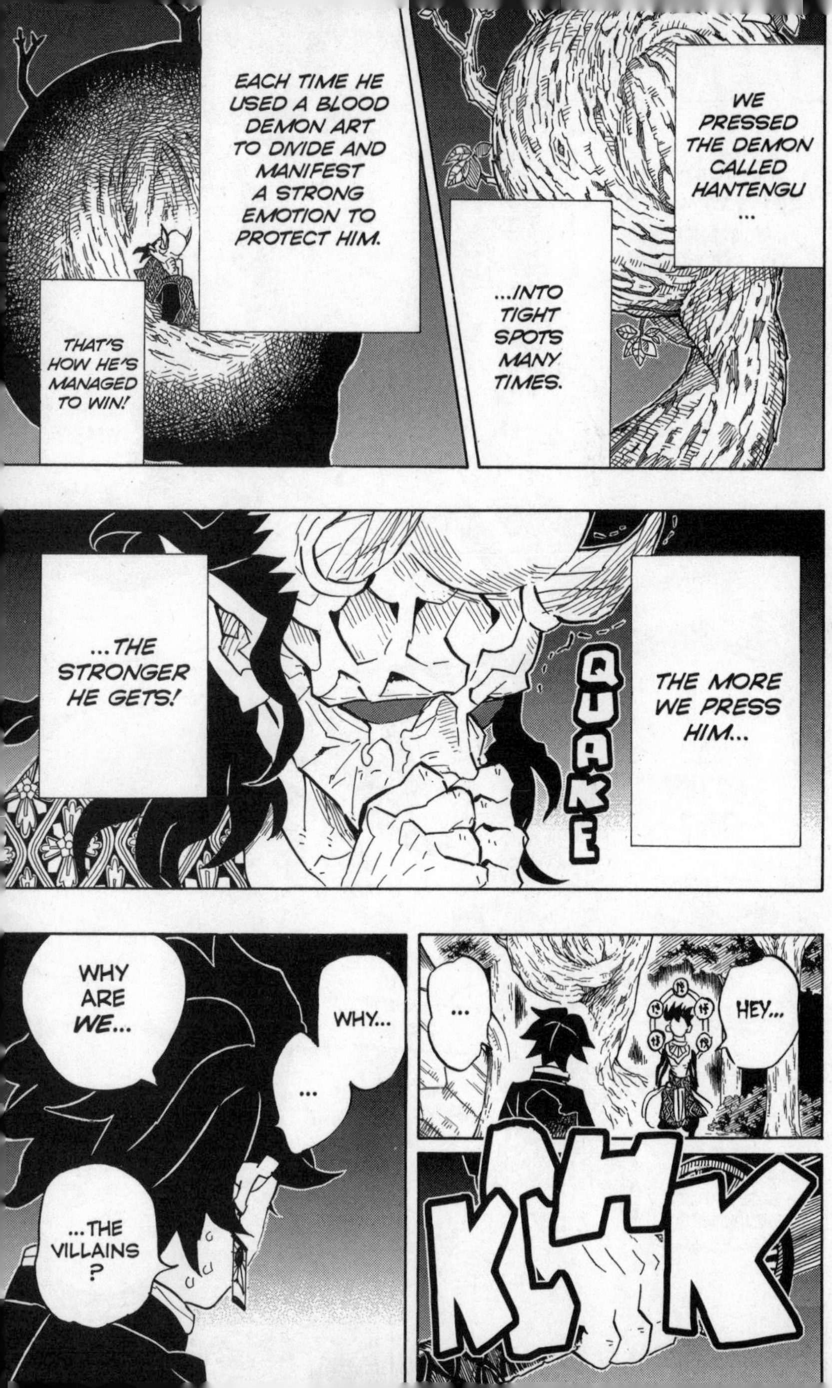
WE PRESSED THE DEMON CALLED HANTENGU ...
...INTO TIGHT SPOTS MANY TIMES.
EACH TIME HE USED A BLOOD DEMON ART TO DIVIDE AND MANIFEST A STRONG EMOTION TO PROTECT HIM.
THAT'S HOW HE'S MANAGED TO WIN!
THE MORE WE PRESS HIM...
QUAKE
...THE STRONGER HE GETS!
HEY...
...
KSHK
WHY...
...
WHY ARE WE...
...THE VILLAINS?

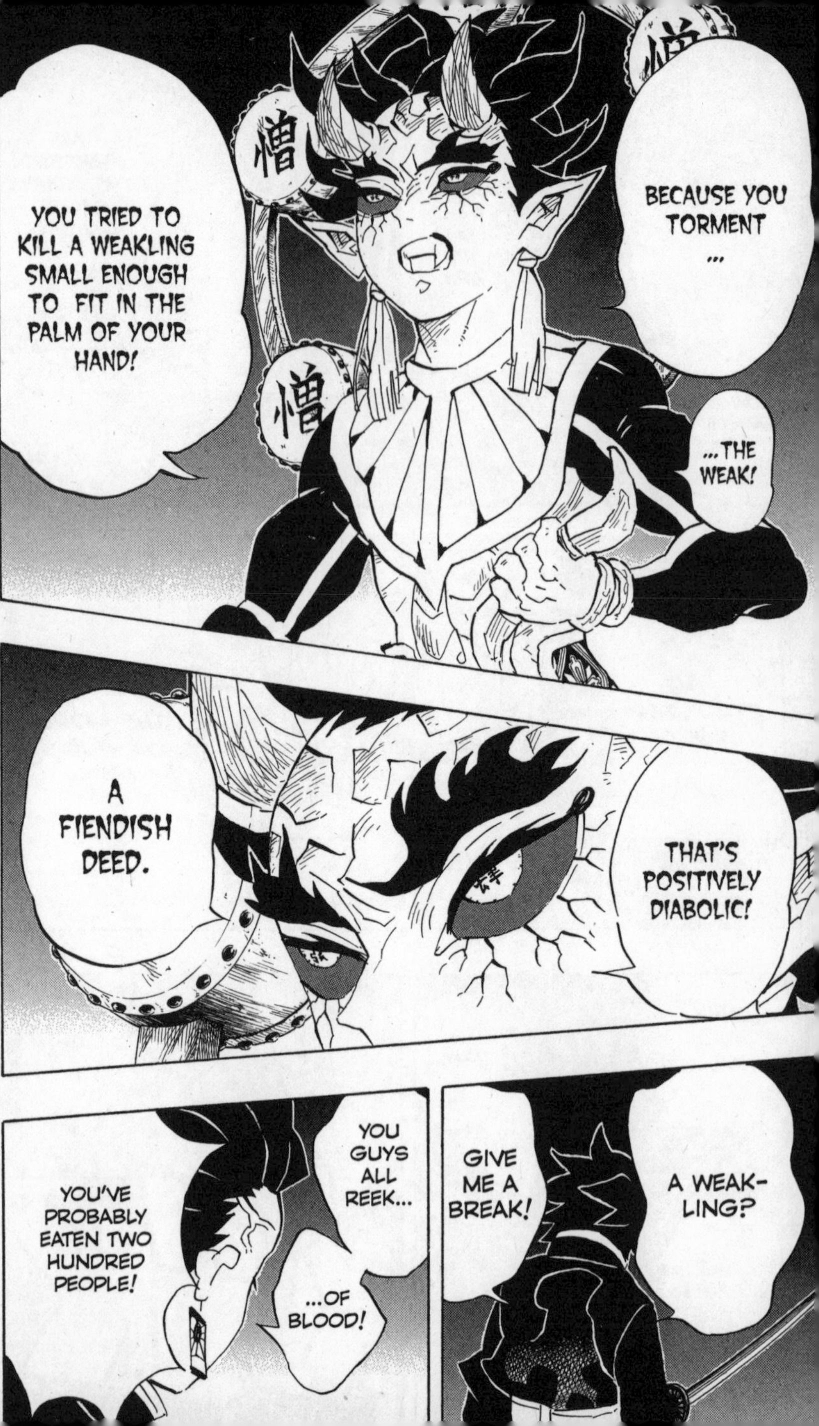
BECAUSE YOU TORMENT ...
...THE WEAK!
YOU TRIED TO KILL A WEAKLING SMALL ENOUGH TO FIT IN THE PALM OF YOUR HAND!
THAT'S POSITIVELY DIABOLIC!
A FIENDISH DEED.
A WEAK-LING?
GIVE ME A BREAK!
YOU GUYS ALL REEK...
...OF BLOOD!
YOU'VE PROBABLY EATEN TWO HUNDRED PEOPLE!

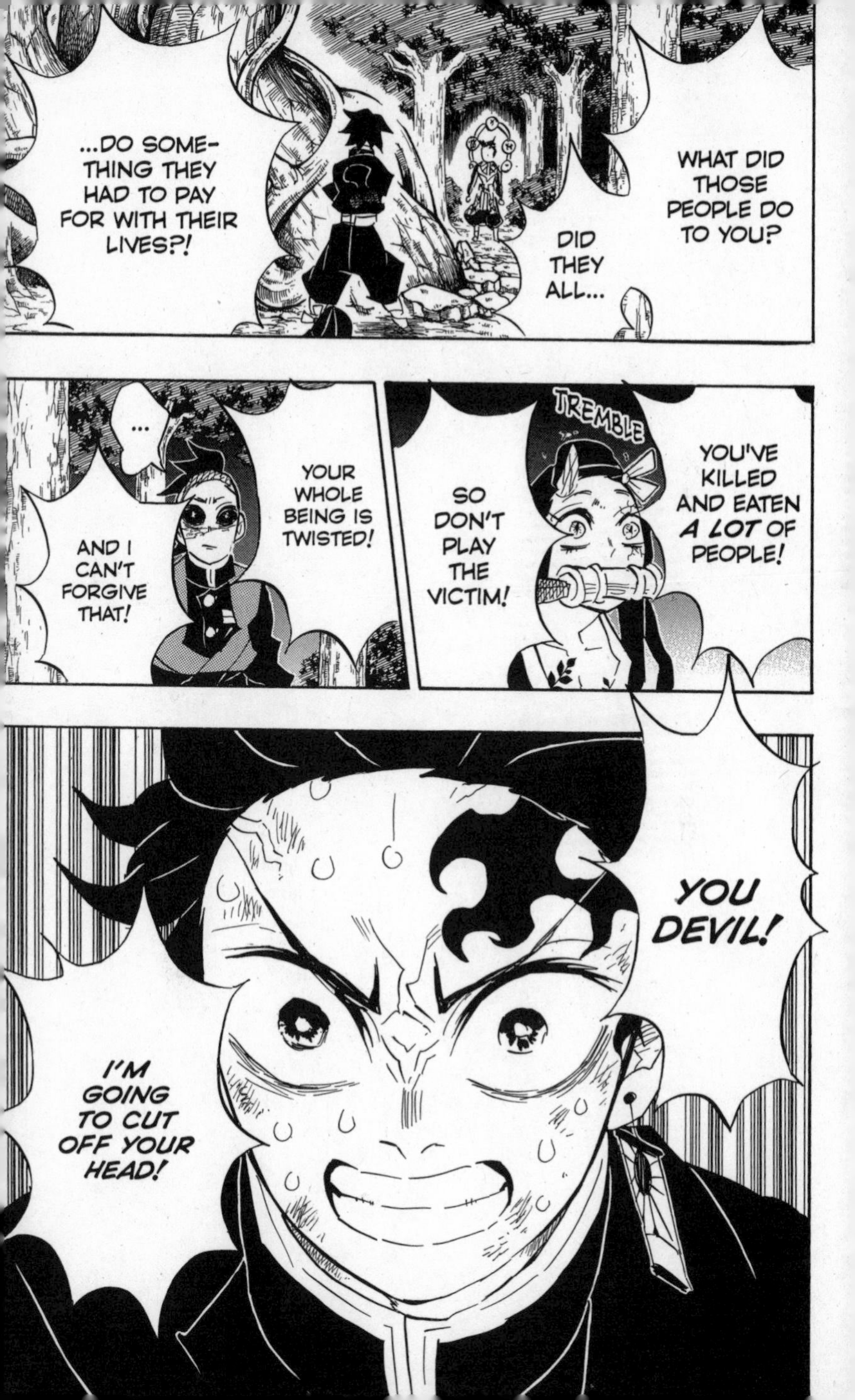
WHAT DID THOSE PEOPLE DO TO YOU?
DID THEY ALL...
...DO SOME-THING THEY HAD TO PAY FOR WITH THEIR LIVES?!
TREMBLE
YOU'VE KILLED AND EATEN *A LOT* OF PEOPLE!
SO DON'T PLAY THE VICTIM!
...
YOUR WHOLE BEING IS TWISTED!
AND I CAN'T FORGIVE THAT!
YOU DEVIL!
I'M GOING TO CUT OFF YOUR HEAD!

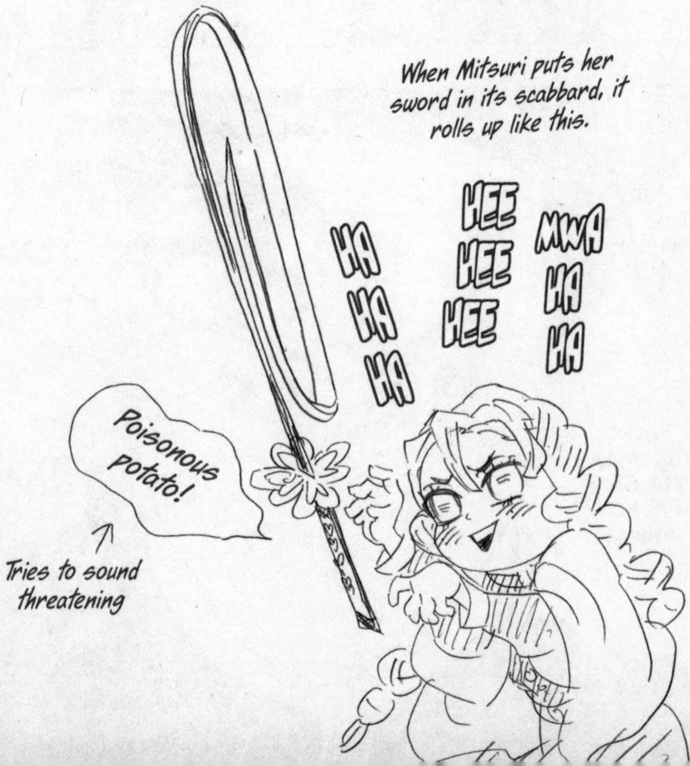

When Mitsuri puts her sword in its scabbard, it rolls up like this.
MWA HA HA
HEE HEE HEE
HA HA HA
Poisonous potato!
Tries to sound threatening

CHAPTER 117: SWORDSMITH

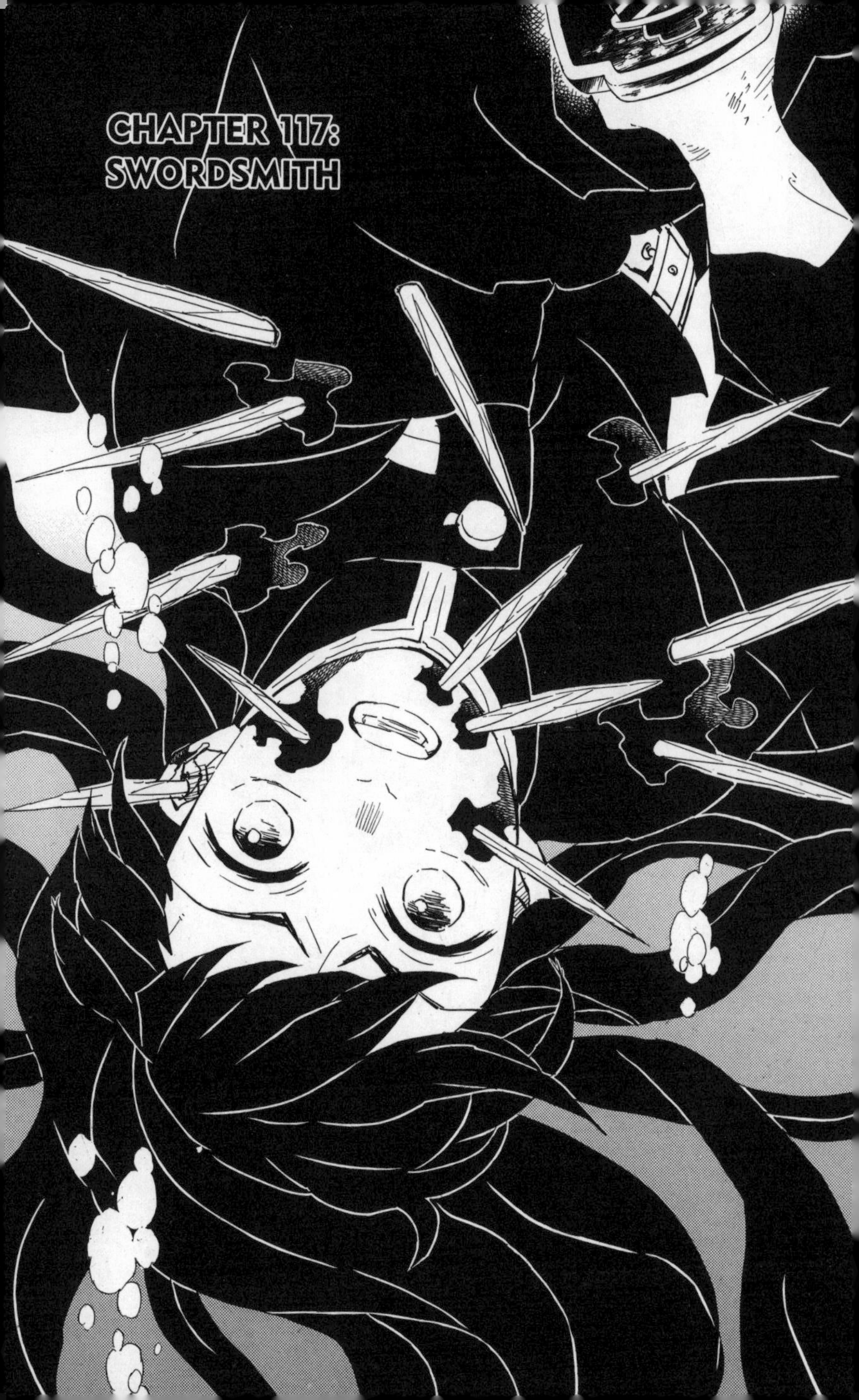

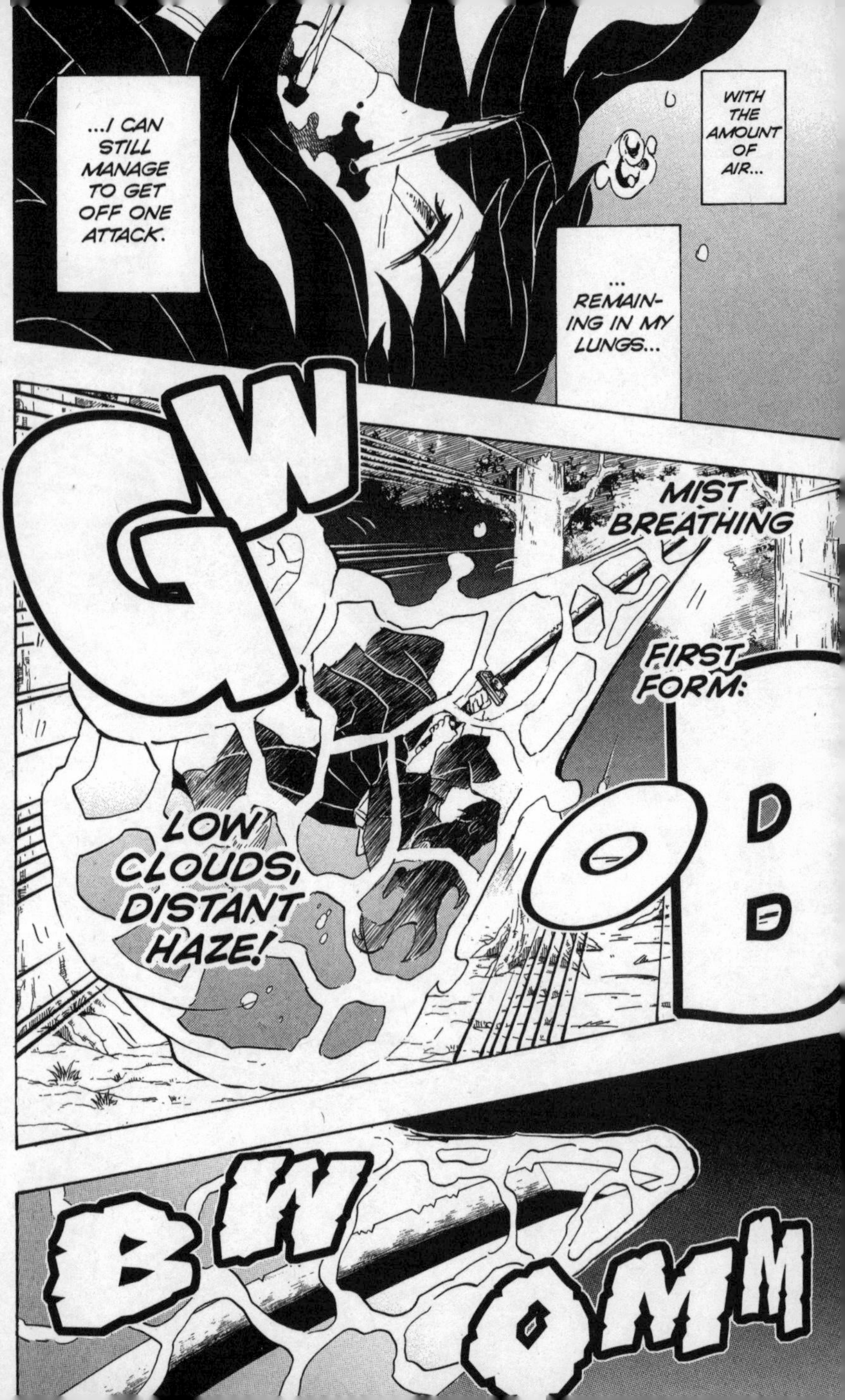
WITH THE AMOUNT OF AIR...
...REMAINING IN MY LUNGS...
...I CAN STILL MANAGE TO GET OFF ONE ATTACK.
MIST BREATHING
FIRST FORM:
LOW CLOUDS, DISTANT HAZE!
BWOMMM

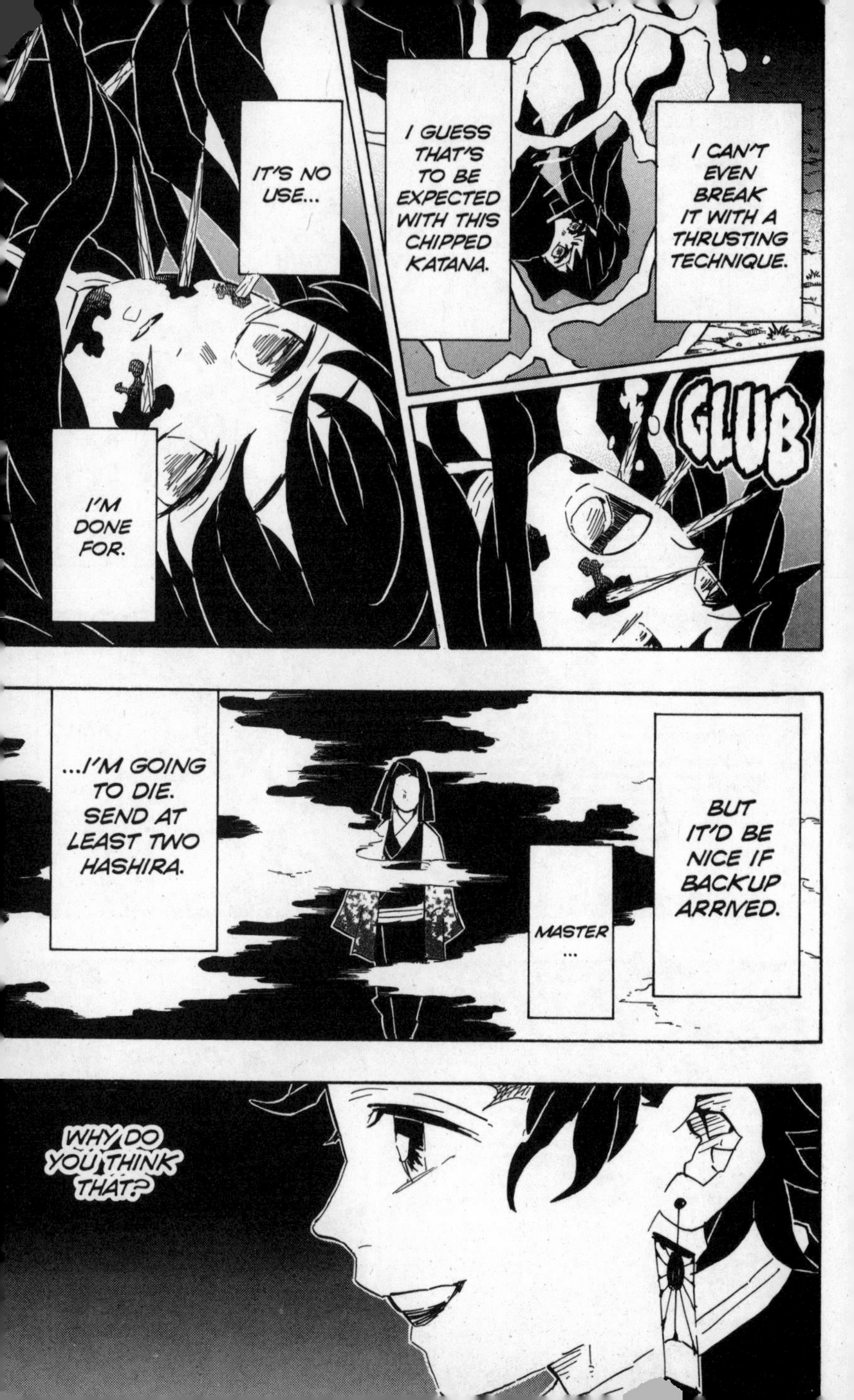
I CAN'T EVEN BREAK IT WITH A THRUSTING TECHNIQUE.
I GUESS THAT'S TO BE EXPECTED WITH THIS CHIPPED KATANA.
GLUB
IT'S NO USE...
I'M DONE FOR.
BUT IT'D BE NICE IF BACKUP ARRIVED.
MASTER...
...I'M GOING TO DIE. SEND AT LEAST TWO HASHIRA.
WHY DO YOU THINK THAT?

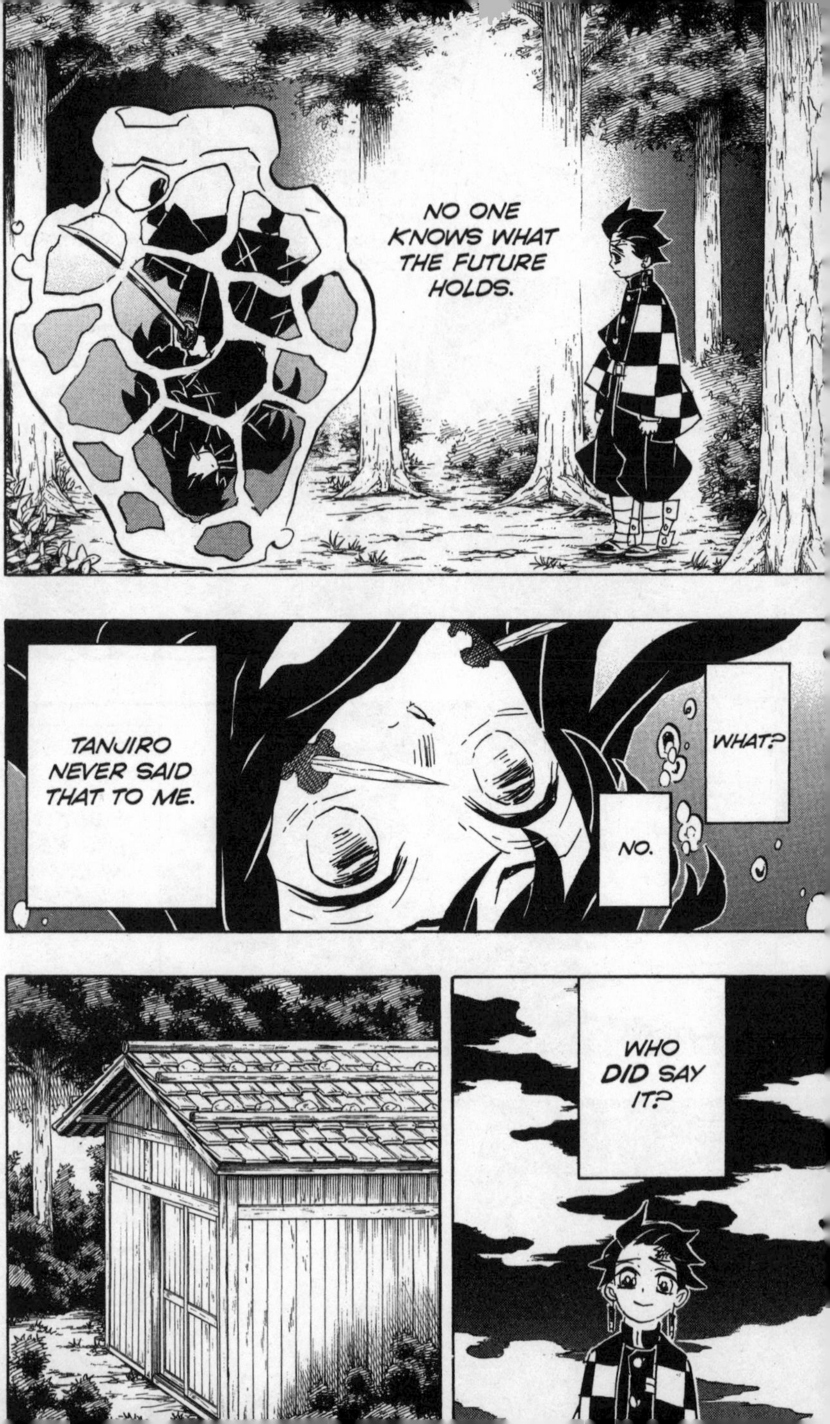
NO ONE KNOWS WHAT THE FUTURE HOLDS.
WHAT?
NO.
TANJIRO NEVER SAID THAT TO ME.
WHO DID SAY IT?

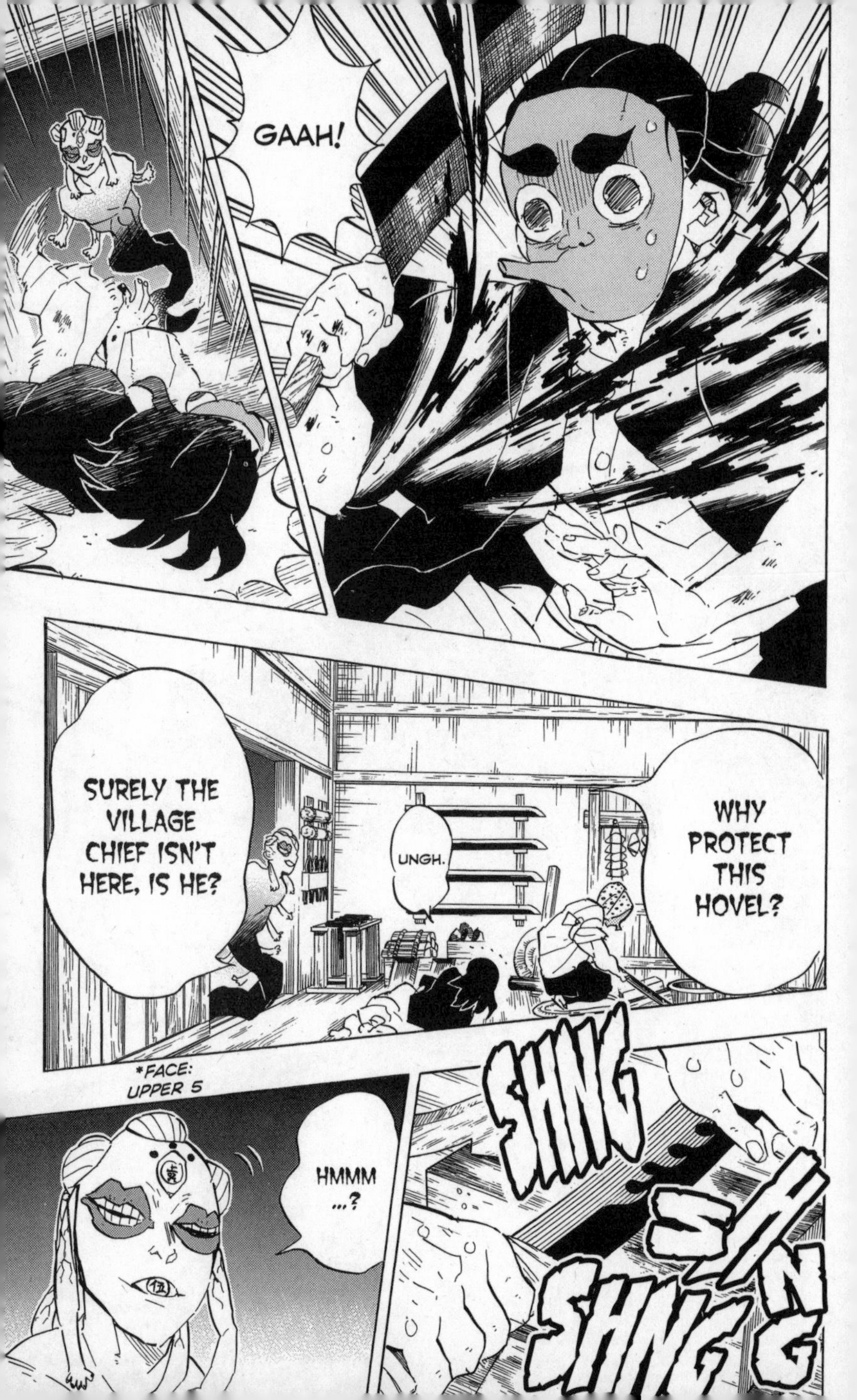
GAAH!
WHY PROTECT THIS HOVEL?
UNGH.
SURELY THE VILLAGE CHIEF ISN'T HERE, IS HE?
SHING
SHING
SHING
*FACE: UPPER 5
HMMM ...?

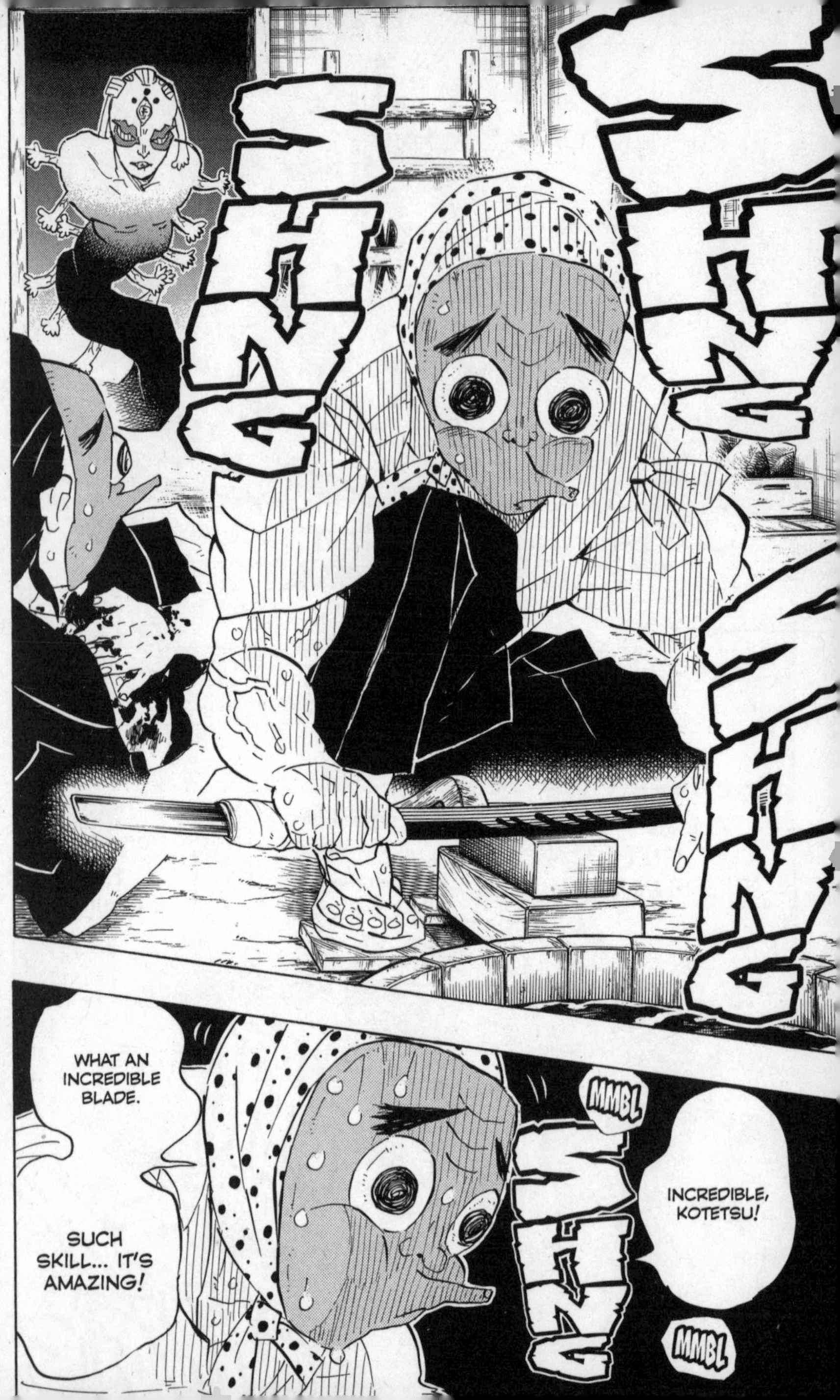
SHING
SHING
SHING
MMBL
INCREDIBLE, KOTETSU!
SHING
MMBL
WHAT AN INCREDIBLE BLADE.
SUCH SKILL... IT'S AMAZING!

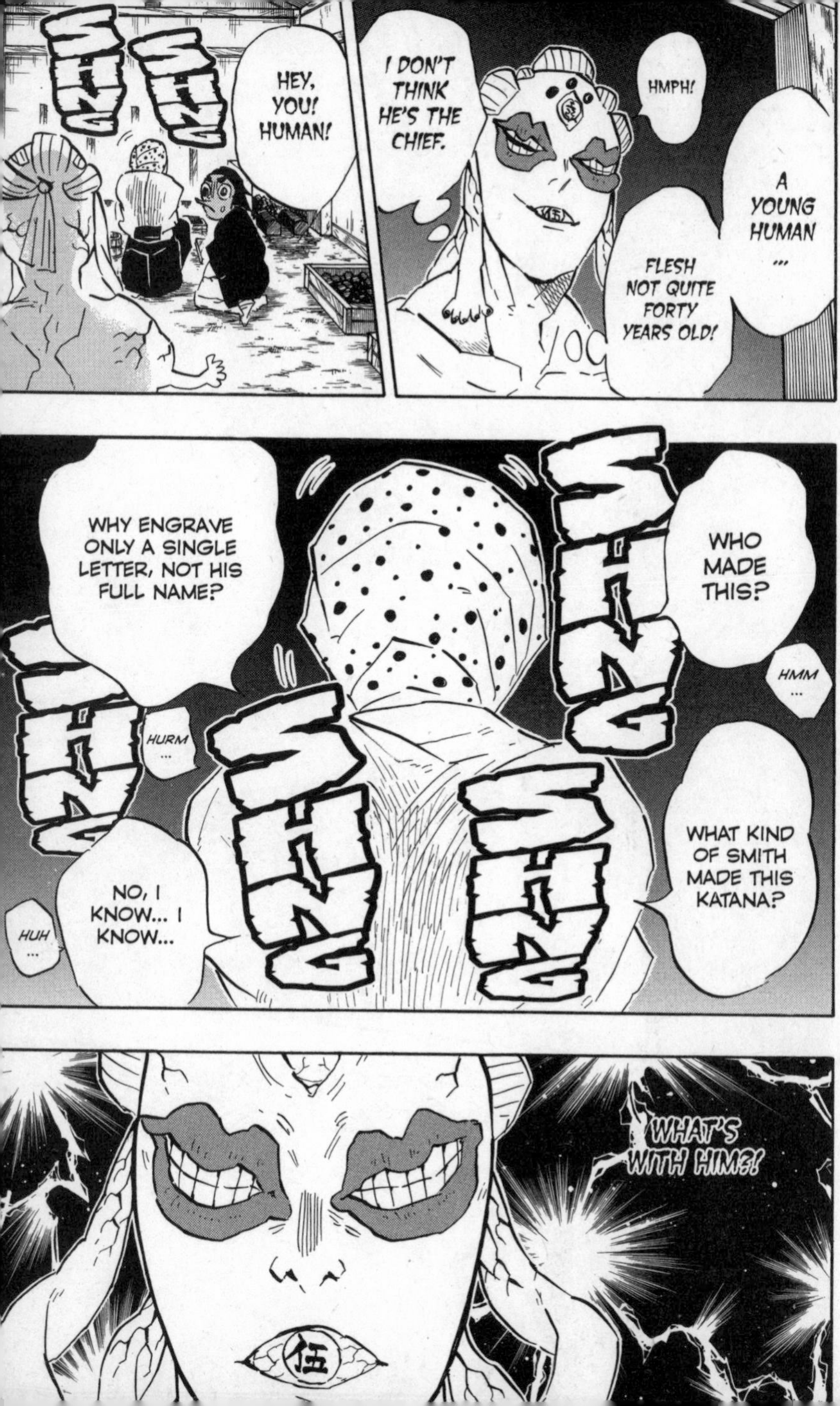
HMPH!
A YOUNG HUMAN ...
FLESH NOT QUITE FORTY YEARS OLD!
I DON'T THINK HE'S THE CHIEF.
HEY, YOU! HUMAN!
SHING
SHING
WHO MADE THIS?
SHING
HMM ...
WHAT KIND OF SMITH MADE THIS KATANA?
SHING
SHING
WHY ENGRAVE ONLY A SINGLE LETTER, NOT HIS FULL NAME?
SHING
HURM ...
NO, I KNOW... I KNOW...
HUH ...
WHAT'S WITH HIM?!

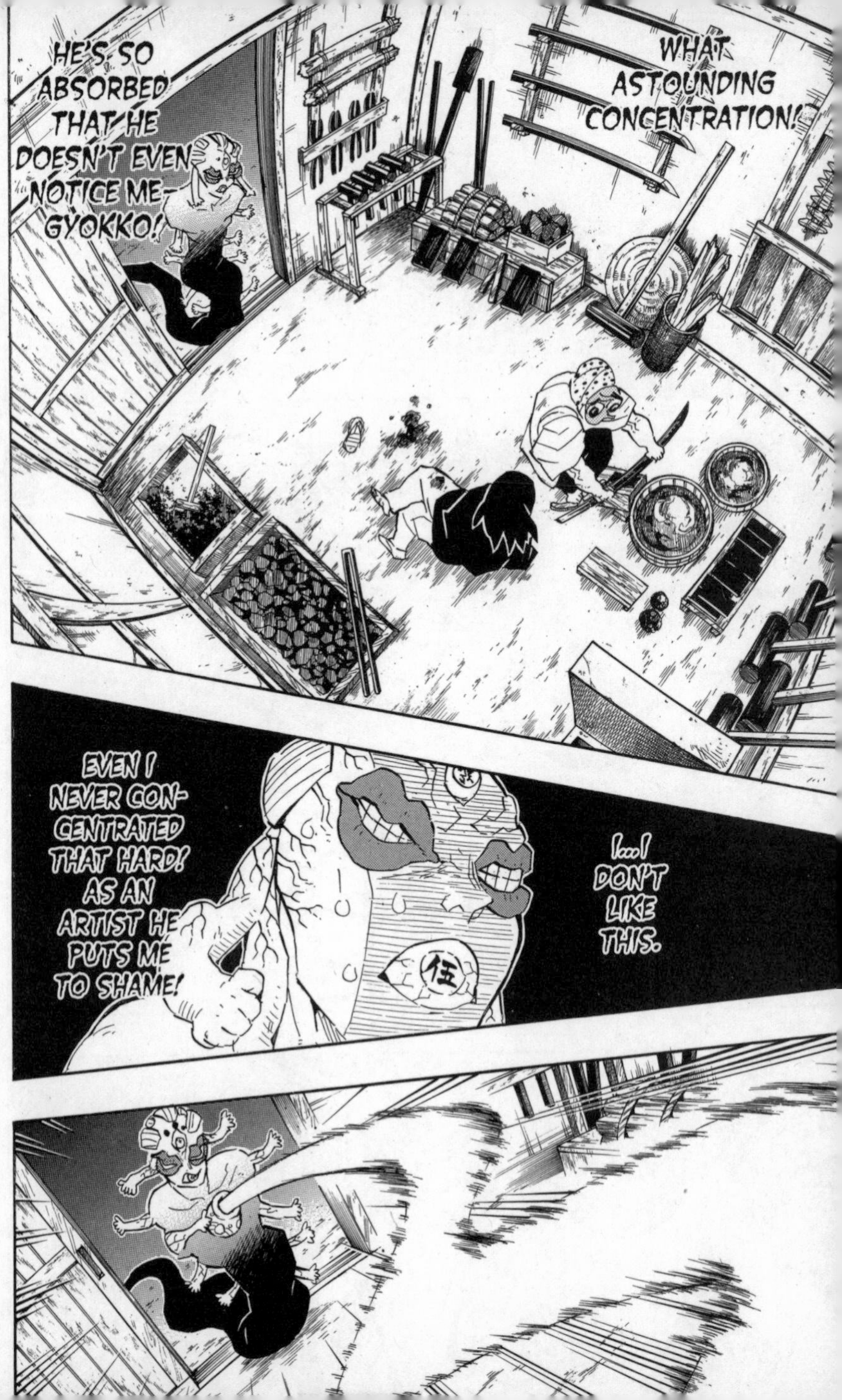
WHAT ASTOUNDING CONCENTRATION!
HE'S SO ABSORBED THAT HE DOESN'T EVEN NOTICE ME—GYOKKO!
I...I DON'T LIKE THIS.
EVEN I NEVER CONCENTRATED THAT HARD! AS AN ARTIST HE PUTS ME TO SHAME!

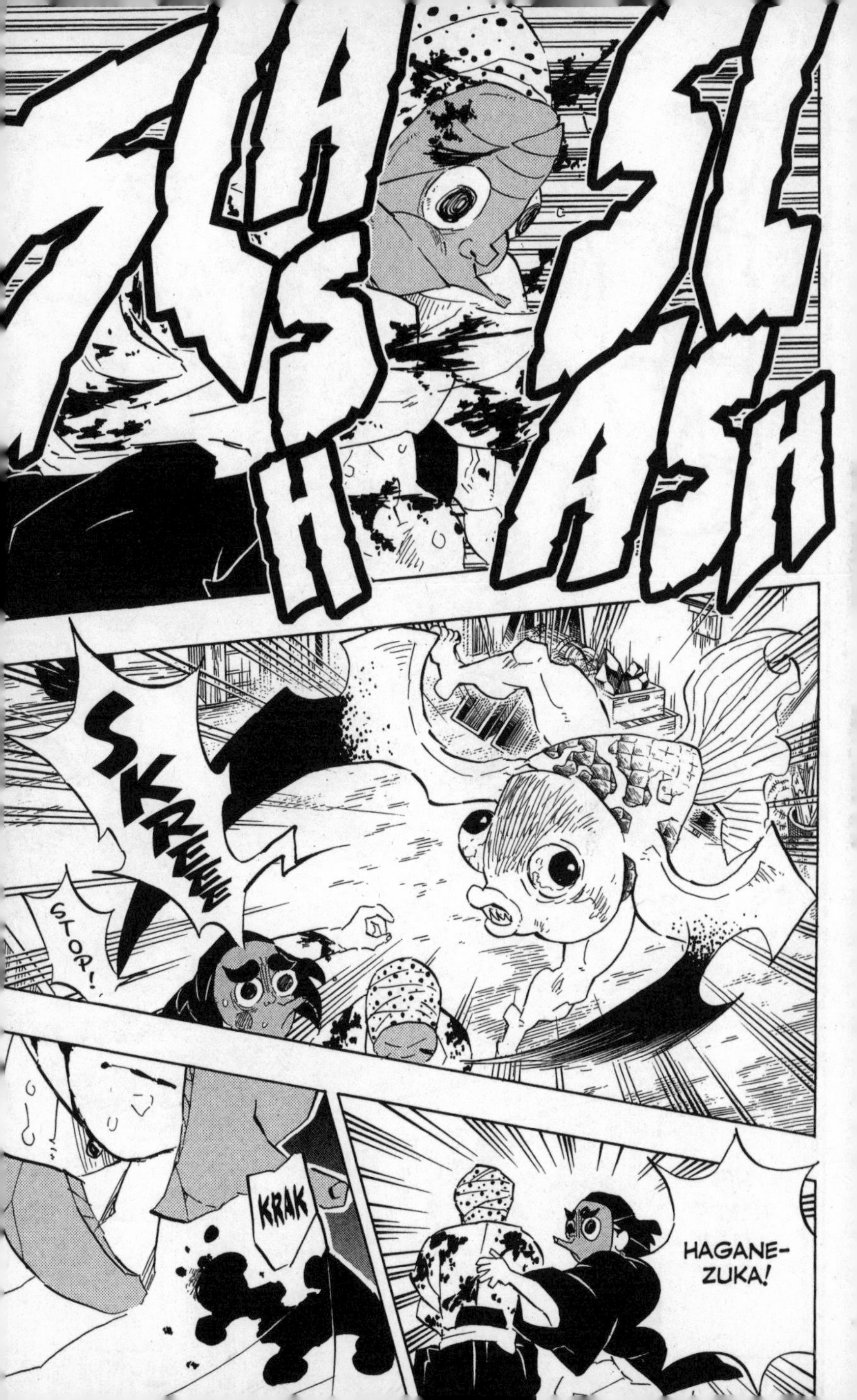
SKREEE
STOP!
HAGANE-
ZUKA!
KRAK

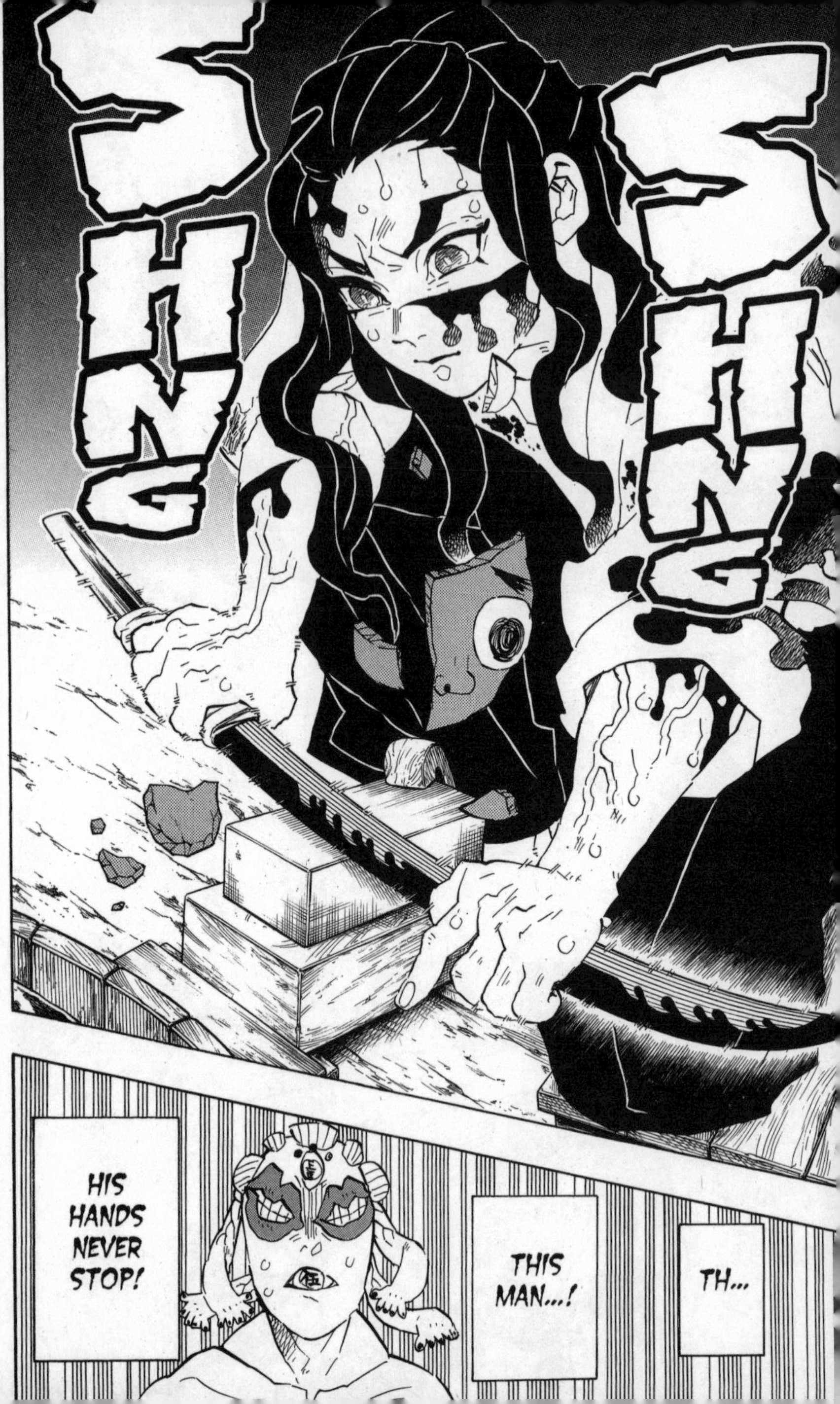
SHING
SHING
TH...
THIS MAN...!
HIS HANDS NEVER STOP!

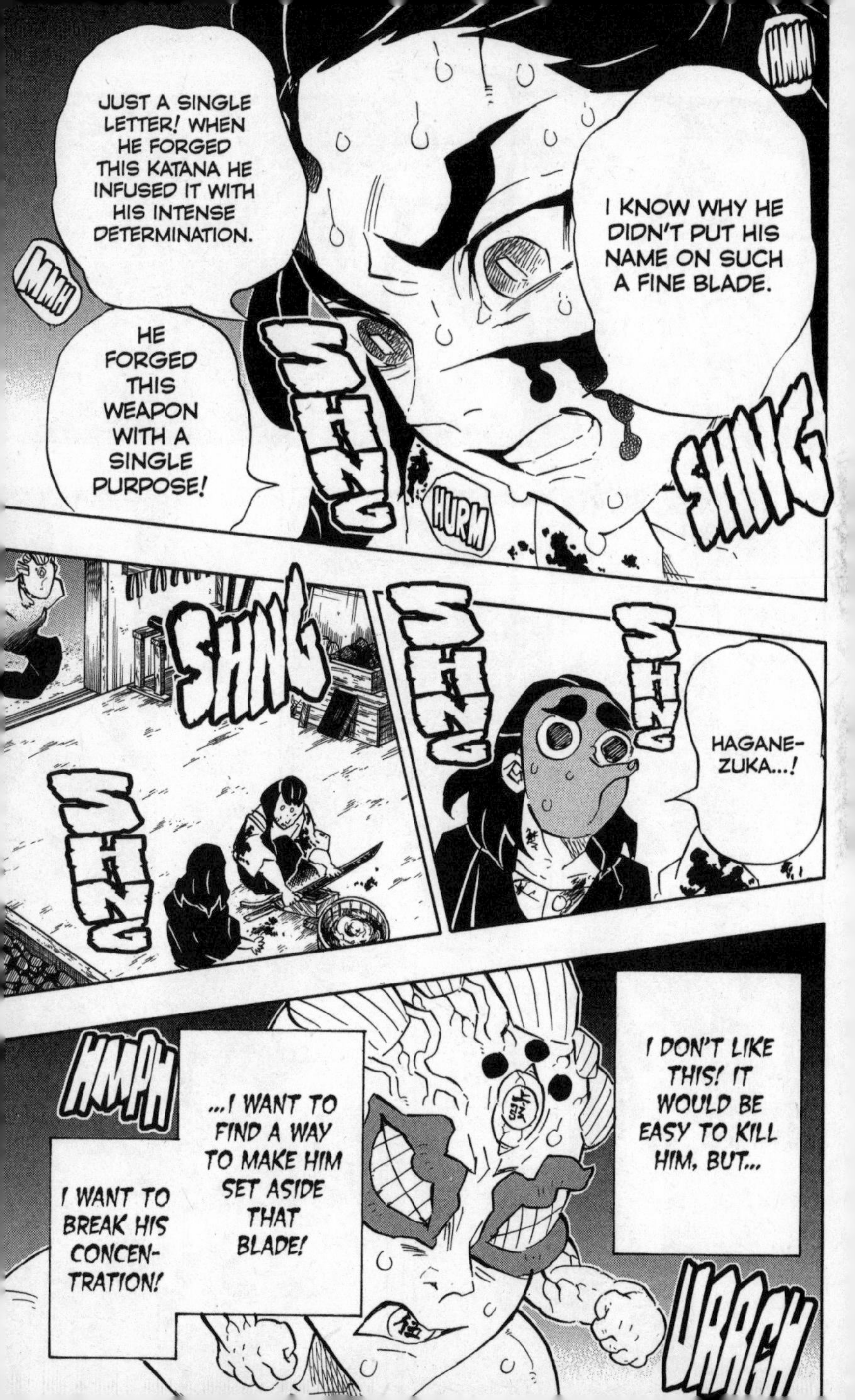
HMM
I KNOW WHY HE DIDN'T PUT HIS NAME ON SUCH A FINE BLADE.
JUST A SINGLE LETTER! WHEN HE FORGED THIS KATANA HE INFUSED IT WITH HIS INTENSE DETERMINATION.
MMH
HE FORGED THIS WEAPON WITH A SINGLE PURPOSE!
SHNG
SHNG
HURM
SHNG
SHNG
HAGANE-ZUKA...!
SHNG
SHNG
I DON'T LIKE THIS! IT WOULD BE EASY TO KILL HIM, BUT...
...I WANT TO FIND A WAY TO MAKE HIM SET ASIDE THAT BLADE!
I WANT TO BREAK HIS CONCENTRATION!
HMPH
URRGH

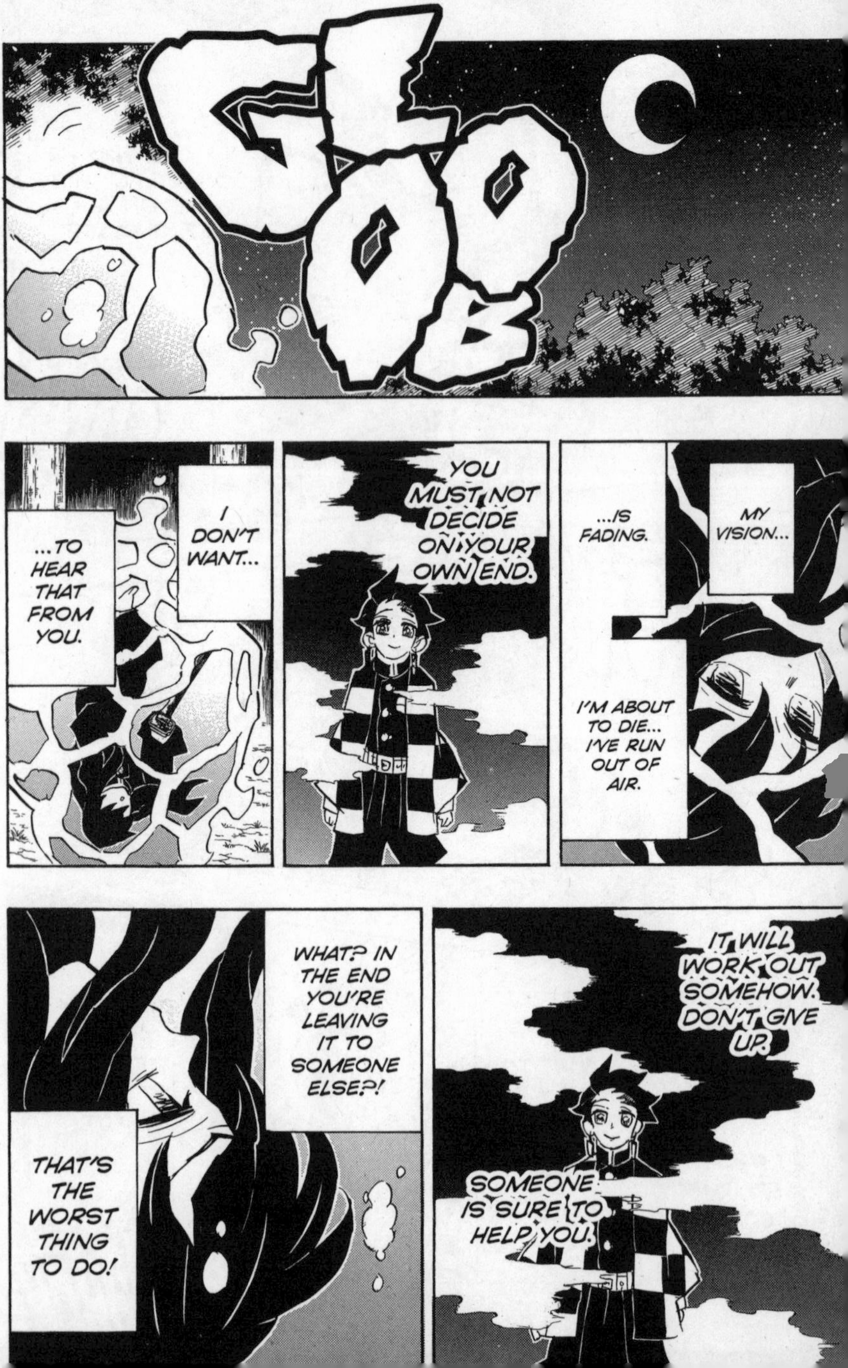
GLOOB
MY VISION...
...IS FADING.
I'M ABOUT TO DIE... I'VE RUN OUT OF AIR.
YOU MUST NOT DECIDE ON YOUR OWN END.
I DON'T WANT...
...TO HEAR THAT FROM YOU.
IT WILL WORK OUT SOMEHOW. DON'T GIVE UP.
SOMEONE IS SURE TO HELP YOU.
WHAT? IN THE END YOU'RE LEAVING IT TO SOMEONE ELSE?!
THAT'S THE WORST THING TO DO!

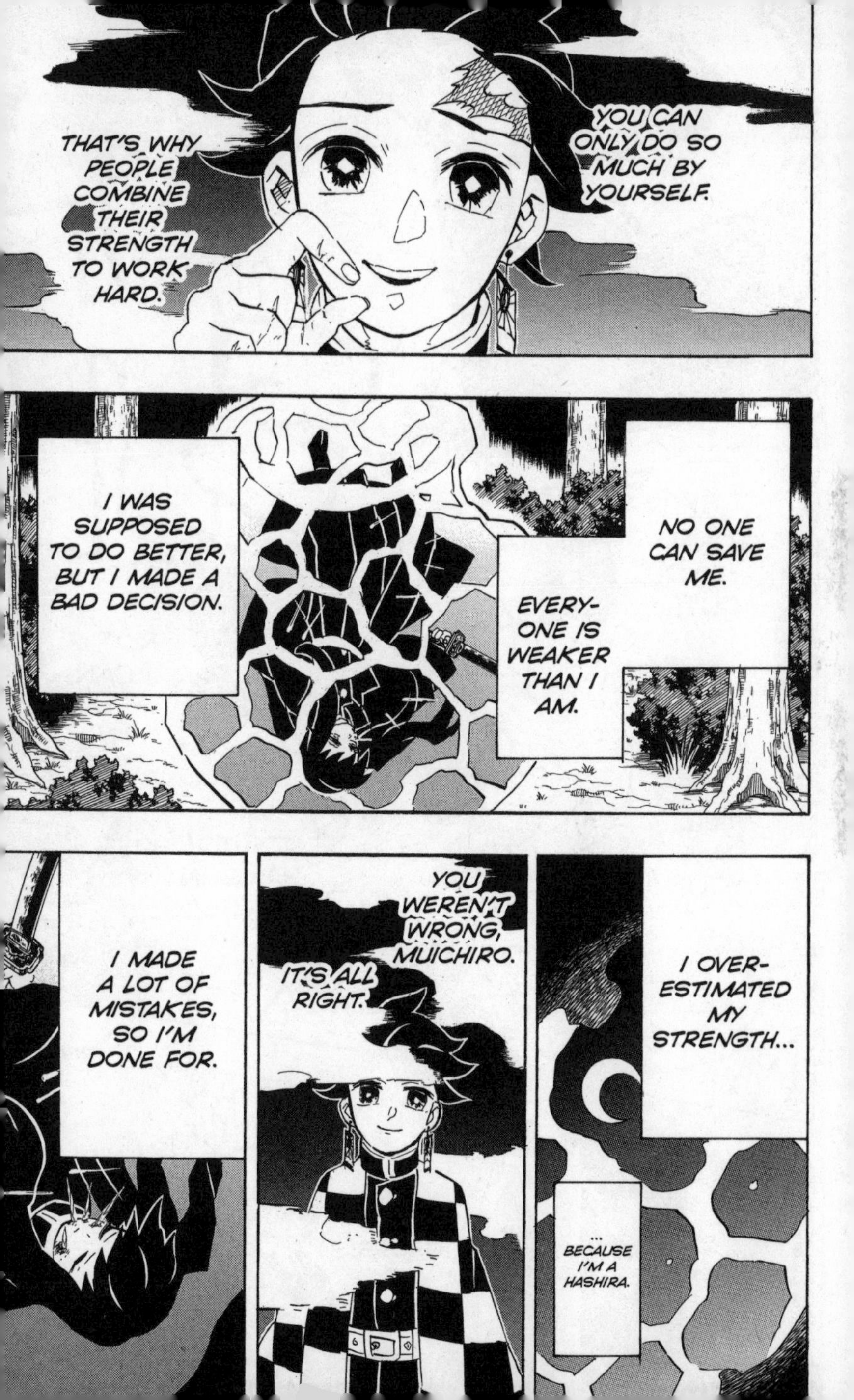
YOU CAN ONLY DO SO MUCH BY YOURSELF.
THAT'S WHY PEOPLE COMBINE THEIR STRENGTH TO WORK HARD.
NO ONE CAN SAVE ME.
EVERY-ONE IS WEAKER THAN I AM.
I WAS SUPPOSED TO DO BETTER, BUT I MADE A BAD DECISION.
I OVER-ESTIMATED MY STRENGTH...
...BECAUSE I'M A HASHIRA.
YOU WEREN'T WRONG, MUICHIRO.
IT'S ALL RIGHT.
I MADE A LOT OF MISTAKES, SO I'M DONE FOR.

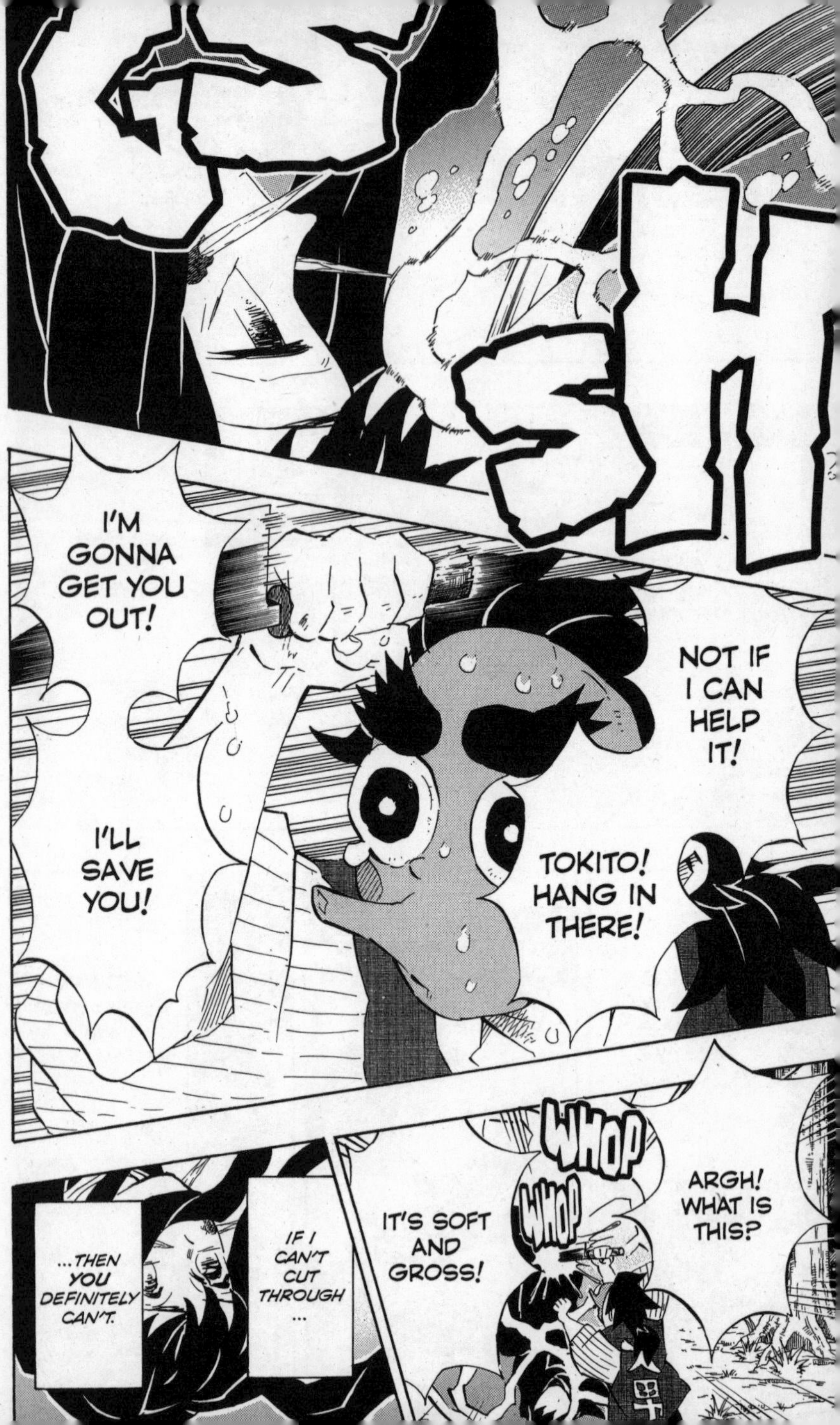
SH
NOT IF I CAN HELP IT!
TOKITO! HANG IN THERE!
I'M GONNA GET YOU OUT!
I'LL SAVE YOU!
WHOP
WHOP
ARGH! WHAT IS THIS?
IT'S SOFT AND GROSS!
IF I CAN'T CUT THROUGH...
...THEN YOU DEFINITELY CAN'T.

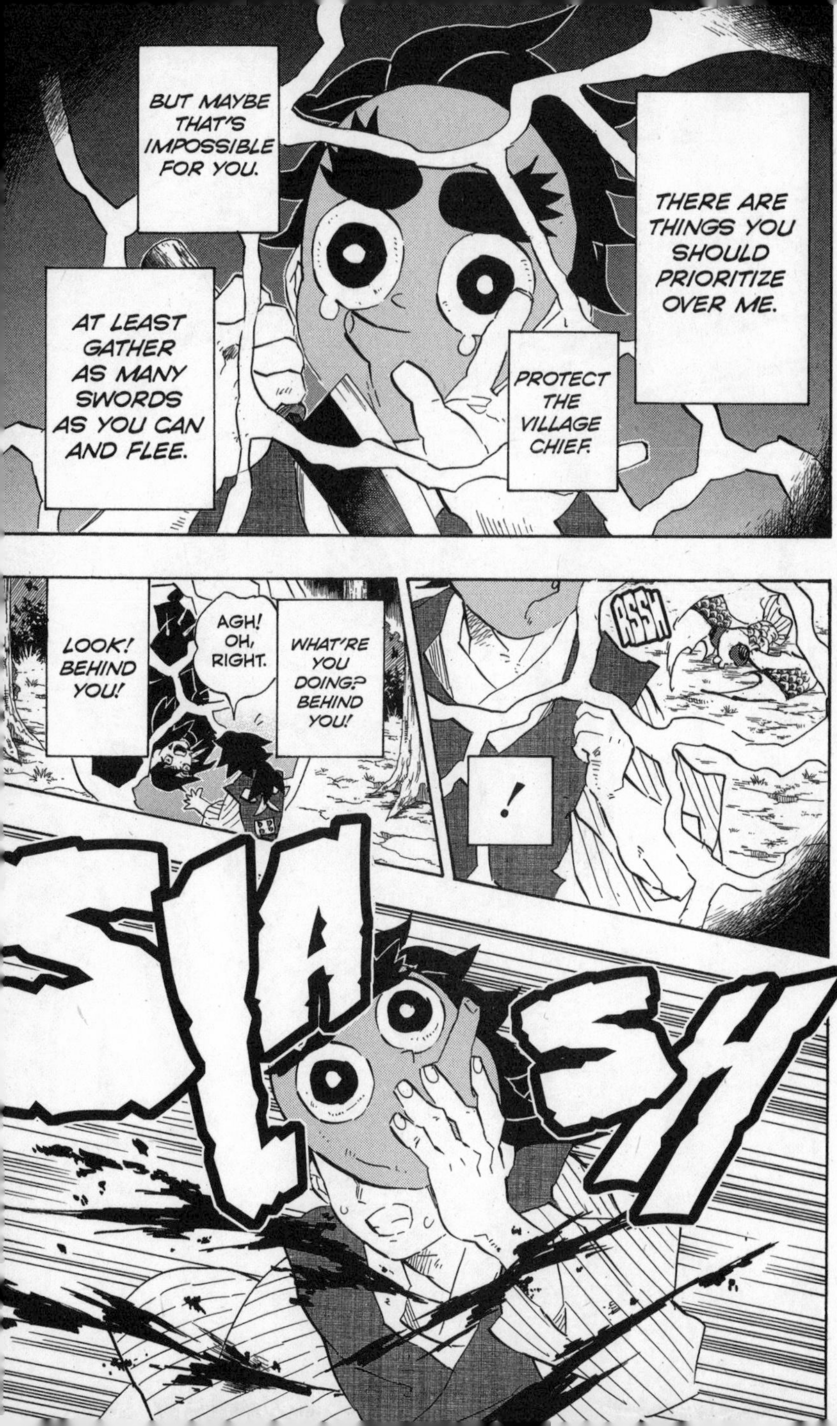
THERE ARE THINGS YOU SHOULD PRIORITIZE OVER ME.
PROTECT THE VILLAGE CHIEF.
BUT MAYBE THAT'S IMPOSSIBLE FOR YOU.
AT LEAST GATHER AS MANY SWORDS AS YOU CAN AND FLEE.
RSSH
!
WHAT'RE YOU DOING? BEHIND YOU!
AGH! OH, RIGHT.
LOOK! BEHIND YOU!
SLASH

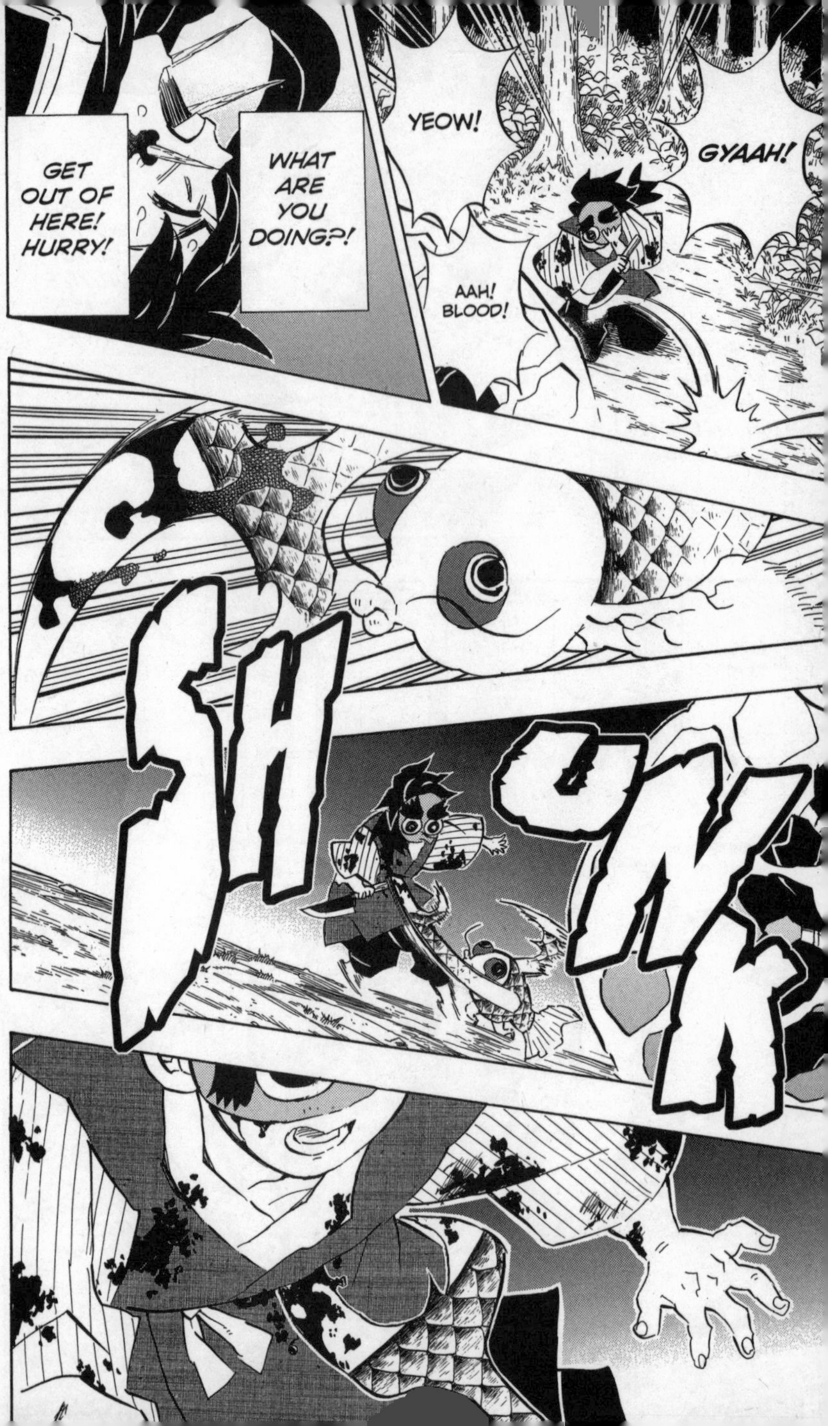
GYAAH!
YEOW!
AAH! BLOOD!
WHAT ARE YOU DOING?!
GET OUT OF HERE! HURRY!
SHUNK

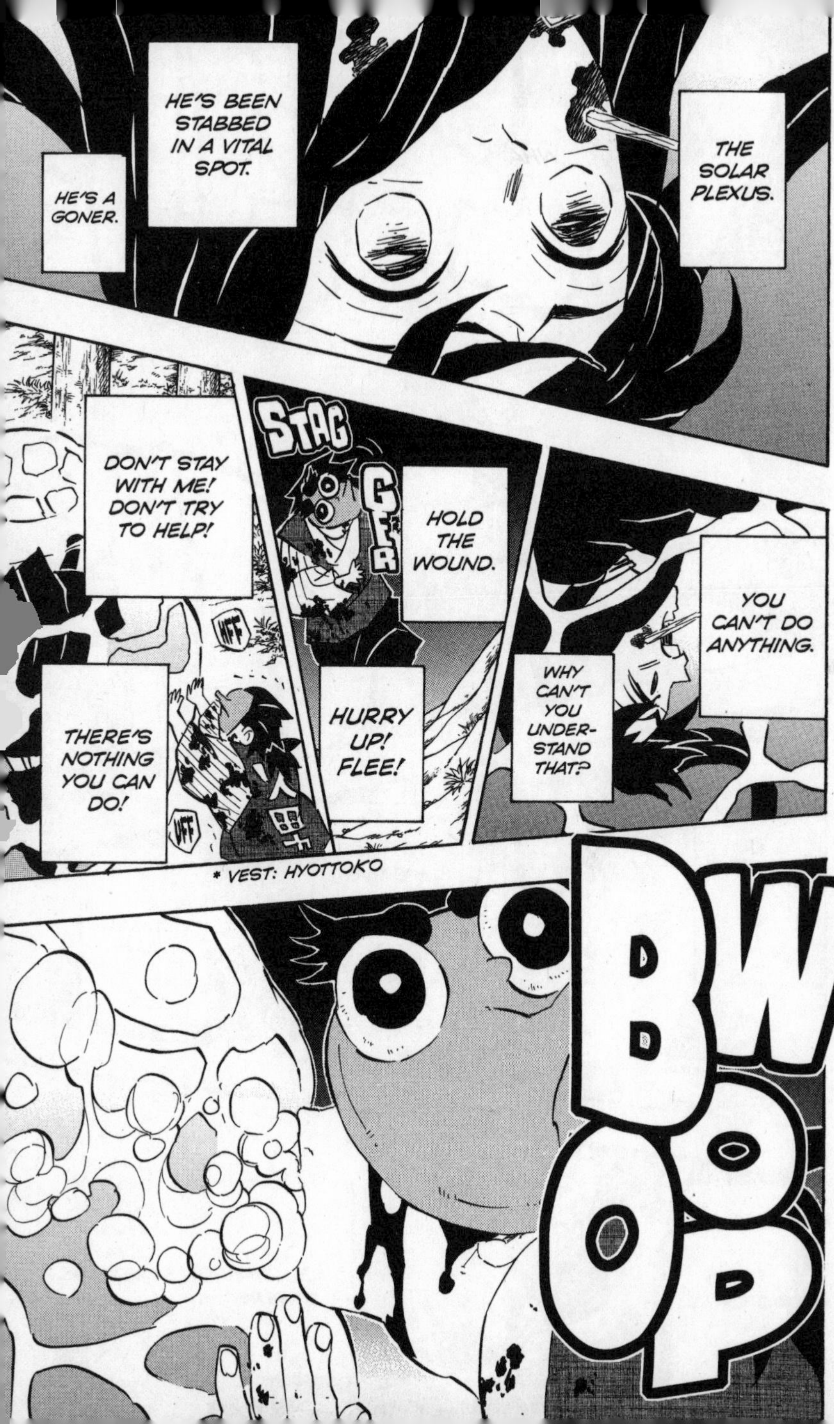
THE SOLAR PLEXUS.
HE'S BEEN STABBED IN A VITAL SPOT.
HE'S A GONER.
YOU CAN'T DO ANYTHING.
WHY CAN'T YOU UNDERSTAND THAT?
STAGGER
HOLD THE WOUND.
HURRY UP! FLEE!
DON'T STAY WITH ME! DON'T TRY TO HELP!
HFF
THERE'S NOTHING YOU CAN DO!
UFF
* VEST: HYOTTOKO
BWOOP

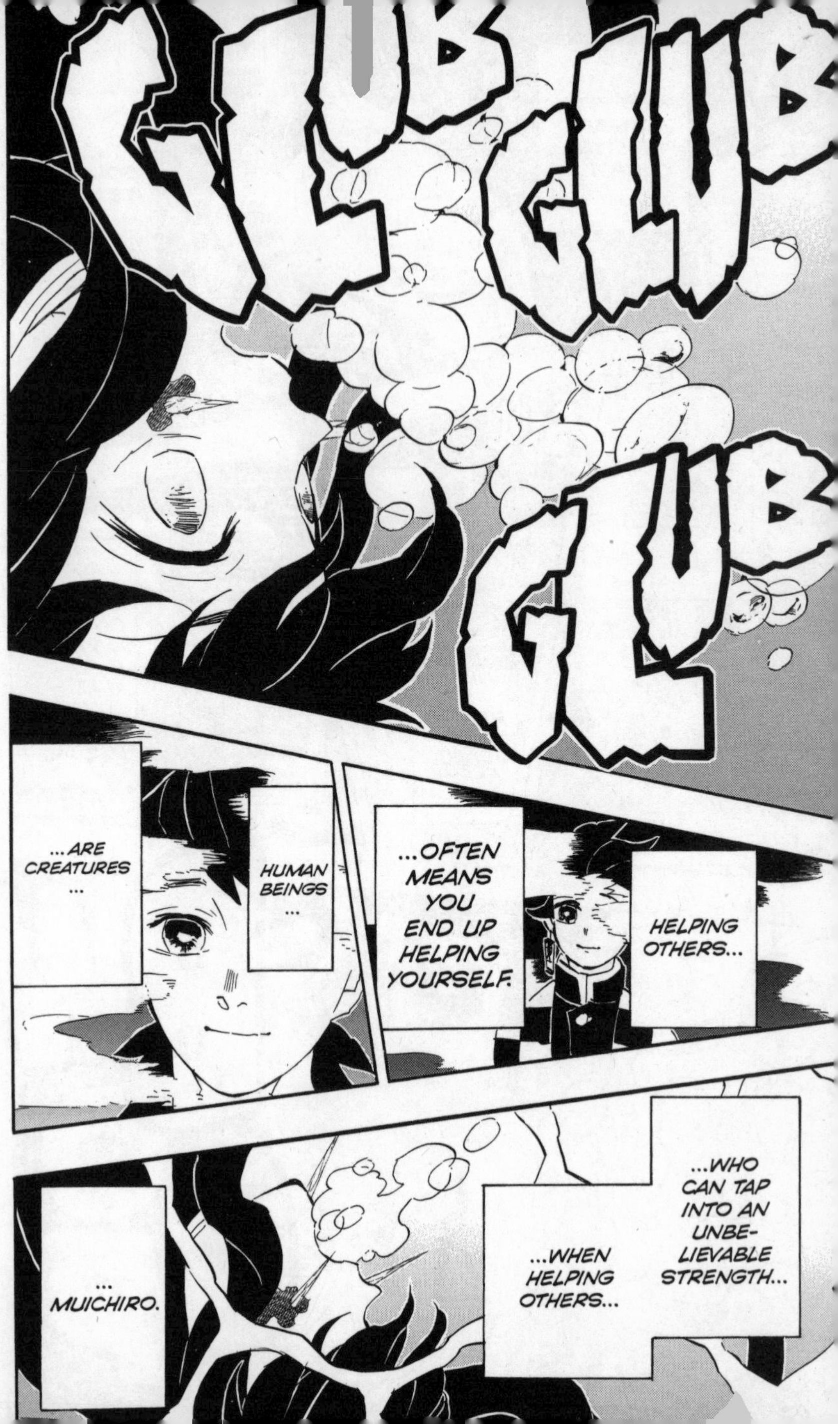
GLUB
GLUB
GLUB
HELPING OTHERS...
...OFTEN MEANS YOU END UP HELPING YOURSELF.
HUMAN BEINGS...
...ARE CREATURES...
...WHO CAN TAP INTO AN UNBELIEVABLE STRENGTH...
...WHEN HELPING OTHERS...
... MUICHIRO.

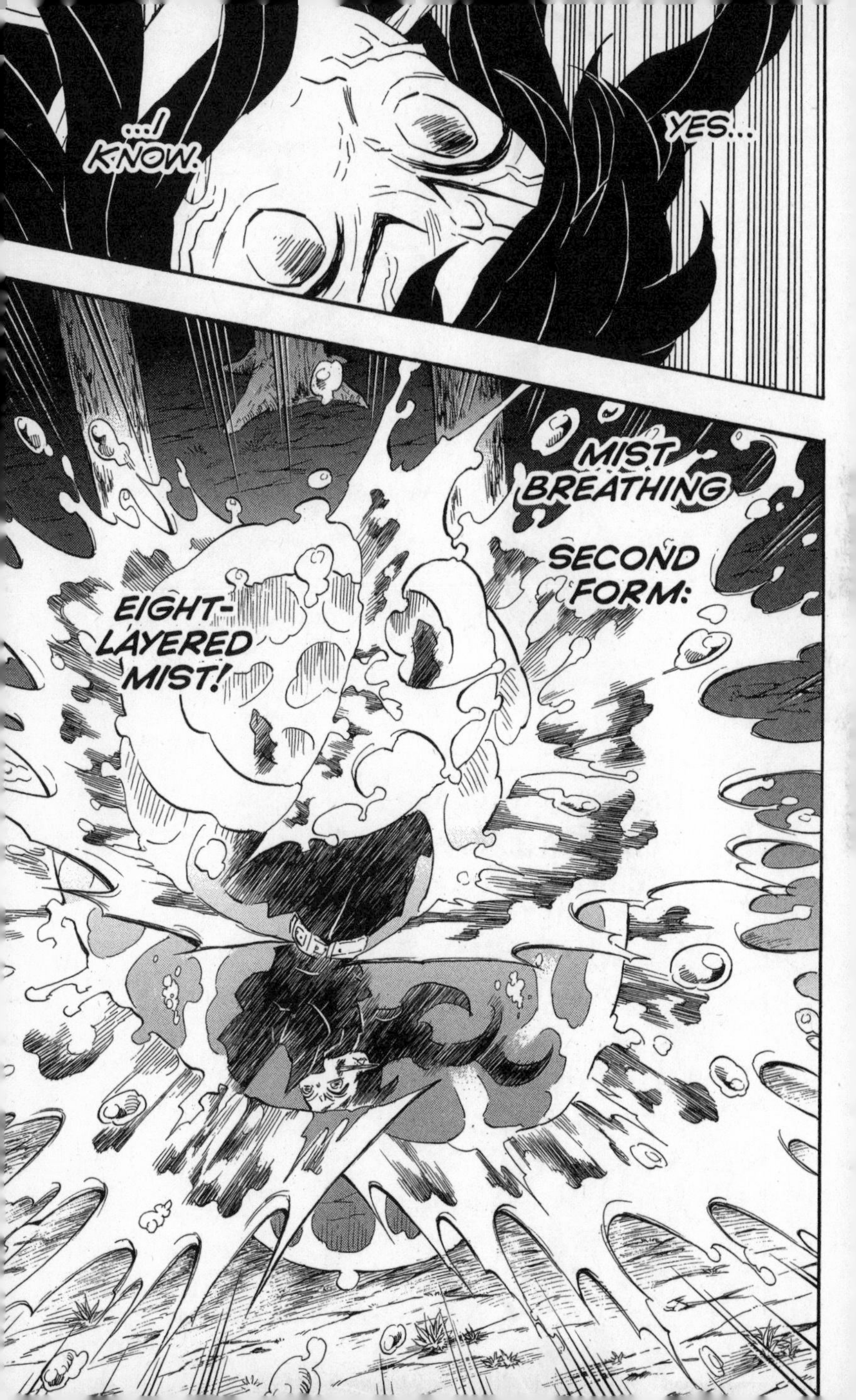
YES...
...I KNOW.
MIST BREATHING
SECOND FORM:
EIGHT-LAYERED MIST!

Illustration for Shueisha's
2019 New Year's postcard.

HAPPY NEW YEAR
HEADLONG RUSH!
DEMON SLAYER
KIMETSU
KOYOHARU
GOTOUGE

January
2019 *Shonen Jump* issue 1
bonus illustration.

CHAPTER 118: THE MU OF MUICHIRO

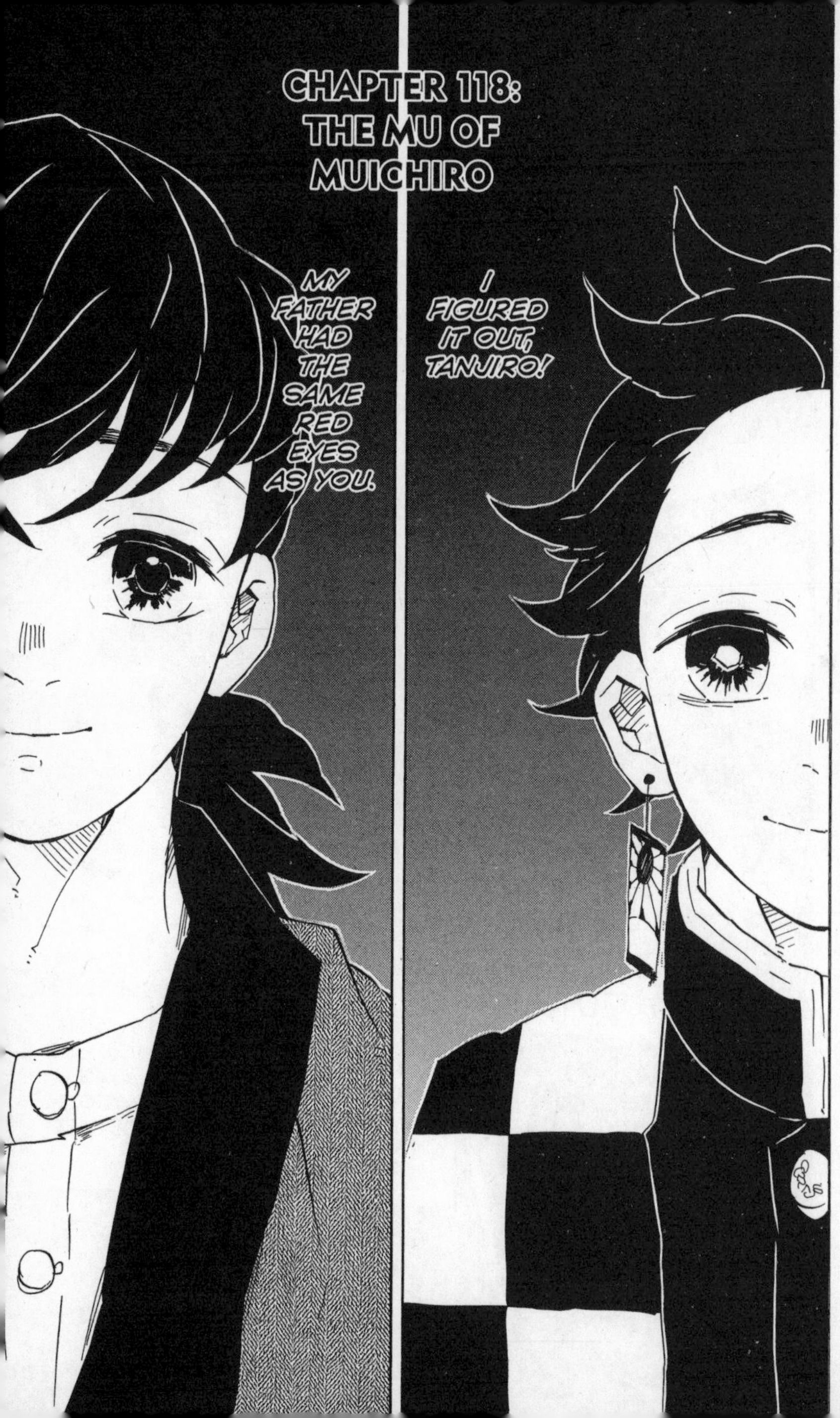
I FIGURED IT OUT, TANJIRO!
MY FATHER HAD THE SAME RED EYES AS YOU.

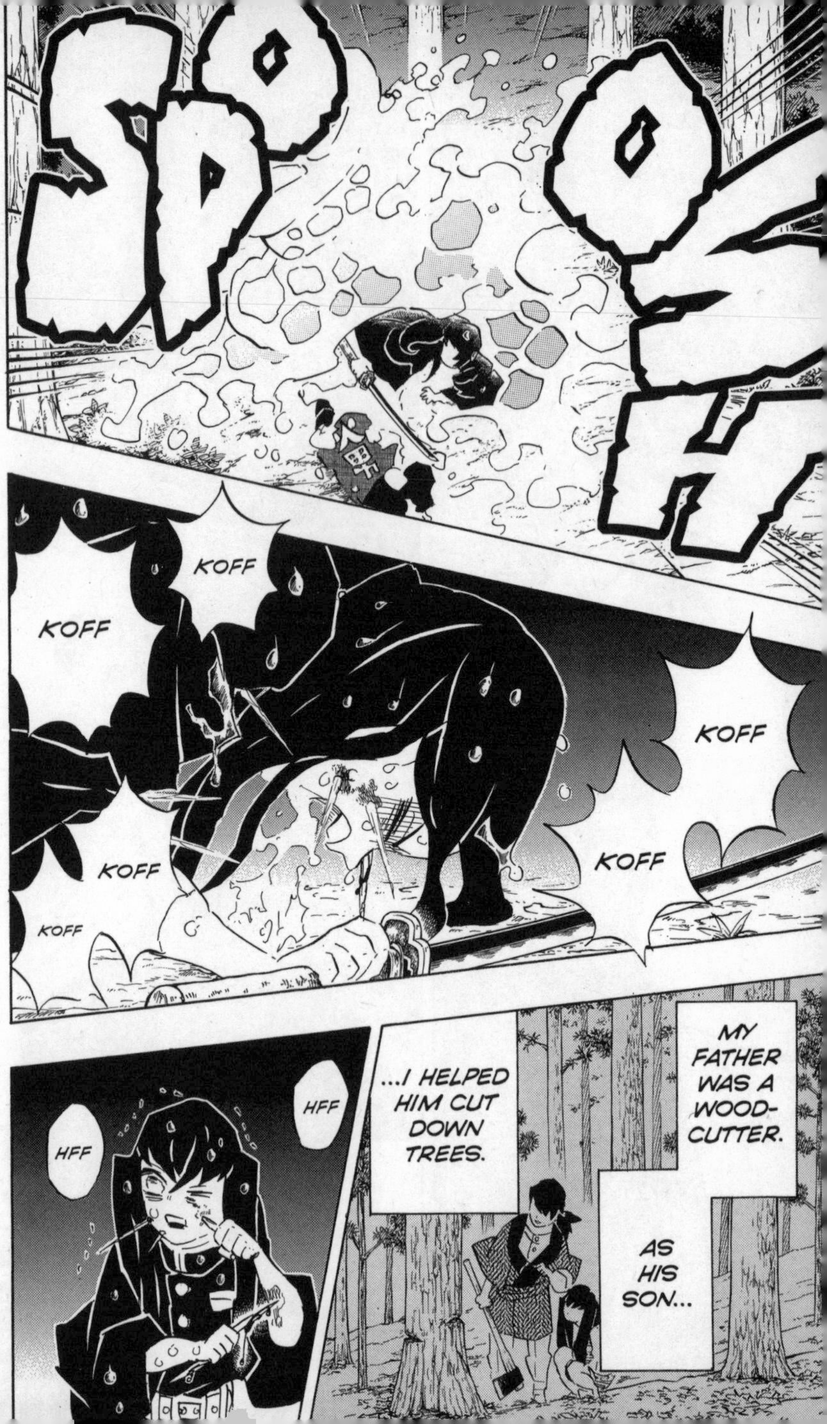
KOFF
KOFF
KOFF
KOFF
KOFF
KOFF
MY FATHER WAS A WOOD-CUTTER.
AS HIS SON...
...I HELPED HIM CUT DOWN TREES.
HFF
HFF

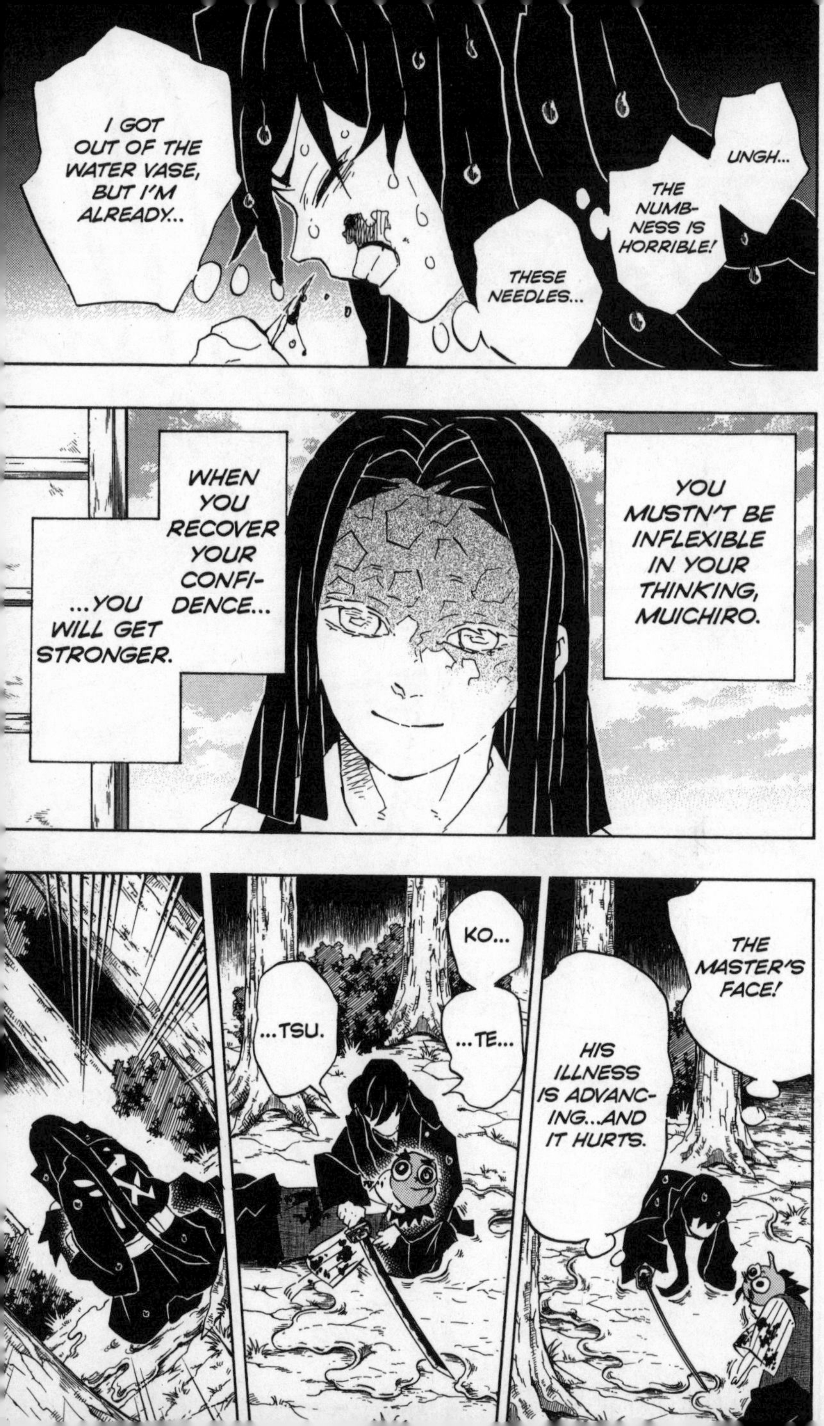
UNGH...
THE NUMBNESS IS HORRIBLE!
THESE NEEDLES...
I GOT OUT OF THE WATER VASE, BUT I'M ALREADY...
YOU MUSTN'T BE INFLEXIBLE IN YOUR THINKING, MUICHIRO.
WHEN YOU RECOVER YOUR CONFIDENCE...
...YOU WILL GET STRONGER.
THE MASTER'S FACE!
HIS ILLNESS IS ADVANCING...AND IT HURTS.
KO...
...TE...
...TSU.

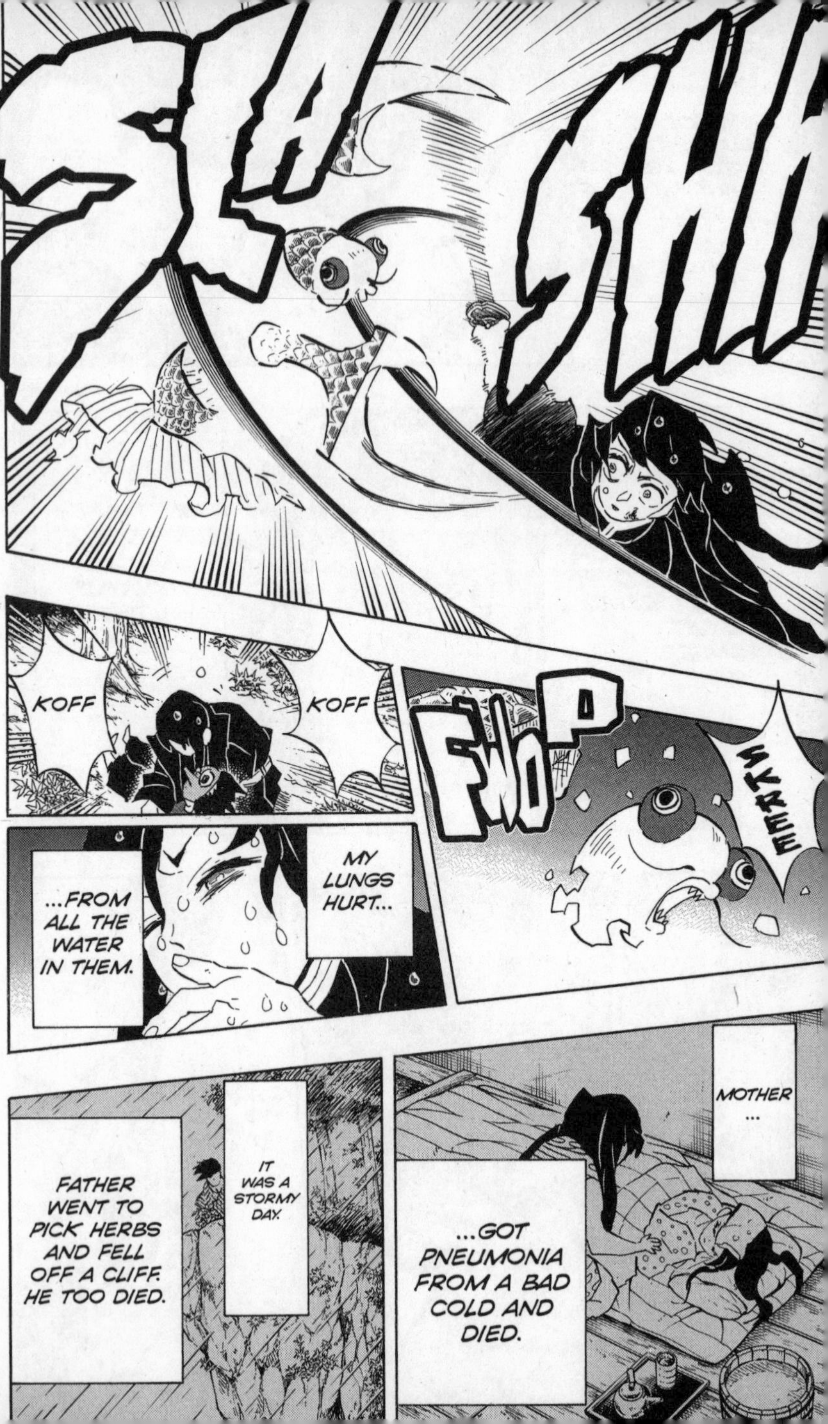
SHA
SHA
FWOP
SKREE
KOFF
KOFF
MY LUNGS HURT...
...FROM ALL THE WATER IN THEM.
MOTHER ...
...GOT PNEUMONIA FROM A BAD COLD AND DIED.
IT WAS A STORMY DAY.
FATHER WENT TO PICK HERBS AND FELL OFF A CLIFF. HE TOO DIED.

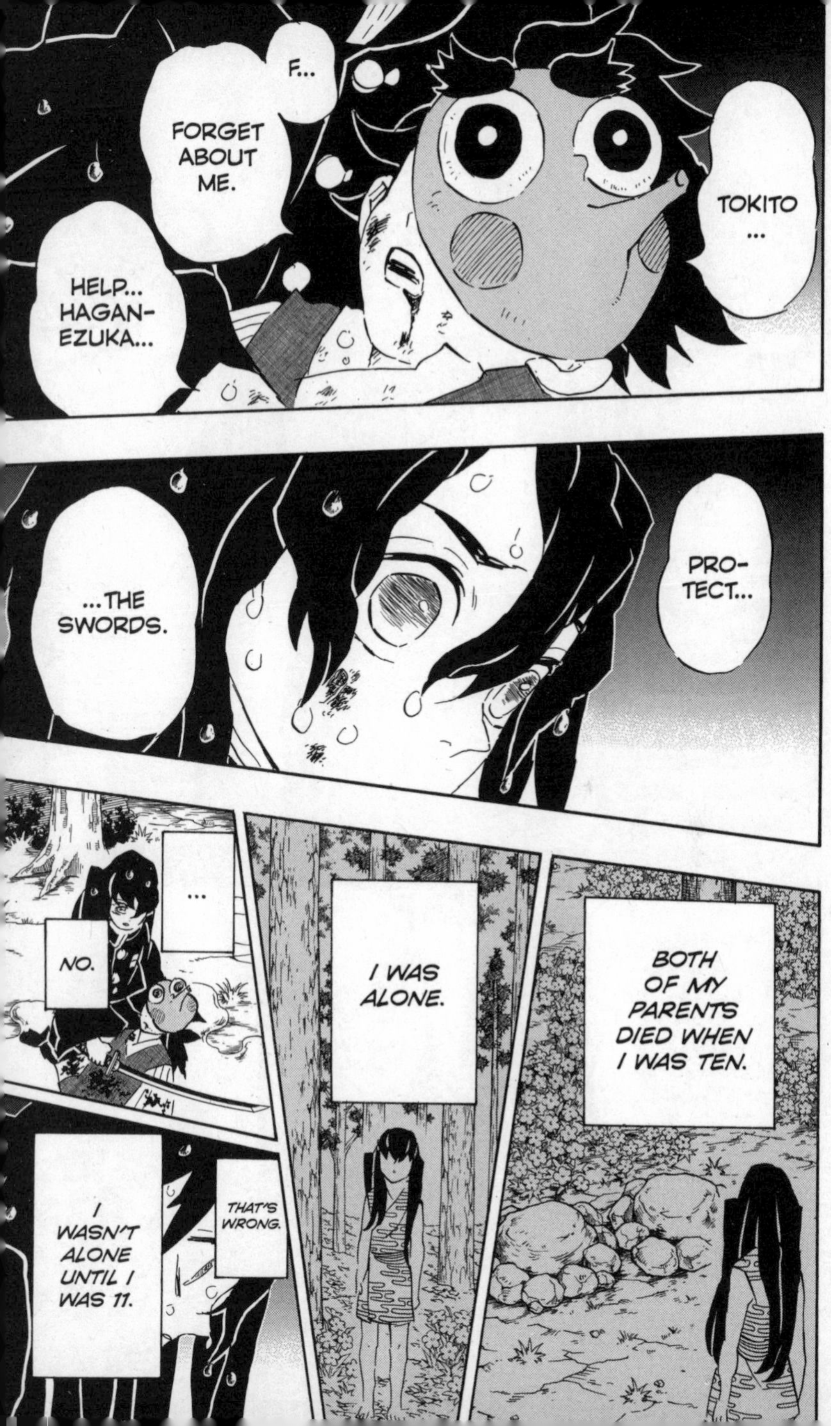
TOKITO ...
F...
FORGET ABOUT ME.
HELP... HAGAN-EZUKA...
PRO-TECT...
...THE SWORDS.
BOTH OF MY PARENTS DIED WHEN I WAS TEN.
I WAS ALONE.
...
NO.
THAT'S WRONG.
I WASN'T ALONE UNTIL I WAS 11.

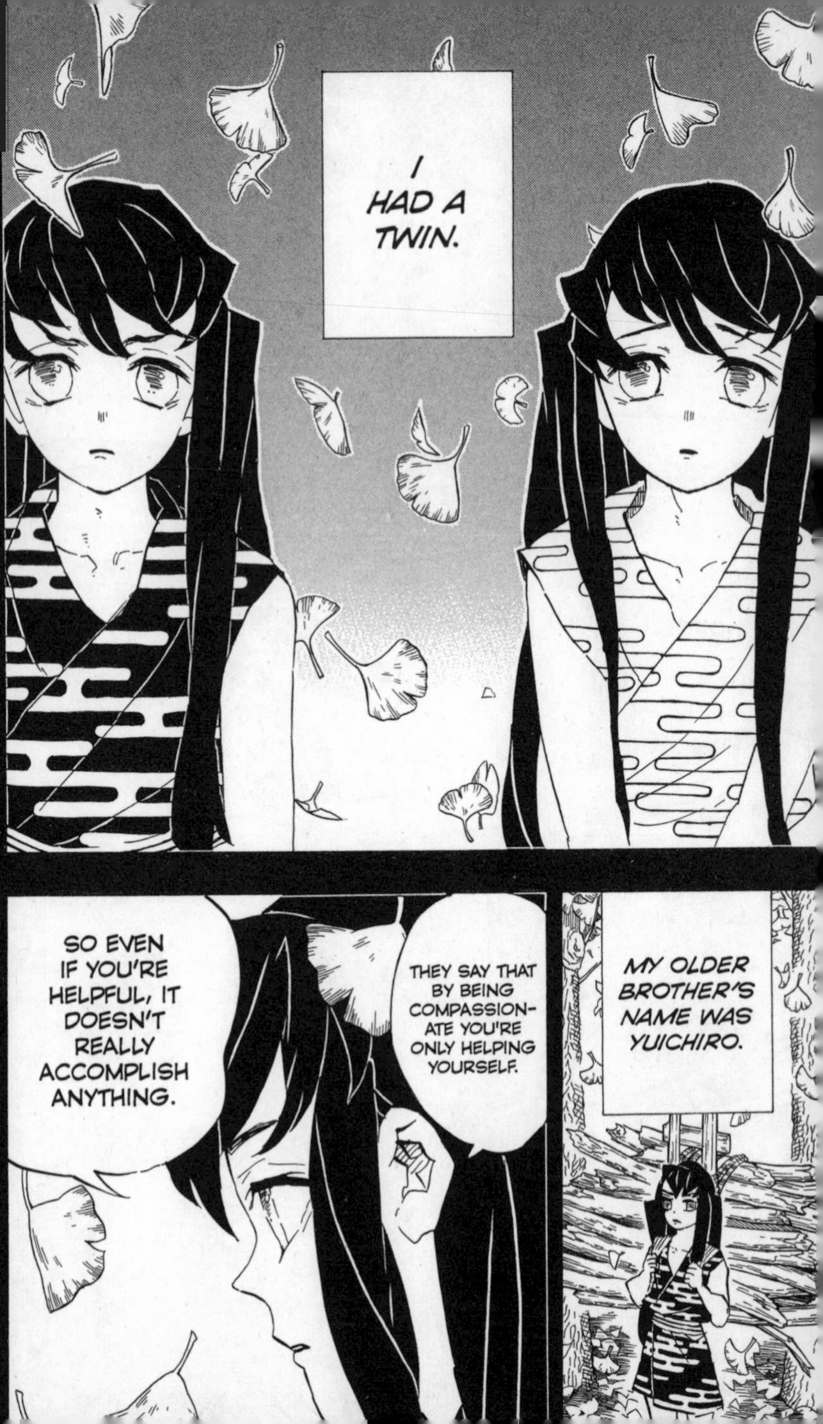
I HAD A TWIN.
MY OLDER BROTHER'S NAME WAS YUICHIRO.
THEY SAY THAT BY BEING COMPASSIONATE YOU'RE ONLY HELPING YOURSELF.
SO EVEN IF YOU'RE HELPFUL, IT DOESN'T REALLY ACCOMPLISH ANYTHING.

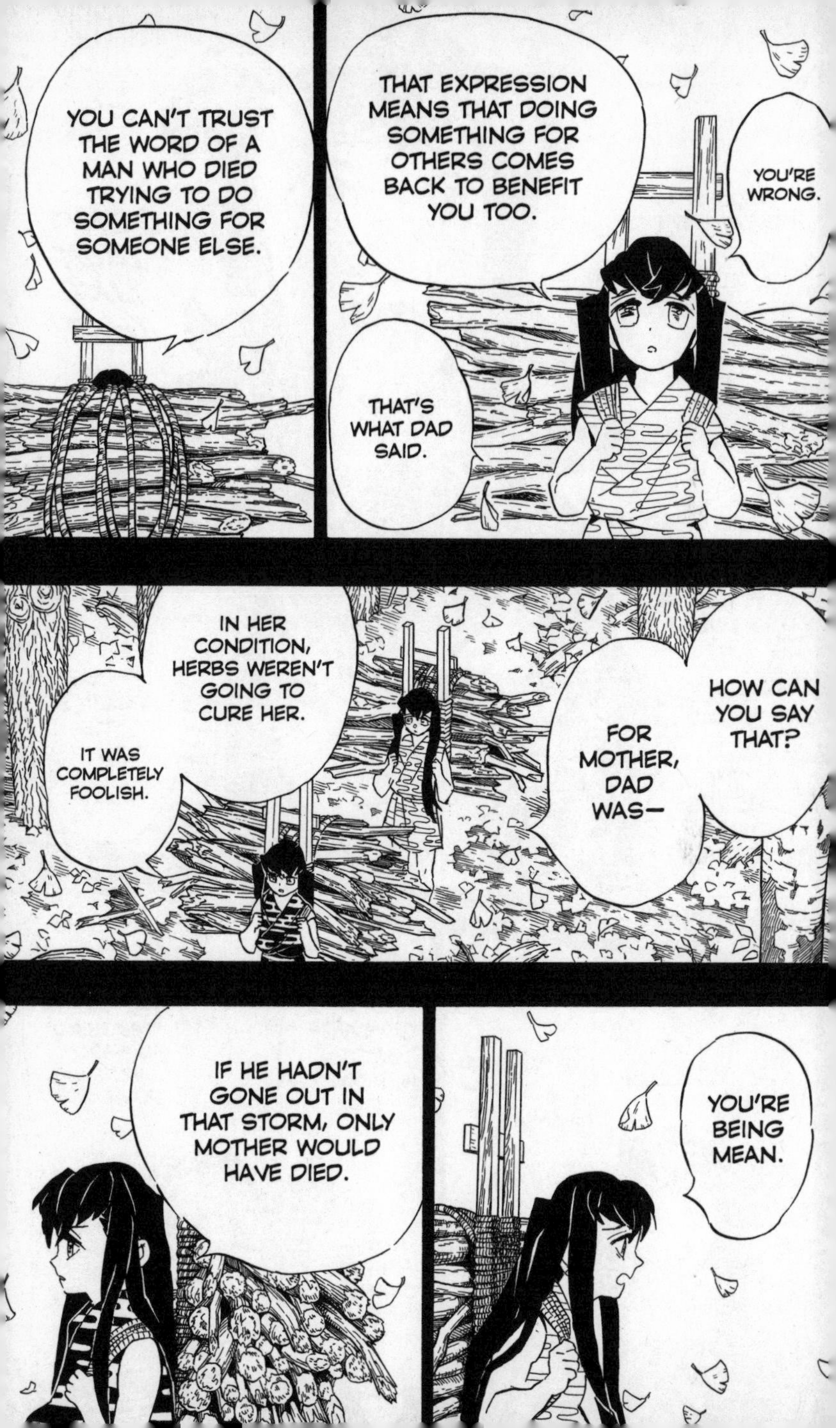
YOU'RE WRONG.
THAT EXPRESSION MEANS THAT DOING SOMETHING FOR OTHERS COMES BACK TO BENEFIT YOU TOO.
THAT'S WHAT DAD SAID.
YOU CAN'T TRUST THE WORD OF A MAN WHO DIED TRYING TO DO SOMETHING FOR SOMEONE ELSE.
HOW CAN YOU SAY THAT?
FOR MOTHER, DAD WAS—
IN HER CONDITION, HERBS WEREN'T GOING TO CURE HER.
IT WAS COMPLETELY FOOLISH.
YOU'RE BEING MEAN.
IF HE HADN'T GONE OUT IN THAT STORM, ONLY MOTHER WOULD HAVE DIED.

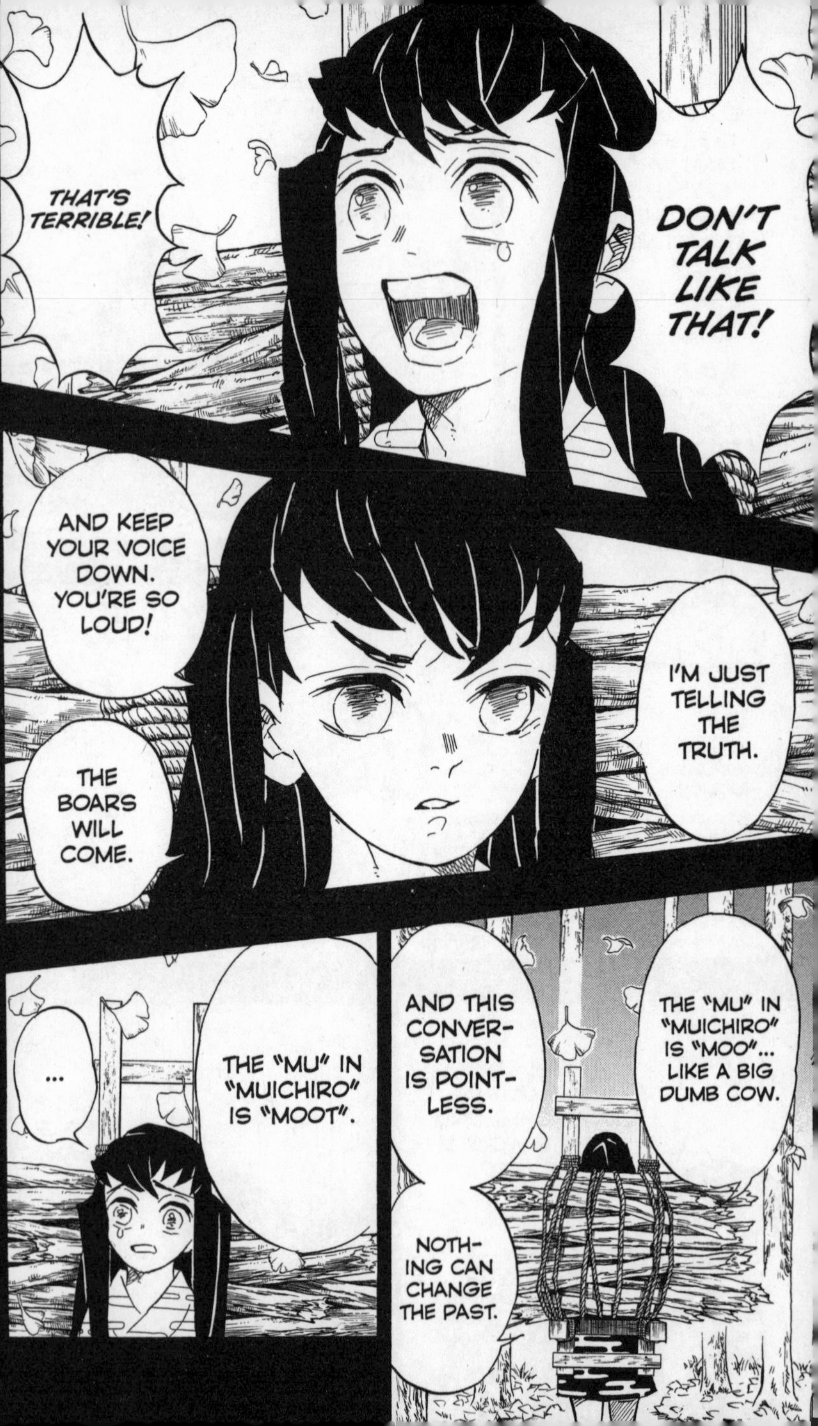
DON'T TALK LIKE THAT!
THAT'S TERRIBLE!
I'M JUST TELLING THE TRUTH.
AND KEEP YOUR VOICE DOWN. YOU'RE SO LOUD!
THE BOARS WILL COME.
THE "MU" IN "MUICHIRO" IS "MOO"... LIKE A BIG DUMB COW.
AND THIS CONVER-SATION IS POINT-LESS.
NOTH-ING CAN CHANGE THE PAST.
THE "MU" IN "MUICHIRO" IS "MOOT".
...

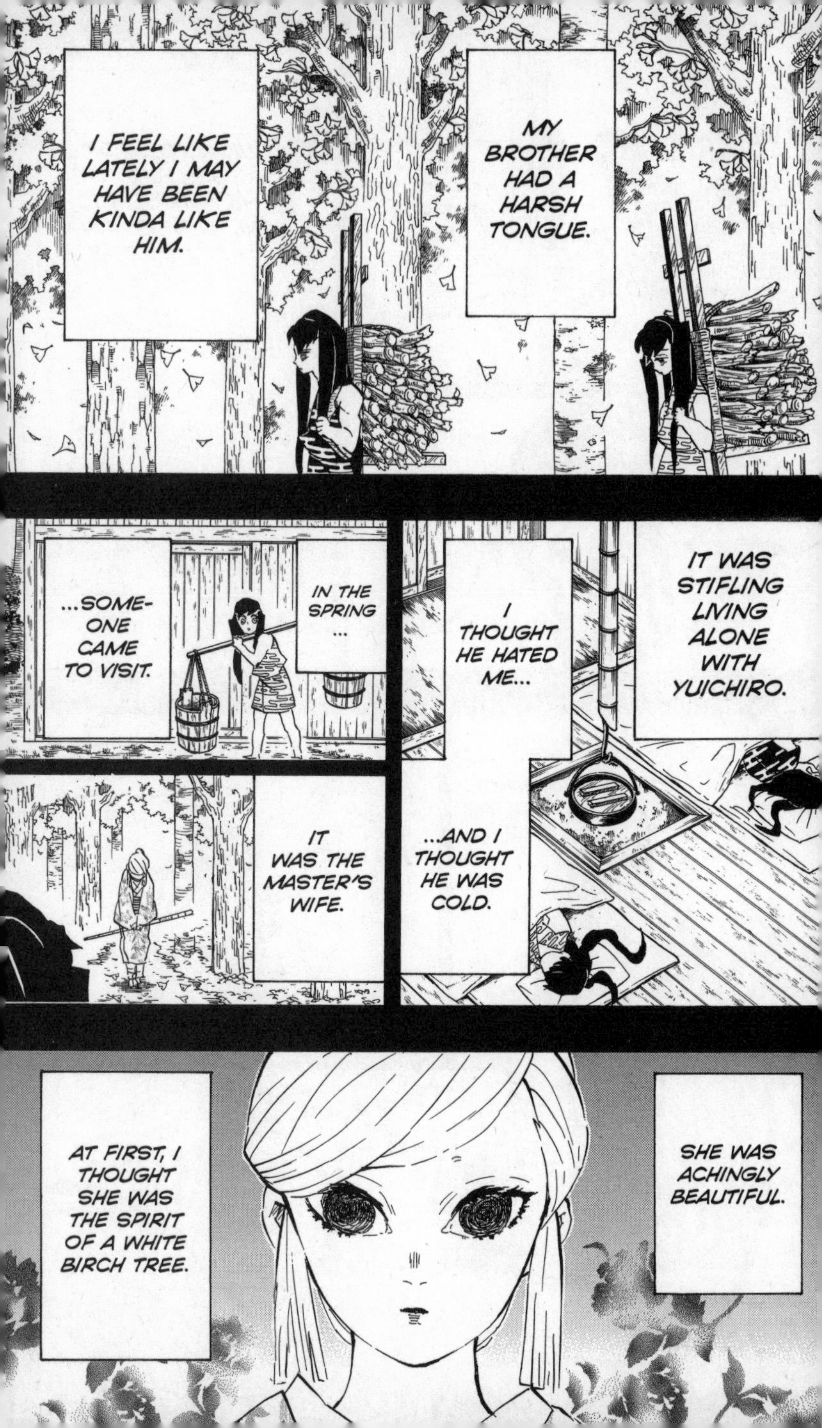
MY BROTHER HAD A HARSH TONGUE.
I FEEL LIKE LATELY I MAY HAVE BEEN KINDA LIKE HIM.
IT WAS STIFLING LIVING ALONE WITH YUICHIRO.
I THOUGHT HE HATED ME...
...AND I THOUGHT HE WAS COLD.
IN THE SPRING ...
...SOME-ONE CAME TO VISIT.
IT WAS THE MASTER'S WIFE.
SHE WAS ACHINGLY BEAUTIFUL.
AT FIRST, I THOUGHT SHE WAS THE SPIRIT OF A WHITE BIRCH TREE.

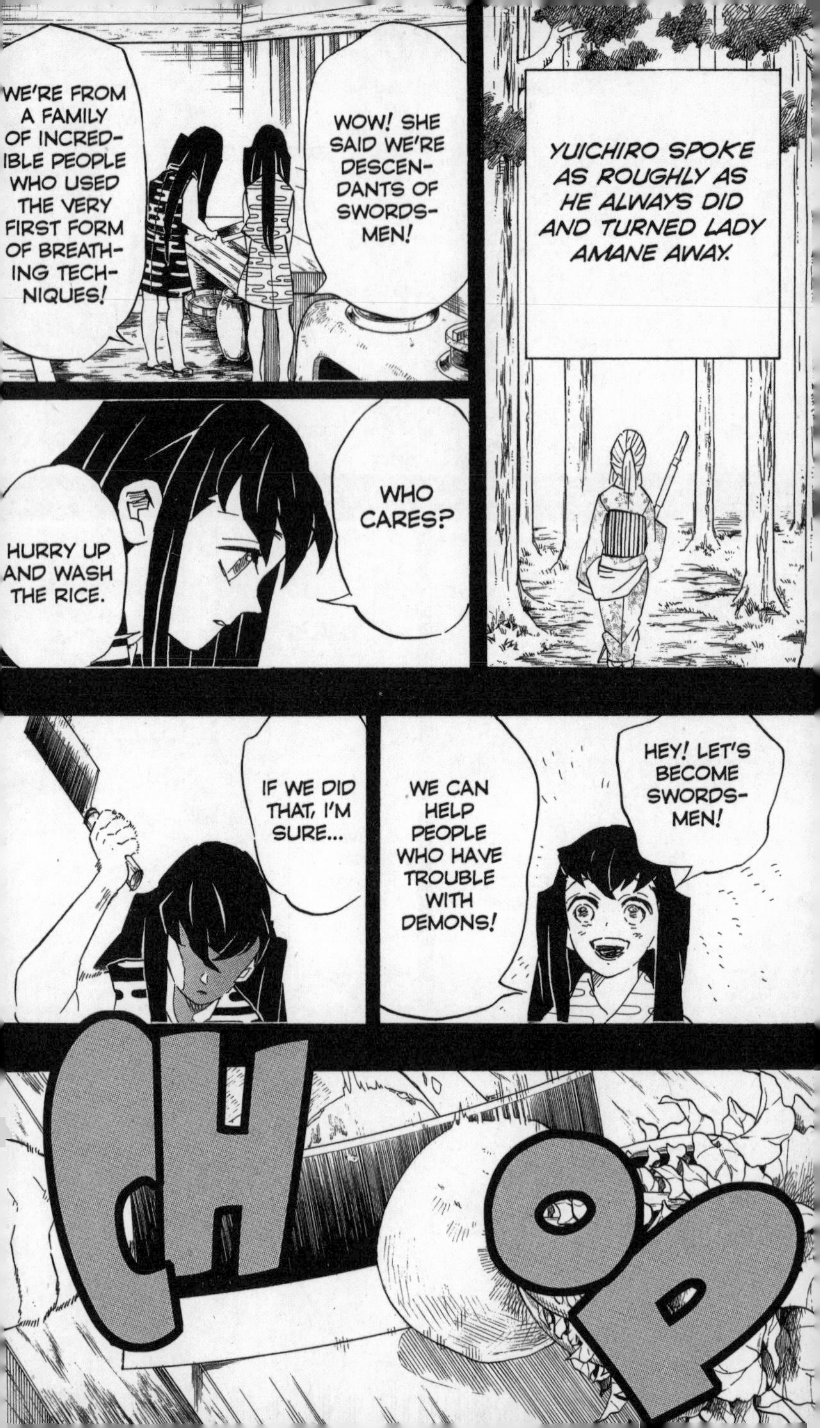
YUICHIRO SPOKE AS ROUGHLY AS HE ALWAYS DID AND TURNED LADY AMANE AWAY.
WOW! SHE SAID WE'RE DESCEN-DANTS OF SWORDS-MEN!
WE'RE FROM A FAMILY OF INCRED-IBLE PEOPLE WHO USED THE VERY FIRST FORM OF BREATH-ING TECH-NIQUES!
WHO CARES?
HURRY UP AND WASH THE RICE.
HEY! LET'S BECOME SWORDS-MEN!
WE CAN HELP PEOPLE WHO HAVE TROUBLE WITH DEMONS!
IF WE DID THAT, I'M SURE...
CHOP

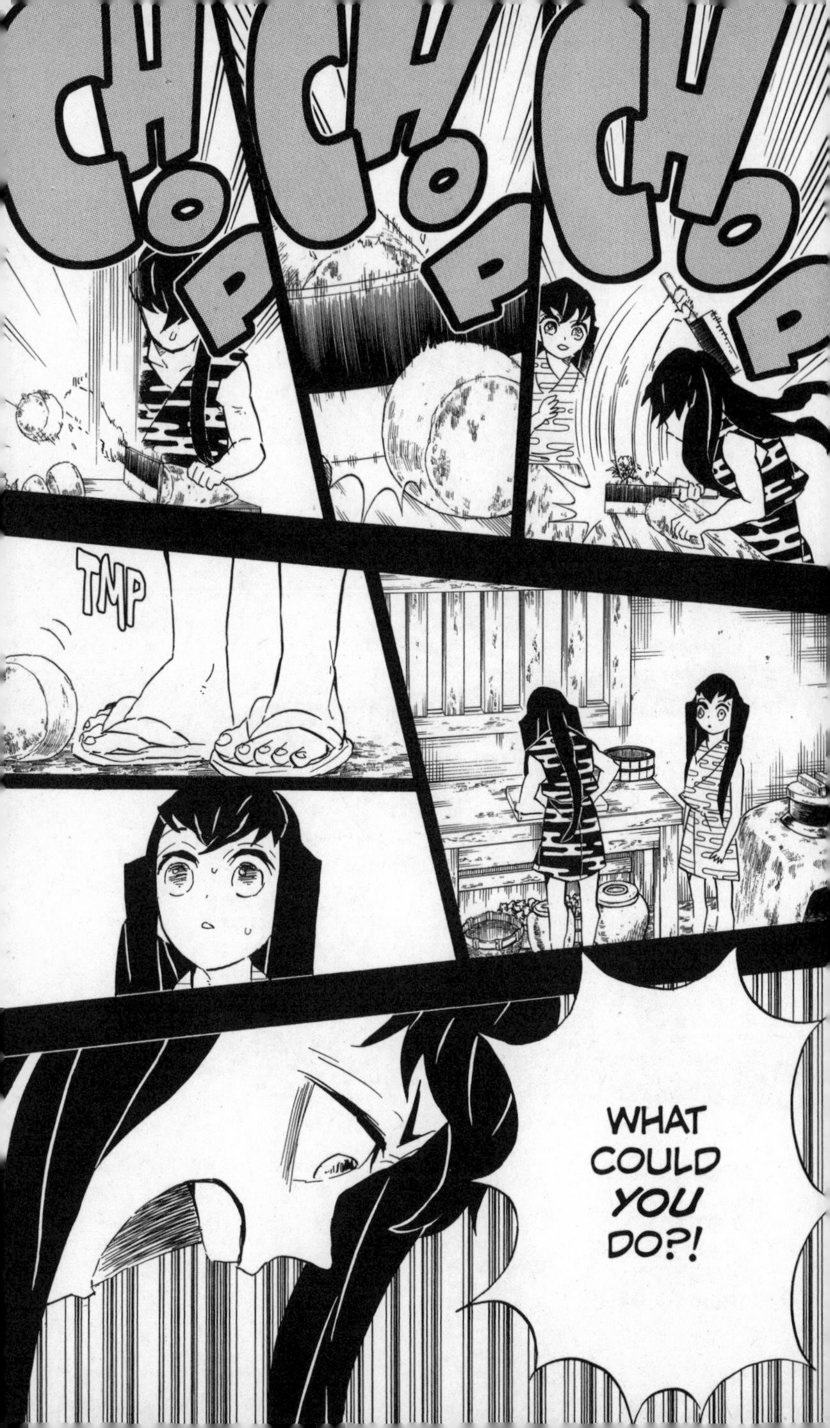
CHOP CHOP CHOP
TMP
WHAT COULD YOU DO?!

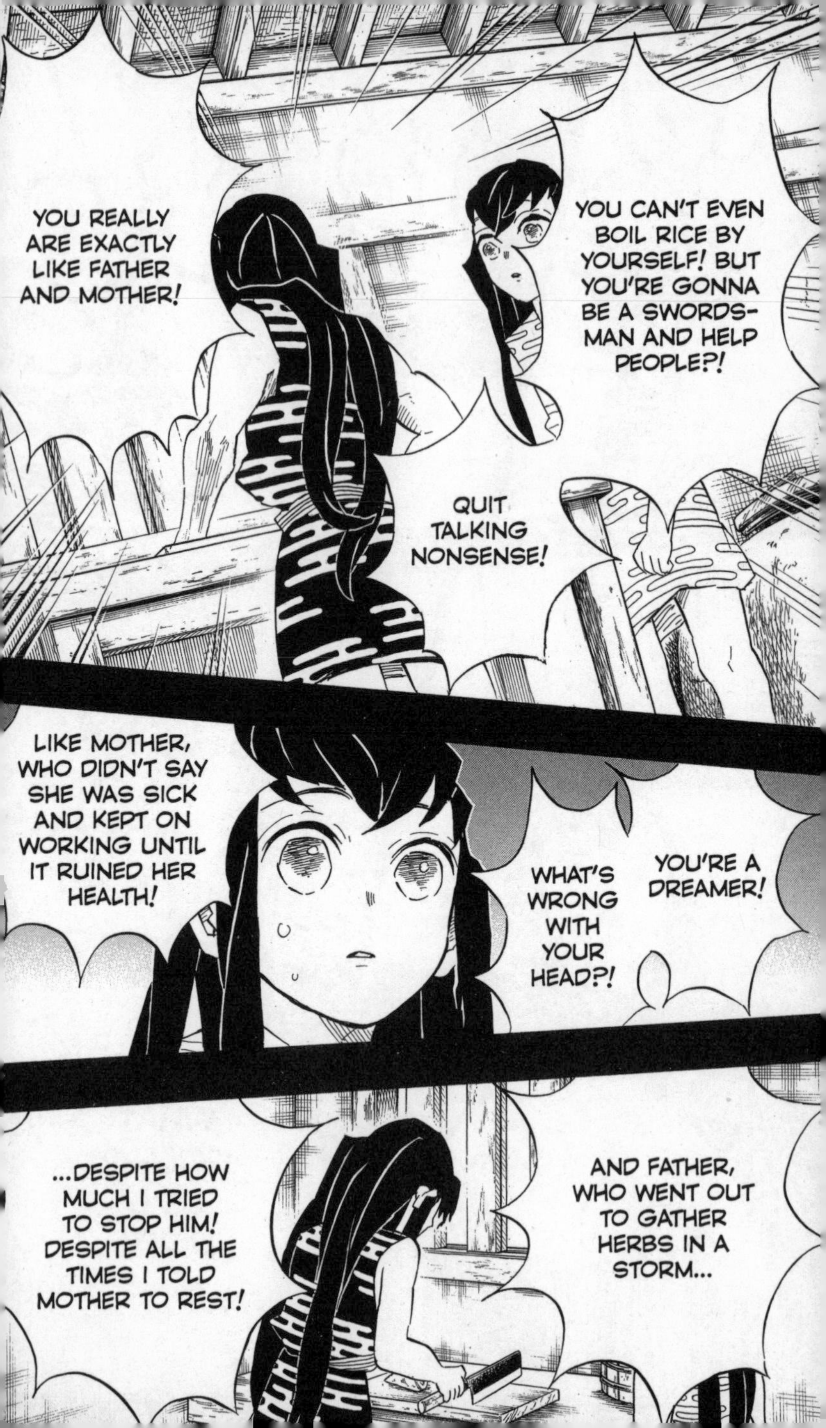
YOU CAN'T EVEN BOIL RICE BY YOURSELF! BUT YOU'RE GONNA BE A SWORDS-MAN AND HELP PEOPLE?!
YOU REALLY ARE EXACTLY LIKE FATHER AND MOTHER!
QUIT TALKING NONSENSE!
YOU'RE A DREAMER!
WHAT'S WRONG WITH YOUR HEAD?!
LIKE MOTHER, WHO DIDN'T SAY SHE WAS SICK AND KEPT ON WORKING UNTIL IT RUINED HER HEALTH!
AND FATHER, WHO WENT OUT TO GATHER HERBS IN A STORM...
...DESPITE HOW MUCH I TRIED TO STOP HIM! DESPITE ALL THE TIMES I TOLD MOTHER TO REST!

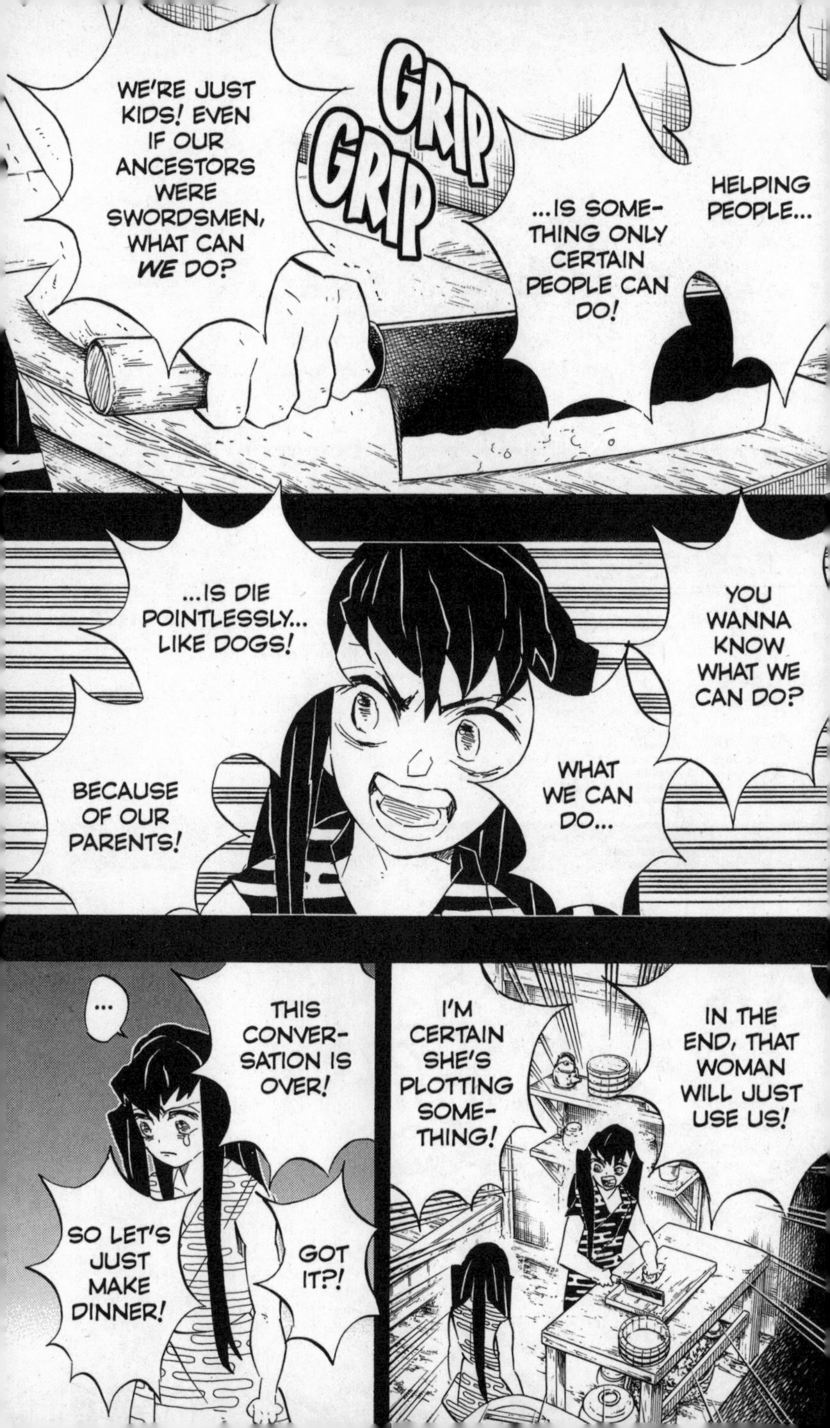
HELPING PEOPLE...
...IS SOMETHING ONLY CERTAIN PEOPLE CAN DO!
GRIP GRIP
WE'RE JUST KIDS! EVEN IF OUR ANCESTORS WERE SWORDSMEN, WHAT CAN *WE* DO?
YOU WANNA KNOW WHAT WE CAN DO?
WHAT WE CAN DO...
...IS DIE POINTLESSLY... LIKE DOGS!
BECAUSE OF OUR PARENTS!
IN THE END, THAT WOMAN WILL JUST USE US!
I'M CERTAIN SHE'S PLOTTING SOMETHING!
THIS CONVERSATION IS OVER!
...
GOT IT?!
SO LET'S JUST MAKE DINNER!

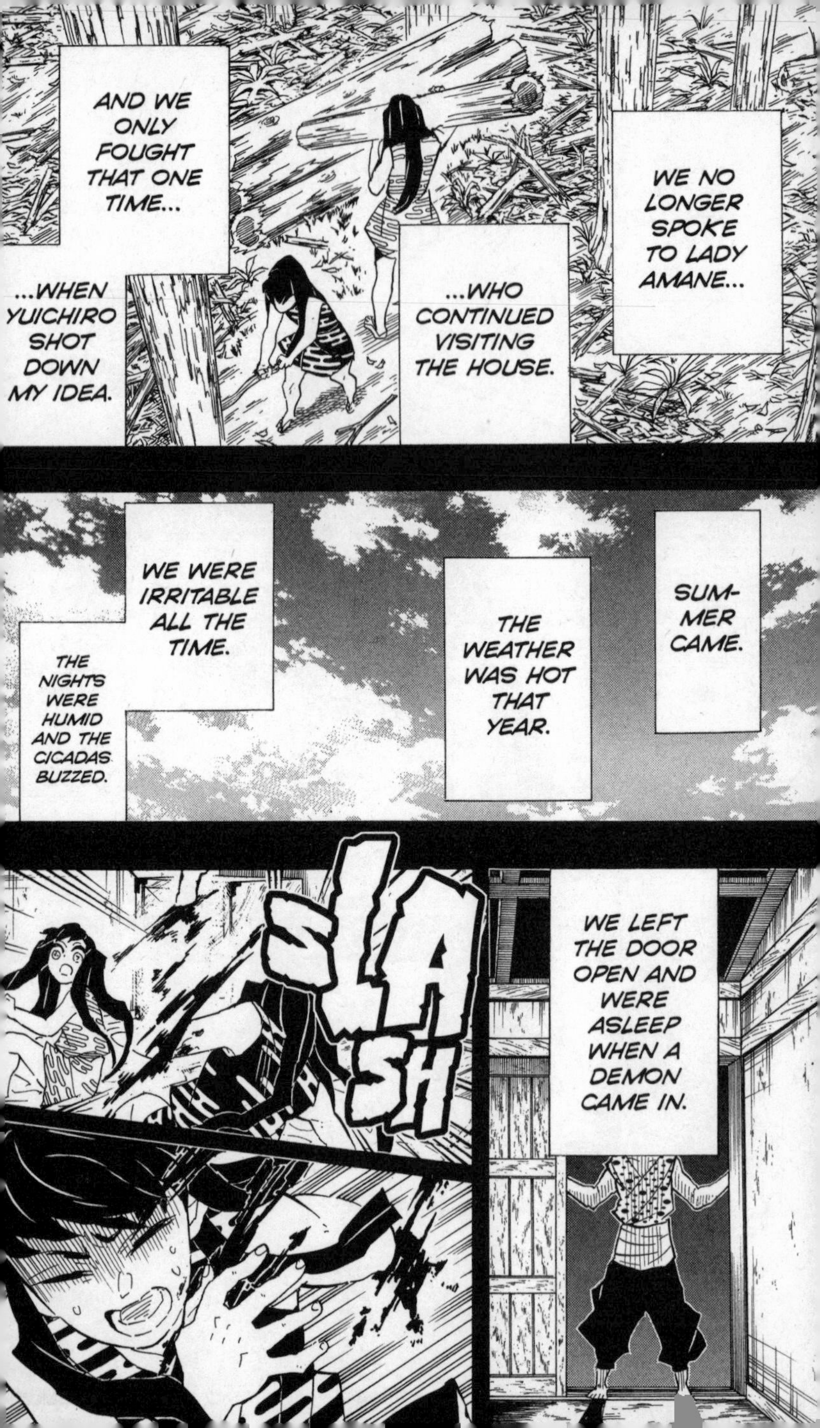
WE NO LONGER SPOKE TO LADY AMANE...
...WHO CONTINUED VISITING THE HOUSE.
AND WE ONLY FOUGHT THAT ONE TIME...
...WHEN YUICHIRO SHOT DOWN MY IDEA.
SUMMER CAME.
THE WEATHER WAS HOT THAT YEAR.
WE WERE IRRITABLE ALL THE TIME.
THE NIGHTS WERE HUMID AND THE CICADAS BUZZED.
WE LEFT THE DOOR OPEN AND WERE ASLEEP WHEN A DEMON CAME IN.
SLASH

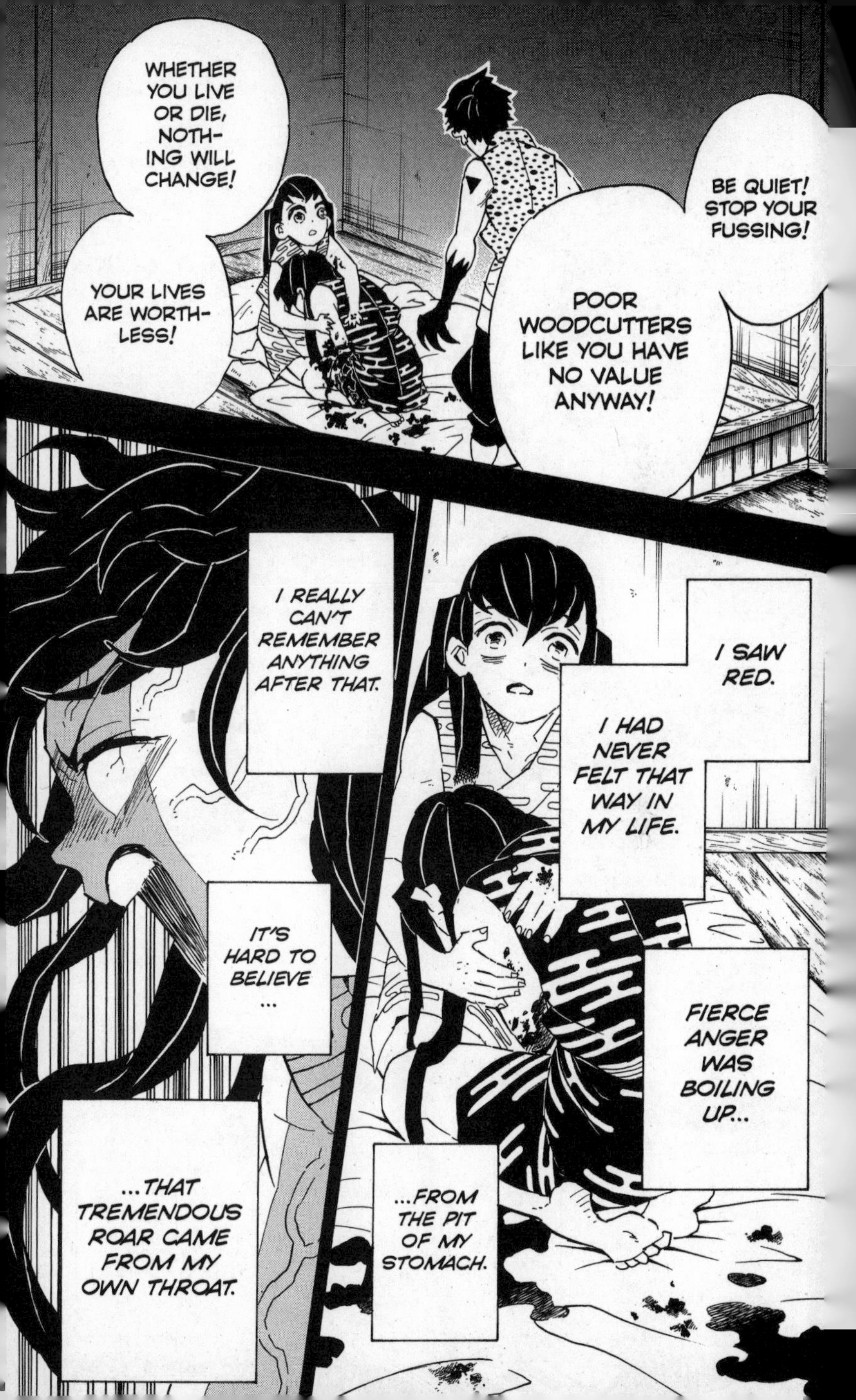
BE QUIET! STOP YOUR FUSSING!
POOR WOODCUTTERS LIKE YOU HAVE NO VALUE ANYWAY!
WHETHER YOU LIVE OR DIE, NOTHING WILL CHANGE!
YOUR LIVES ARE WORTHLESS!
I SAW RED.
I HAD NEVER FELT THAT WAY IN MY LIFE.
FIERCE ANGER WAS BOILING UP...
...FROM THE PIT OF MY STOMACH.
I REALLY CAN'T REMEMBER ANYTHING AFTER THAT.
IT'S HARD TO BELIEVE...
...THAT TREMENDOUS ROAR CAME FROM MY OWN THROAT.

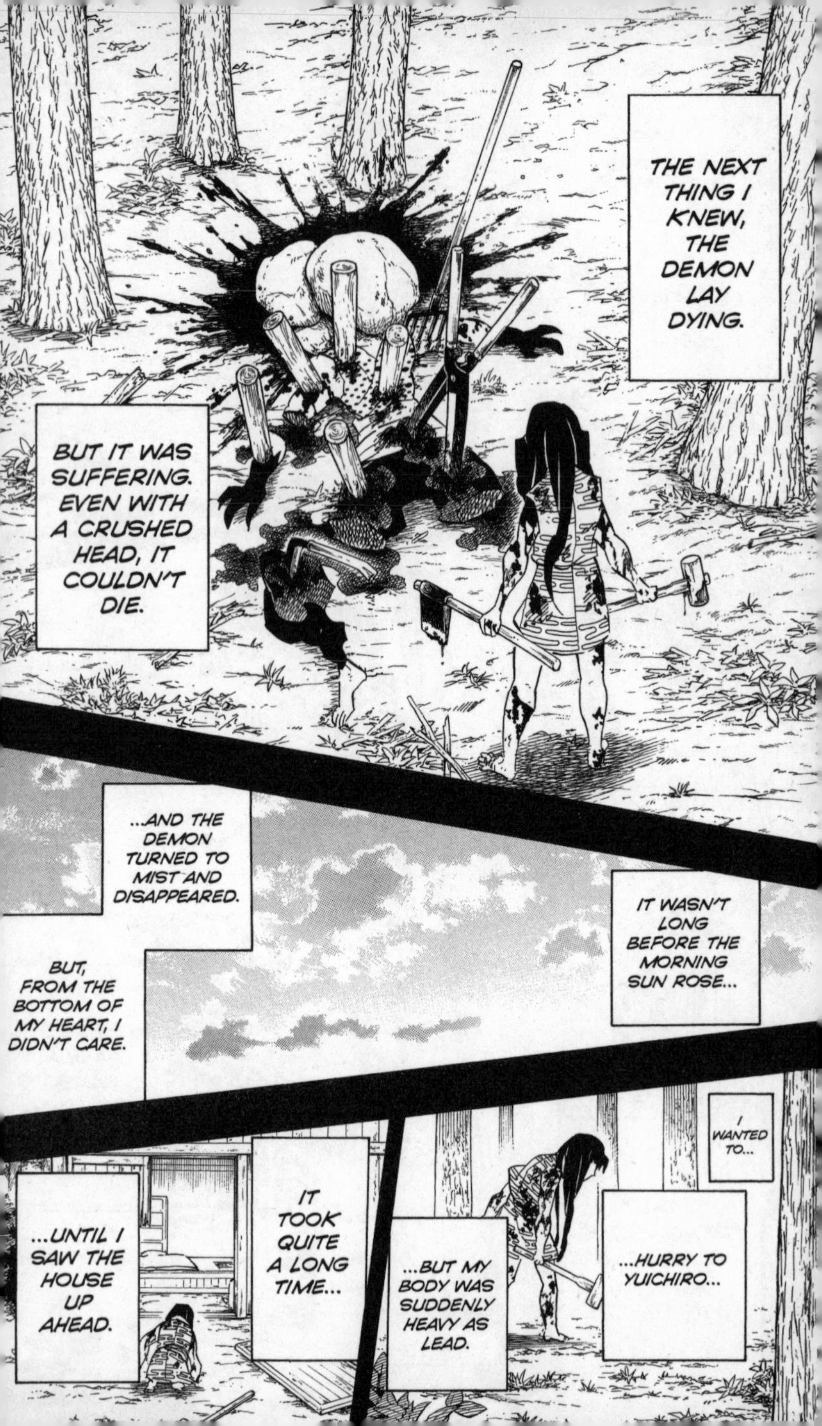
THE NEXT THING I KNEW, THE DEMON LAY DYING.
BUT IT WAS SUFFERING. EVEN WITH A CRUSHED HEAD, IT COULDN'T DIE.
IT WASN'T LONG BEFORE THE MORNING SUN ROSE...
...AND THE DEMON TURNED TO MIST AND DISAPPEARED.
BUT, FROM THE BOTTOM OF MY HEART, I DIDN'T CARE.
I WANTED TO...
...HURRY TO YUICHIRO...
...BUT MY BODY WAS SUDDENLY HEAVY AS LEAD.
IT TOOK QUITE A LONG TIME...
...UNTIL I SAW THE HOUSE UP AHEAD.

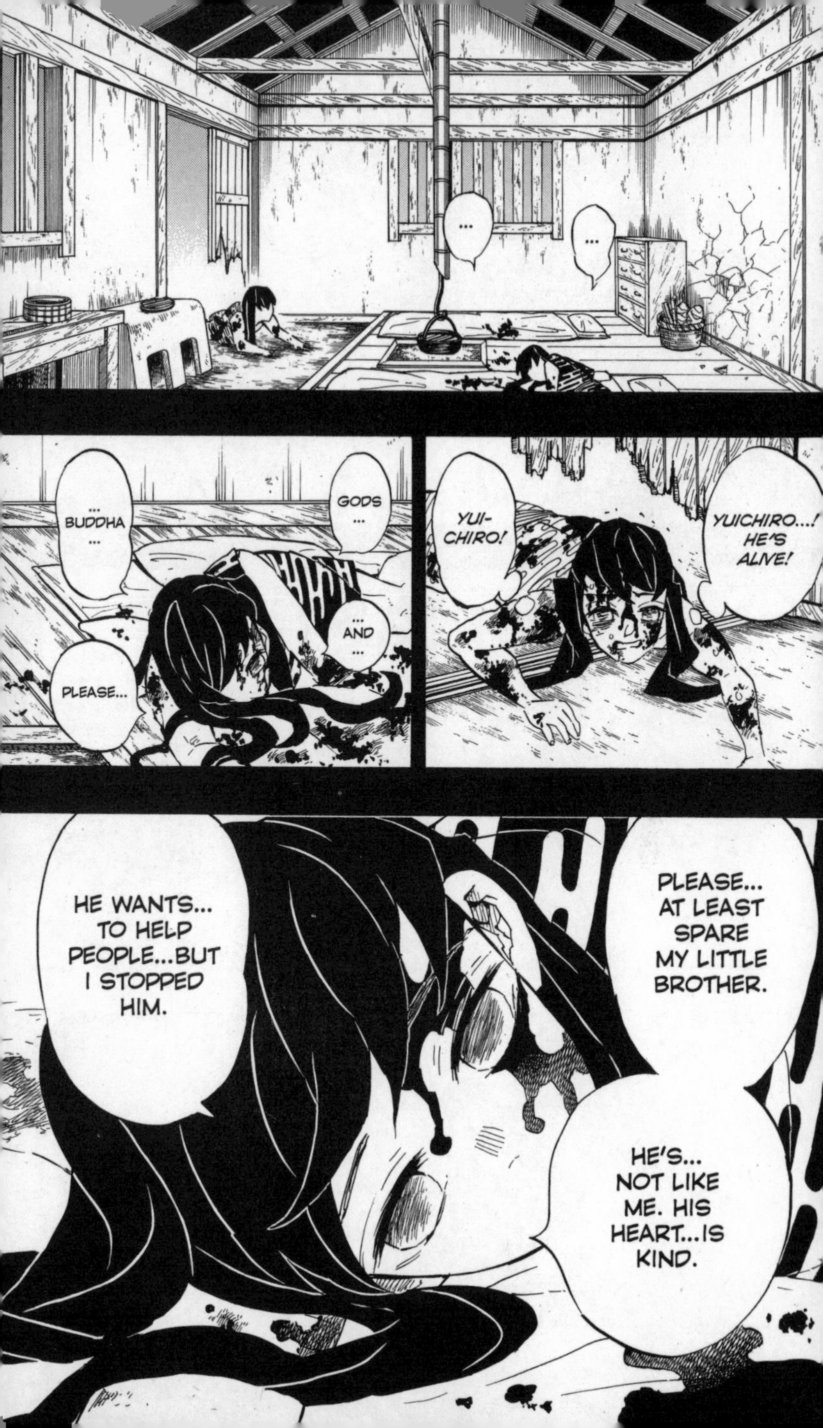
...
...
YUICHIRO...! HE'S ALIVE!
YUI-CHIRO!
GODS...
...BUDDHA...
...AND...
PLEASE...
PLEASE... AT LEAST SPARE MY LITTLE BROTHER.
HE WANTS... TO HELP PEOPLE...BUT I STOPPED HIM.
HE'S... NOT LIKE ME. HIS HEART...IS KIND.

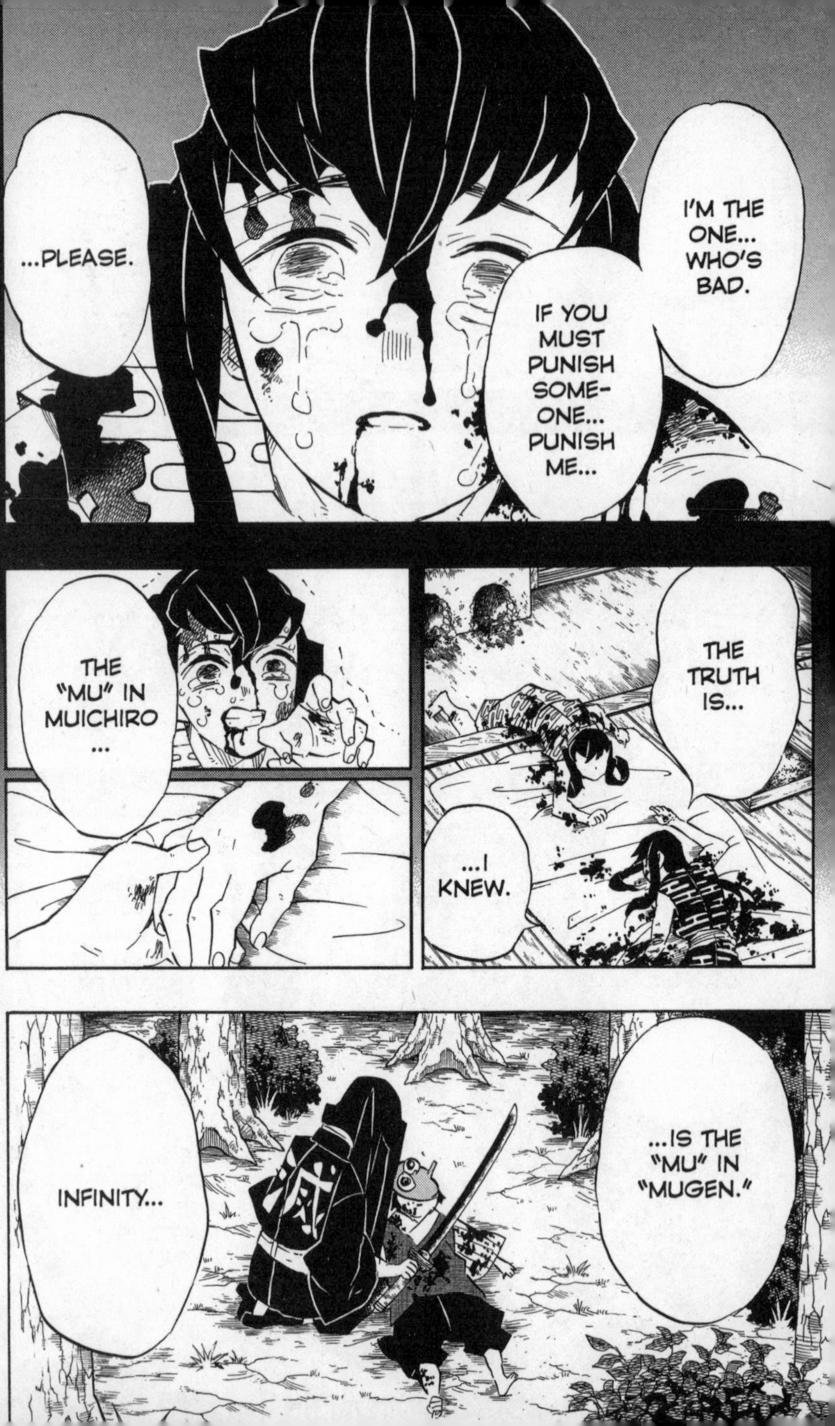
I'M THE ONE... WHO'S BAD.
IF YOU MUST PUNISH SOME-ONE... PUNISH ME...
...PLEASE.
THE TRUTH IS...
...I KNEW.
THE "MU" IN MUICHIRO ...
...IS THE "MU" IN "MUGEN."
INFINITY...

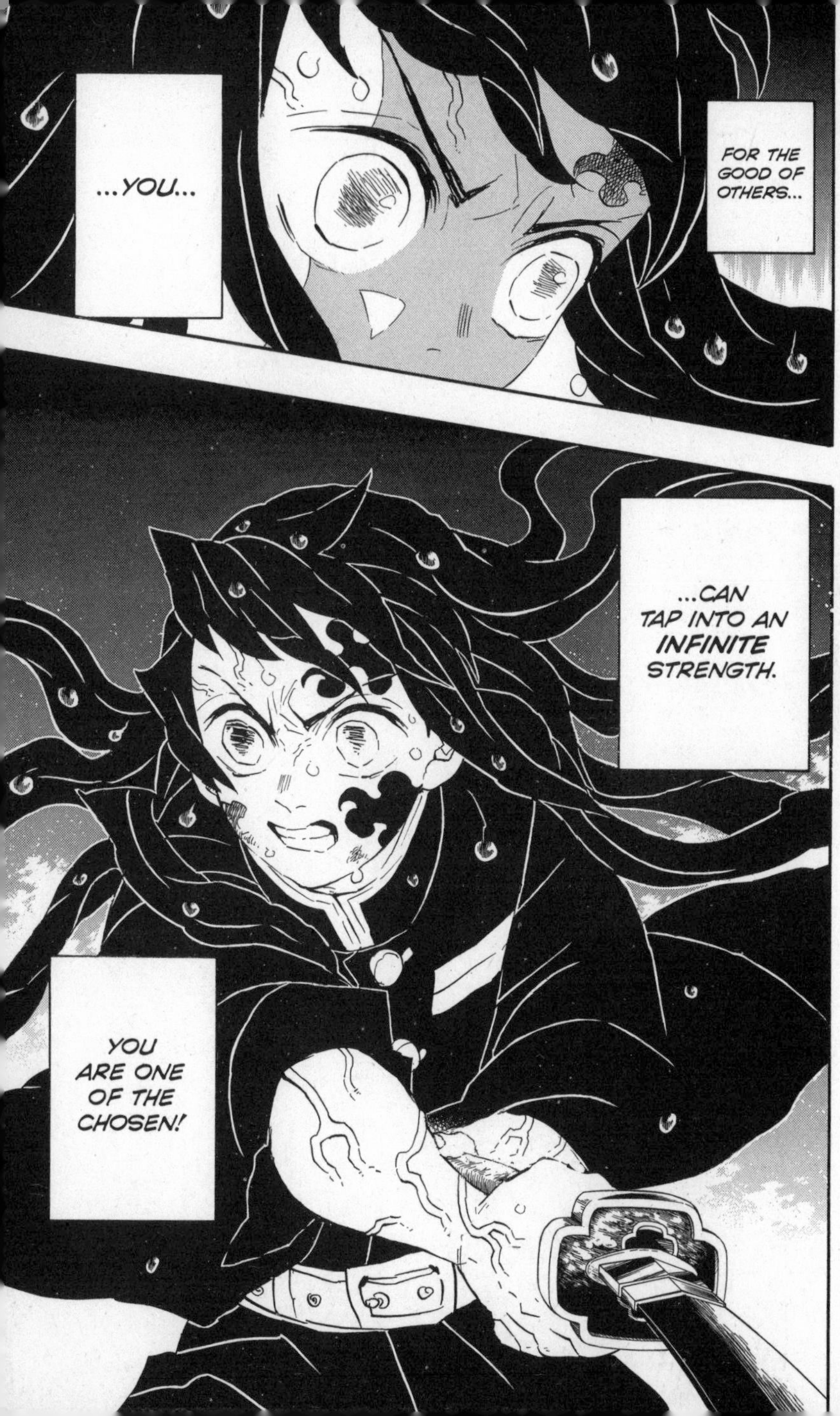
FOR THE GOOD OF OTHERS...
...YOU...
...CAN TAP INTO AN INFINITE STRENGTH.
YOU ARE ONE OF THE CHOSEN!

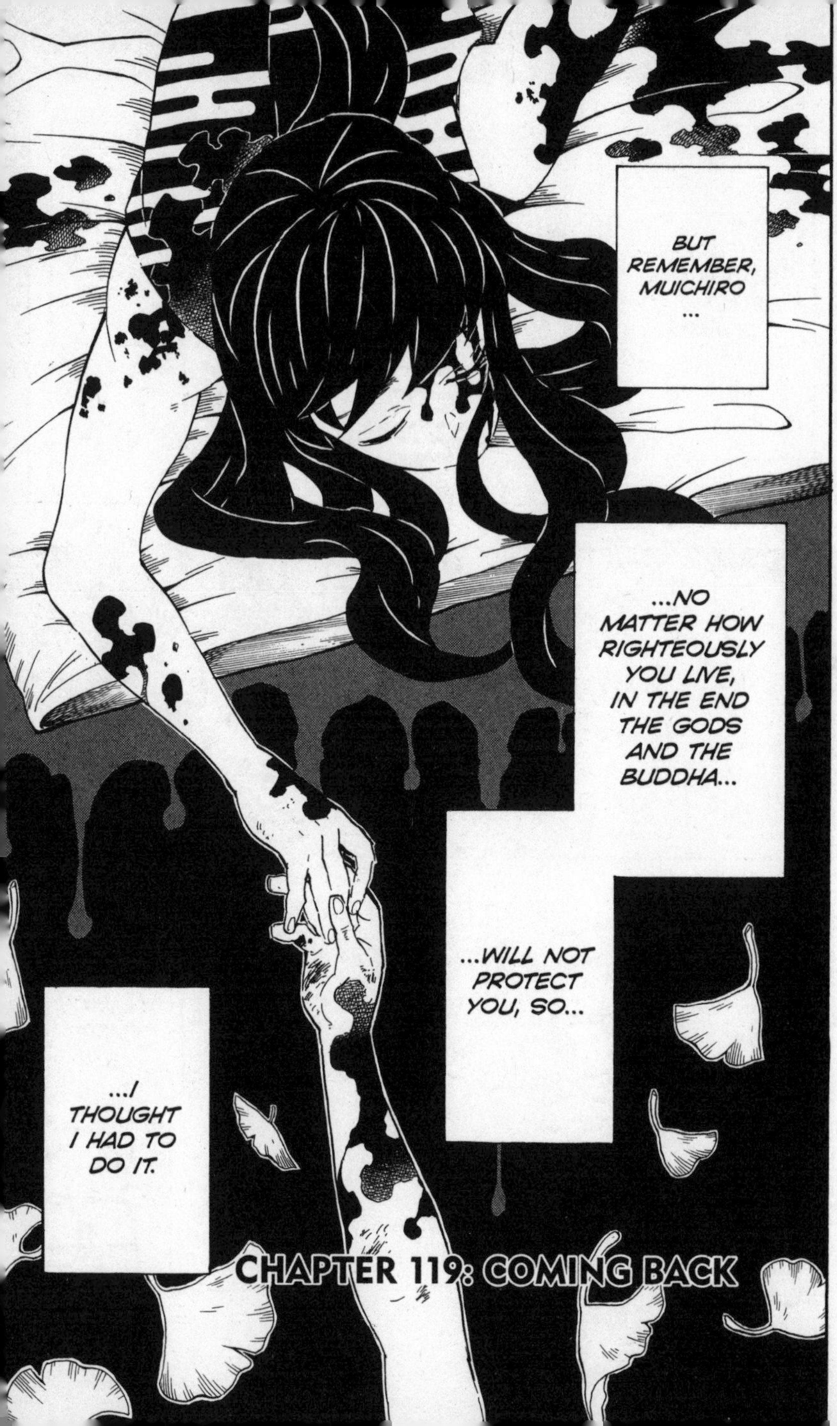
BUT REMEMBER, MUICHIRO ...
...NO MATTER HOW RIGHTEOUSLY YOU LIVE, IN THE END THE GODS AND THE BUDDHA...
...WILL NOT PROTECT YOU, SO...
...I THOUGHT I HAD TO DO IT.

CHAPTER 119: COMING BACK

ONLY CHOSEN SOULS CAN BE KIND TO OTHERS.

I'M SORRY I COULDN'T BE KINDER.

I COULDN'T AFFORD TO.

URRRGH

*EYE: CRESCENT MOON

THIS HUMAN!

I CAN'T STAND IT!

THIS MAN!

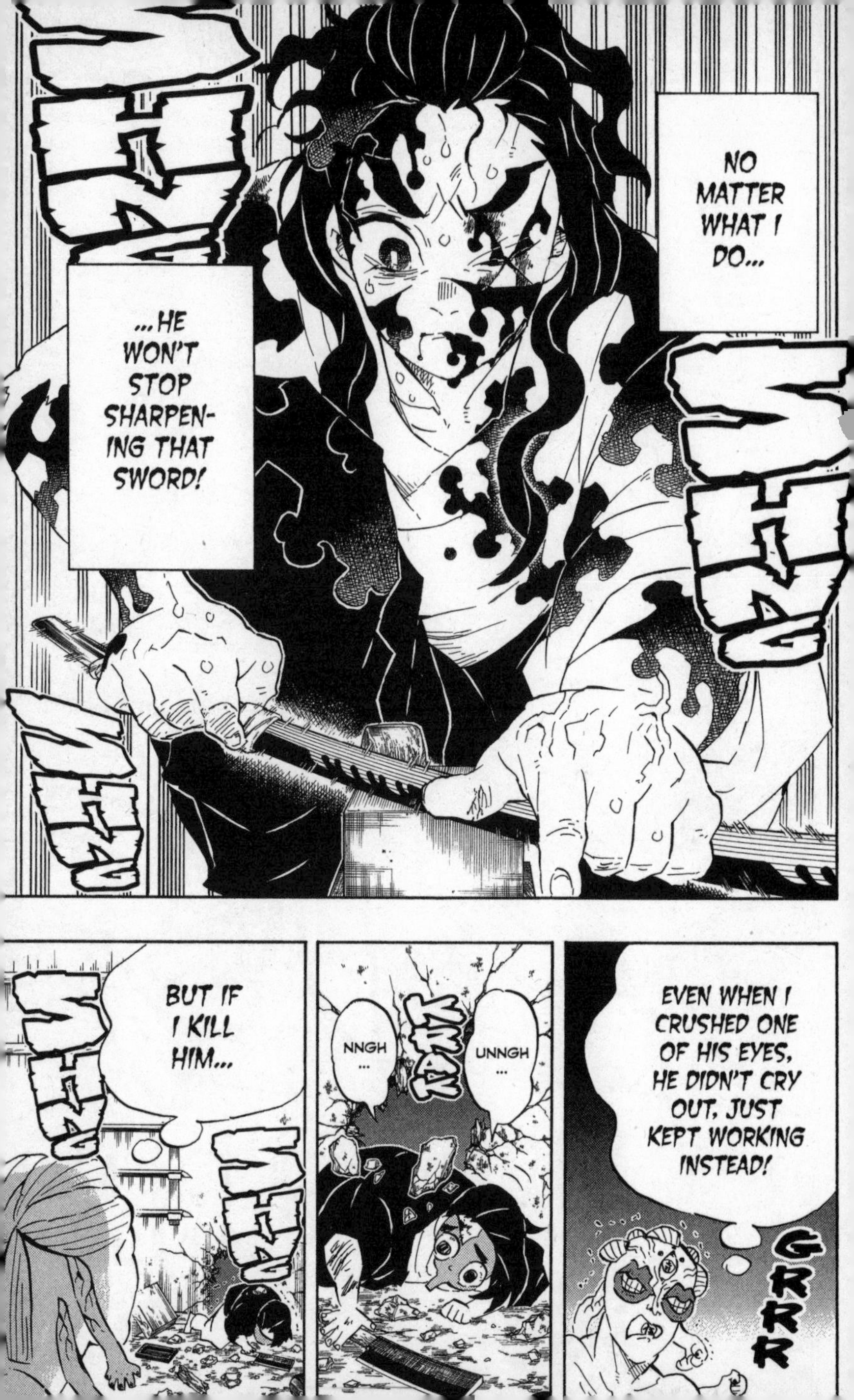
NO MATTER WHAT I DO...
...HE WON'T STOP SHARPENING THAT SWORD!
EVEN WHEN I CRUSHED ONE OF HIS EYES, HE DIDN'T CRY OUT, JUST KEPT WORKING INSTEAD!
GRRR
UNNGH...
NNGH...
BUT IF I KILL HIM...

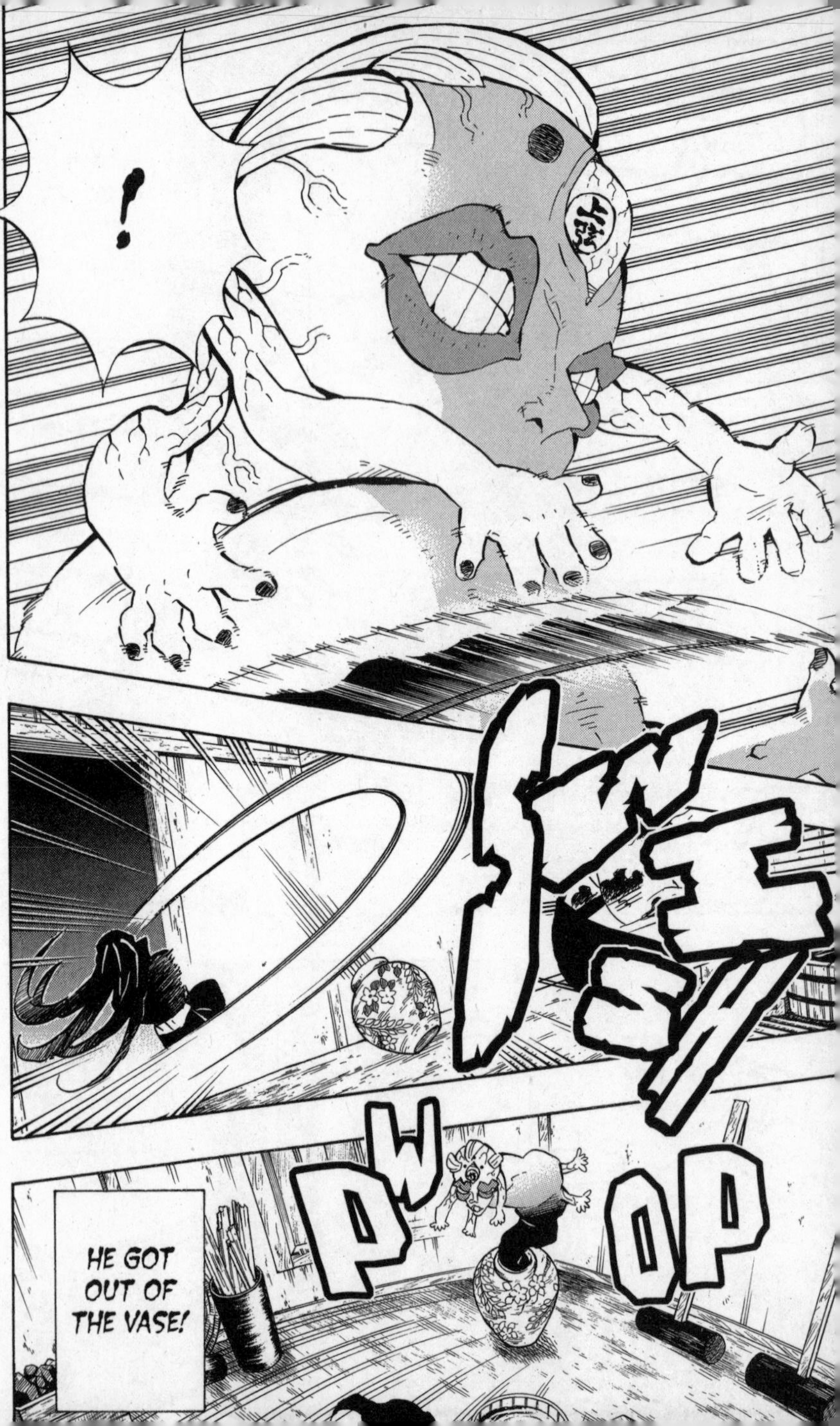
!
FWEESH
PWOP
HE GOT OUT OF THE VASE!

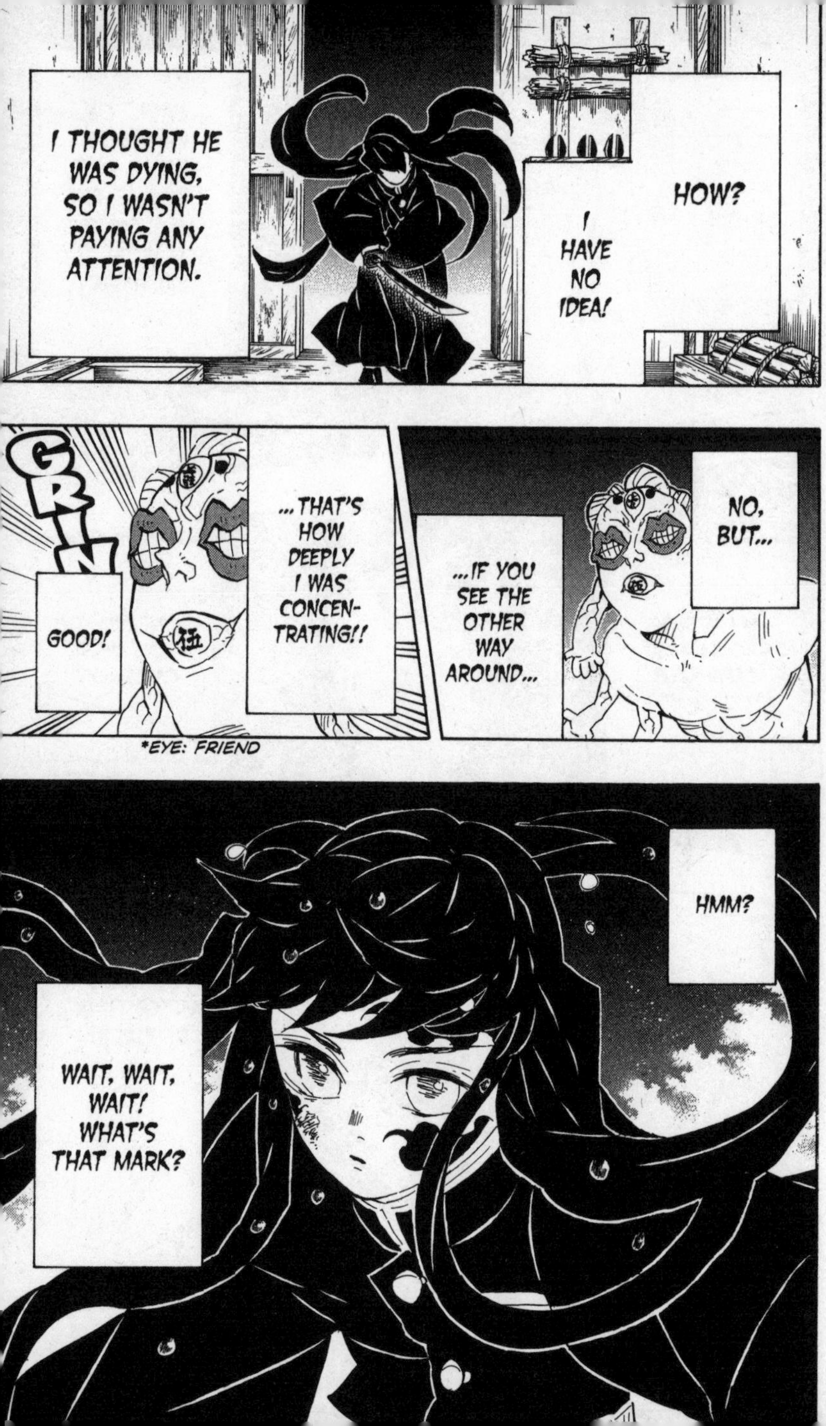
HOW?
I HAVE NO IDEA!
I THOUGHT HE WAS DYING, SO I WASN'T PAYING ANY ATTENTION.
NO, BUT...
...IF YOU SEE THE OTHER WAY AROUND...
...THAT'S HOW DEEPLY I WAS CONCEN-TRATING!!
GRIN
GOOD!
*EYE: FRIEND
HMM?
WAIT, WAIT, WAIT! WHAT'S THAT MARK?

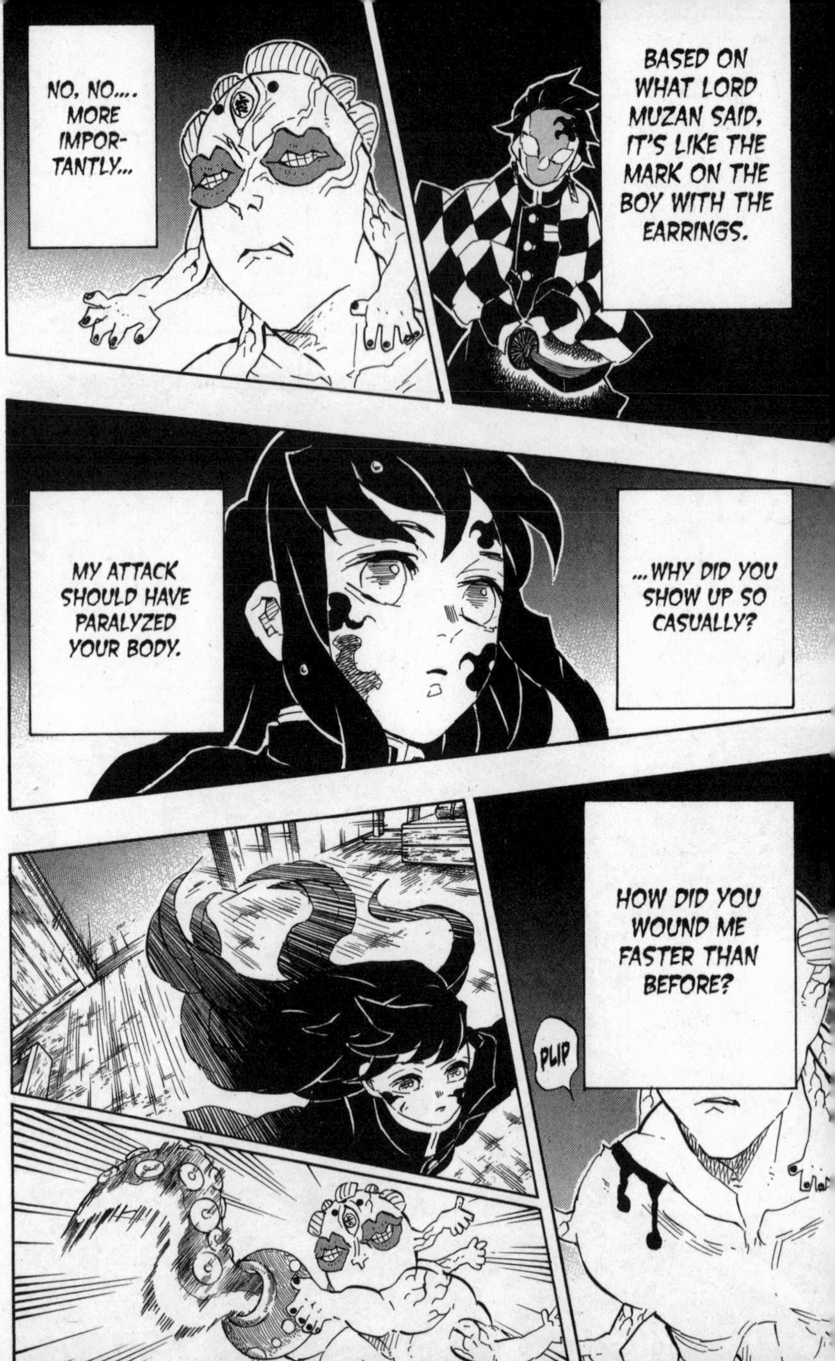
BASED ON WHAT LORD MUZAN SAID, IT'S LIKE THE MARK ON THE BOY WITH THE EARRINGS.
NO, NO.... MORE IMPORTANTLY...
...WHY DID YOU SHOW UP SO CASUALLY?
MY ATTACK SHOULD HAVE PARALYZED YOUR BODY.
HOW DID YOU WOUND ME FASTER THAN BEFORE?
PLIP

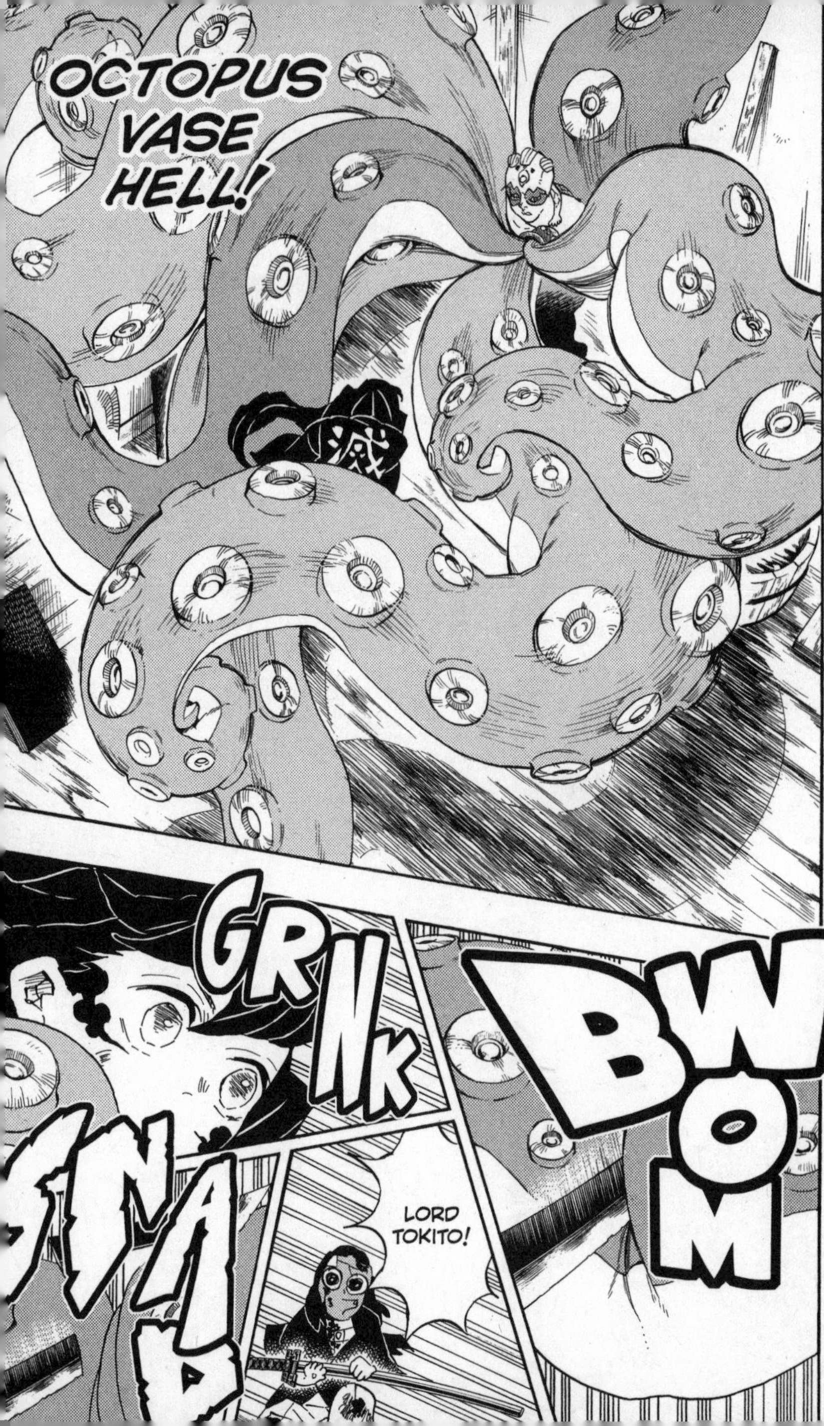
OCTOPUS VASE HELL!
BWOOM
GRINK
LORD TOKITO!

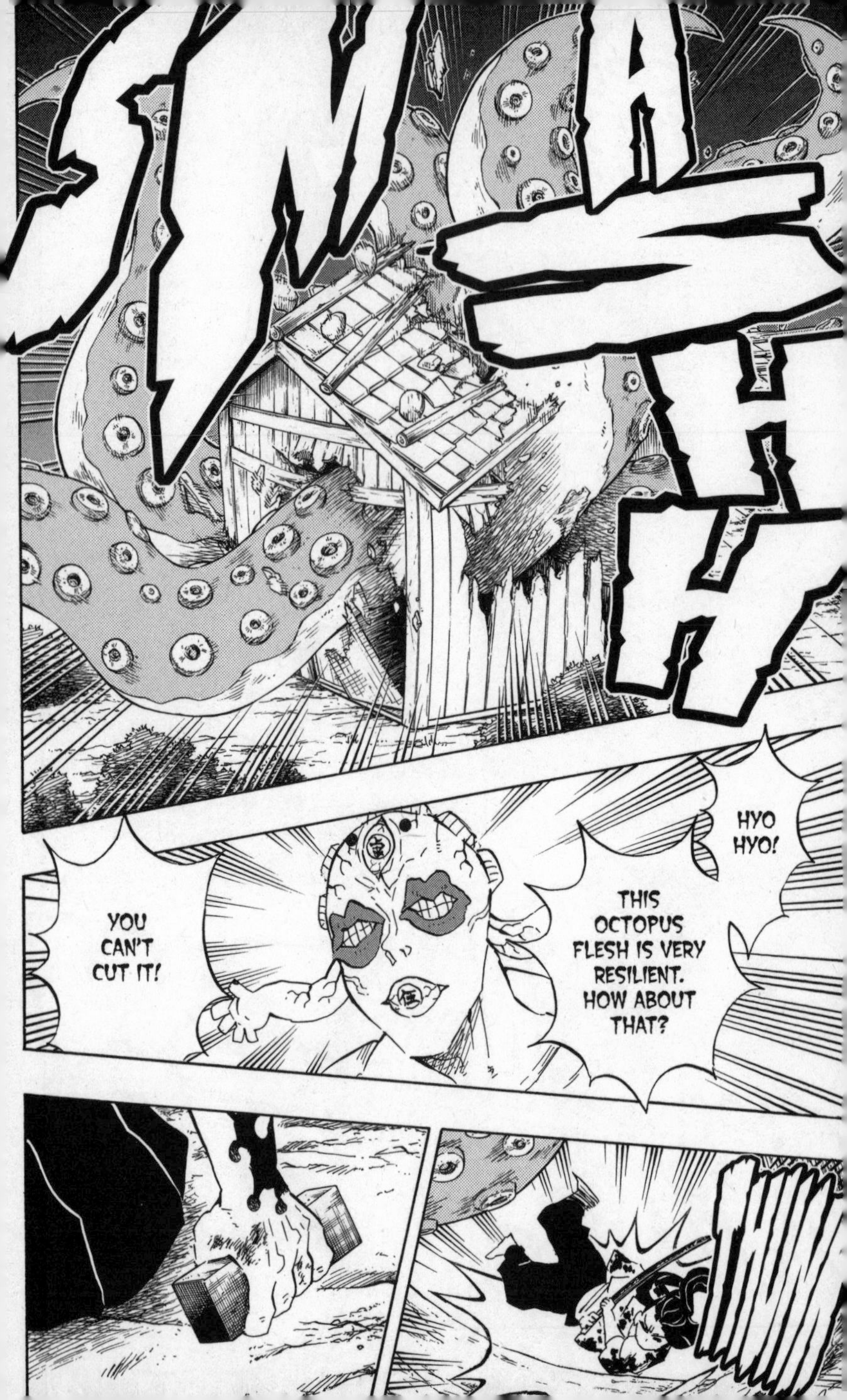
HYO HYO!
THIS OCTOPUS FLESH IS VERY RESILIENT. HOW ABOUT THAT?
YOU CAN'T CUT IT!

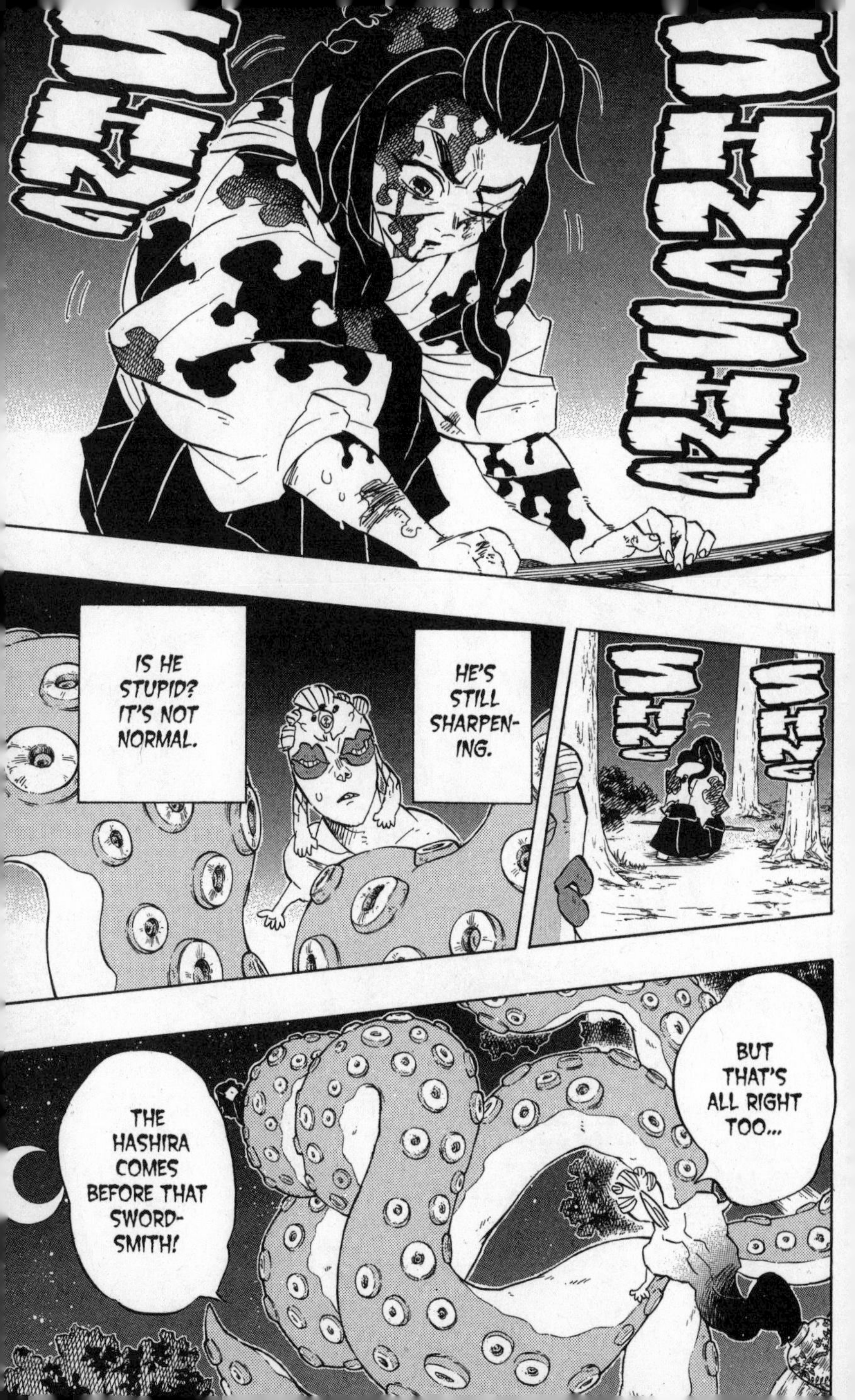
SHING SHING
SHING
SHING
SHING
HE'S STILL SHARPEN-ING.
IS HE STUPID? IT'S NOT NORMAL.
BUT THAT'S ALL RIGHT TOO...
THE HASHIRA COMES BEFORE THAT SWORD-SMITH!

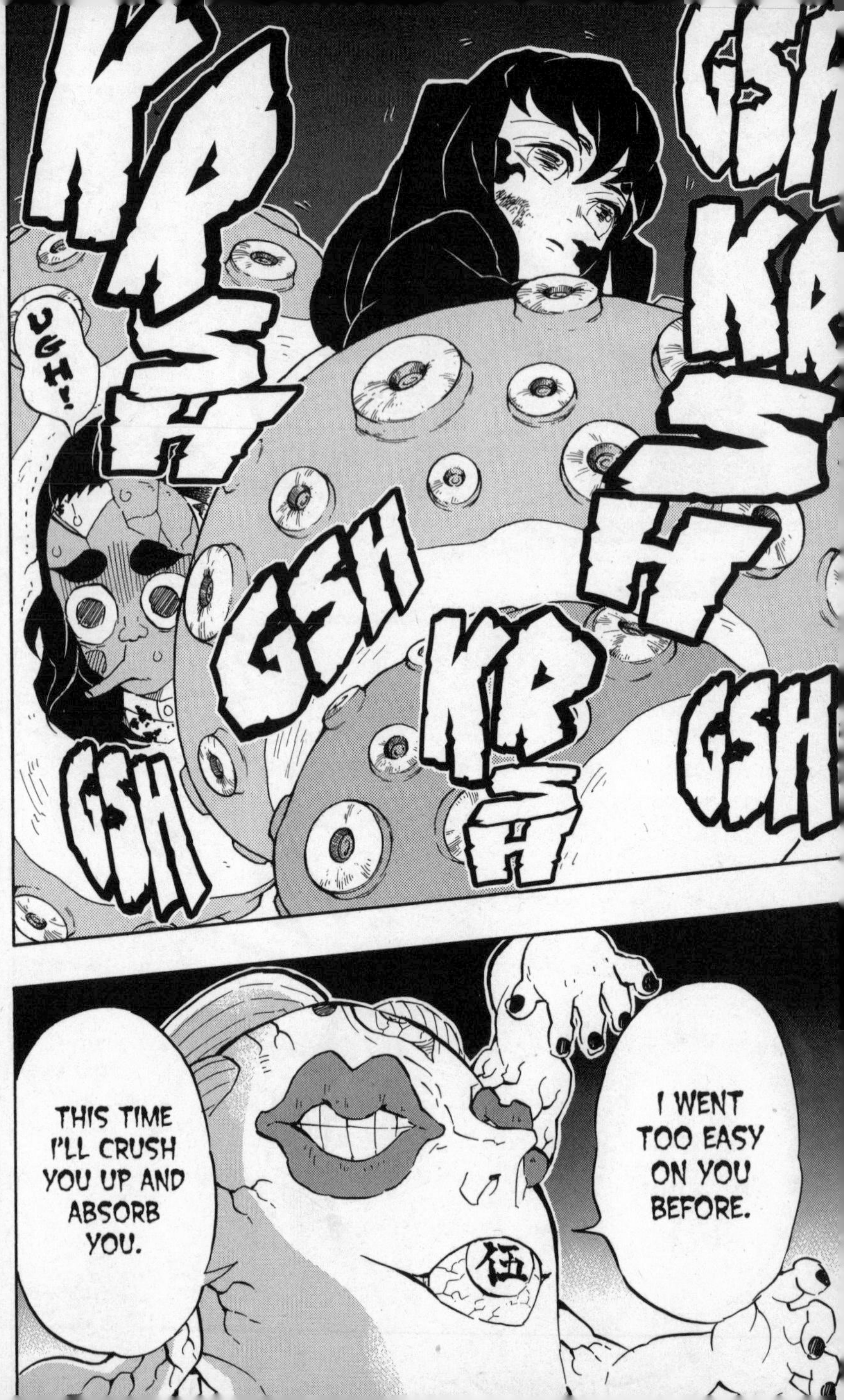
KRSH
GSH
KRSH
GSH
KRSH
UGH!
GSH
I WENT TOO EASY ON YOU BEFORE.
THIS TIME I'LL CRUSH YOU UP AND ABSORB YOU.

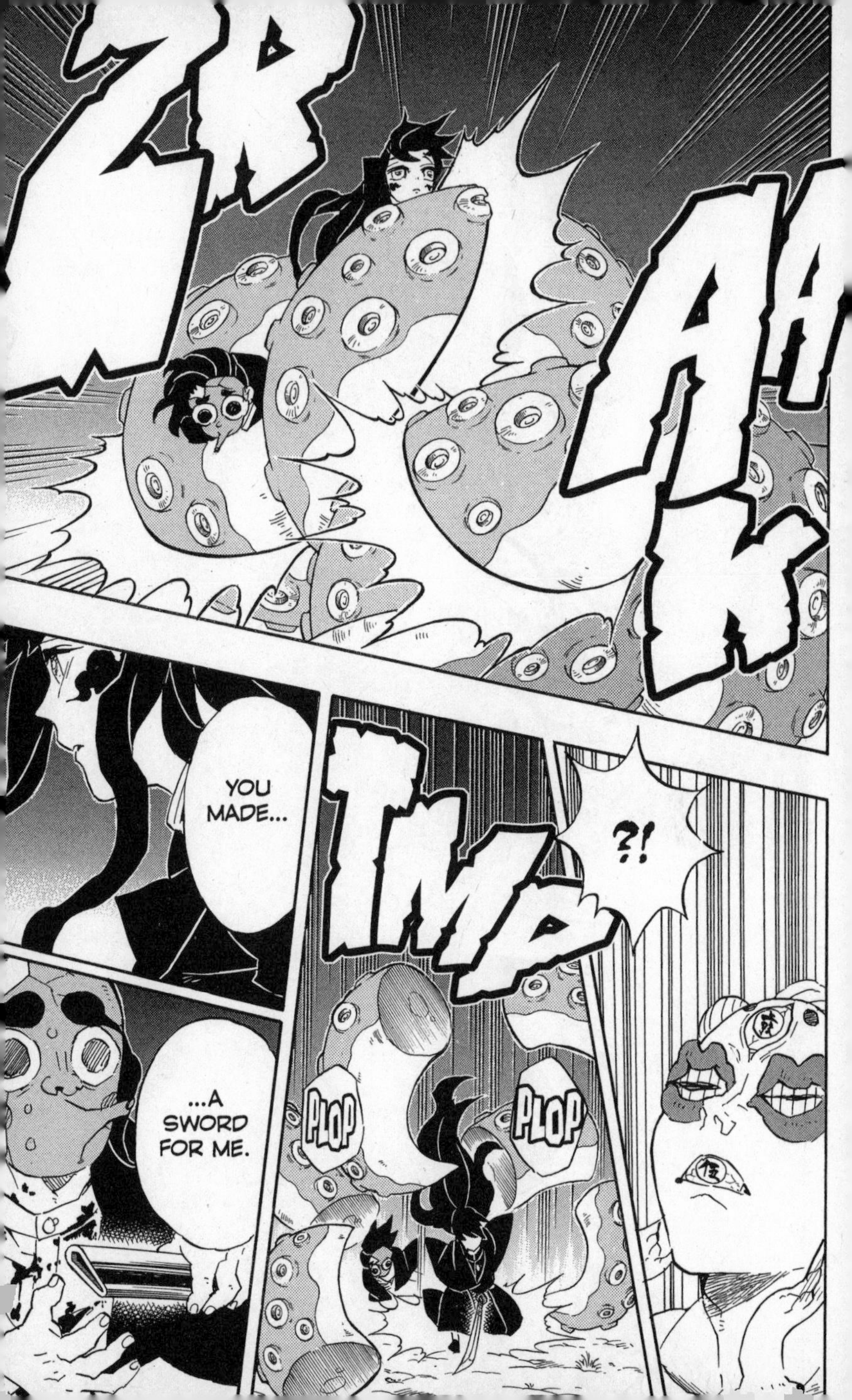
ZRAAK
?!
TMP
PLOP
PLOP
YOU MADE...
...A SWORD FOR ME.

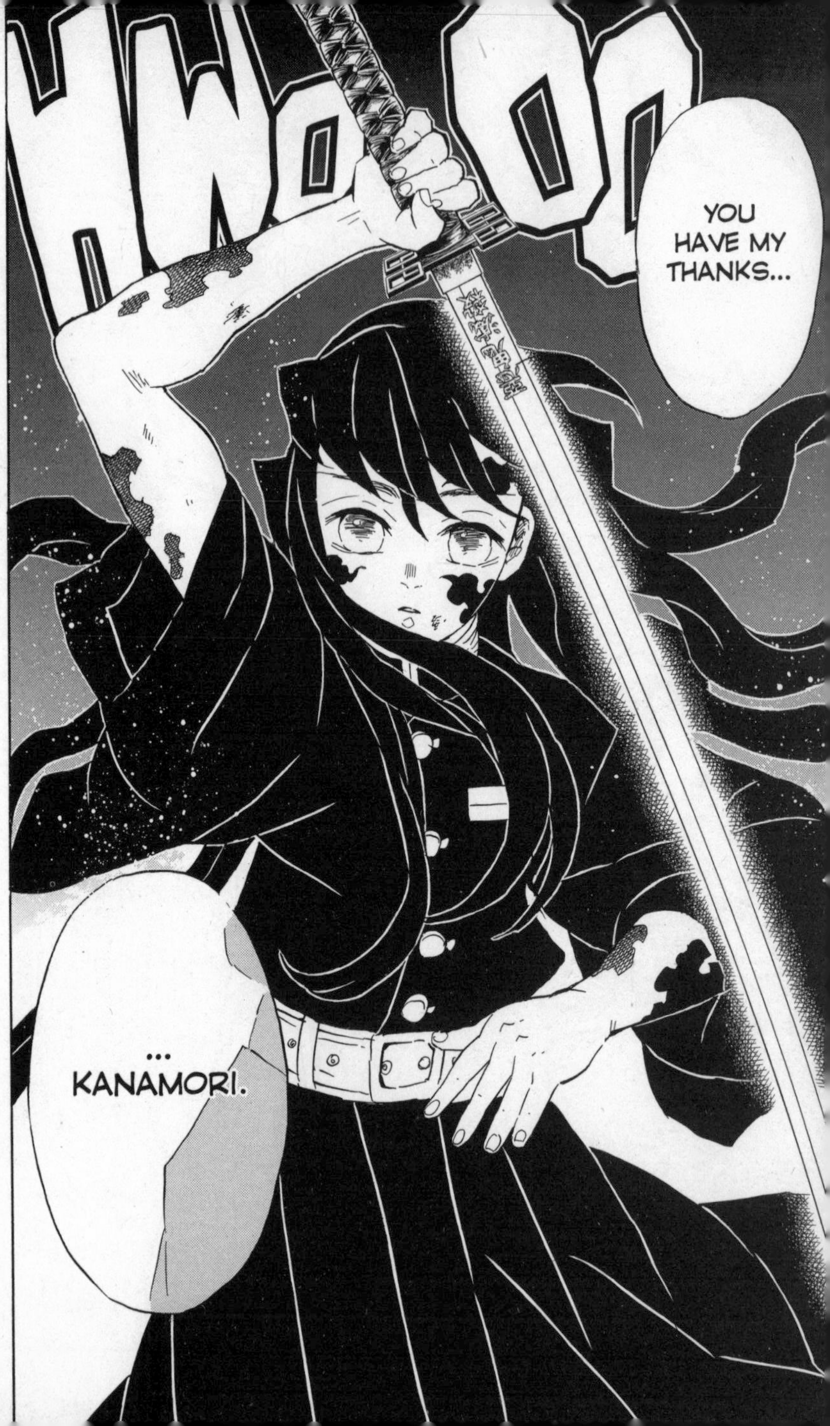
KWOOO
YOU HAVE MY THANKS...
... KANAMORI.

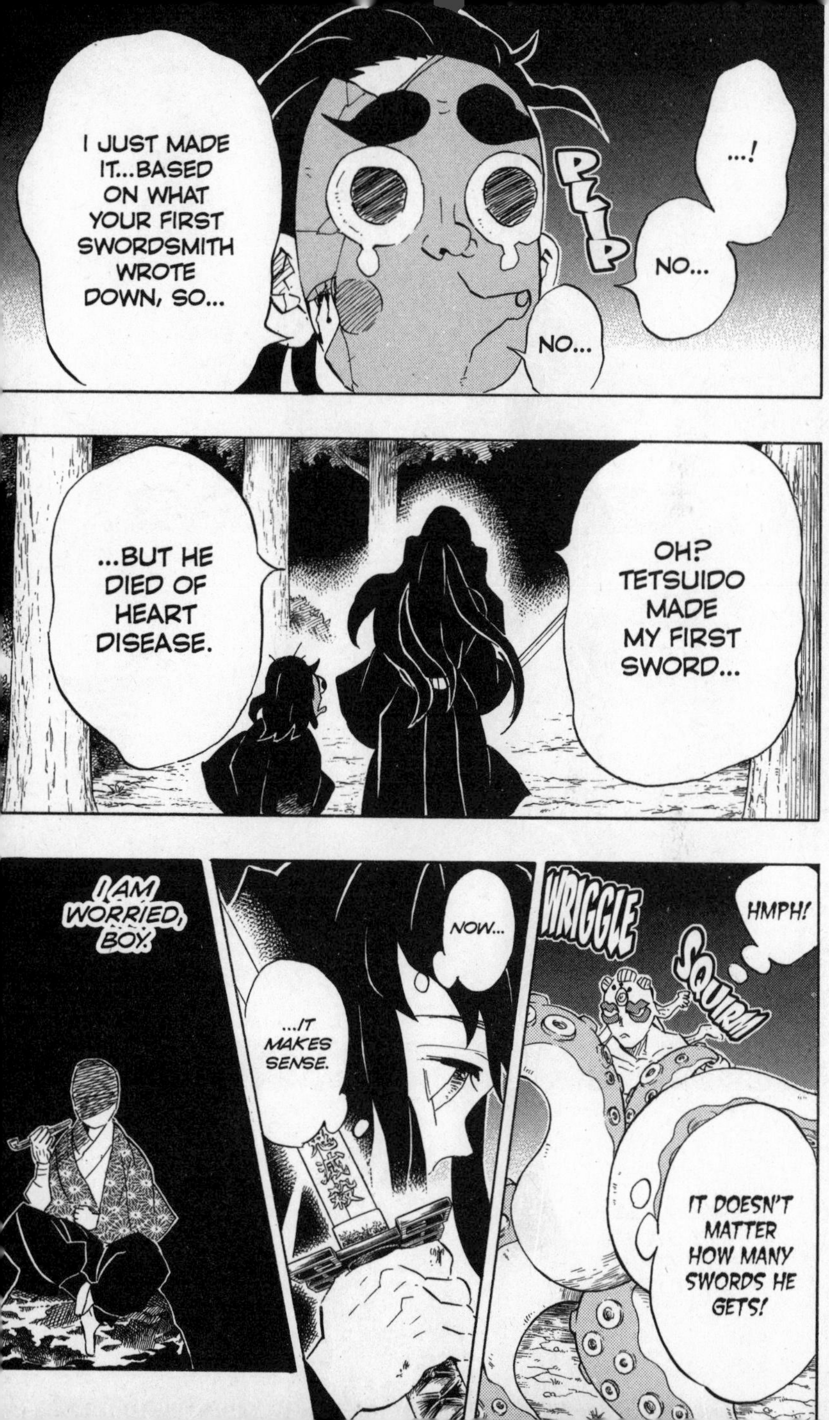
...!
NO...
PLIP
NO...
I JUST MADE IT...BASED ON WHAT YOUR FIRST SWORDSMITH WROTE DOWN, SO...
OH? TETSUIDO MADE MY FIRST SWORD...
...BUT HE DIED OF HEART DISEASE.
HMPH!
WRIGGLE
SQUIRM
IT DOESN'T MATTER HOW MANY SWORDS HE GETS!
NOW...
...IT MAKES SENSE.
I AM WORRIED, BOY.

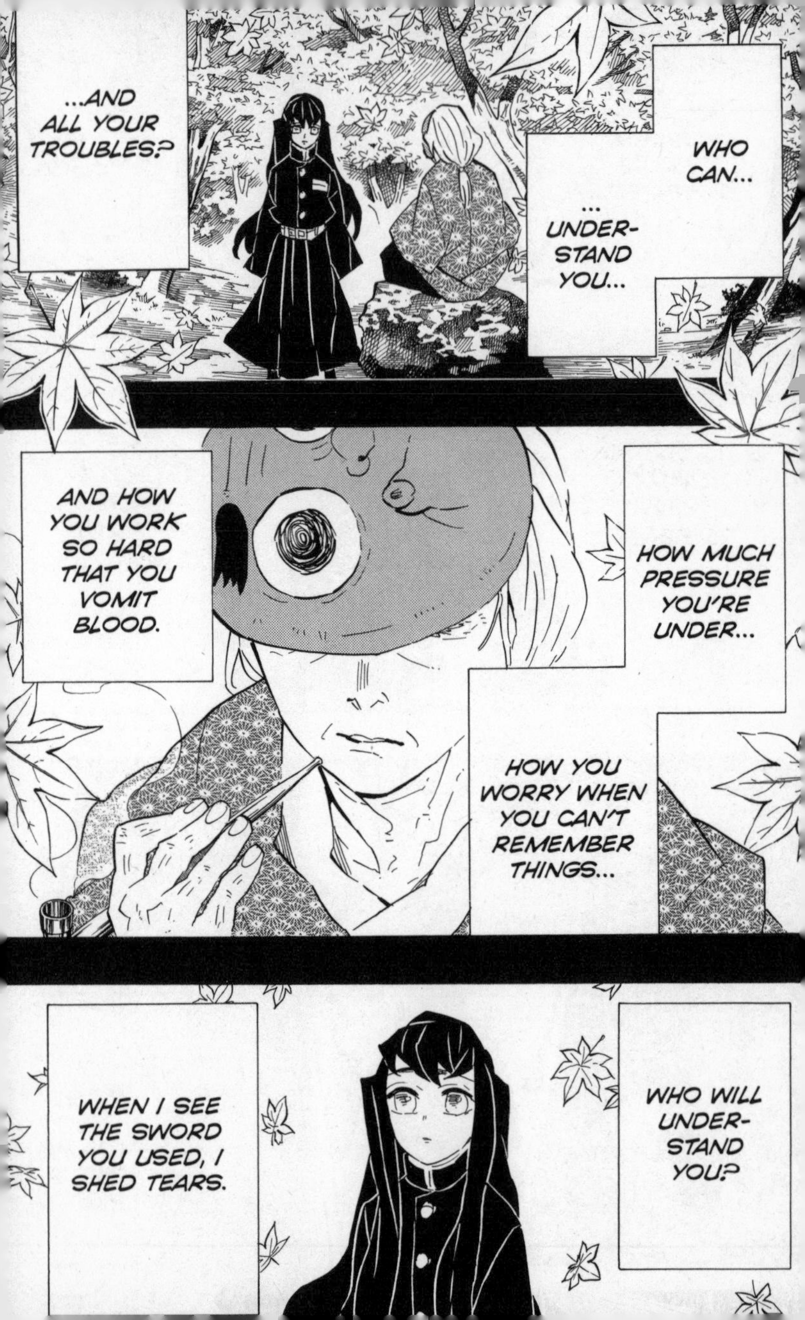
WHO CAN...
... UNDER-STAND YOU...
...AND ALL YOUR TROUBLES?
HOW MUCH PRESSURE YOU'RE UNDER...
HOW YOU WORRY WHEN YOU CAN'T REMEMBER THINGS...
AND HOW YOU WORK SO HARD THAT YOU VOMIT BLOOD.
WHO WILL UNDER-STAND YOU?
WHEN I SEE THE SWORD YOU USED, I SHED TEARS.

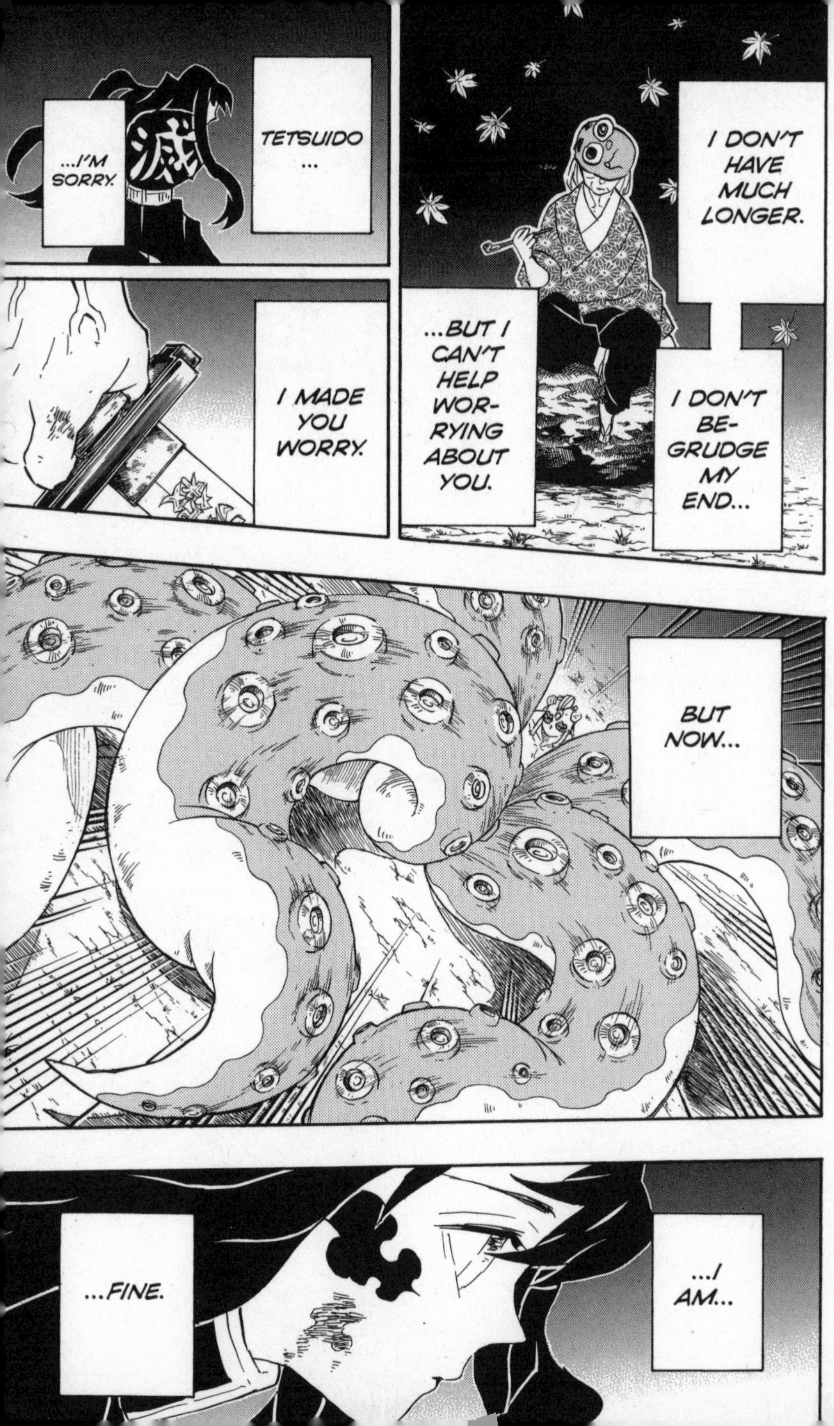
I DON'T HAVE MUCH LONGER.
I DON'T BEGRUDGE MY END...
...BUT I CAN'T HELP WORRYING ABOUT YOU.
TETSUIDO ...
...I'M SORRY.
I MADE YOU WORRY.
BUT NOW...
...I AM...
...FINE.

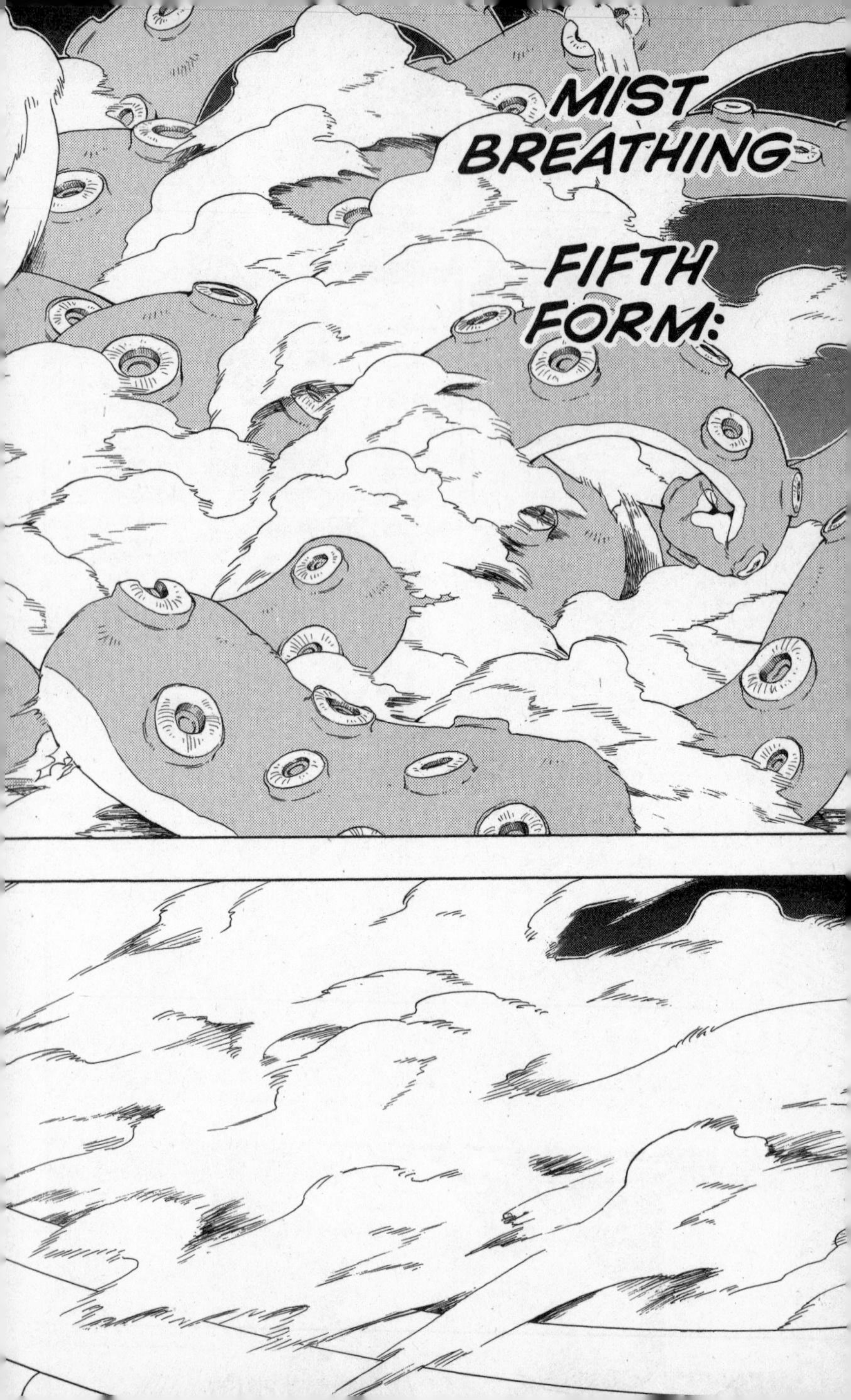
MIST BREATHING
FIFTH FORM:

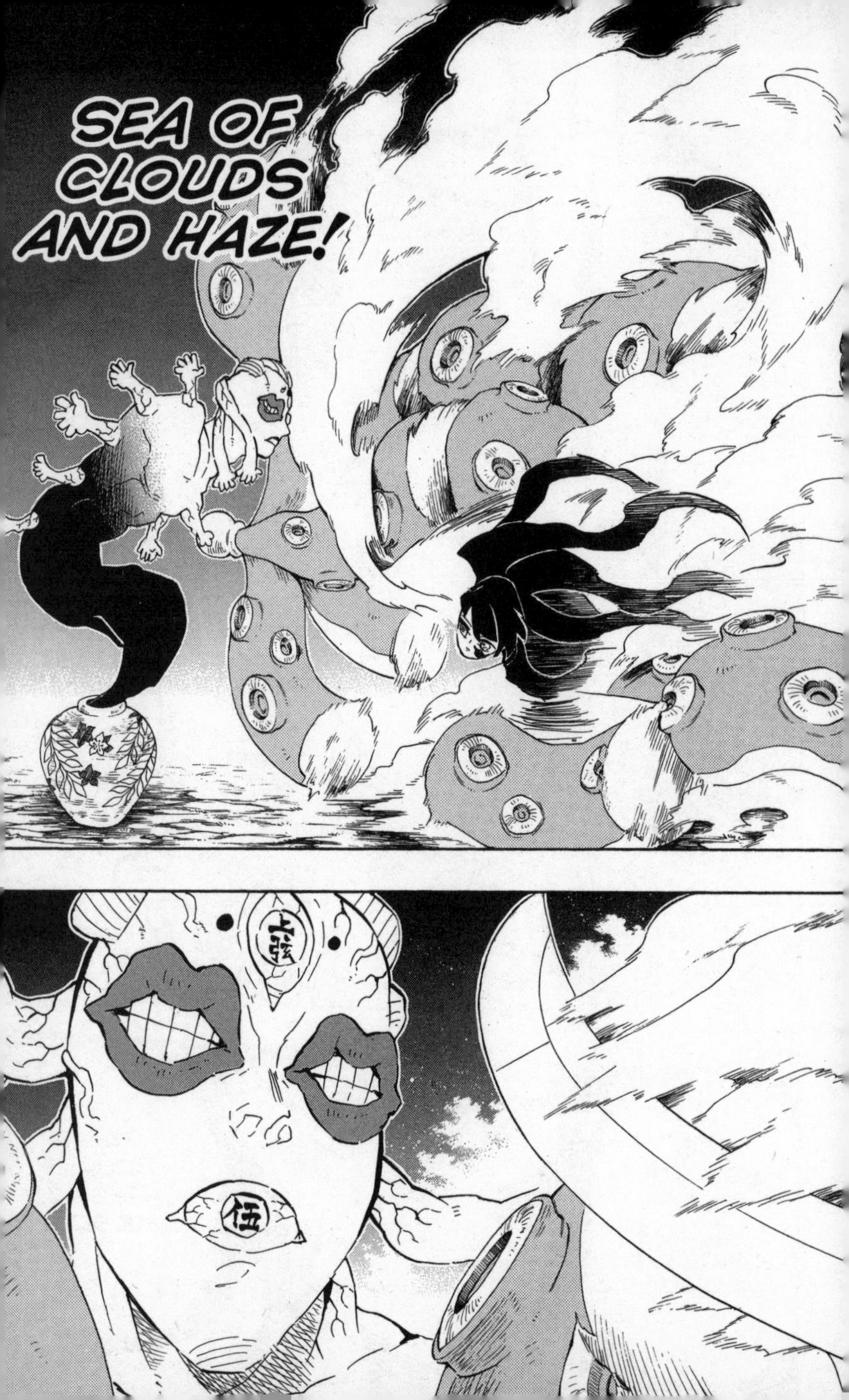
SEA OF CLOUDS AND HAZE!
上弦
伍

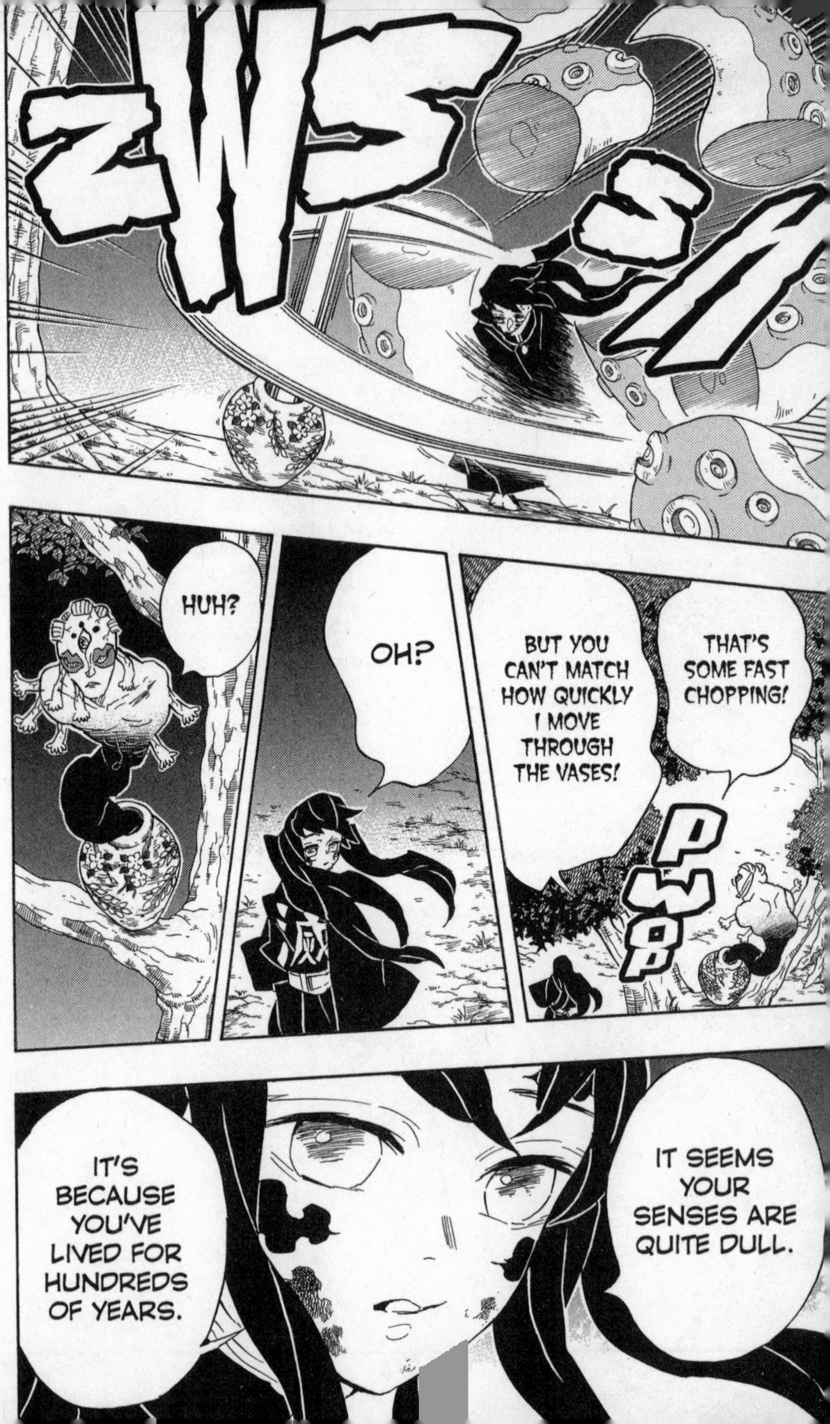
ZWSSH
THAT'S SOME FAST CHOPPING!
BUT YOU CAN'T MATCH HOW QUICKLY I MOVE THROUGH THE VASES!
PWOP
OH?
HUH?
IT SEEMS YOUR SENSES ARE QUITE DULL.
IT'S BECAUSE YOU'VE LIVED FOR HUNDREDS OF YEARS.

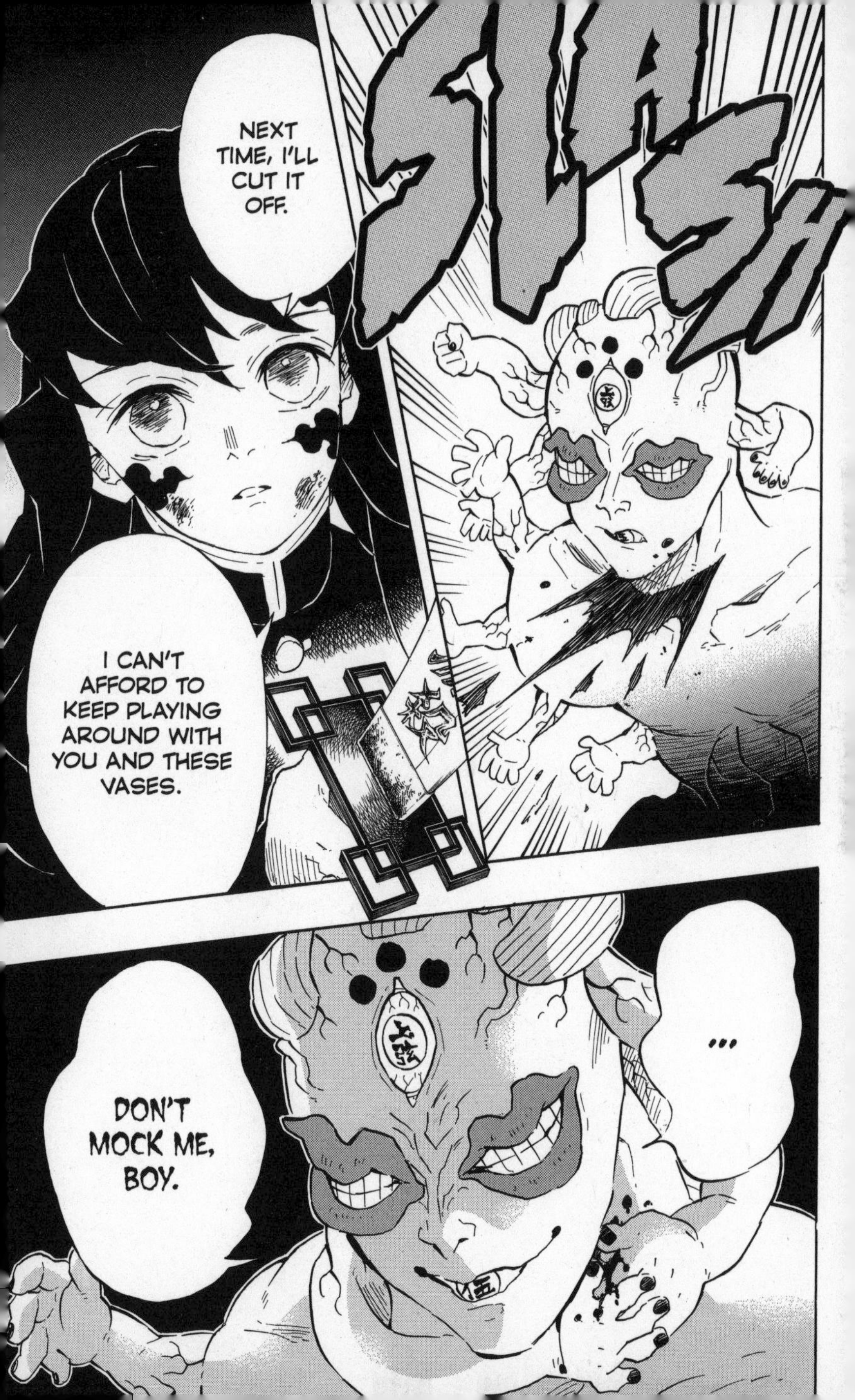
SLASH
NEXT TIME, I'LL CUT IT OFF.
I CAN'T AFFORD TO KEEP PLAYING AROUND WITH YOU AND THESE VASES.
...
DON'T MOCK ME, BOY.

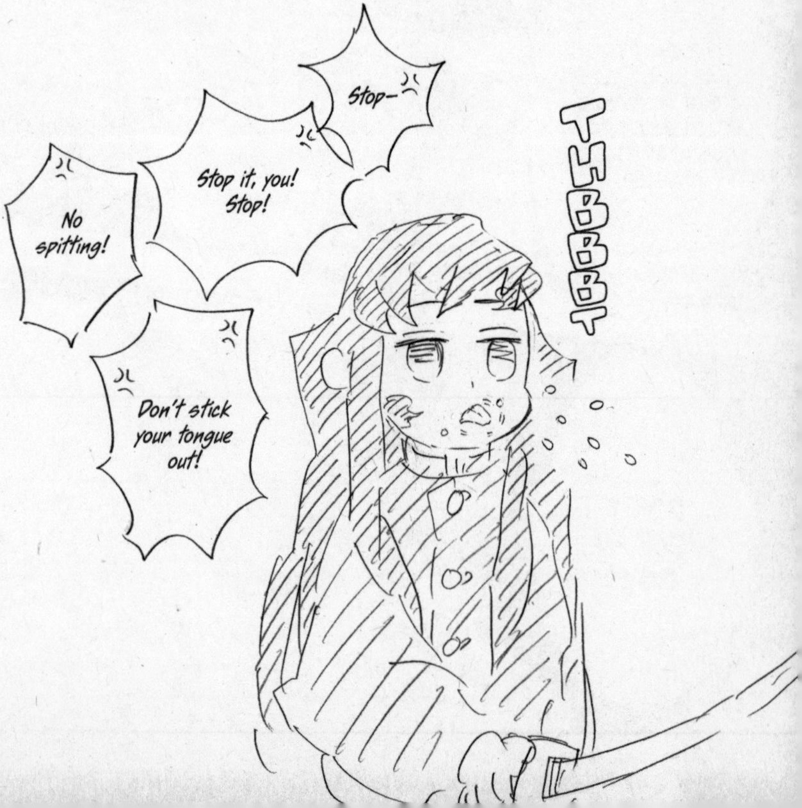
Stop–
THBBBT
Stop it, you! Stop!
No spitting!
Don't stick your tongue out!

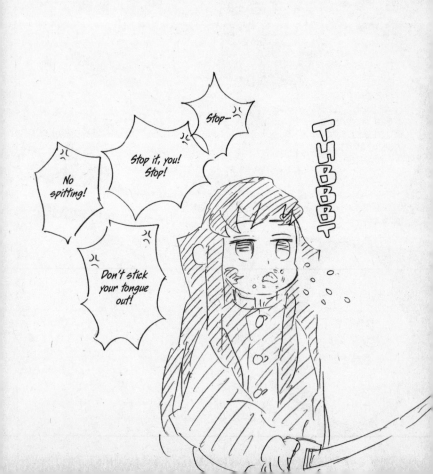

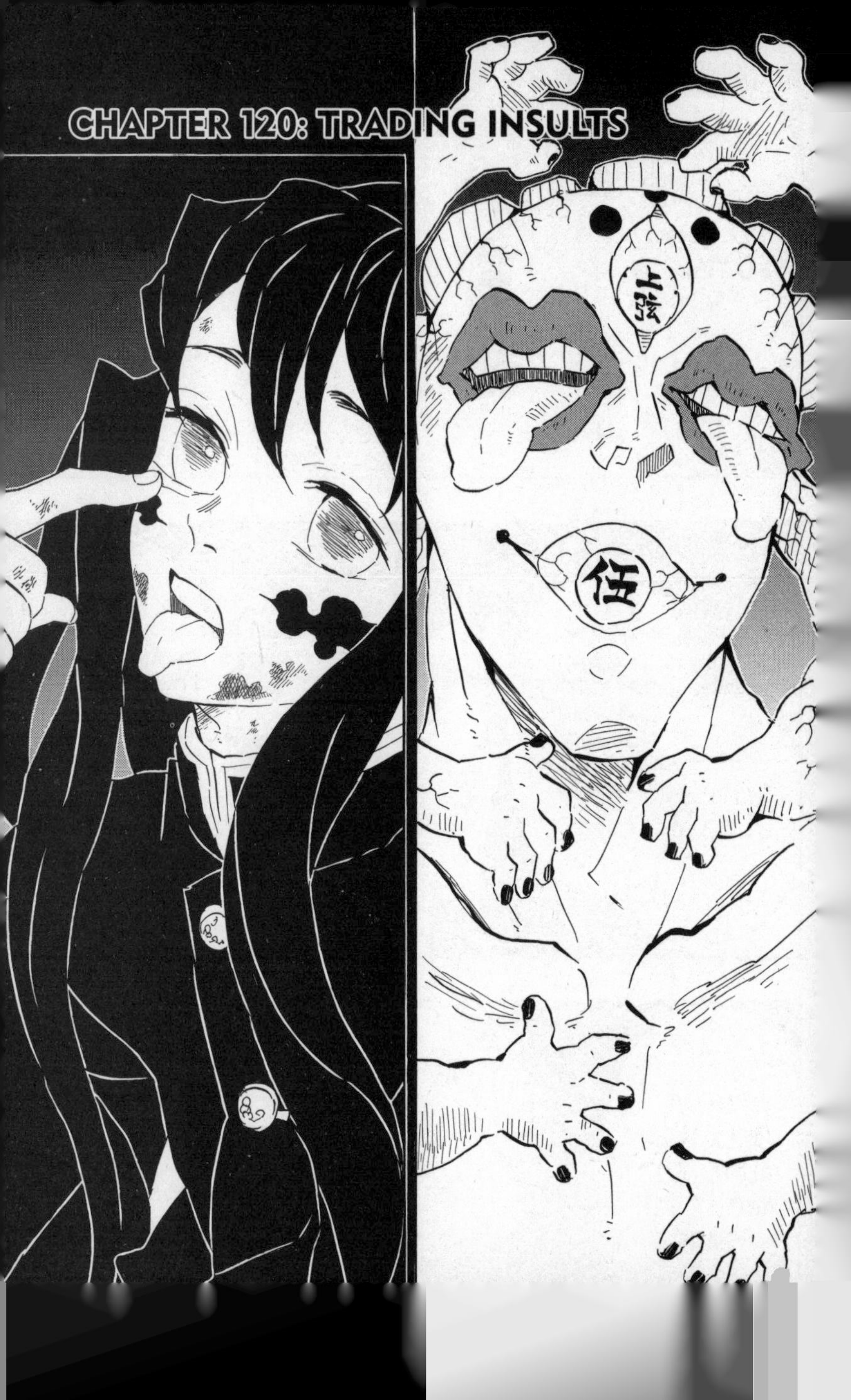
CHAPTER 120: TRADING INSULTS
上弦
伍

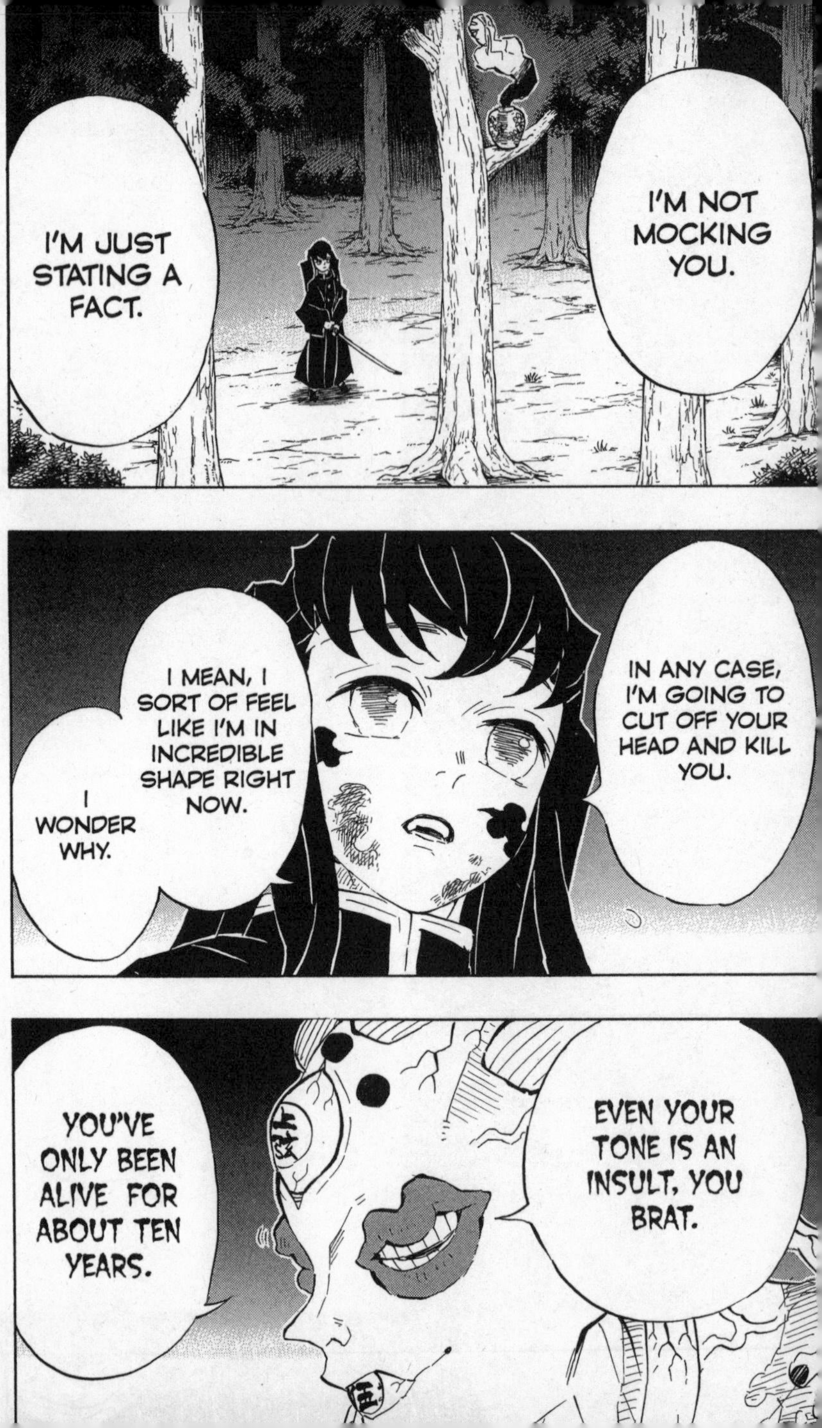
I'M NOT MOCKING YOU.
I'M JUST STATING A FACT.
IN ANY CASE, I'M GOING TO CUT OFF YOUR HEAD AND KILL YOU.
I MEAN, I SORT OF FEEL LIKE I'M IN INCREDIBLE SHAPE RIGHT NOW.
I WONDER WHY.
EVEN YOUR TONE IS AN INSULT, YOU BRAT.
YOU'VE ONLY BEEN ALIVE FOR ABOUT TEN YEARS.

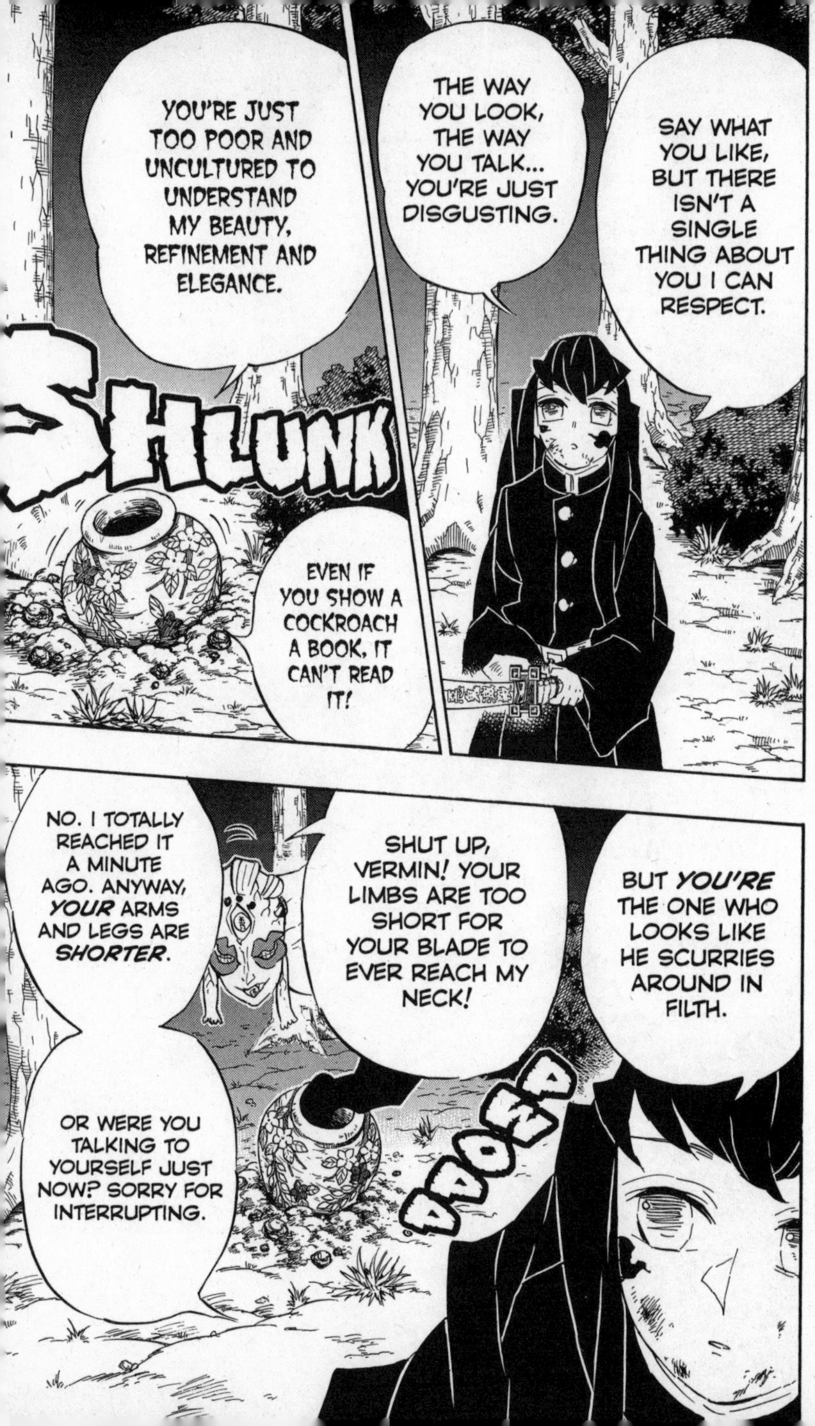
SAY WHAT YOU LIKE, BUT THERE ISN'T A SINGLE THING ABOUT YOU I CAN RESPECT.
THE WAY YOU LOOK, THE WAY YOU TALK... YOU'RE JUST DISGUSTING.
YOU'RE JUST TOO POOR AND UNCULTURED TO UNDERSTAND MY BEAUTY, REFINEMENT AND ELEGANCE.
SHLUNK
EVEN IF YOU SHOW A COCKROACH A BOOK, IT CAN'T READ IT!
BUT *YOU'RE* THE ONE WHO LOOKS LIKE HE SCURRIES AROUND IN FILTH.
SHUT UP, VERMIN! YOUR LIMBS ARE TOO SHORT FOR YOUR BLADE TO EVER REACH MY NECK!
NO. I TOTALLY REACHED IT A MINUTE AGO. ANYWAY, ***YOUR*** ARMS AND LEGS ARE ***SHORTER***.
OR WERE YOU TALKING TO YOURSELF JUST NOW? SORRY FOR INTERRUPTING.

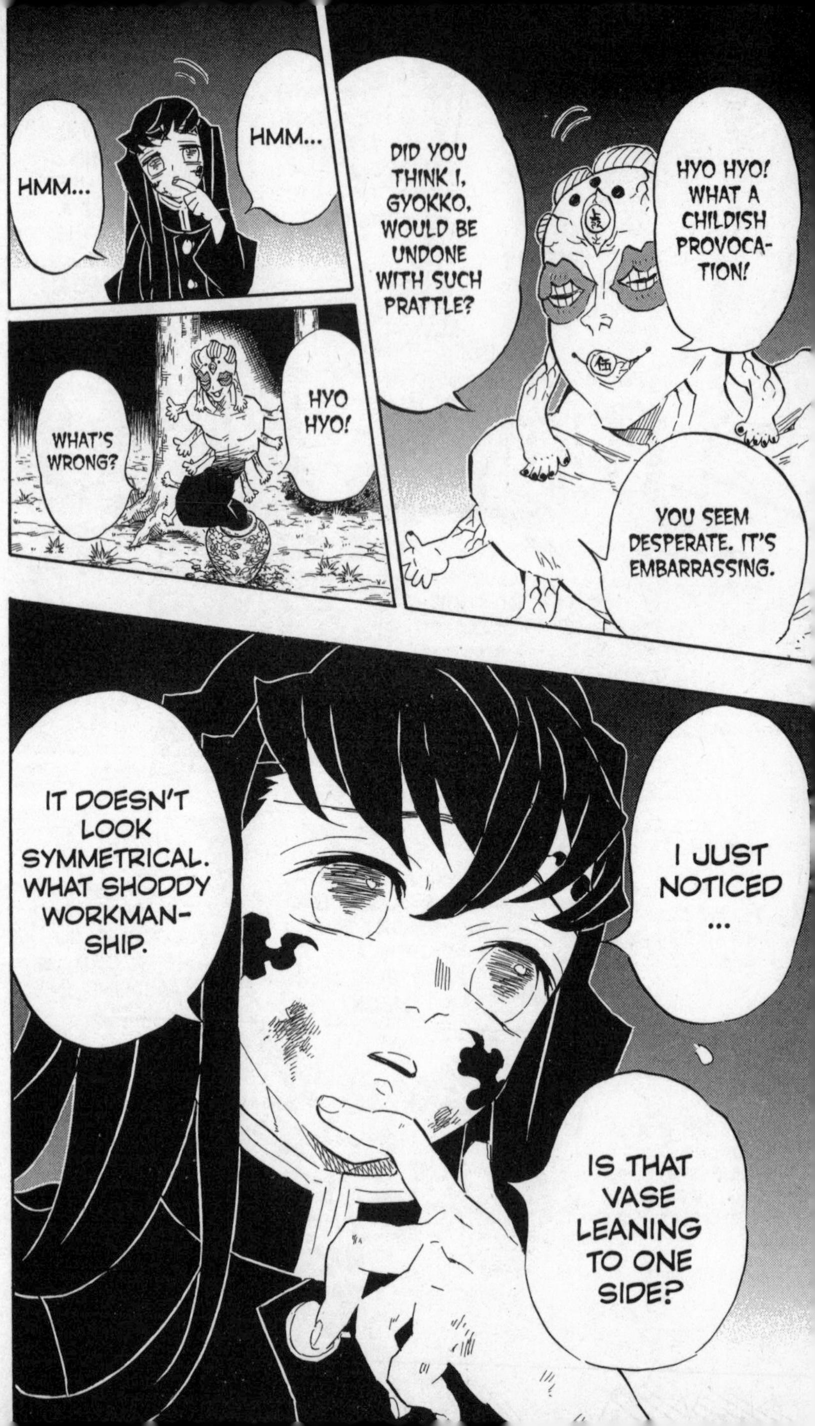
HYO HYO! WHAT A CHILDISH PROVOCATION!
DID YOU THINK I, GYOKKO, WOULD BE UNDONE WITH SUCH PRATTLE?
YOU SEEM DESPERATE. IT'S EMBARRASSING.
HMM...
HMM...
HYO HYO!
WHAT'S WRONG?
I JUST NOTICED ...
IS THAT VASE LEANING TO ONE SIDE?
IT DOESN'T LOOK SYMMETRICAL. WHAT SHODDY WORKMAN-SHIP.

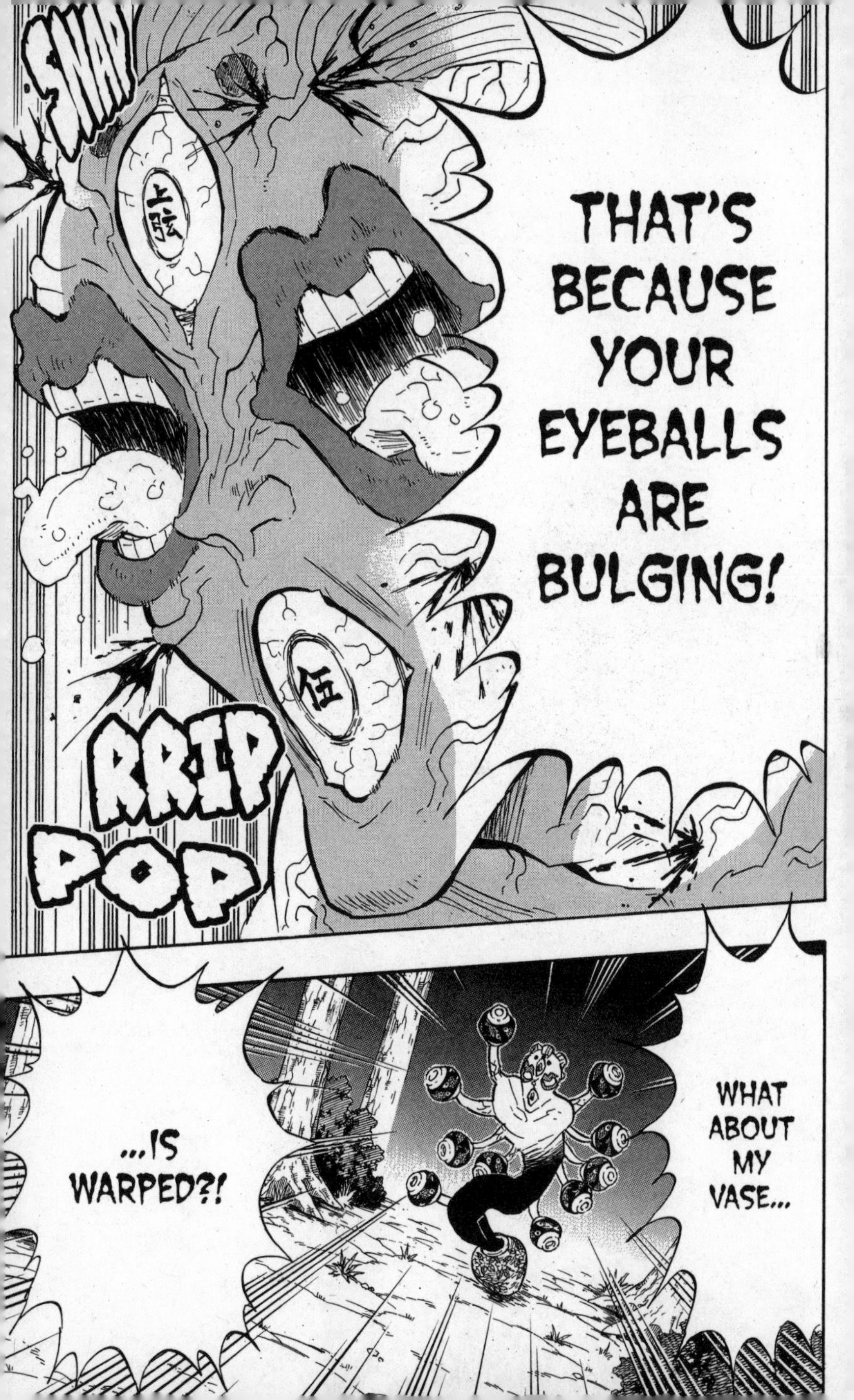
THAT'S BECAUSE YOUR EYEBALLS ARE BULGING!
SNAP
上弦
伍
RRIP
POP
WHAT ABOUT MY VASE...
...IS WARPED?!

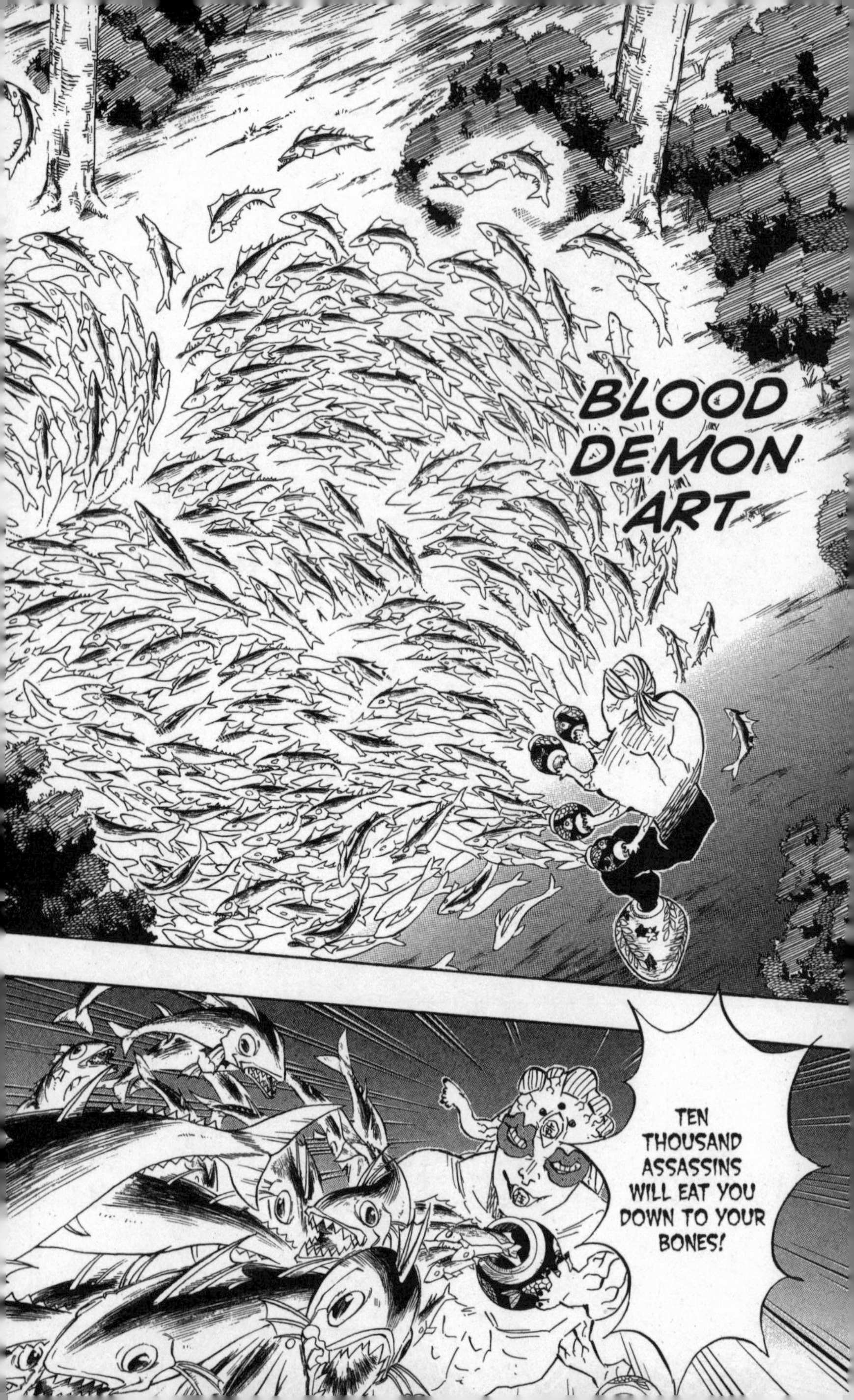
BLOOD DEMON ART
TEN THOUSAND ASSASSINS WILL EAT YOU DOWN TO YOUR BONES!

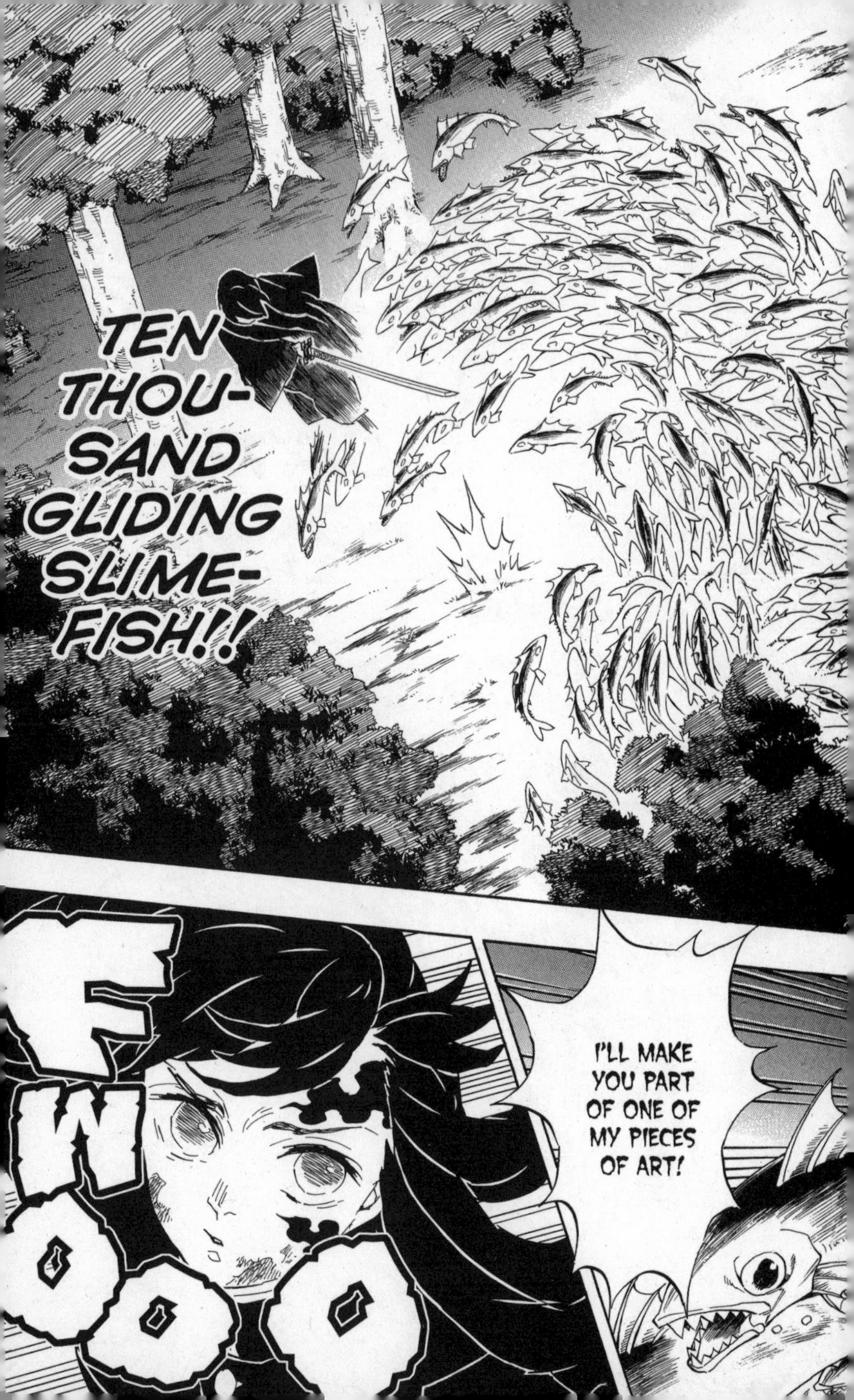
TEN THOU-SAND GLIDING SLIME-FISH!!
I'LL MAKE YOU PART OF ONE OF MY PIECES OF ART!
FWOOO

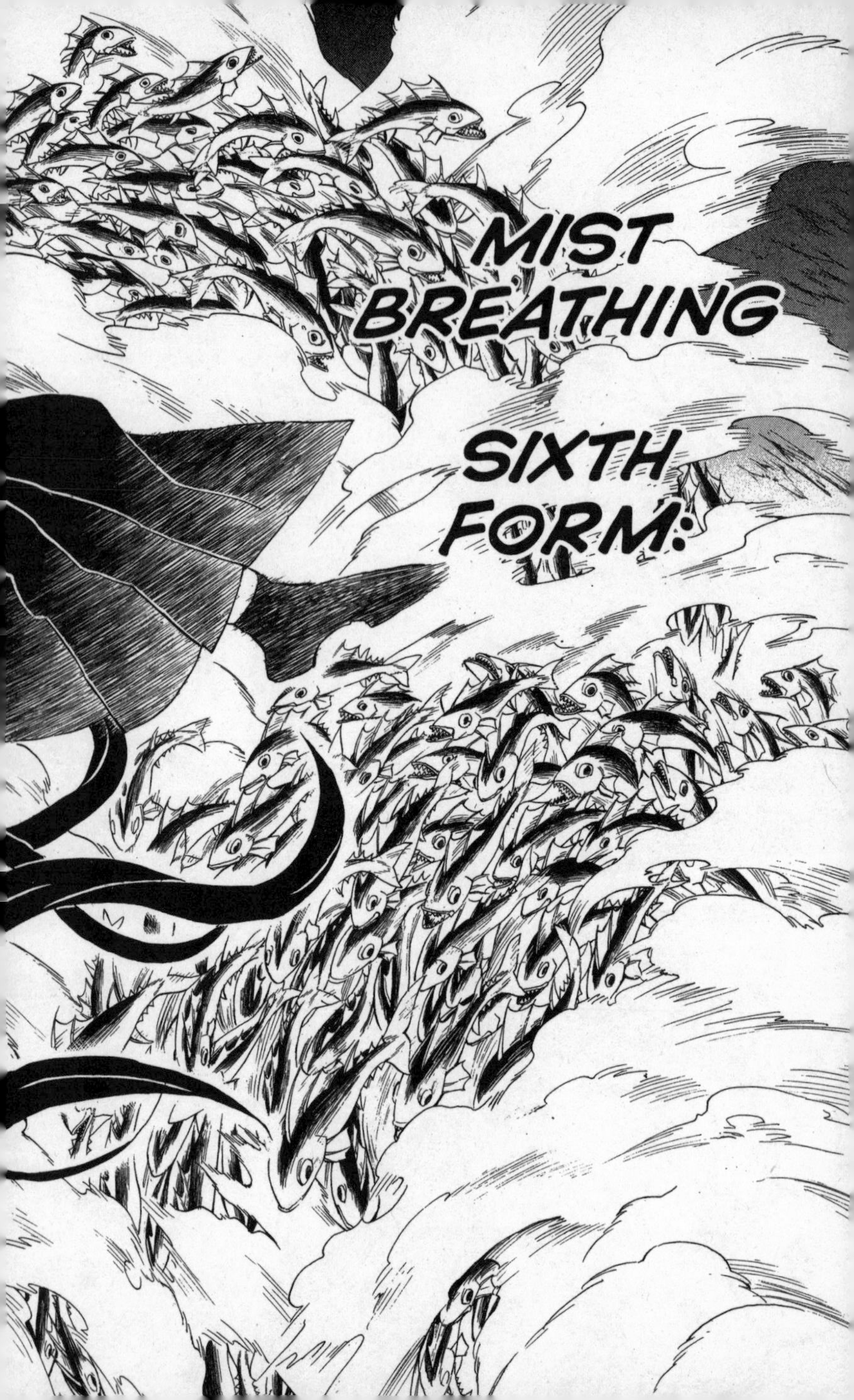
MIST BREATHING
SIXTH FORM:

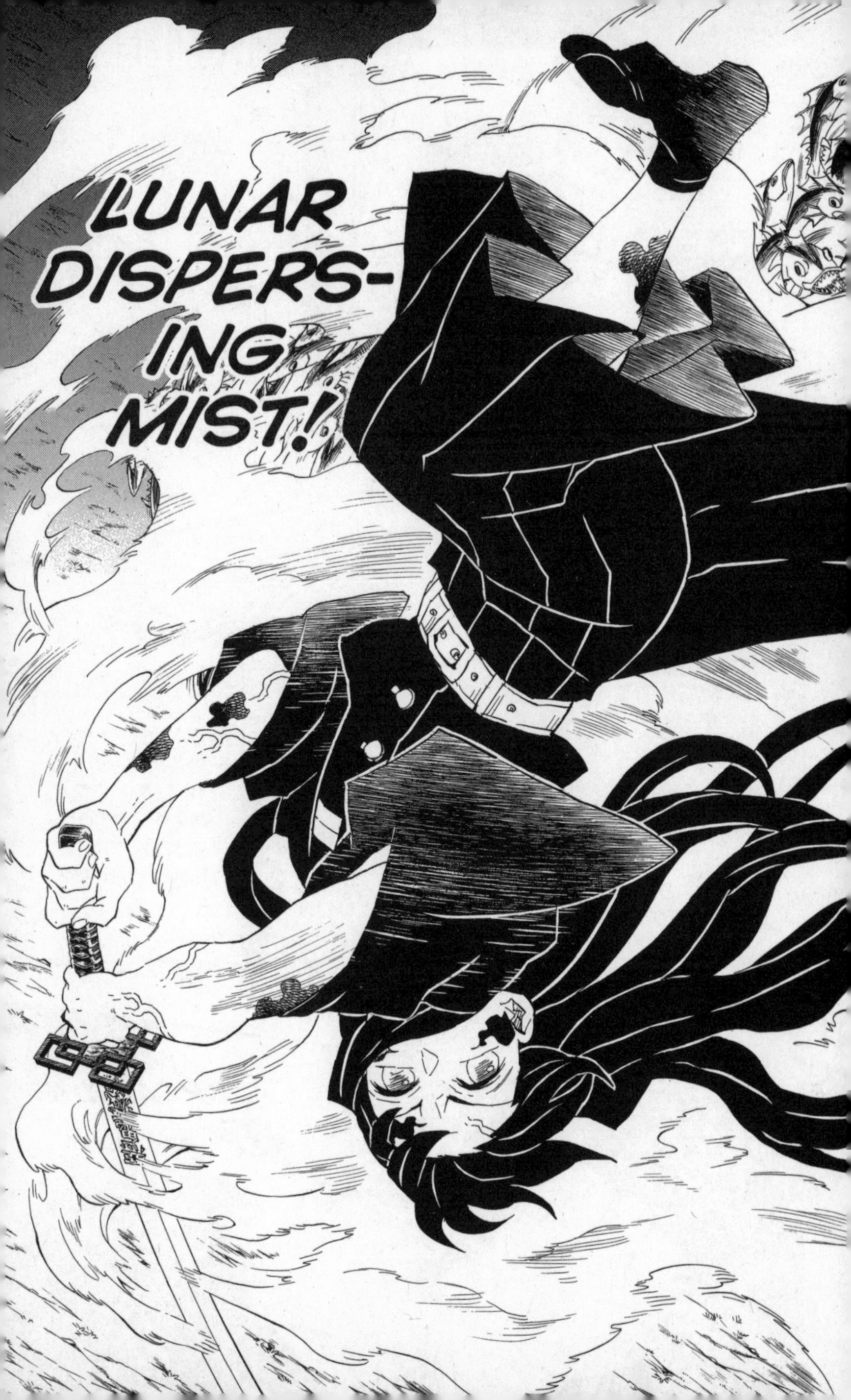
LUNAR DISPERS-ING MIST!

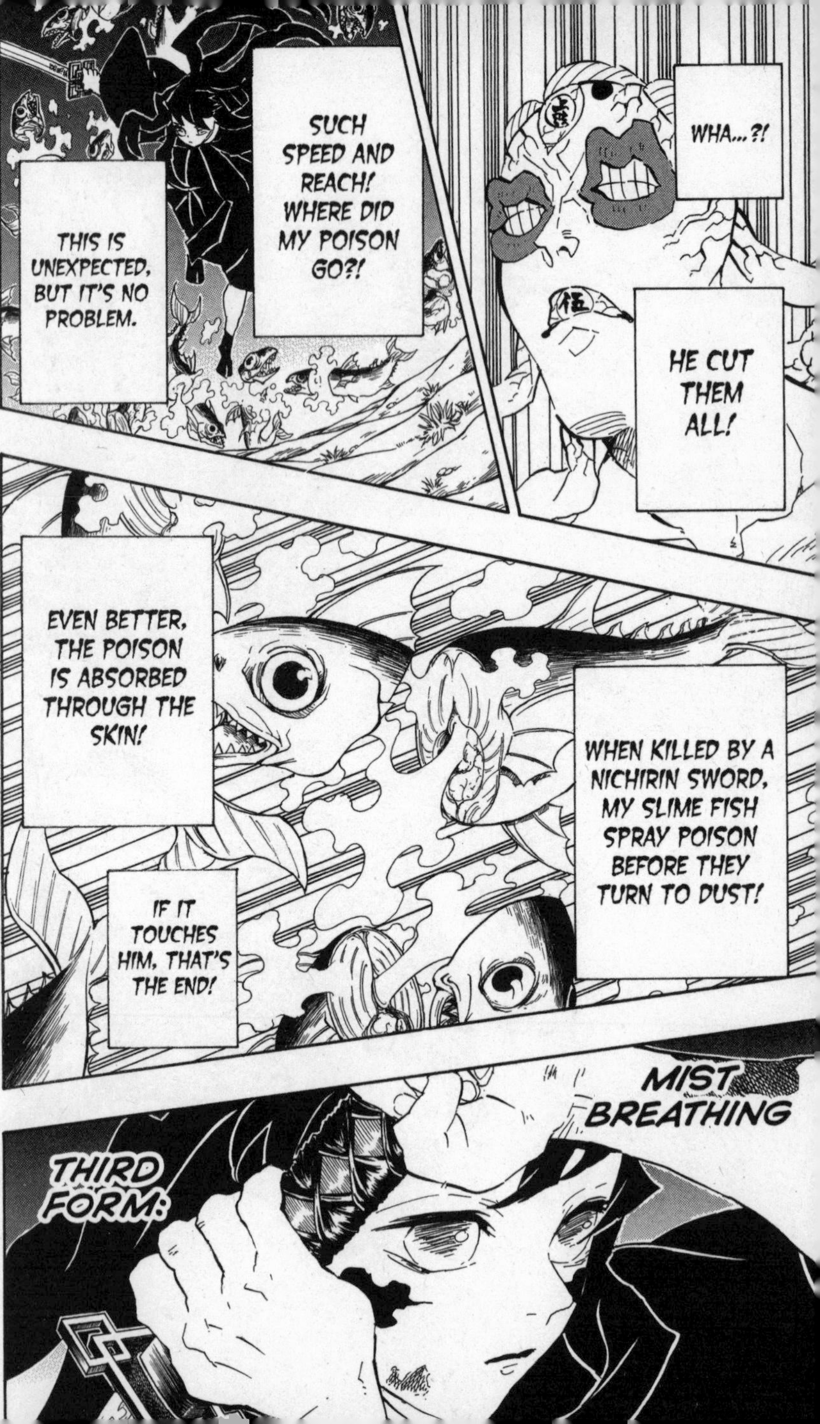

WHA...?!
HE CUT THEM ALL!
SUCH SPEED AND REACH! WHERE DID MY POISON GO?!
THIS IS UNEXPECTED, BUT IT'S NO PROBLEM.
WHEN KILLED BY A NICHIRIN SWORD, MY SLIME FISH SPRAY POISON BEFORE THEY TURN TO DUST!
EVEN BETTER, THE POISON IS ABSORBED THROUGH THE SKIN!
IF IT TOUCHES HIM, THAT'S THE END!
MIST BREATHING
THIRD FORM:

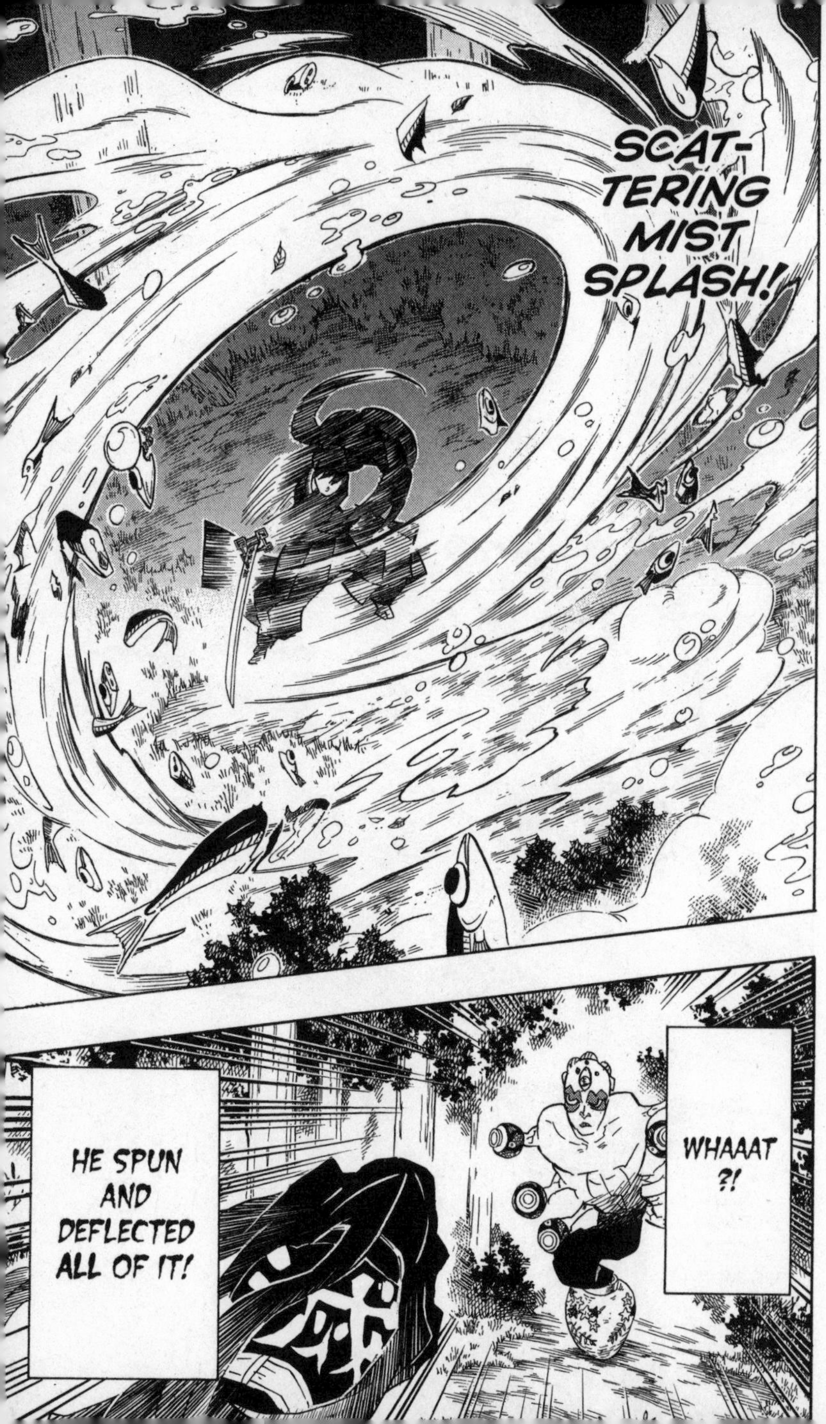
SCAT-TERING MIST SPLASH!
WHAAAT ?!
HE SPUN AND DEFLECTED ALL OF IT!

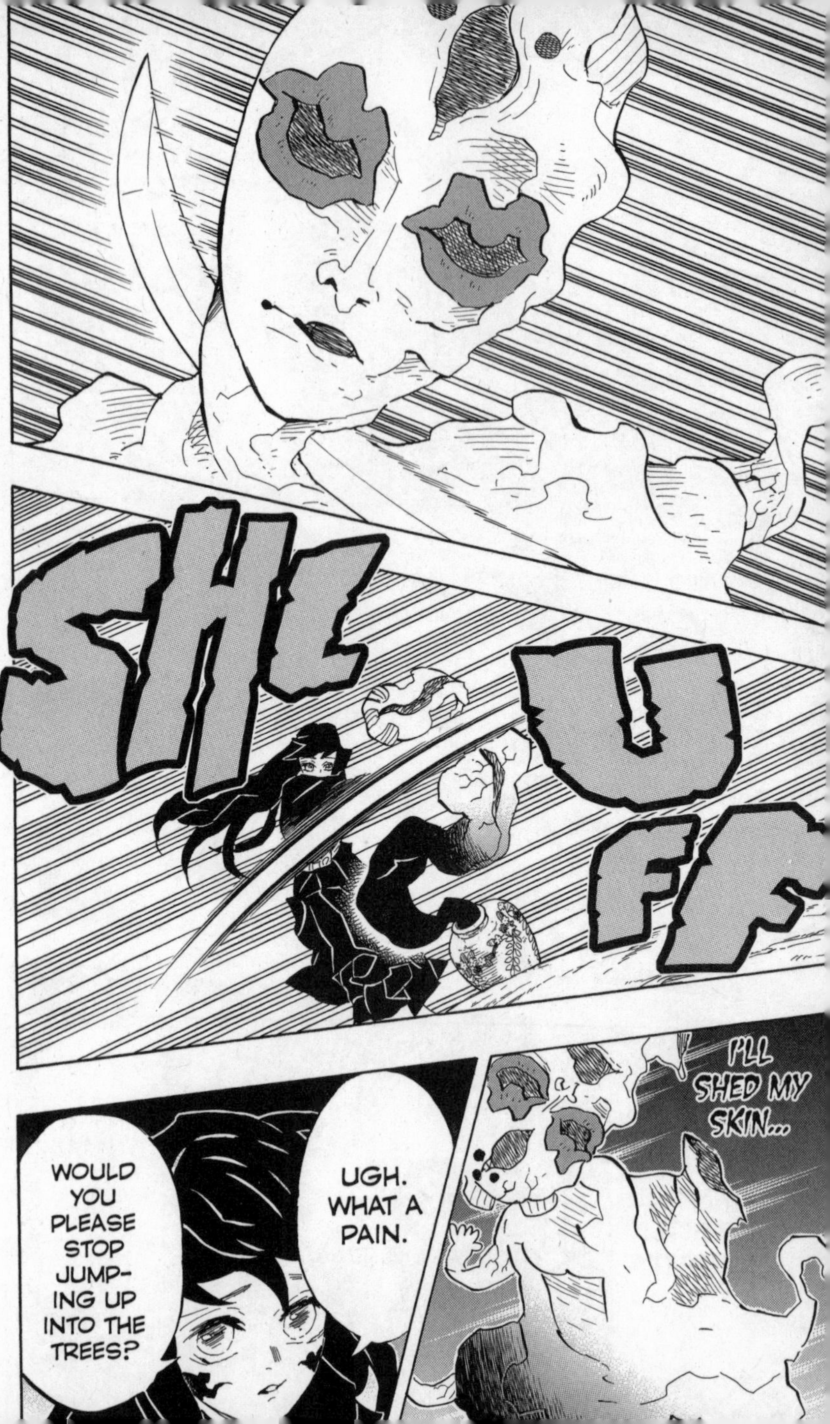
SHLUFF
I'LL SHED MY SKIN...
UGH. WHAT A PAIN.
WOULD YOU PLEASE STOP JUMPING UP INTO THE TREES?

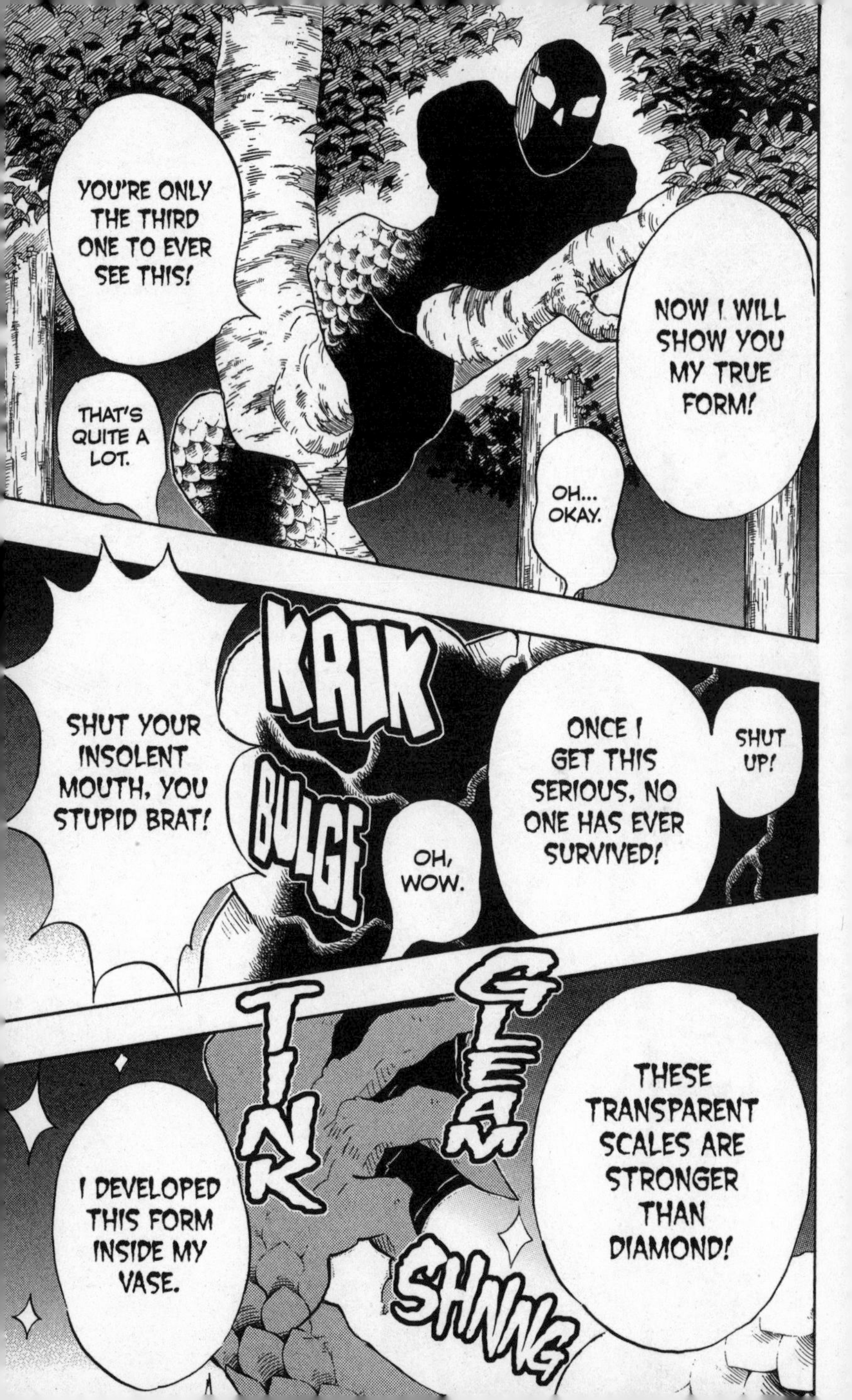
NOW I WILL SHOW YOU MY TRUE FORM!
OH... OKAY.
YOU'RE ONLY THE THIRD ONE TO EVER SEE THIS!
THAT'S QUITE A LOT.
SHUT UP!
ONCE I GET THIS SERIOUS, NO ONE HAS EVER SURVIVED!
OH, WOW.
KRIK
BULGE
SHUT YOUR INSOLENT MOUTH, YOU STUPID BRAT!
THESE TRANSPARENT SCALES ARE STRONGER THAN DIAMOND!
GLEAM
TINK
SHNNG
I DEVELOPED THIS FORM INSIDE MY VASE.

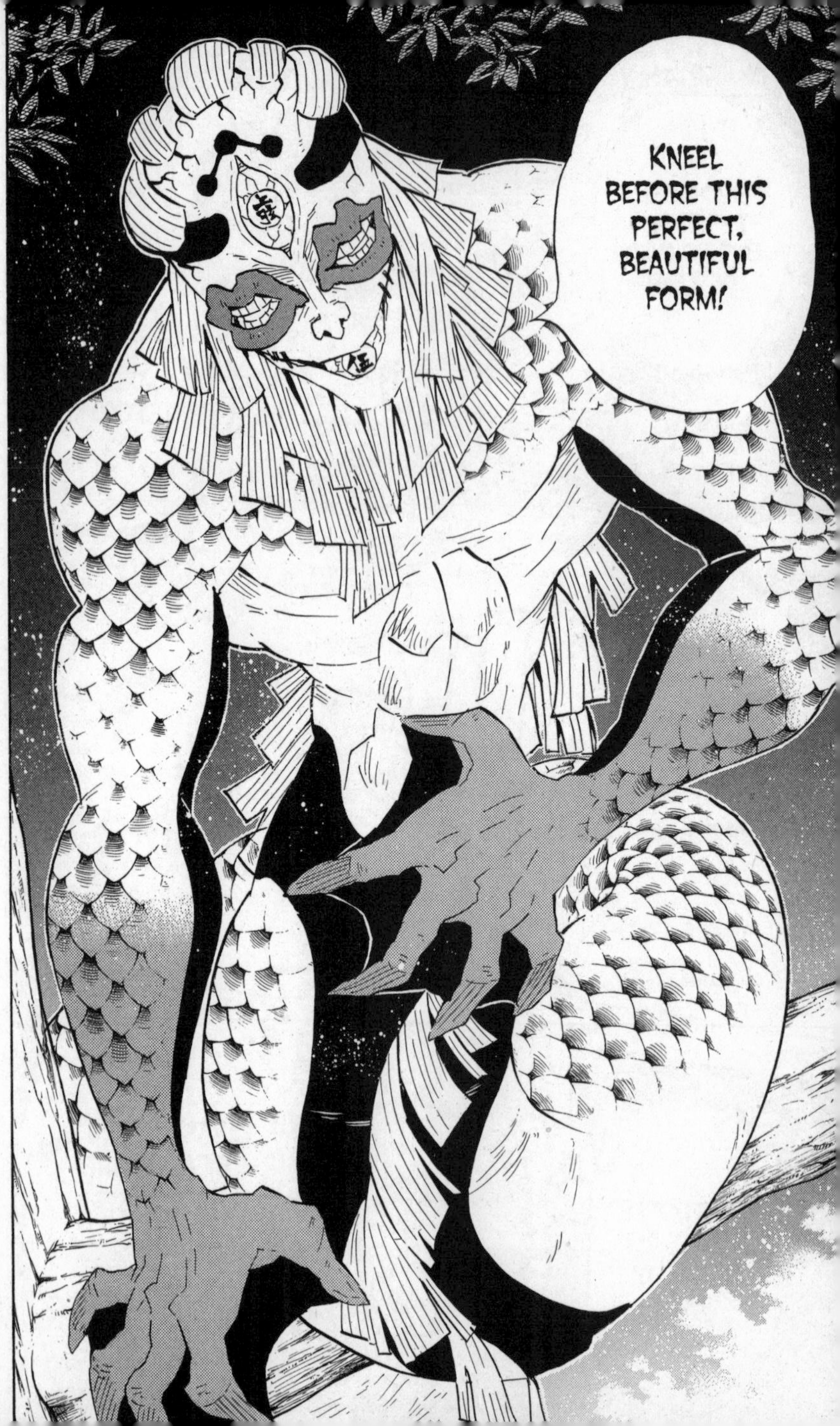
KNEEL BEFORE THIS PERFECT, BEAUTIFUL FORM!

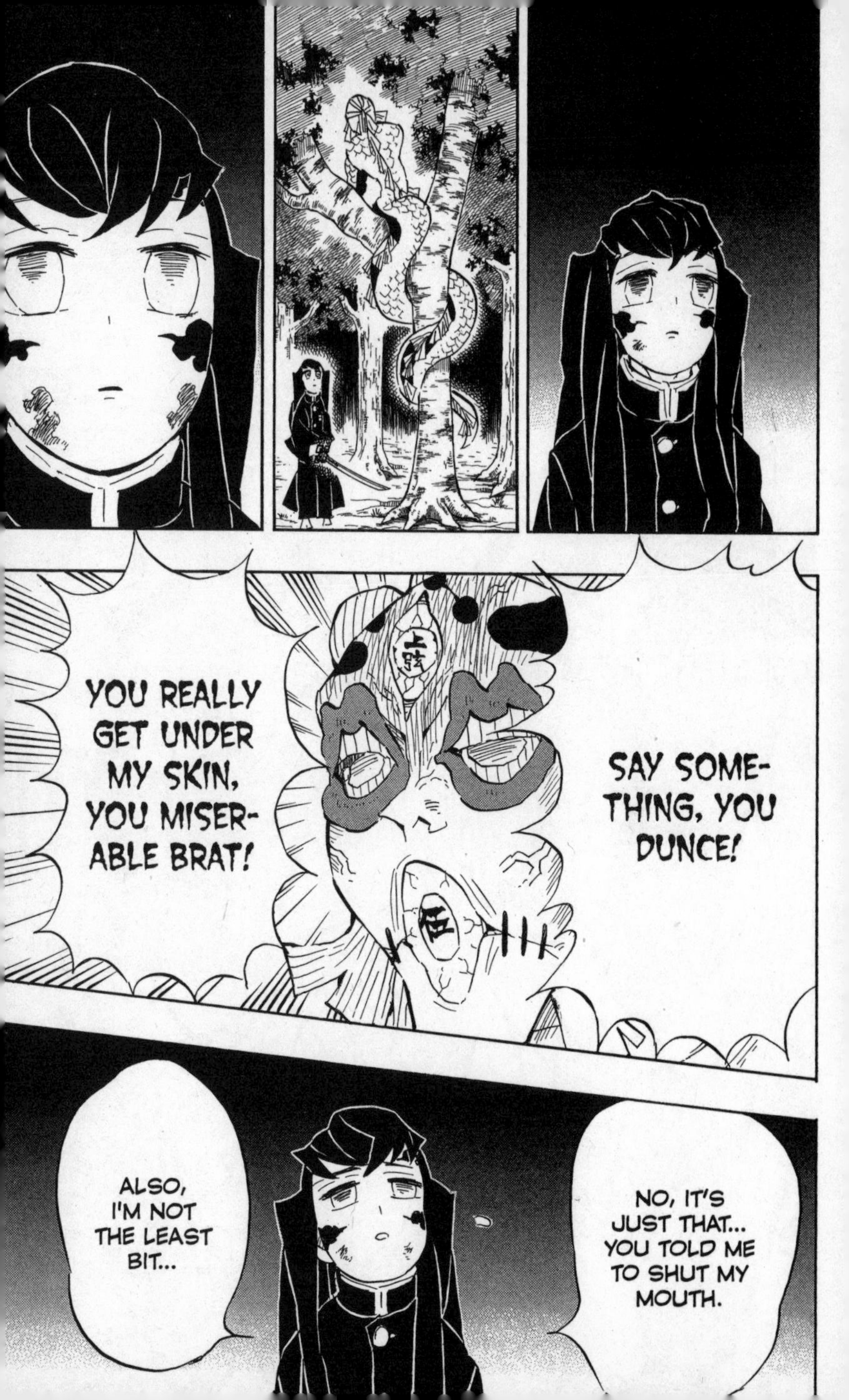
SAY SOME-THING, YOU DUNCE!
YOU REALLY GET UNDER MY SKIN, YOU MISER-ABLE BRAT!
NO, IT'S JUST THAT... YOU TOLD ME TO SHUT MY MOUTH.
ALSO, I'M NOT THE LEAST BIT...

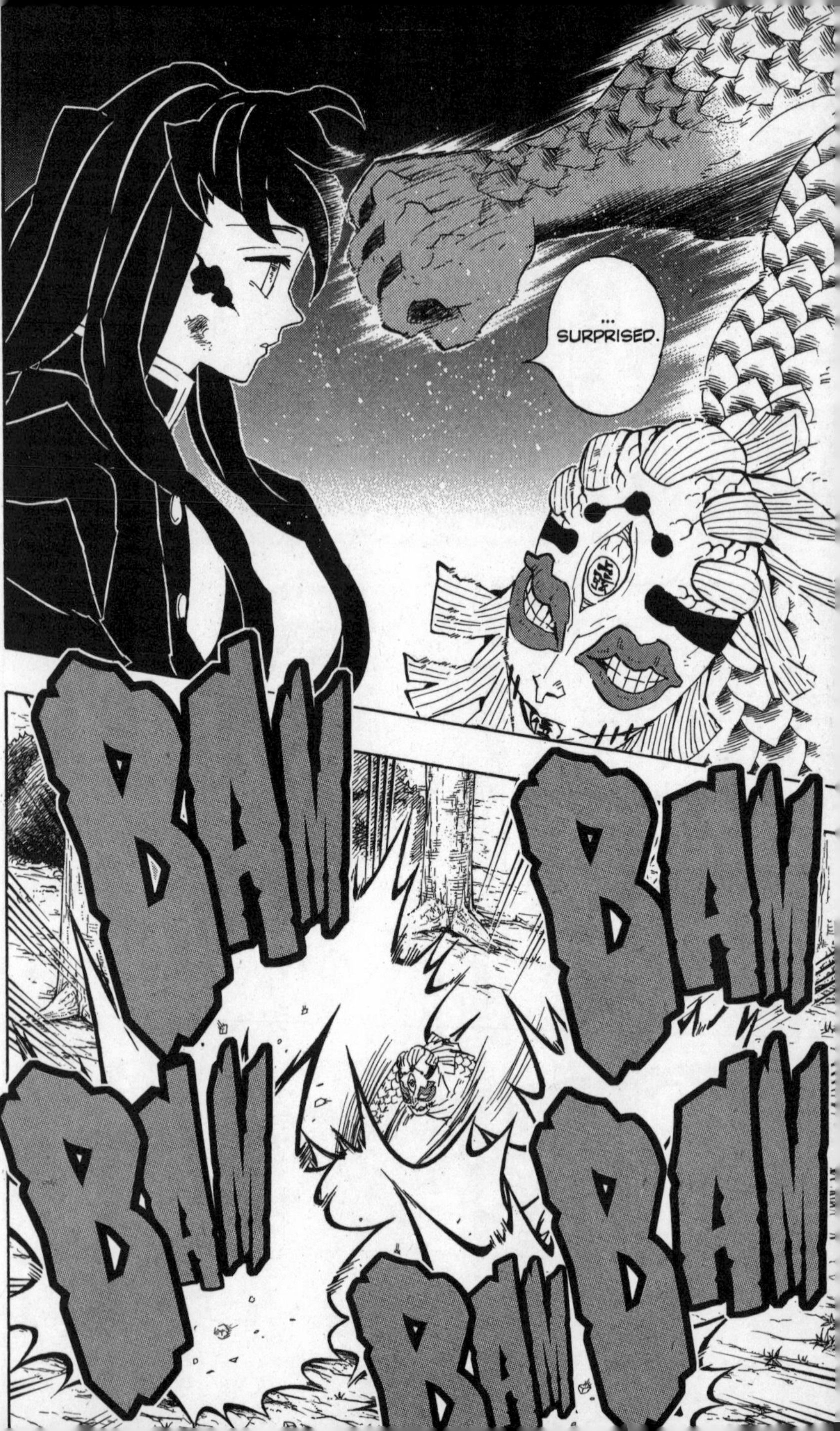

... SURPRISED.
BAM
BAM
BAM
BAM
BAM

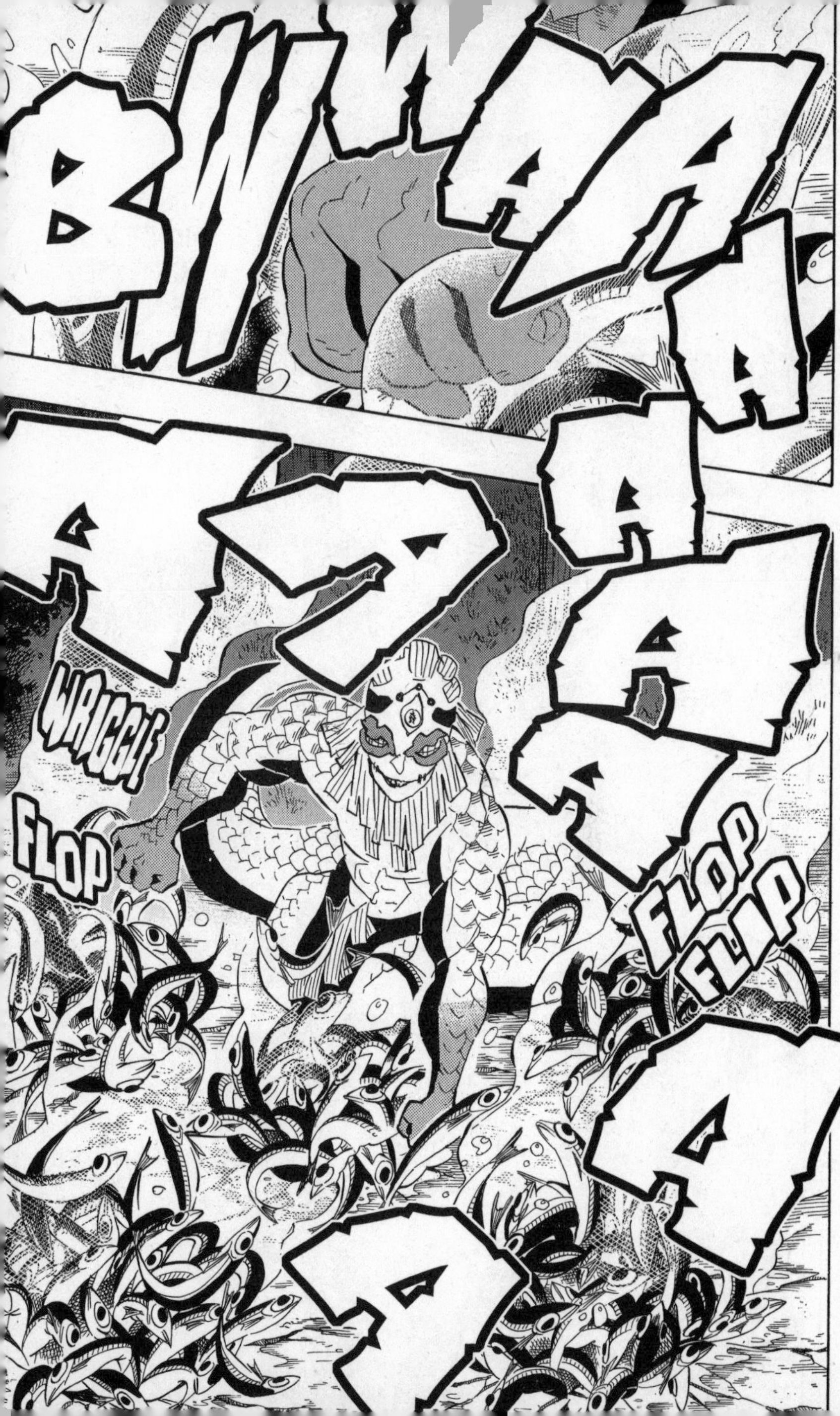
BWAA!
FLOP
FLIP
WRIGGLE
FLOP

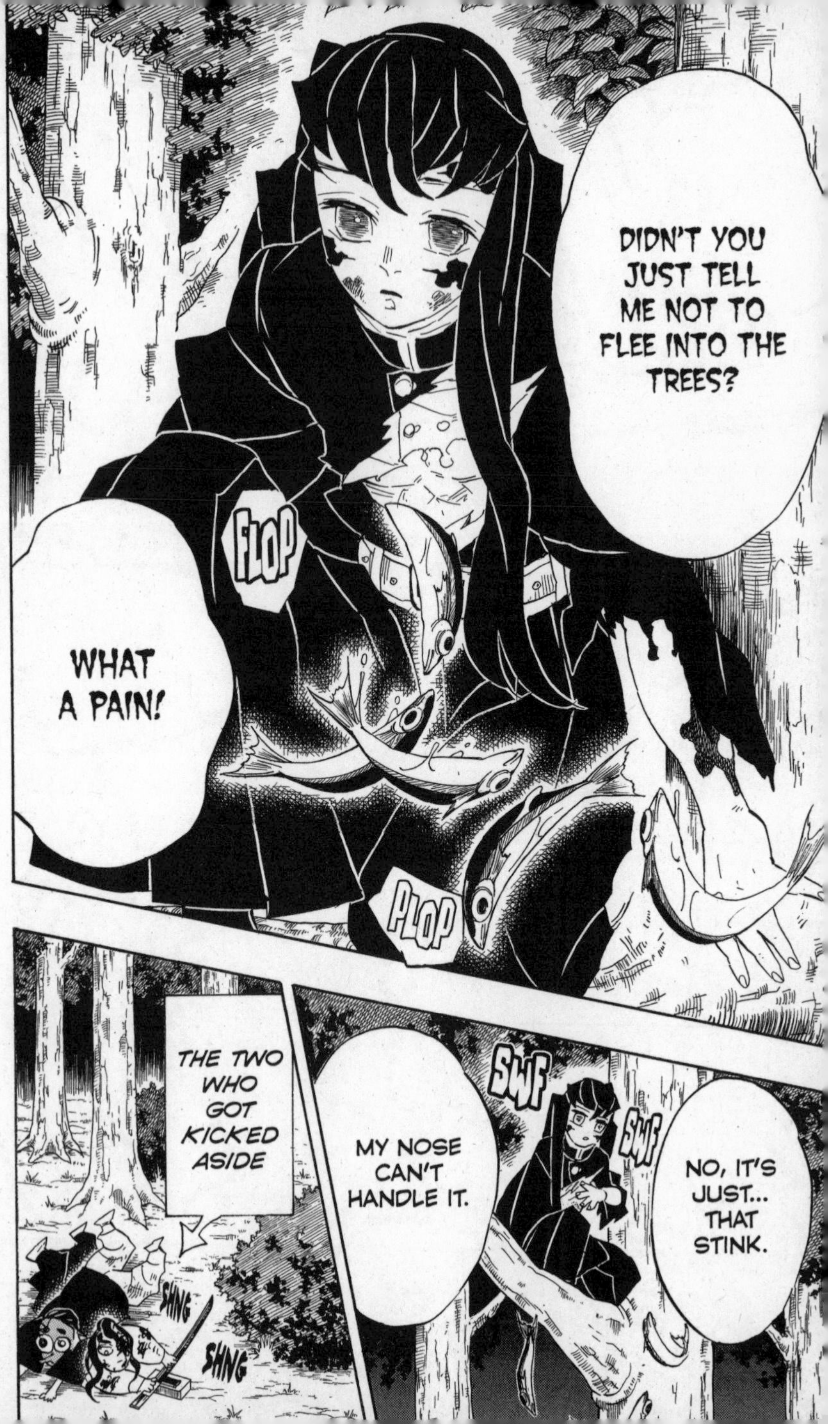
DIDN'T YOU JUST TELL ME NOT TO FLEE INTO THE TREES?
FLOP
WHAT A PAIN!
PLOP
NO, IT'S JUST... THAT STINK.
SWF
SWF
MY NOSE CAN'T HANDLE IT.
THE TWO WHO GOT KICKED ASIDE
SHNG
SHNG

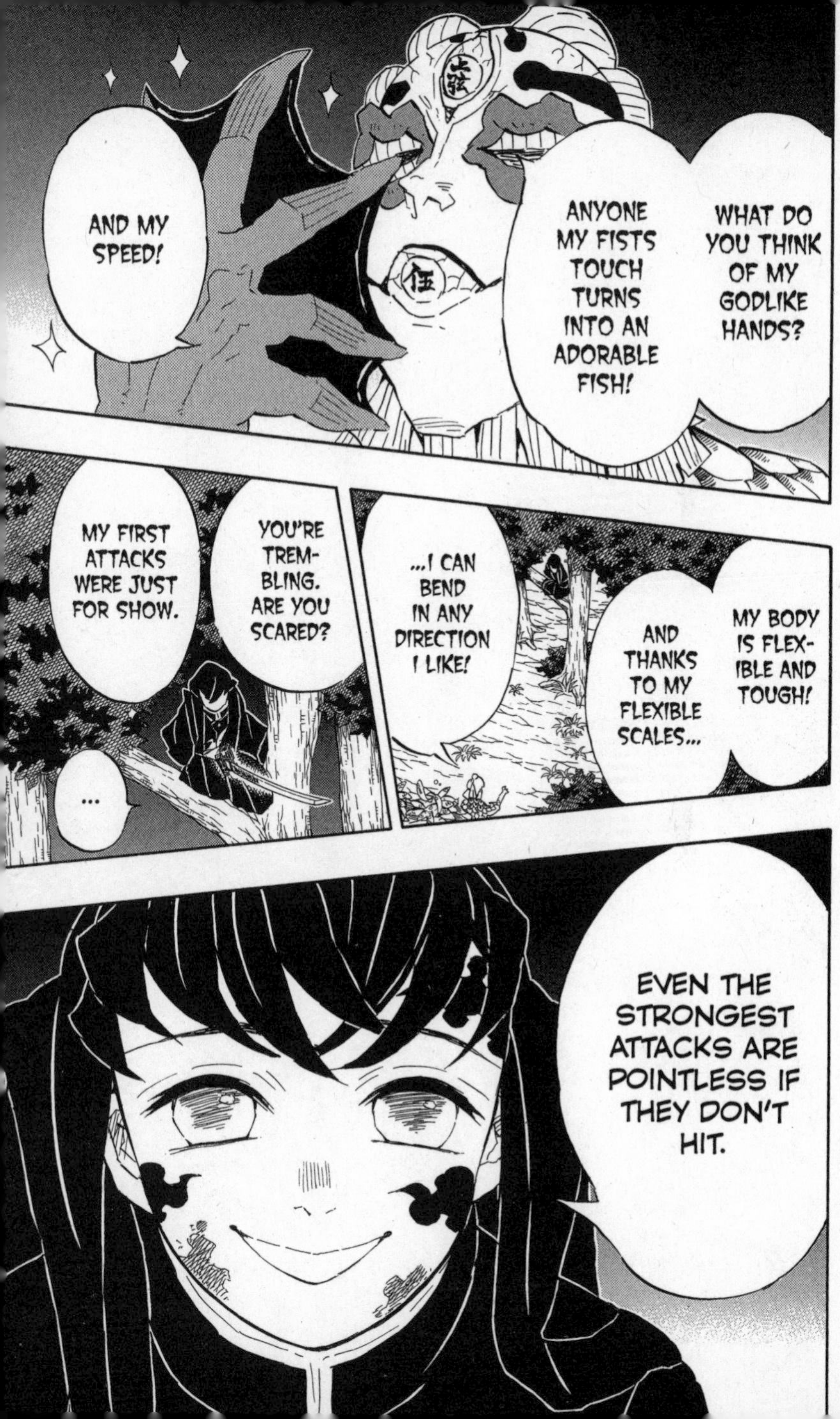
WHAT DO YOU THINK OF MY GODLIKE HANDS?
ANYONE MY FISTS TOUCH TURNS INTO AN ADORABLE FISH!
AND MY SPEED!
MY BODY IS FLEXIBLE AND TOUGH!
AND THANKS TO MY FLEXIBLE SCALES...
...I CAN BEND IN ANY DIRECTION I LIKE!
YOU'RE TREMBLING. ARE YOU SCARED?
MY FIRST ATTACKS WERE JUST FOR SHOW.
...
EVEN THE STRONGEST ATTACKS ARE POINTLESS IF THEY DON'T HIT.

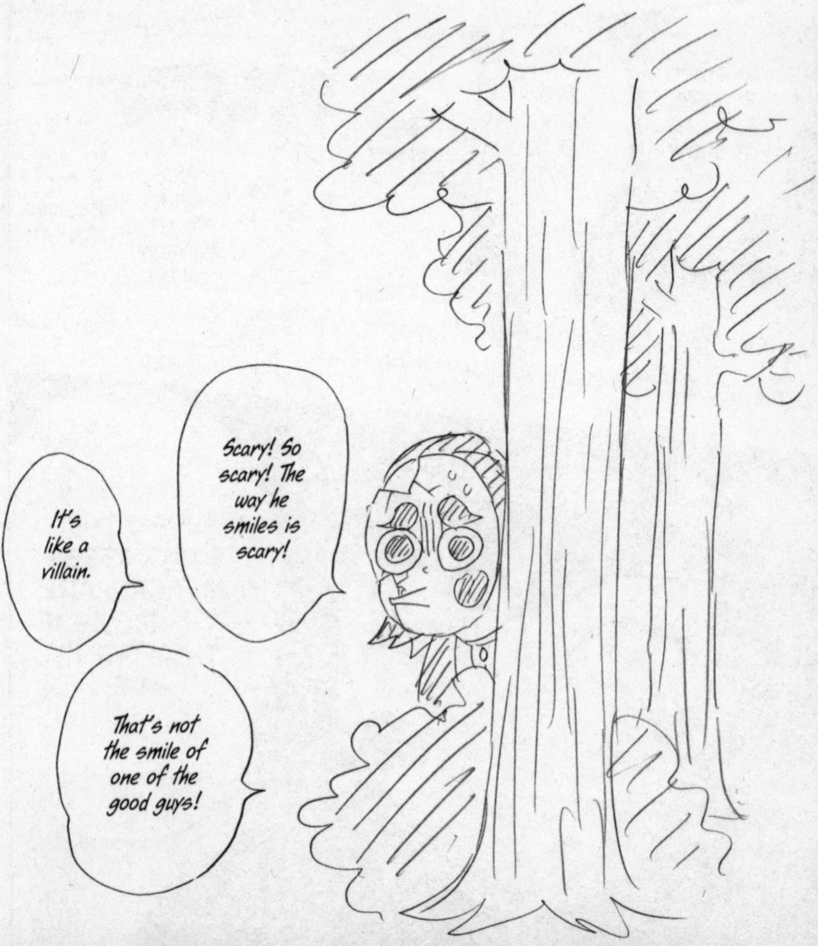
Scary! So scary! The way he smiles is scary!
It's like a villain.
That's not the smile of one of the good guys!

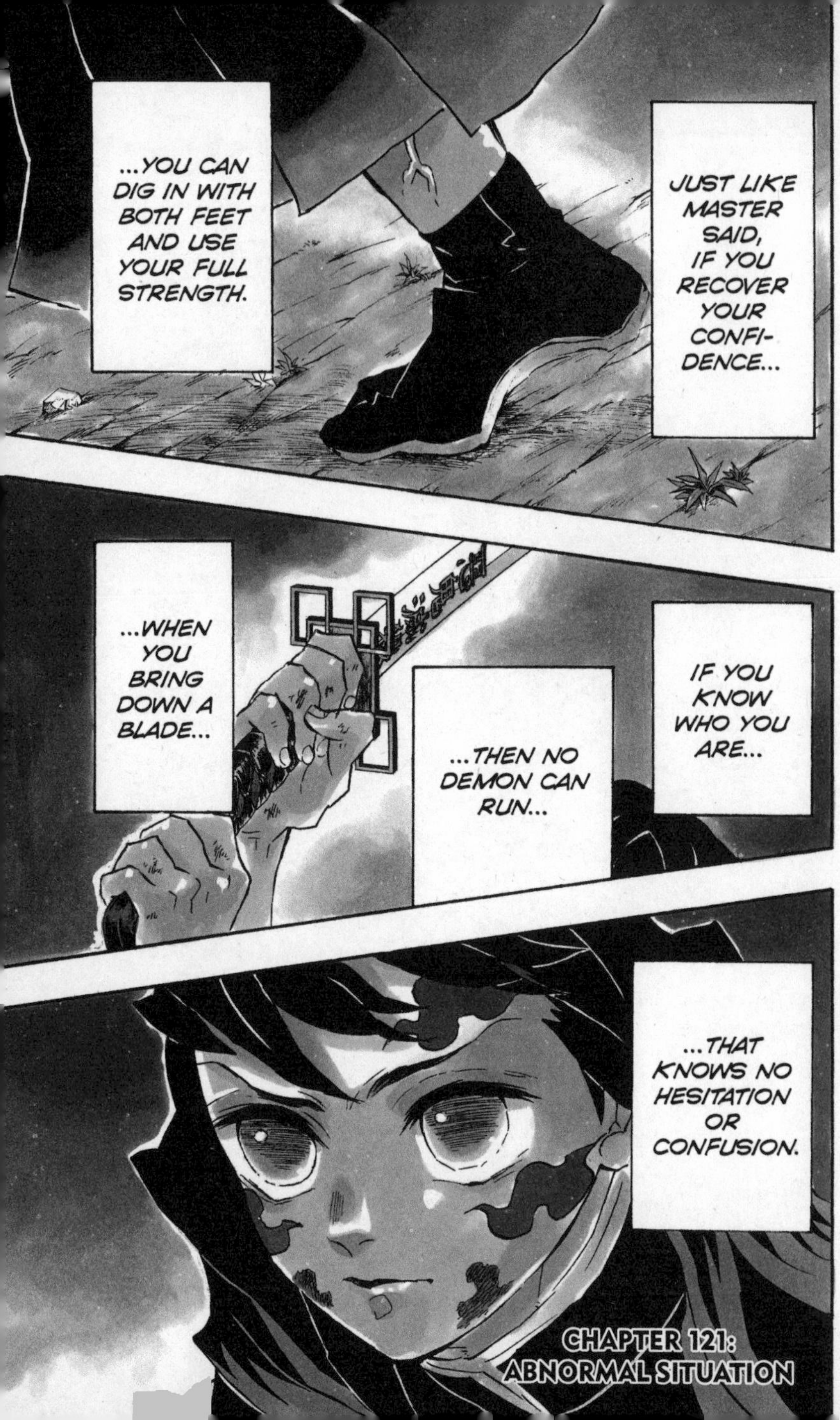
JUST LIKE MASTER SAID, IF YOU RECOVER YOUR CONFIDENCE...
...YOU CAN DIG IN WITH BOTH FEET AND USE YOUR FULL STRENGTH.
IF YOU KNOW WHO YOU ARE...
...THEN NO DEMON CAN RUN...
...WHEN YOU BRING DOWN A BLADE...
...THAT KNOWS NO HESITATION OR CONFUSION.
CHAPTER 121: ABNORMAL SITUATION

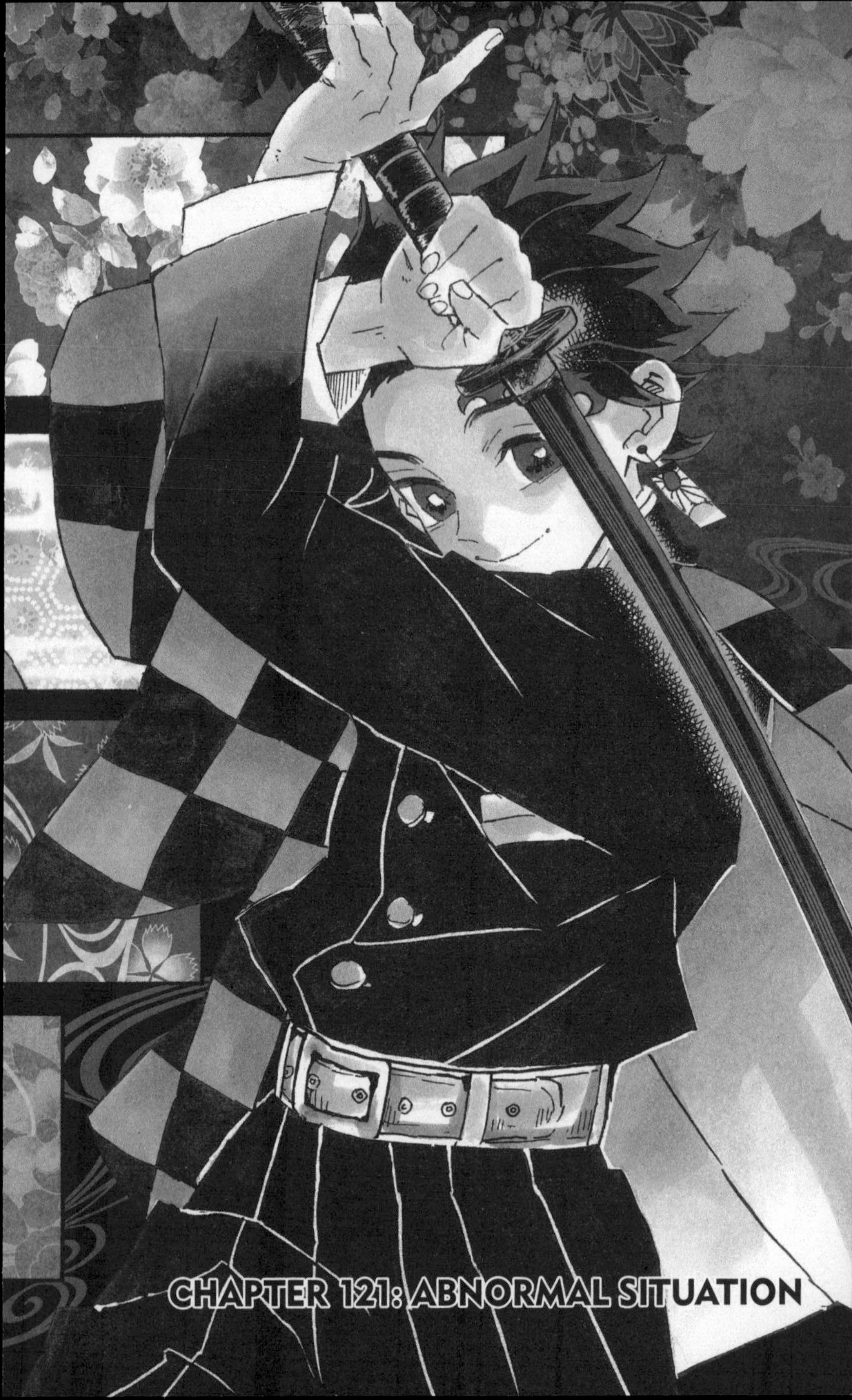

CHAPTER 121: ABNORMAL SITUATION

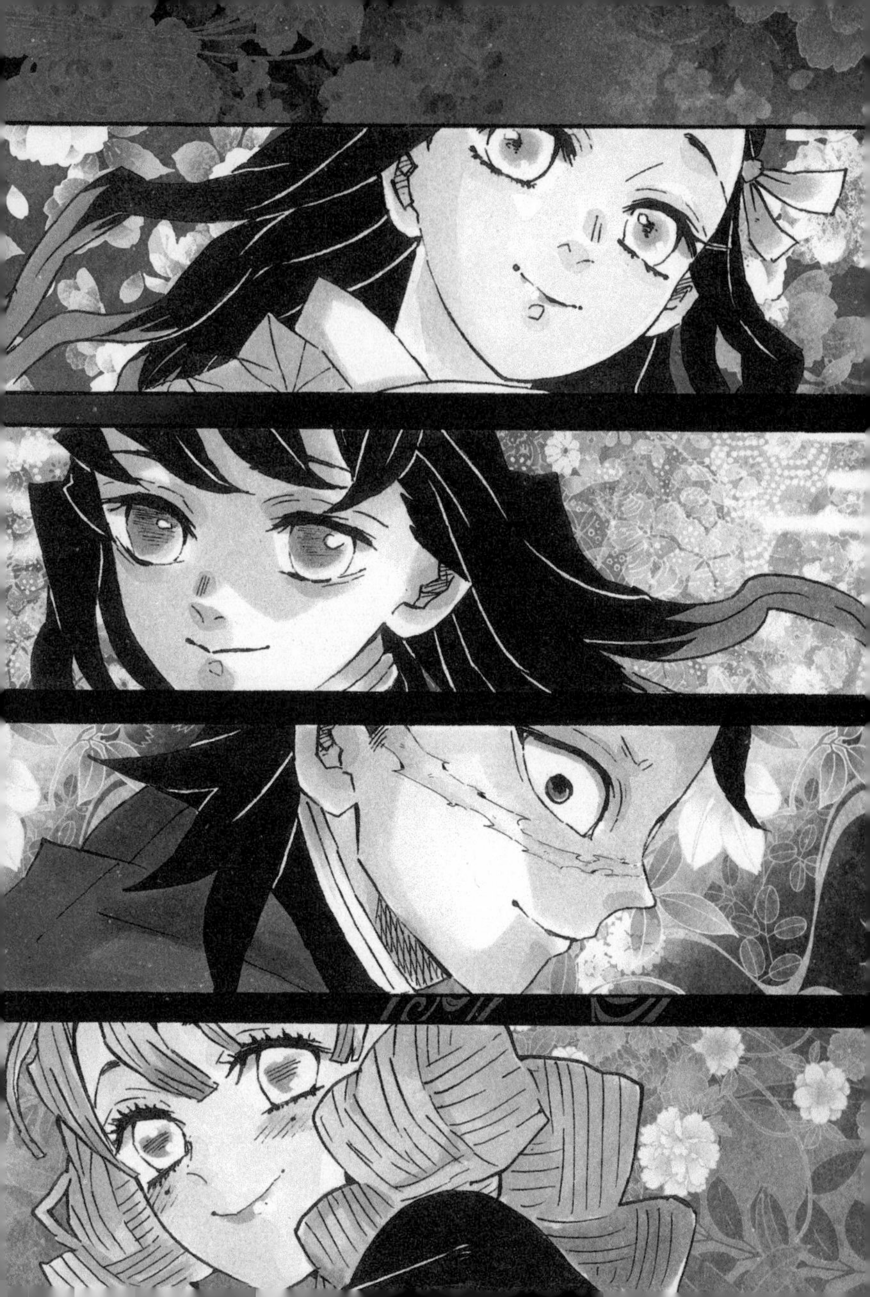

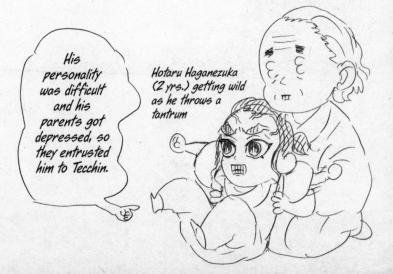

VILLAGE CHIEF TECCHIN'S FACE

Hotaru Haganezuka (2 yrs.) getting wild as he throws a tantrum
His personality was difficult and his parents got depressed, so they entrusted him to Tecchin.

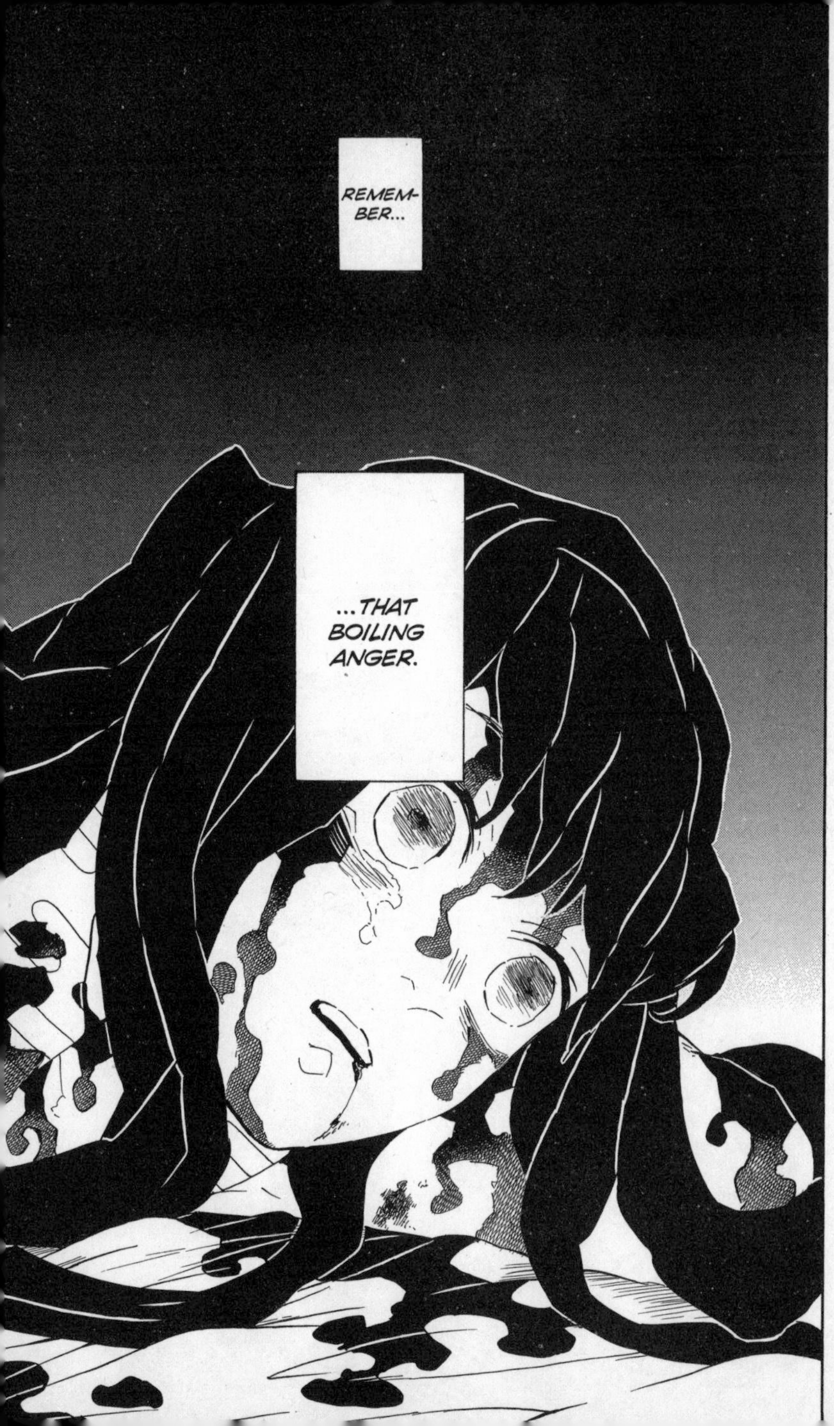
REMEMBER...
...THAT BOILING ANGER.

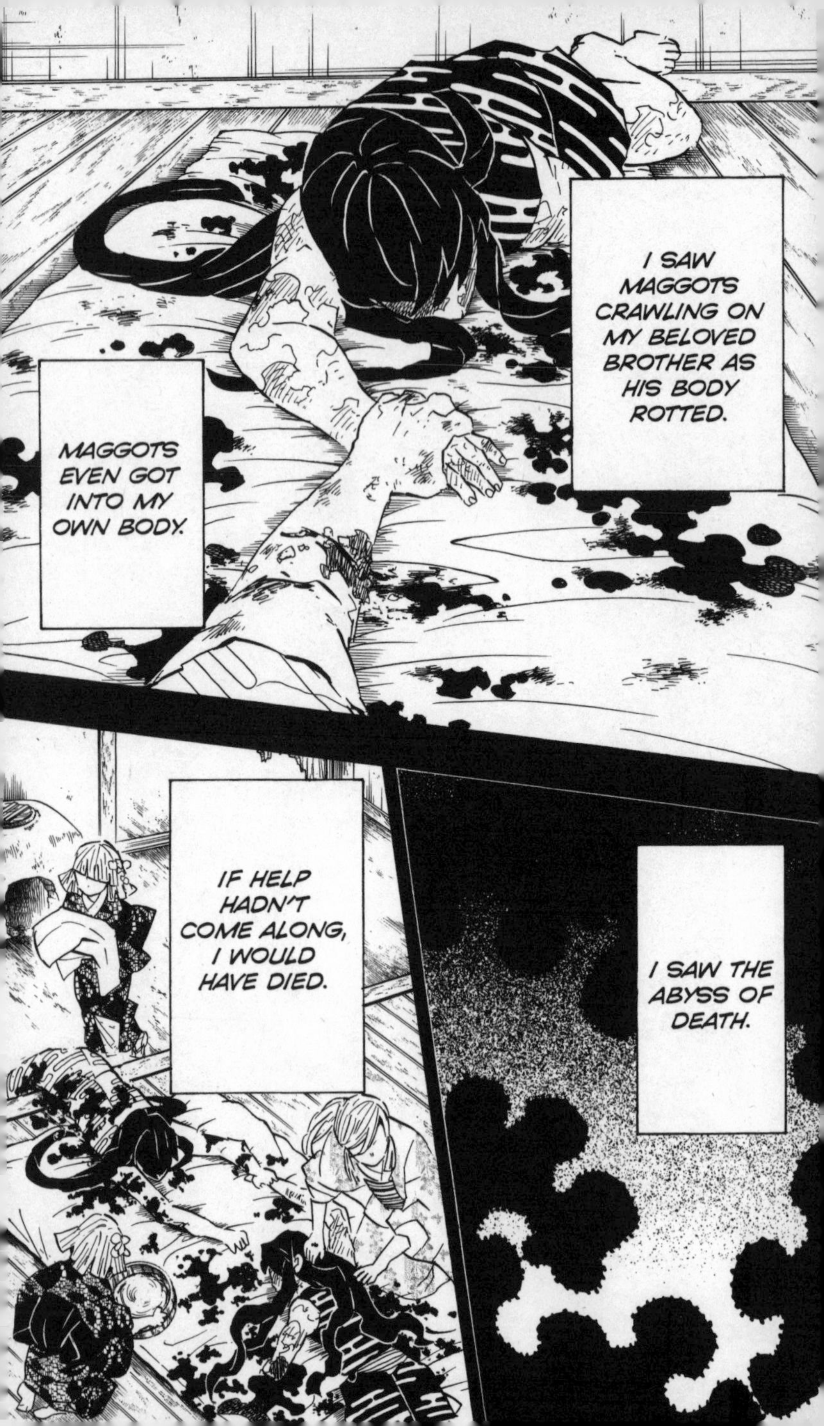
I SAW MAGGOTS CRAWLING ON MY BELOVED BROTHER AS HIS BODY ROTTED.
MAGGOTS EVEN GOT INTO MY OWN BODY.
I SAW THE ABYSS OF DEATH.
IF HELP HADN'T COME ALONG, I WOULD HAVE DIED.

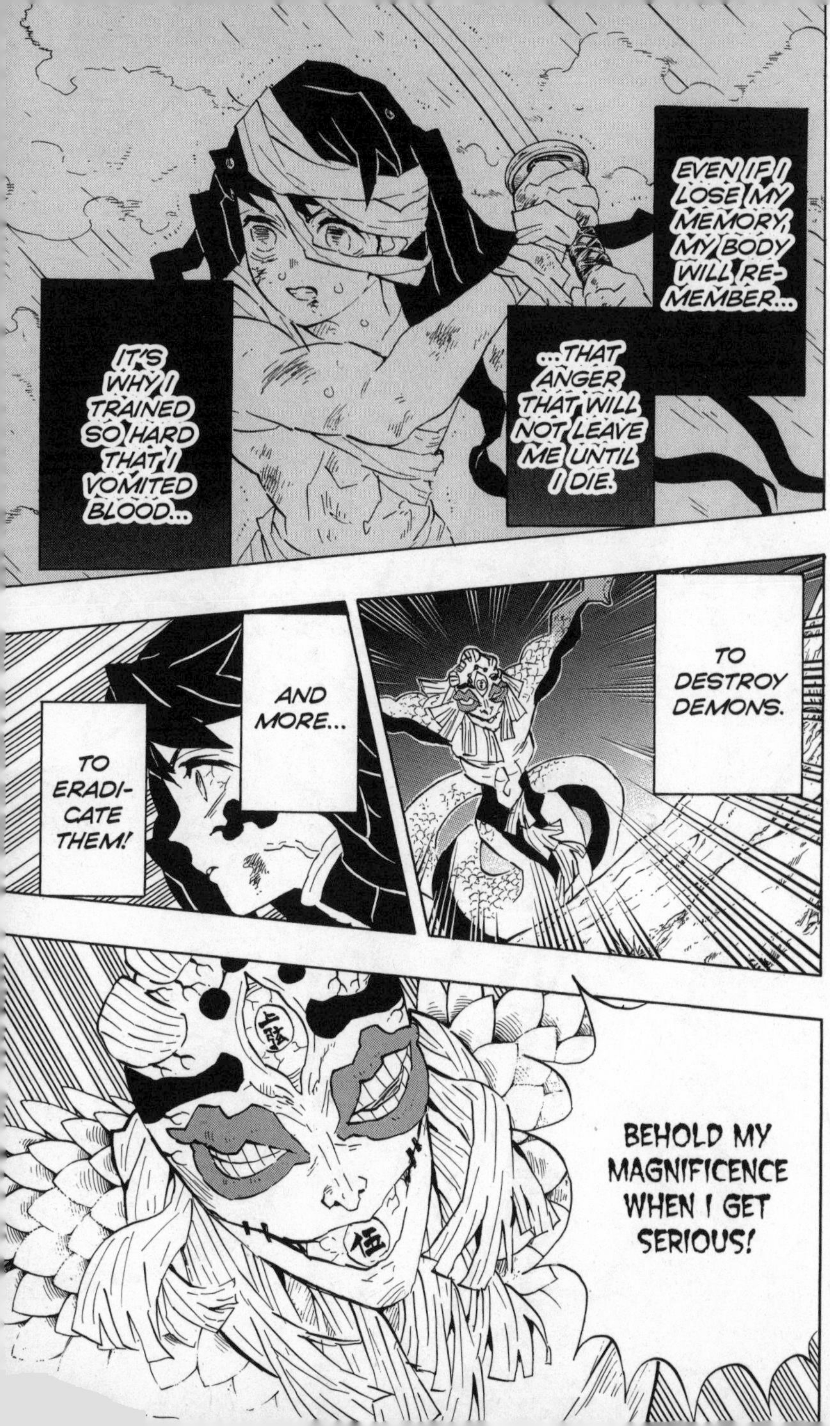
EVEN IF I LOSE MY MEMORY, MY BODY WILL RE-MEMBER...
...THAT ANGER THAT WILL NOT LEAVE ME UNTIL I DIE.
IT'S WHY I TRAINED SO HARD THAT I VOMITED BLOOD...
TO DESTROY DEMONS.
AND MORE...
TO ERADI-CATE THEM!
BEHOLD MY MAGNIFICENCE WHEN I GET SERIOUS!

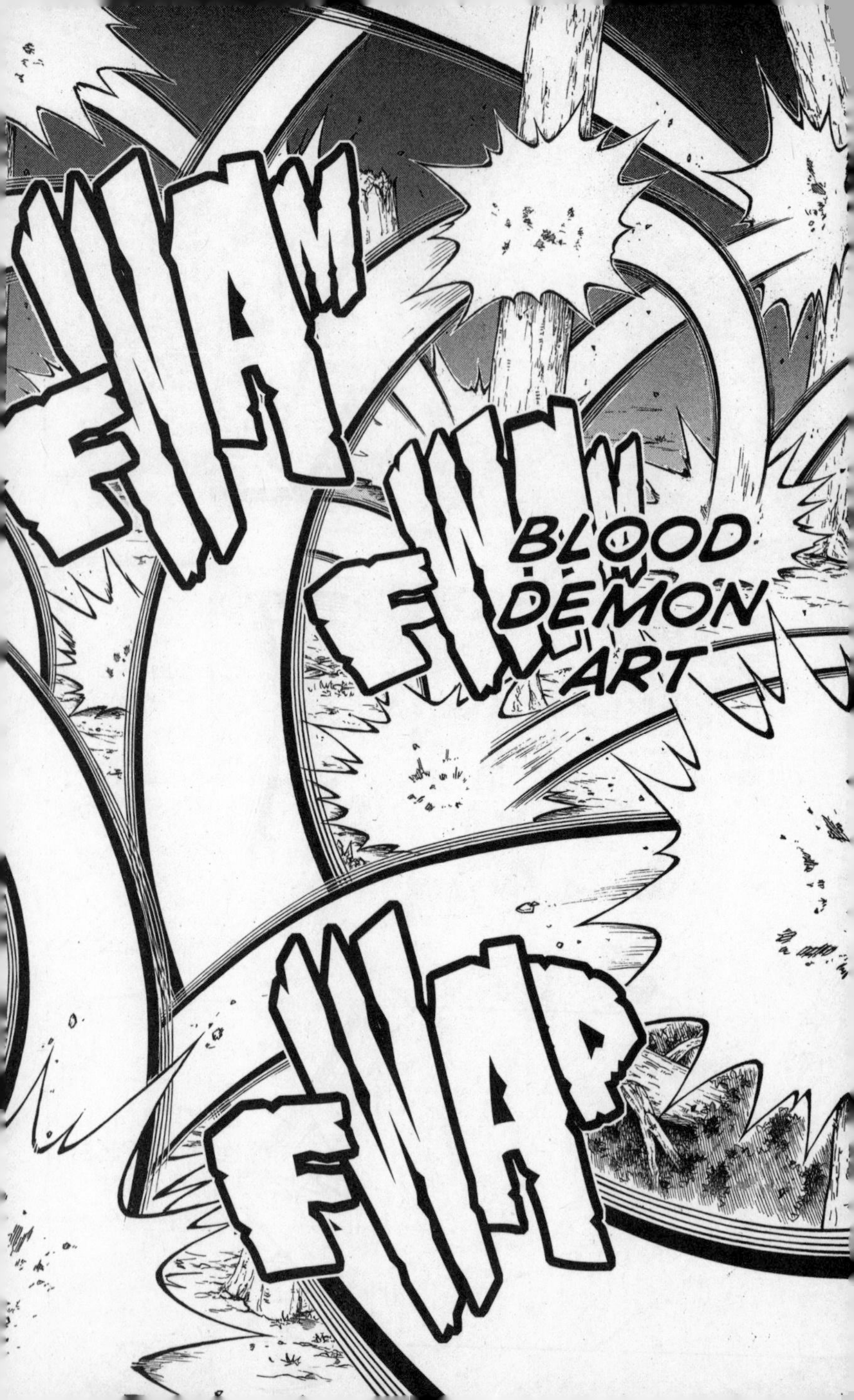
FWAM
FWM
BLOOD DEMON ART
FWAP

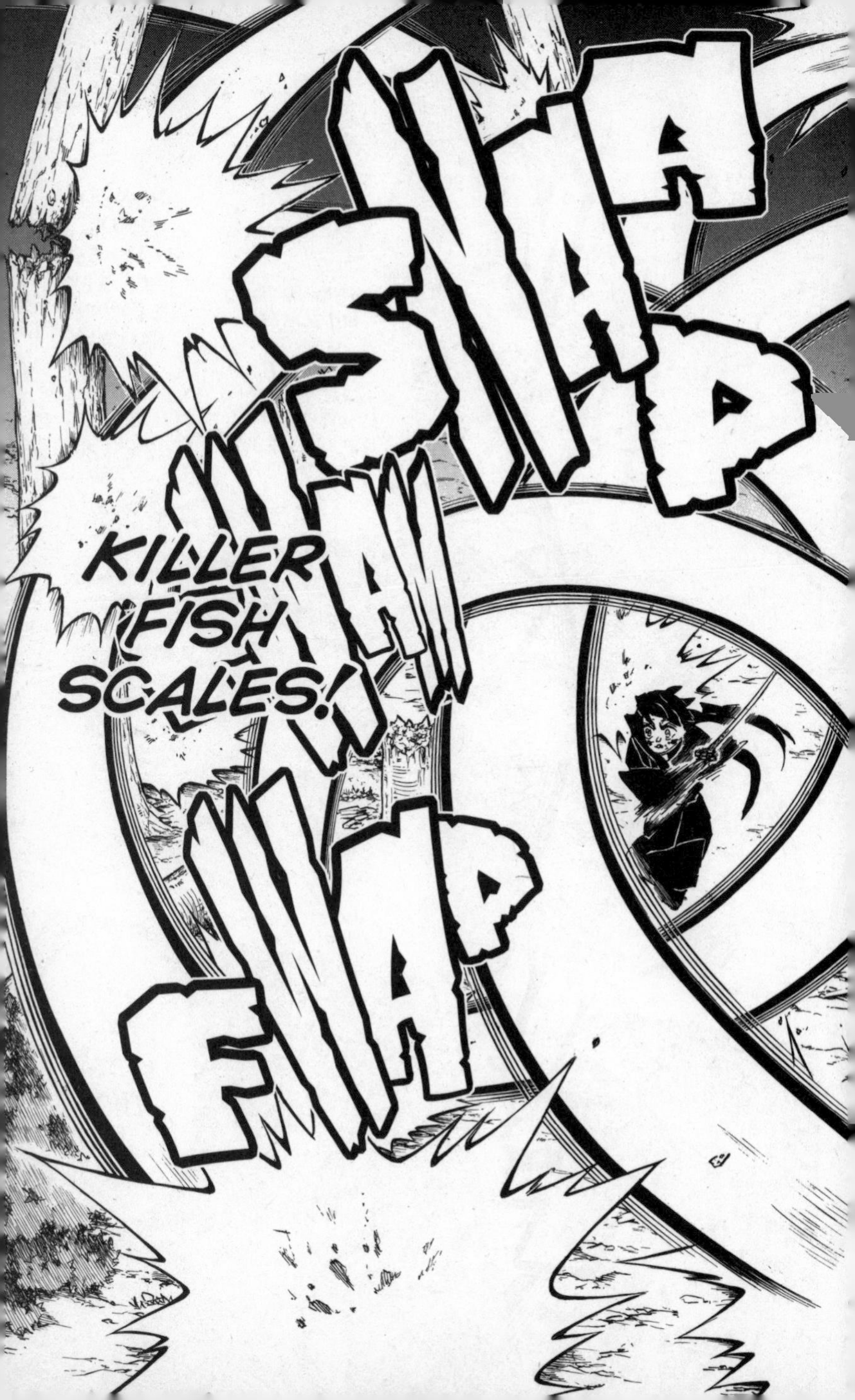
SNAP
KILLER FISH SCALES!

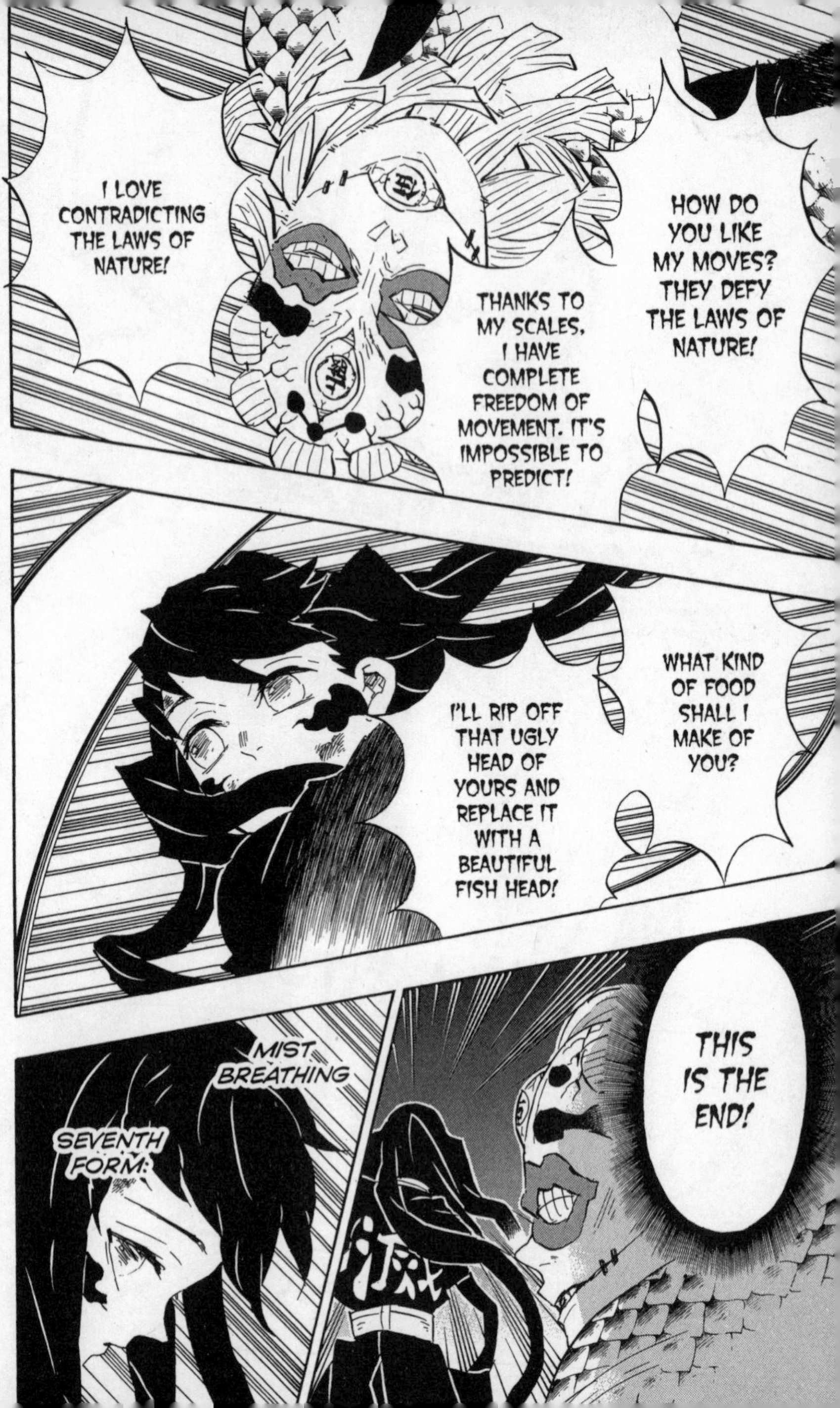
HOW DO YOU LIKE MY MOVES? THEY DEFY THE LAWS OF NATURE!
THANKS TO MY SCALES, I HAVE COMPLETE FREEDOM OF MOVEMENT. IT'S IMPOSSIBLE TO PREDICT!
I LOVE CONTRADICTING THE LAWS OF NATURE!
WHAT KIND OF FOOD SHALL I MAKE OF YOU?
I'LL RIP OFF THAT UGLY HEAD OF YOURS AND REPLACE IT WITH A BEAUTIFUL FISH HEAD!
THIS IS THE END!
MIST BREATHING
SEVENTH FORM:

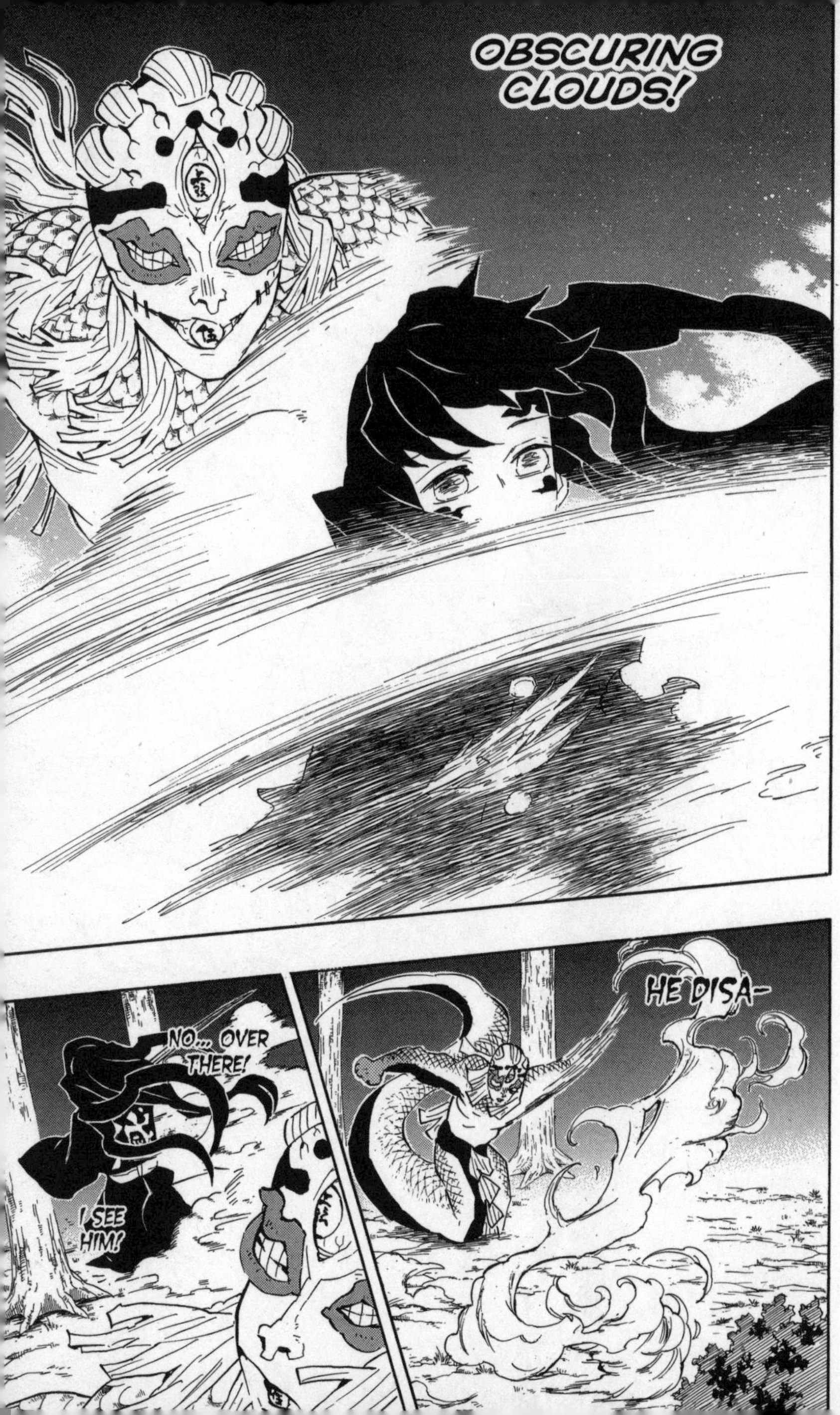
OBSCURING CLOUDS!
HE DISA-
NO... OVER THERE!
I SEE HIM!

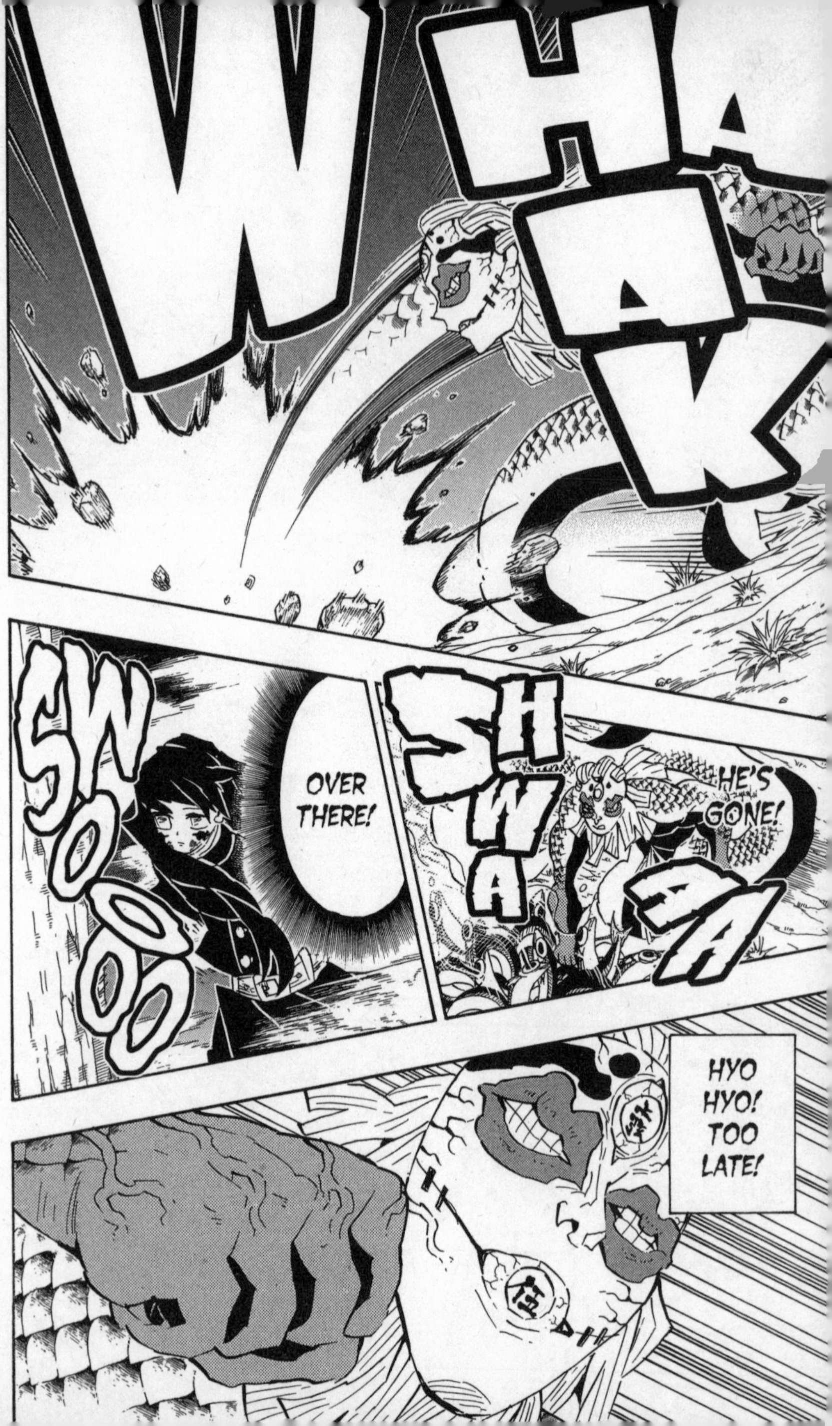
WHAAK
SHWA
HE'S GONE!
A
SWOOOOO
OVER THERE!
HYO HYO! TOO LATE!

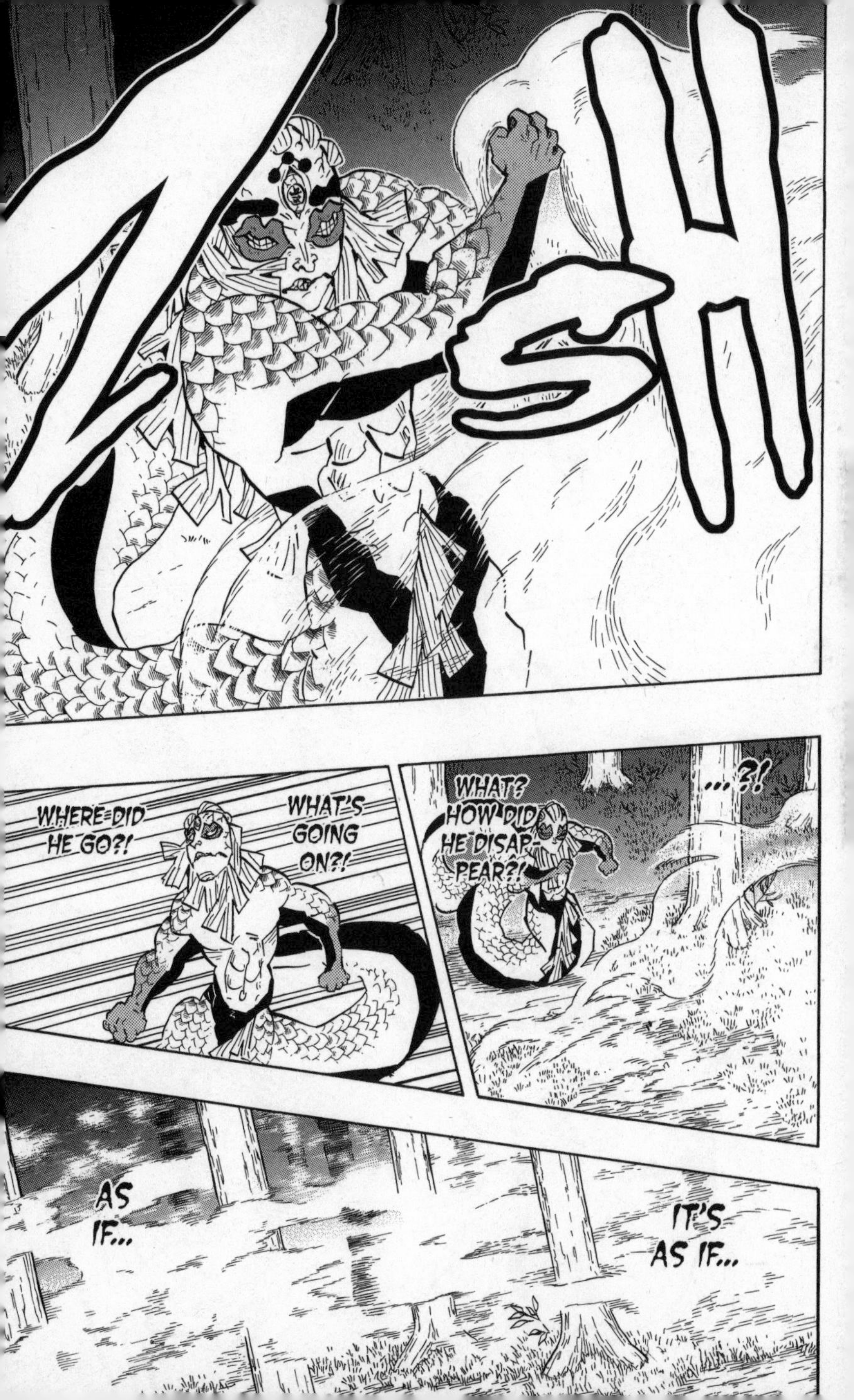
...?!
WHAT? HOW DID HE DISAP-PEAR?!
WHAT'S GOING ON?!
WHERE DID HE GO?!
IT'S AS IF...
AS IF...

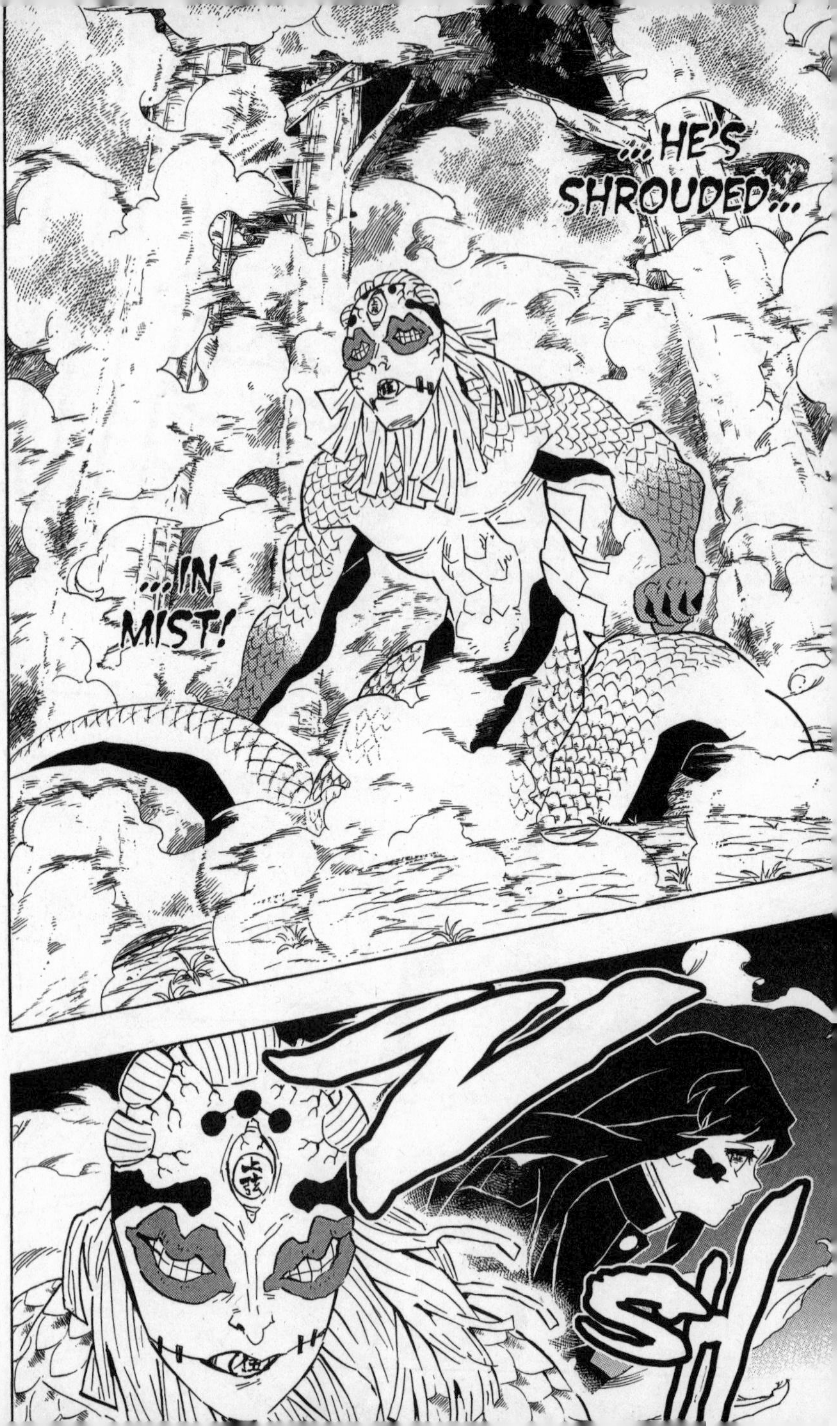
...HE'S SHROUDED...
...IN MIST!
SH

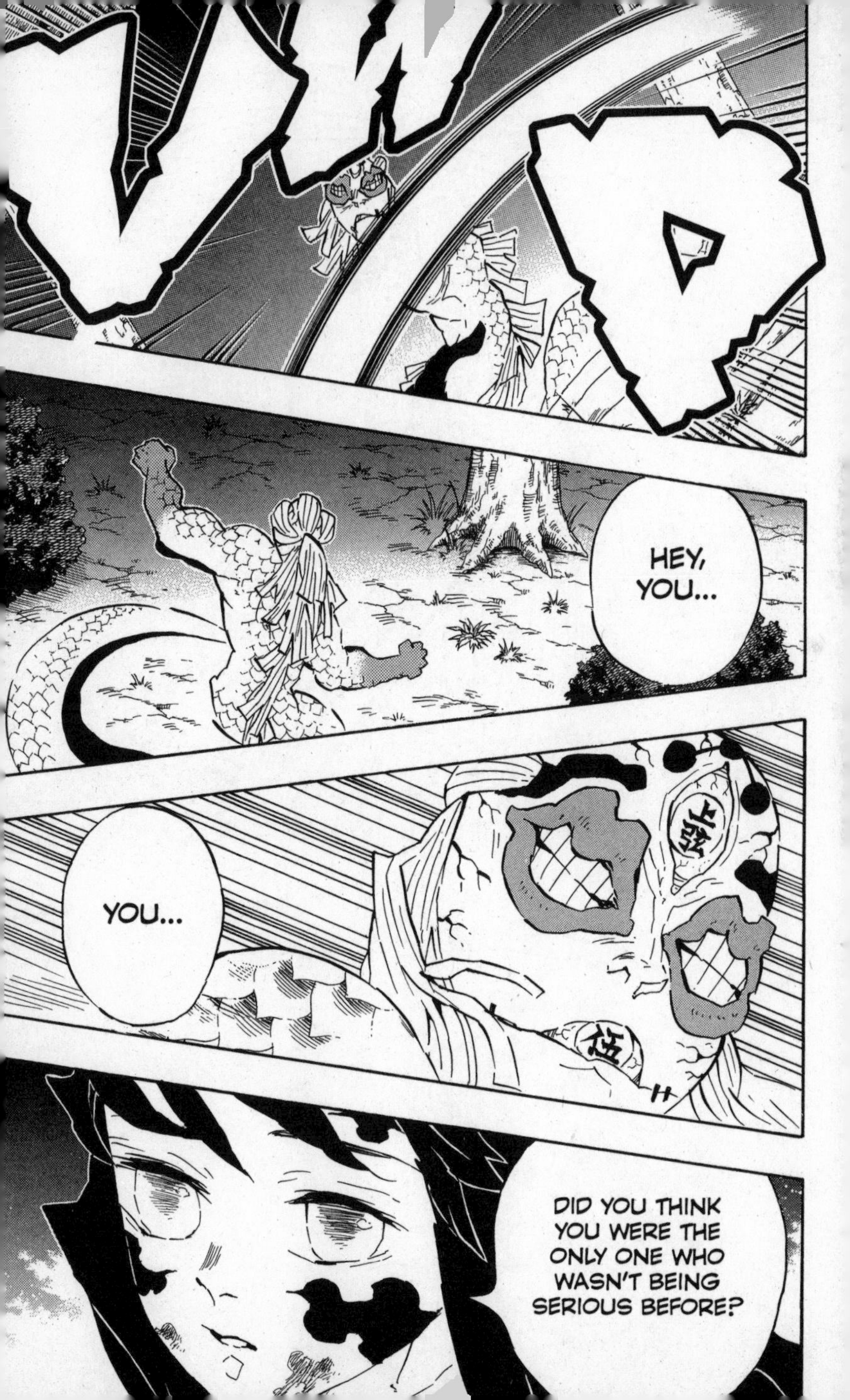
HEY, YOU...
YOU...
DID YOU THINK YOU WERE THE ONLY ONE WHO WASN'T BEING SERIOUS BEFORE?

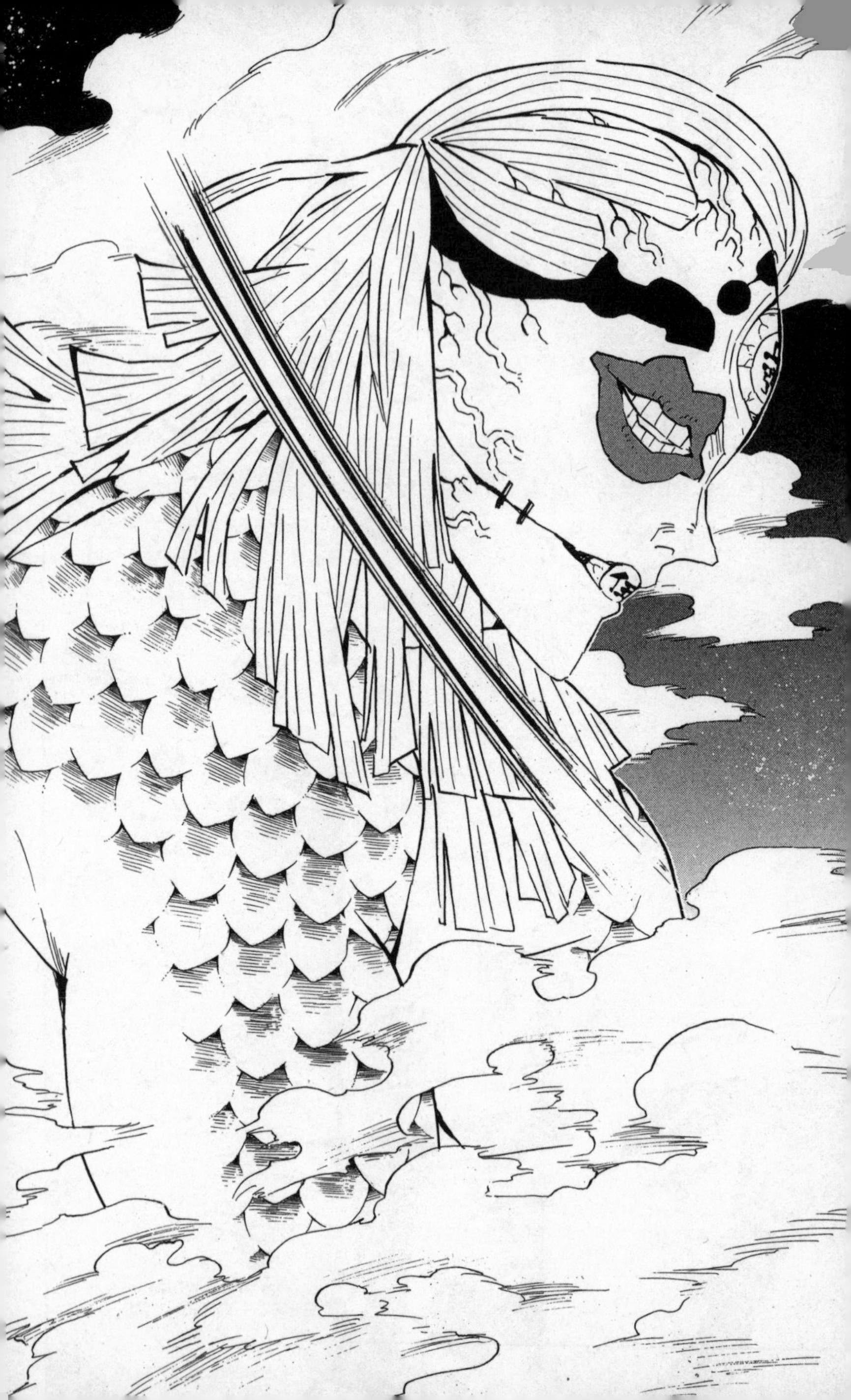

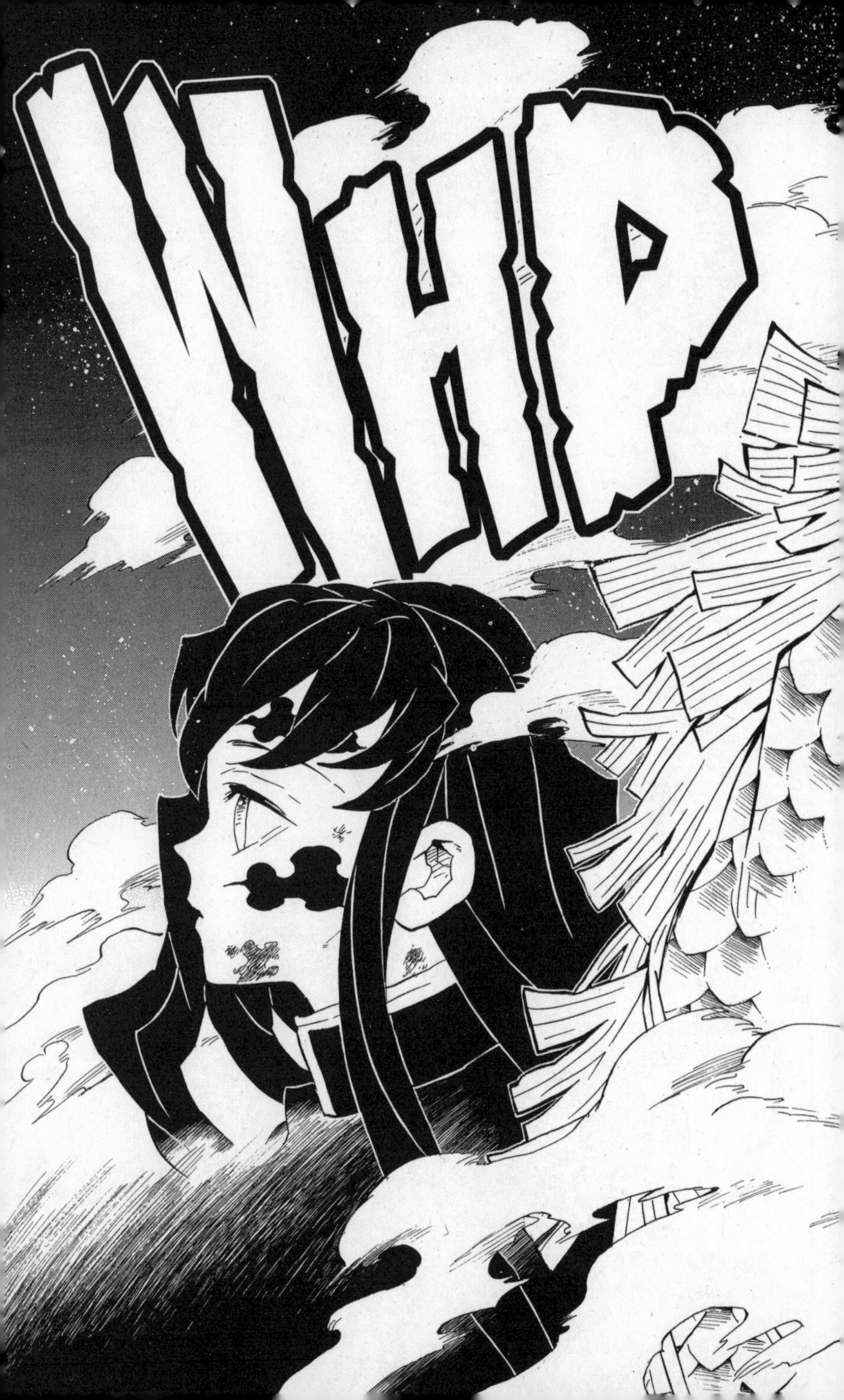
WHIP

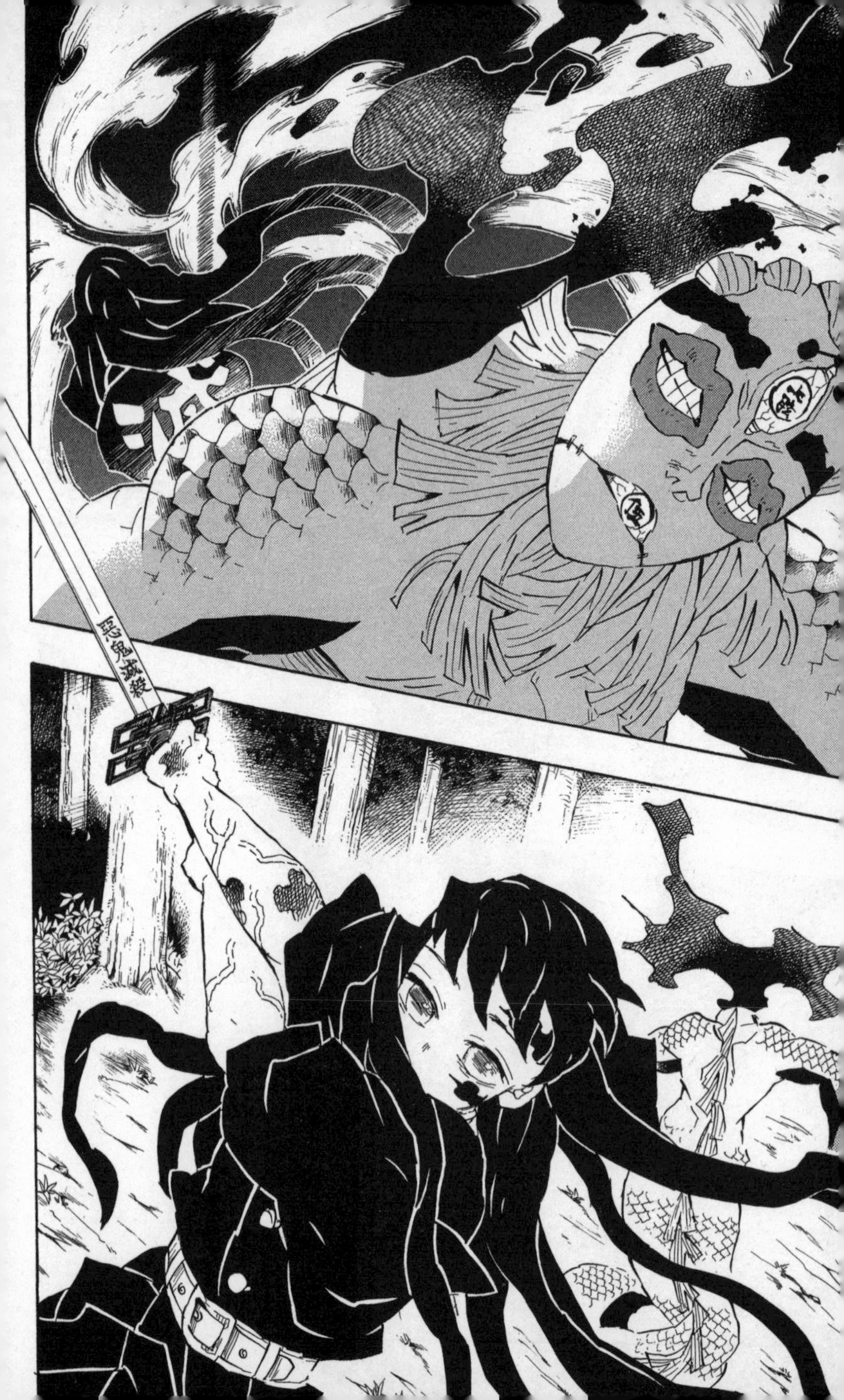
悪鬼滅殺

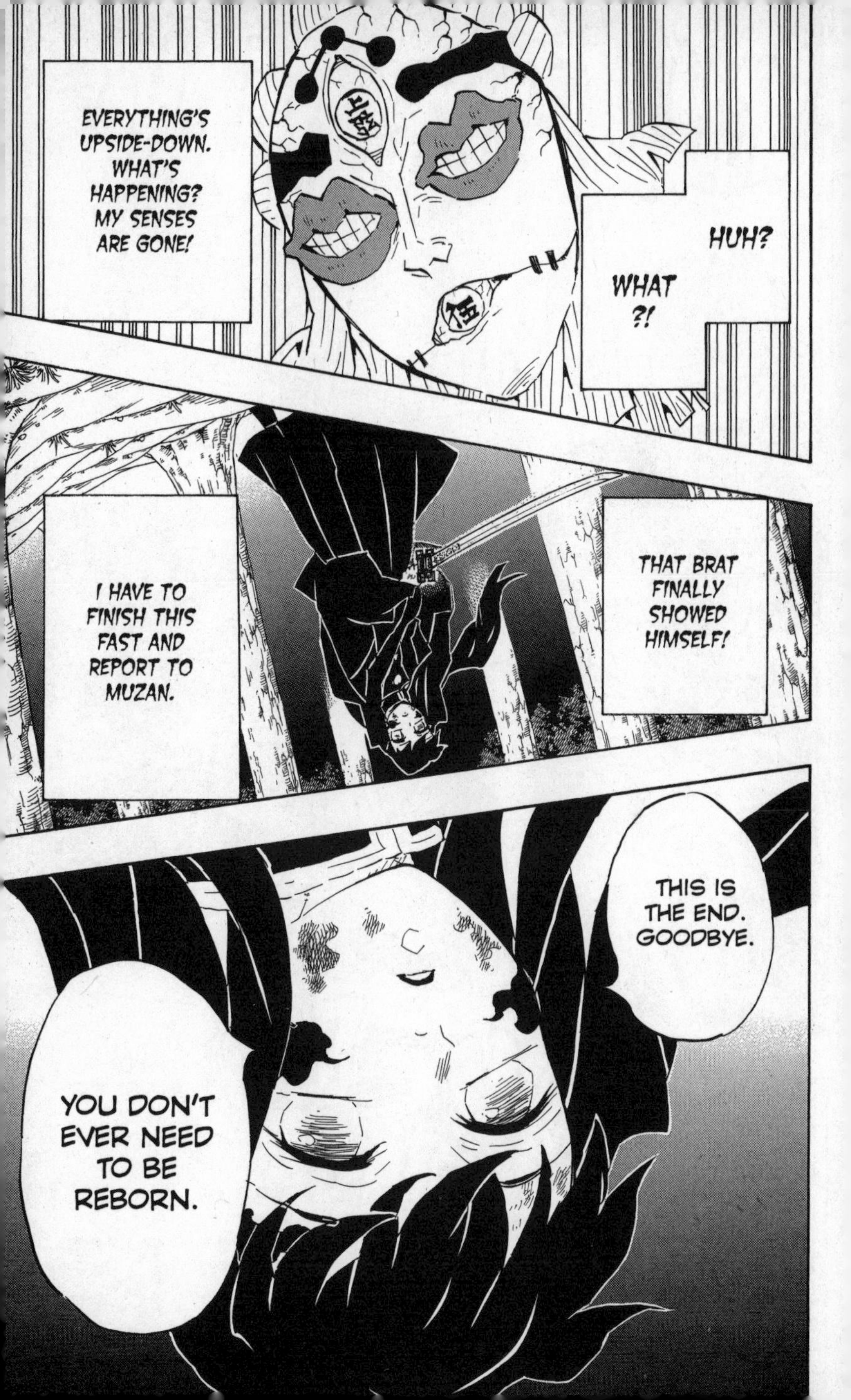
HUH?
WHAT ?!
EVERYTHING'S UPSIDE-DOWN. WHAT'S HAPPENING? MY SENSES ARE GONE!
THAT BRAT FINALLY SHOWED HIMSELF!
I HAVE TO FINISH THIS FAST AND REPORT TO MUZAN.
THIS IS THE END. GOODBYE.
YOU DON'T EVER NEED TO BE REBORN.

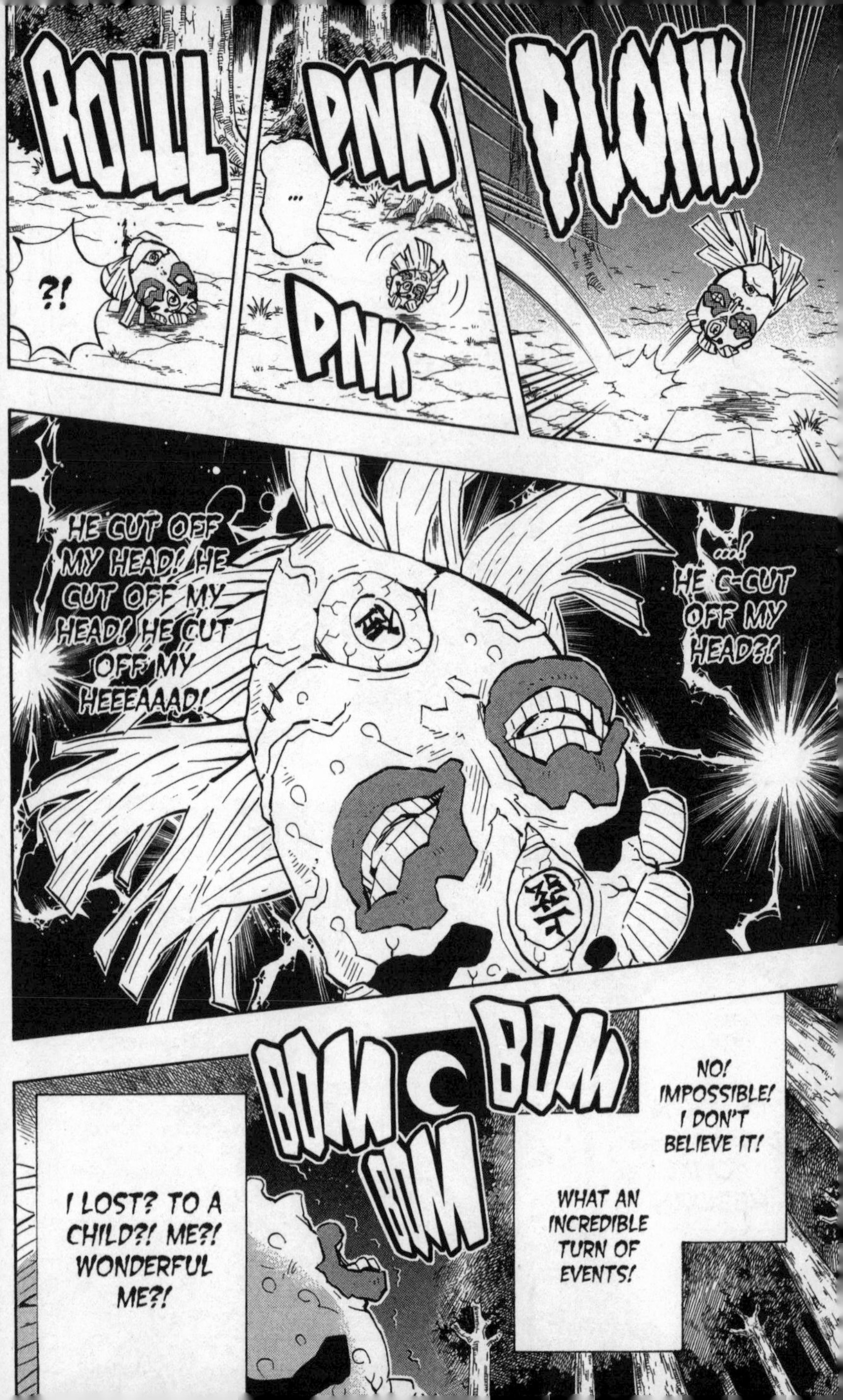
PLONK
...
PNK
PNK
ROLLL
?!
...! HE C-CUT OFF MY HEAD?!
HE CUT OFF MY HEAD! HE CUT OFF MY HEAD! HE CUT OFF MY HEEEAAAD!
BOM
BOM
BOM
NO! IMPOSSIBLE! I DON'T BELIEVE IT!
WHAT AN INCREDIBLE TURN OF EVENTS!
I LOST? TO A CHILD?! ME?! WONDERFUL ME?!

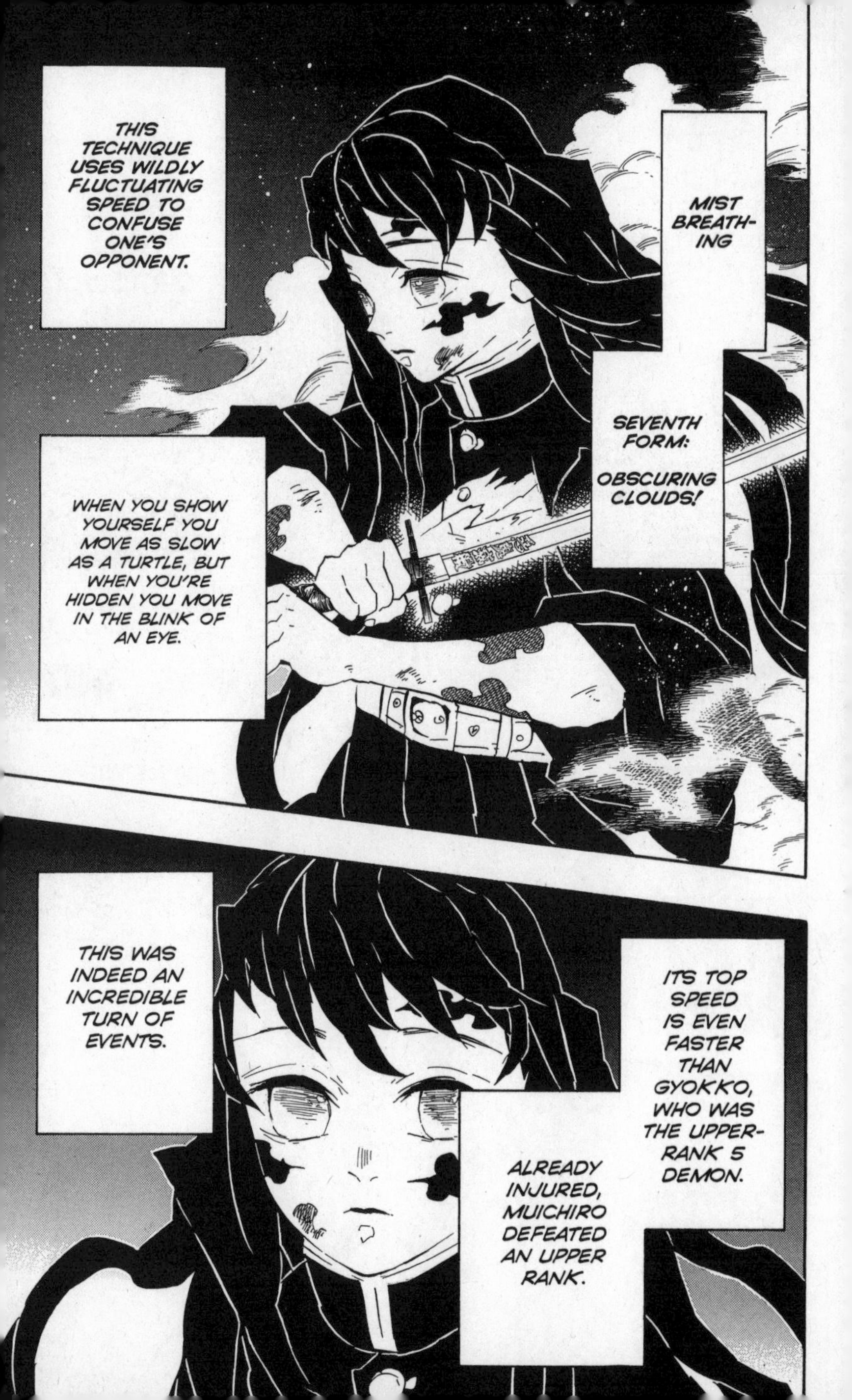
MIST BREATHING
SEVENTH FORM: OBSCURING CLOUDS!
THIS TECHNIQUE USES WILDLY FLUCTUATING SPEED TO CONFUSE ONE'S OPPONENT.
WHEN YOU SHOW YOURSELF YOU MOVE AS SLOW AS A TURTLE, BUT WHEN YOU'RE HIDDEN YOU MOVE IN THE BLINK OF AN EYE.
ITS TOP SPEED IS EVEN FASTER THAN GYOKKO, WHO WAS THE UPPER-RANK 5 DEMON.
ALREADY INJURED, MUICHIRO DEFEATED AN UPPER RANK.
THIS WAS INDEED AN INCREDIBLE TURN OF EVENTS.

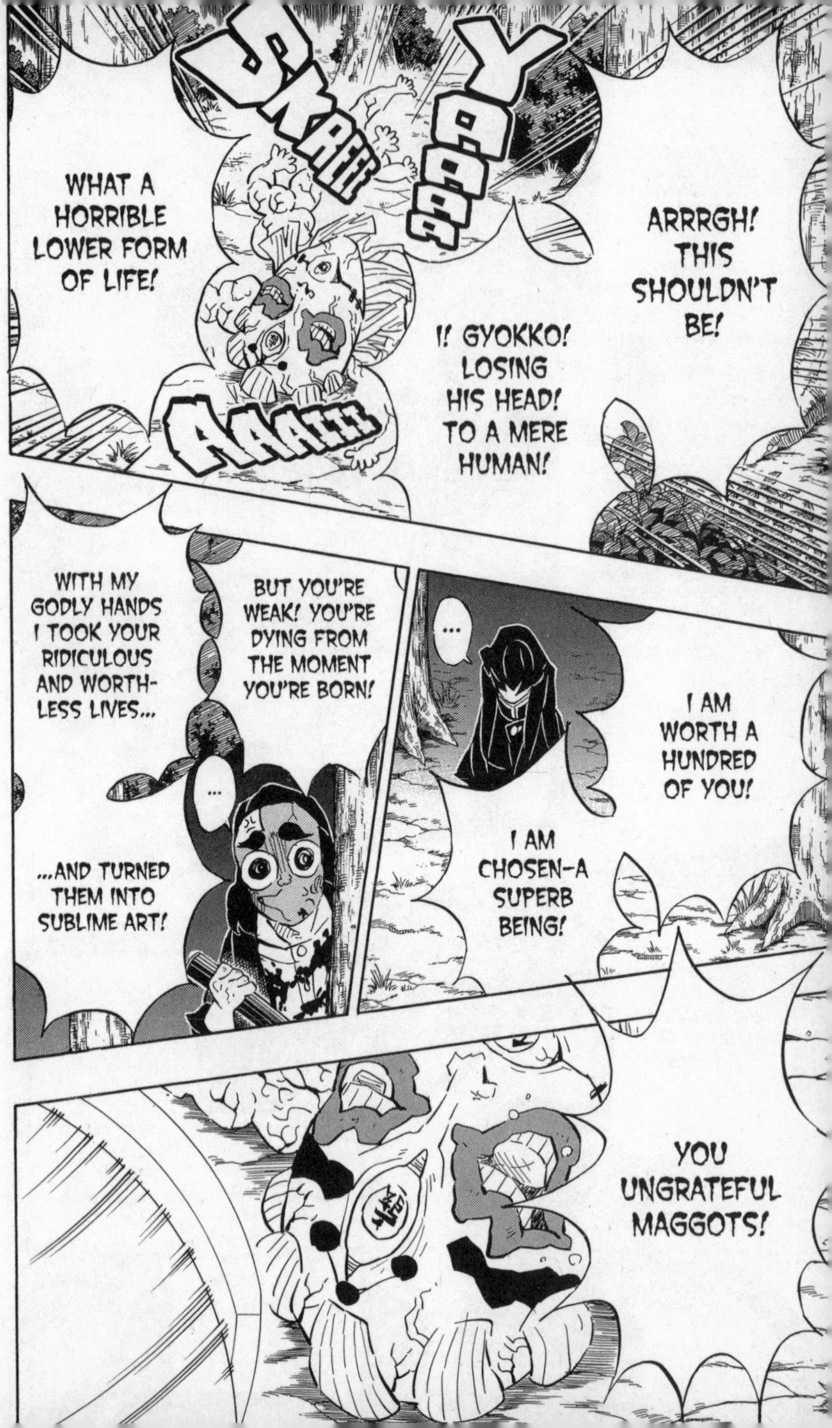
ARRRGH! THIS SHOULDN'T BE!
!! GYOKKO! LOSING HIS HEAD! TO A MERE HUMAN!
WHAT A HORRIBLE LOWER FORM OF LIFE!
I AM WORTH A HUNDRED OF YOU!
...
I AM CHOSEN—A SUPERB BEING!
BUT YOU'RE WEAK! YOU'RE DYING FROM THE MOMENT YOU'RE BORN!
WITH MY GODLY HANDS I TOOK YOUR RIDICULOUS AND WORTHLESS LIVES...
...
...AND TURNED THEM INTO SUBLIME ART!
YOU UNGRATEFUL MAGGOTS!

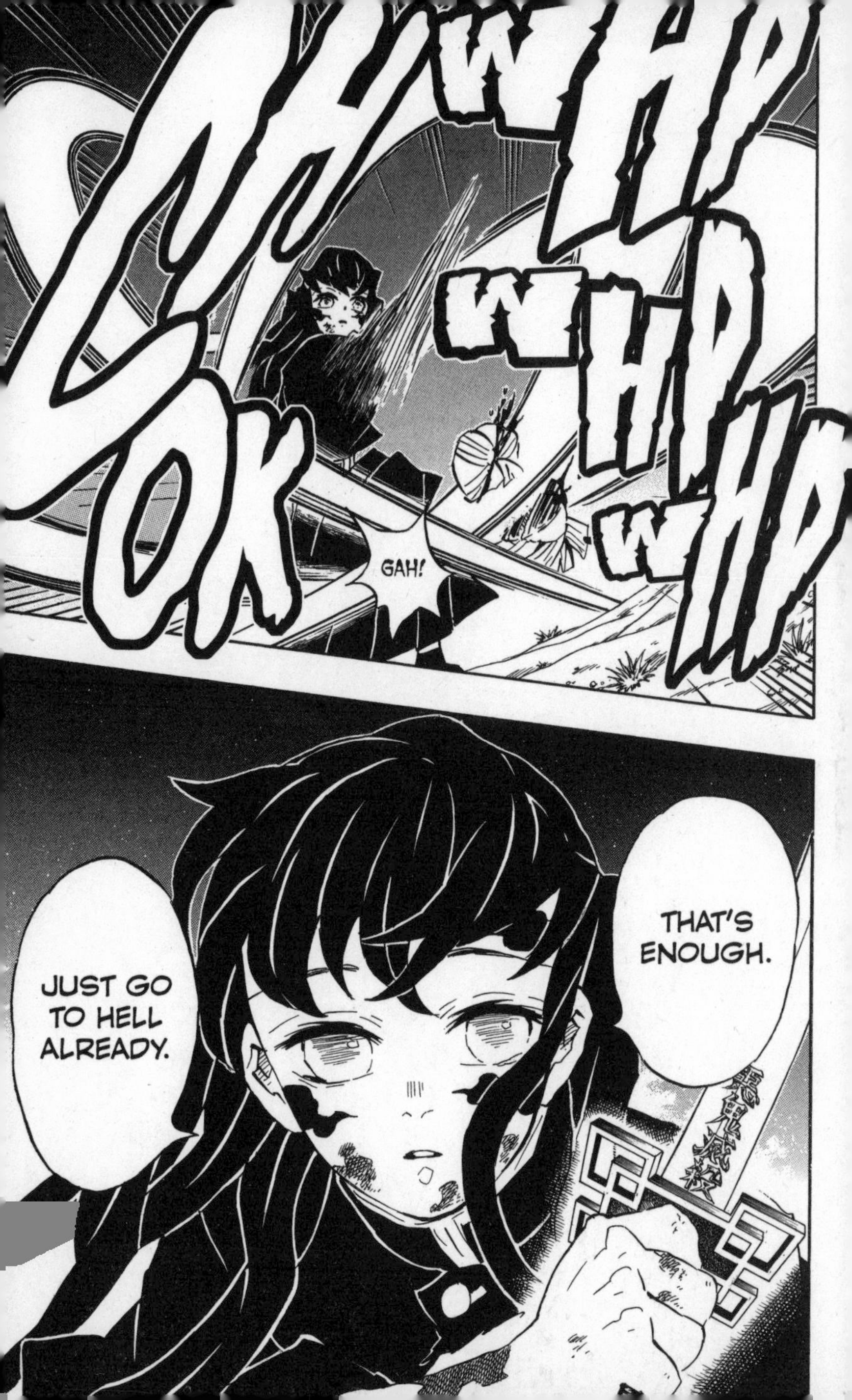
WHAP
WHAP
GAH!
THAT'S ENOUGH.
JUST GO TO HELL ALREADY.

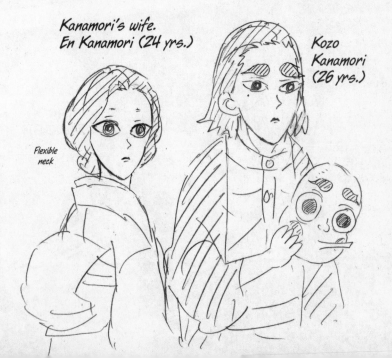

Kanamori's true slender face
Kozo Kanamori (26 yrs.)
Kanamori's wife. En Kanamori (24 yrs.)
Flexible neck

CHAPTER 122: A PASSING MOMENT OF EXCITEMENT

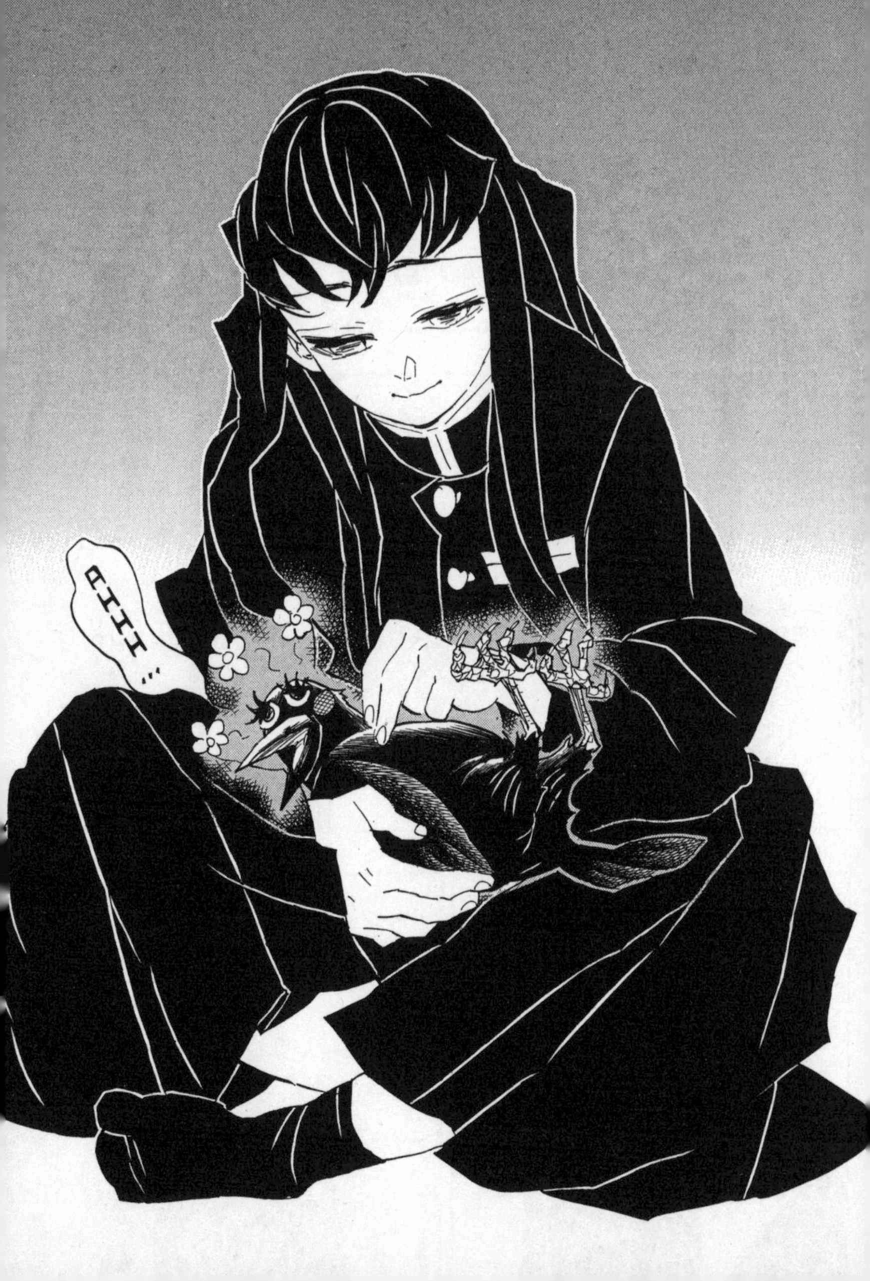
AIIII...

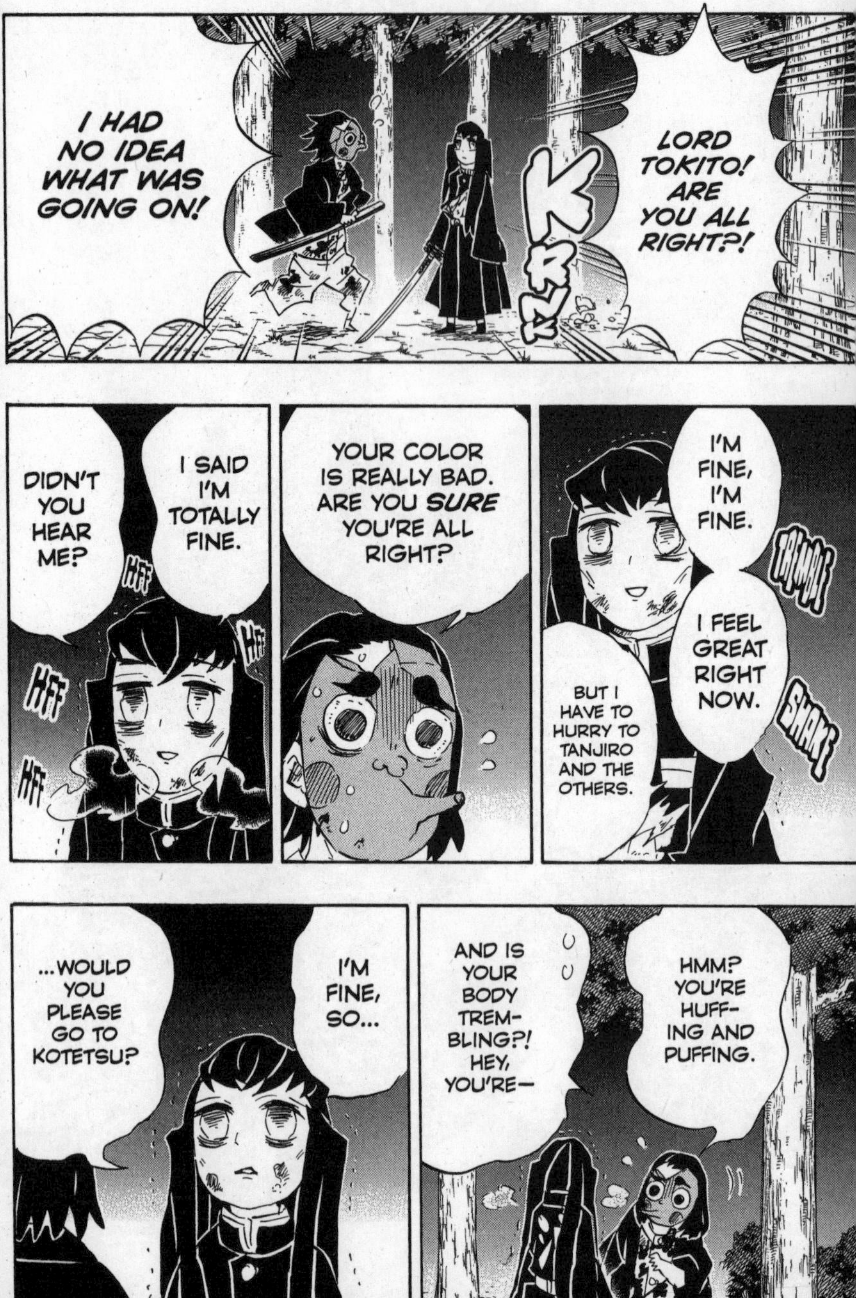
LORD TOKITO! ARE YOU ALL RIGHT?!
I HAD NO IDEA WHAT WAS GOING ON!
I'M FINE, I'M FINE.
TREMBLE
I FEEL GREAT RIGHT NOW.
SHAKE
BUT I HAVE TO HURRY TO TANJIRO AND THE OTHERS.
YOUR COLOR IS REALLY BAD. ARE YOU *SURE* YOU'RE ALL RIGHT?
I SAID I'M TOTALLY FINE.
DIDN'T YOU HEAR ME?
HFF
HFF
HFF
HFF
HMM? YOU'RE HUFF-ING AND PUFFING.
AND IS YOUR BODY TREM-BLING?! HEY, YOU'RE—
I'M FINE, SO...
...WOULD YOU PLEASE GO TO KOTETSU?

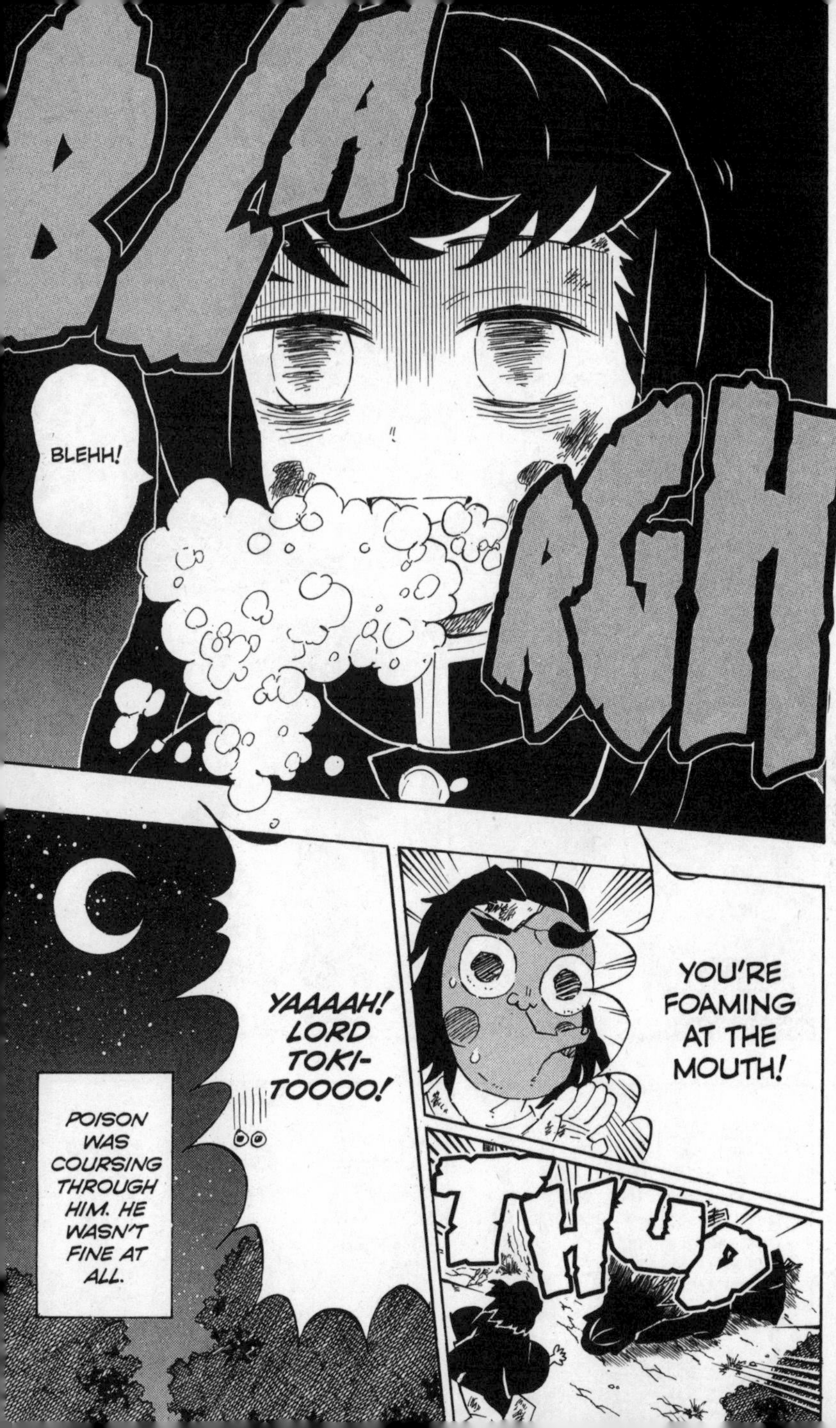
BLARGH
BLEHH!
YOU'RE FOAMING AT THE MOUTH!
YAAAAH! LORD TOKI-TOOOO!
THUD
POISON WAS COURSING THROUGH HIM. HE WASN'T FINE AT ALL.

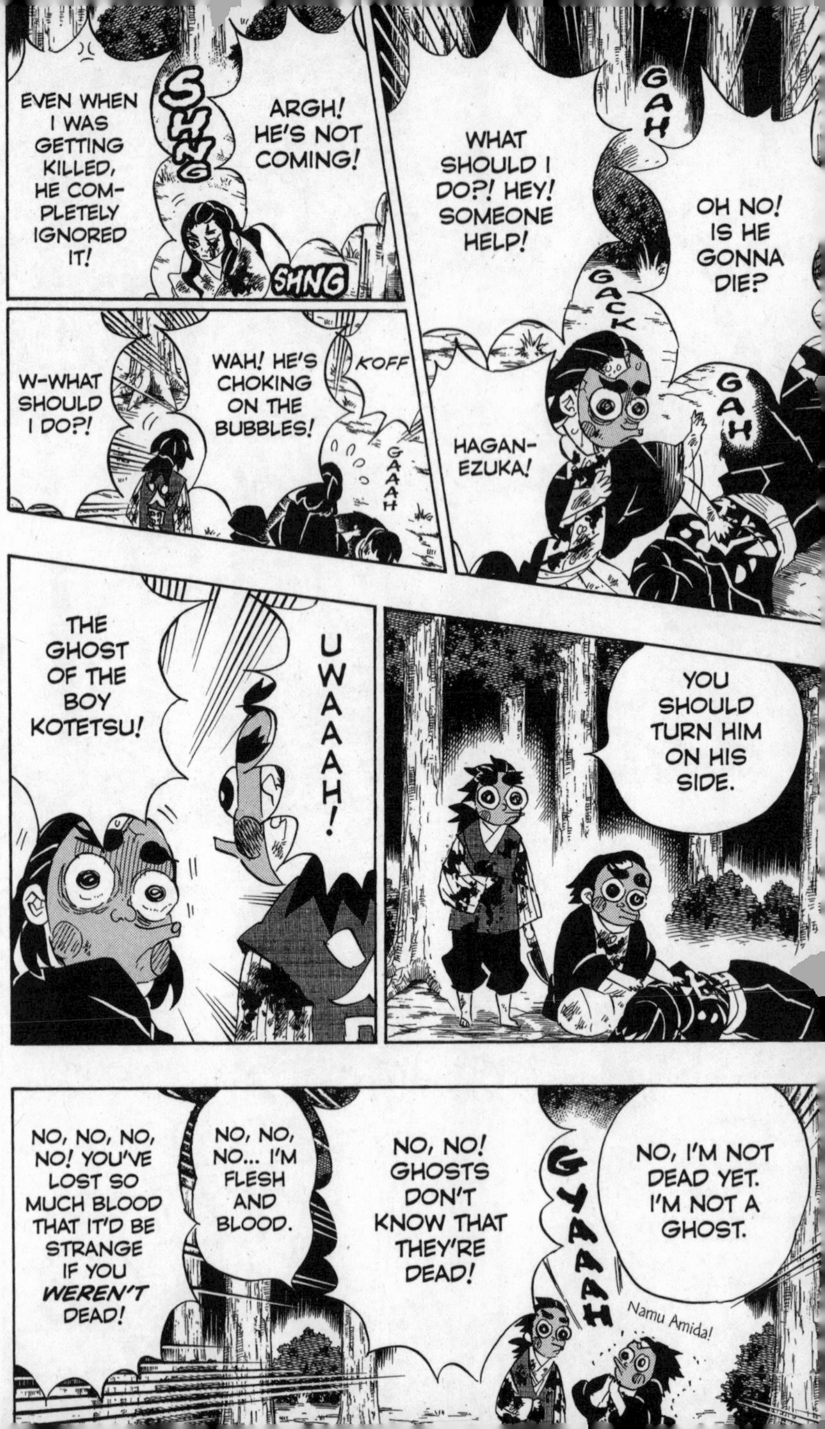
GAH
OH NO! IS HE GONNA DIE?
WHAT SHOULD I DO?! HEY! SOMEONE HELP!
GACK
GAH
HAGAN-EZUKA!
ARGH! HE'S NOT COMING!
SHNG
EVEN WHEN I WAS GETTING KILLED, HE COMPLETELY IGNORED IT!
SHNG
KOFF
WAH! HE'S CHOKING ON THE BUBBLES!
GAAAH
W-WHAT SHOULD I DO?!
YOU SHOULD TURN HIM ON HIS SIDE.
UWAAAAH!
THE GHOST OF THE BOY KOTETSU!
NO, I'M NOT DEAD YET. I'M NOT A GHOST.
GYAAAH
Namu Amida!
NO, NO! GHOSTS DON'T KNOW THAT THEY'RE DEAD!
NO, NO, NO... I'M FLESH AND BLOOD.
NO, NO, NO, NO! YOU'VE LOST SO MUCH BLOOD THAT IT'D BE STRANGE IF YOU *WEREN'T* DEAD!

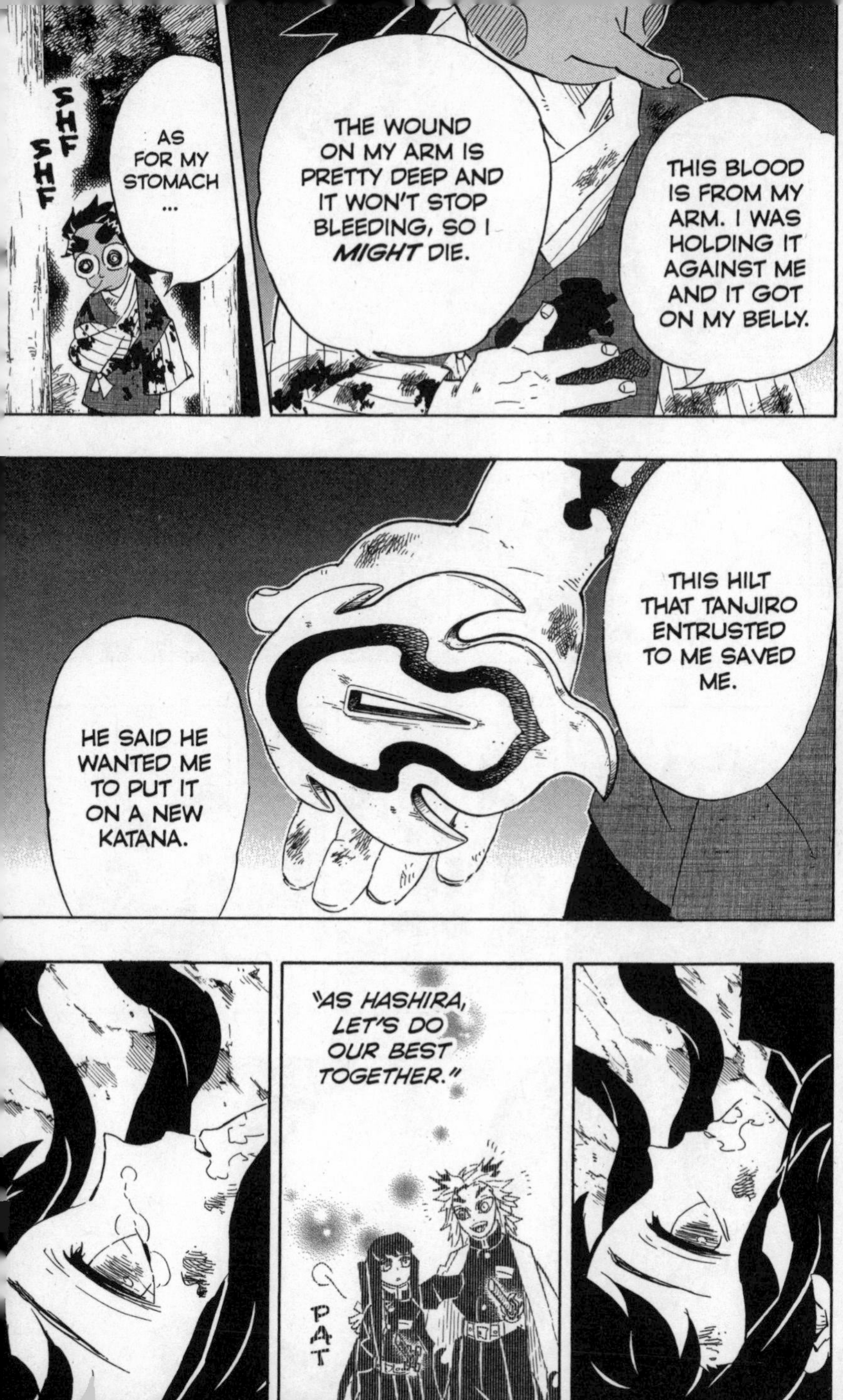
THIS BLOOD IS FROM MY ARM. I WAS HOLDING IT AGAINST ME AND IT GOT ON MY BELLY.
THE WOUND ON MY ARM IS PRETTY DEEP AND IT WON'T STOP BLEEDING, SO I *MIGHT* DIE.
AS FOR MY STOMACH ...
SHF SHF
THIS HILT THAT TANJIRO ENTRUSTED TO ME SAVED ME.
HE SAID HE WANTED ME TO PUT IT ON A NEW KATANA.
"AS HASHIRA, LET'S DO OUR BEST TOGETHER."
PAT

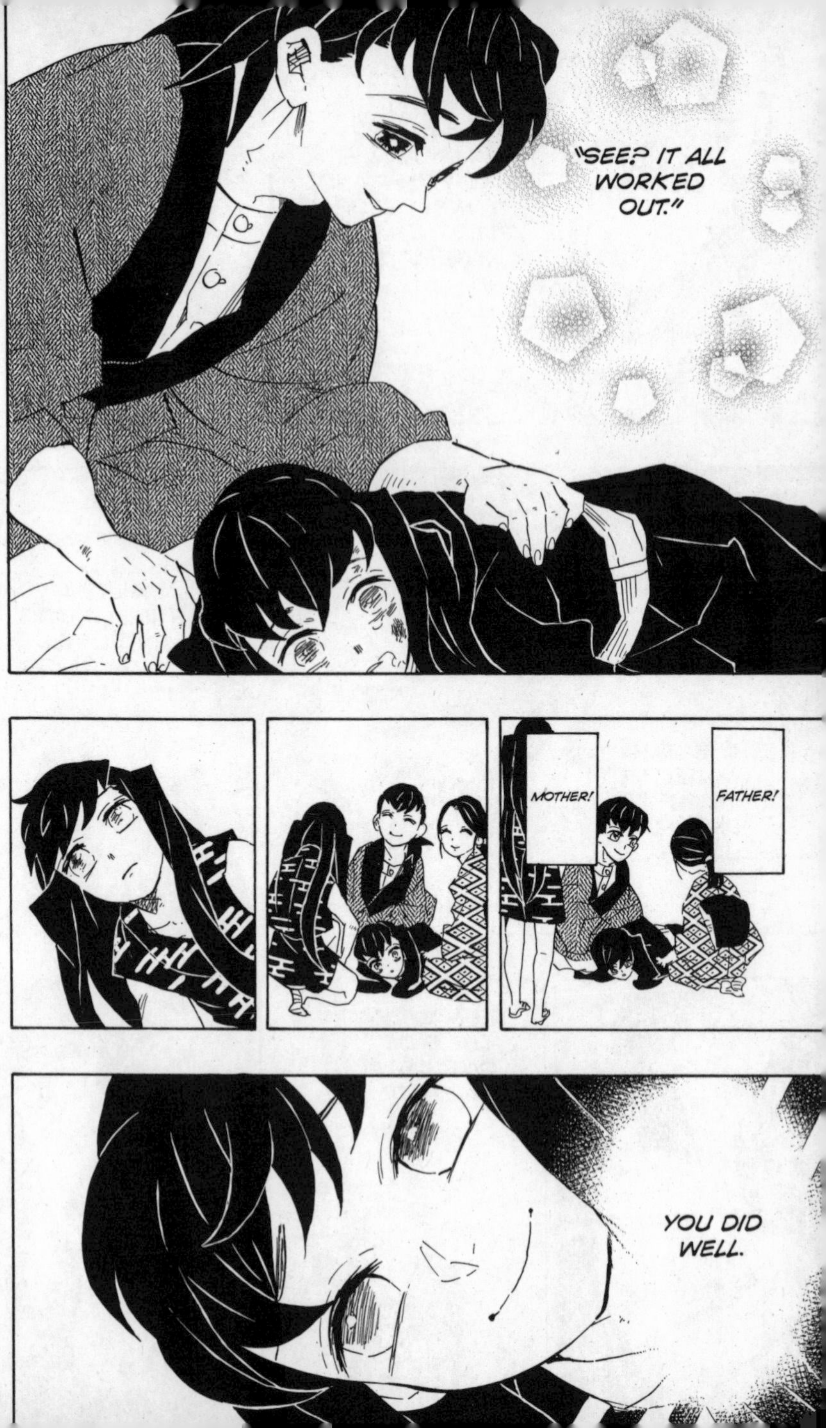
"SEE? IT ALL WORKED OUT."
FATHER!
MOTHER!
YOU DID WELL.

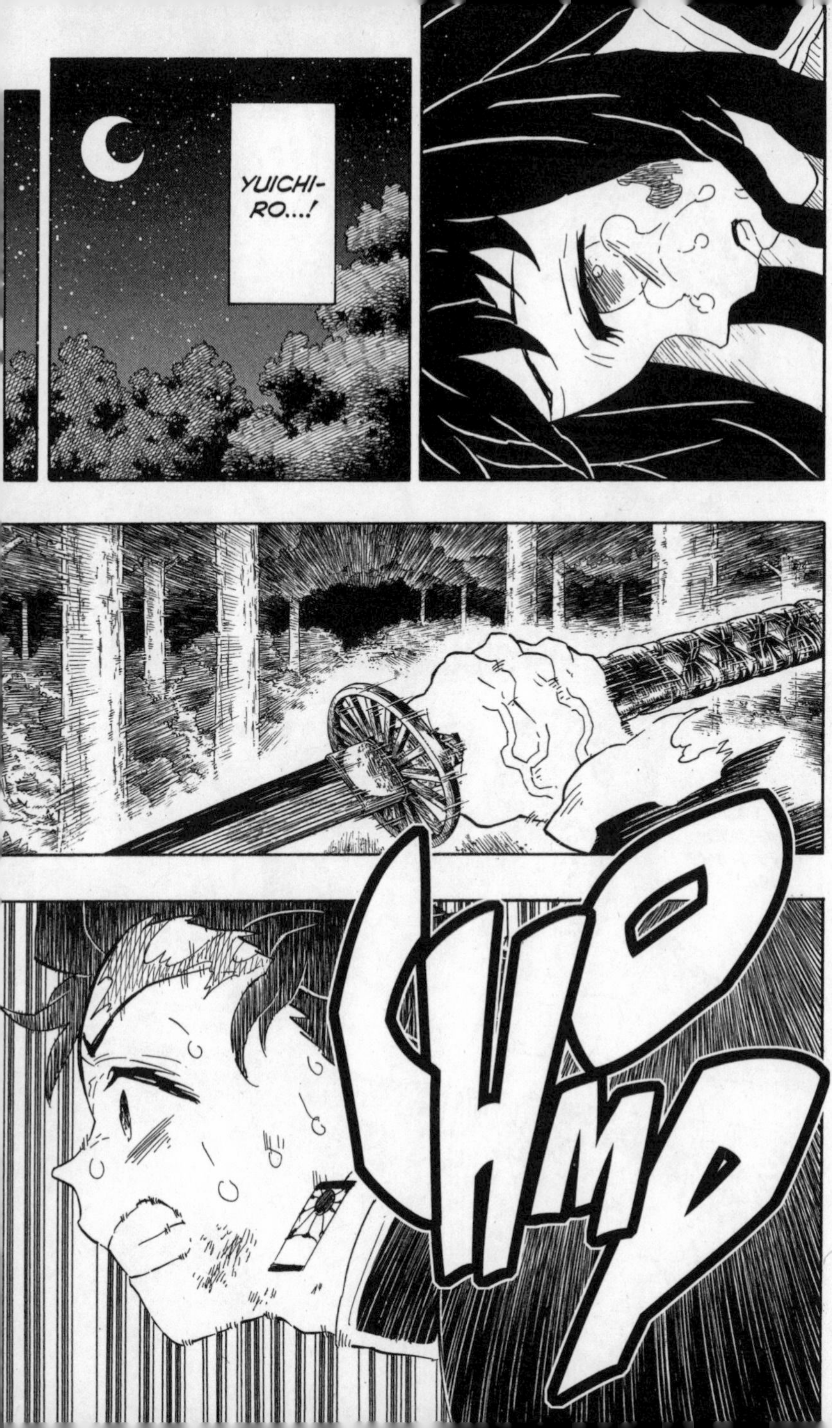
YUICHI-
RO...!
CHMP

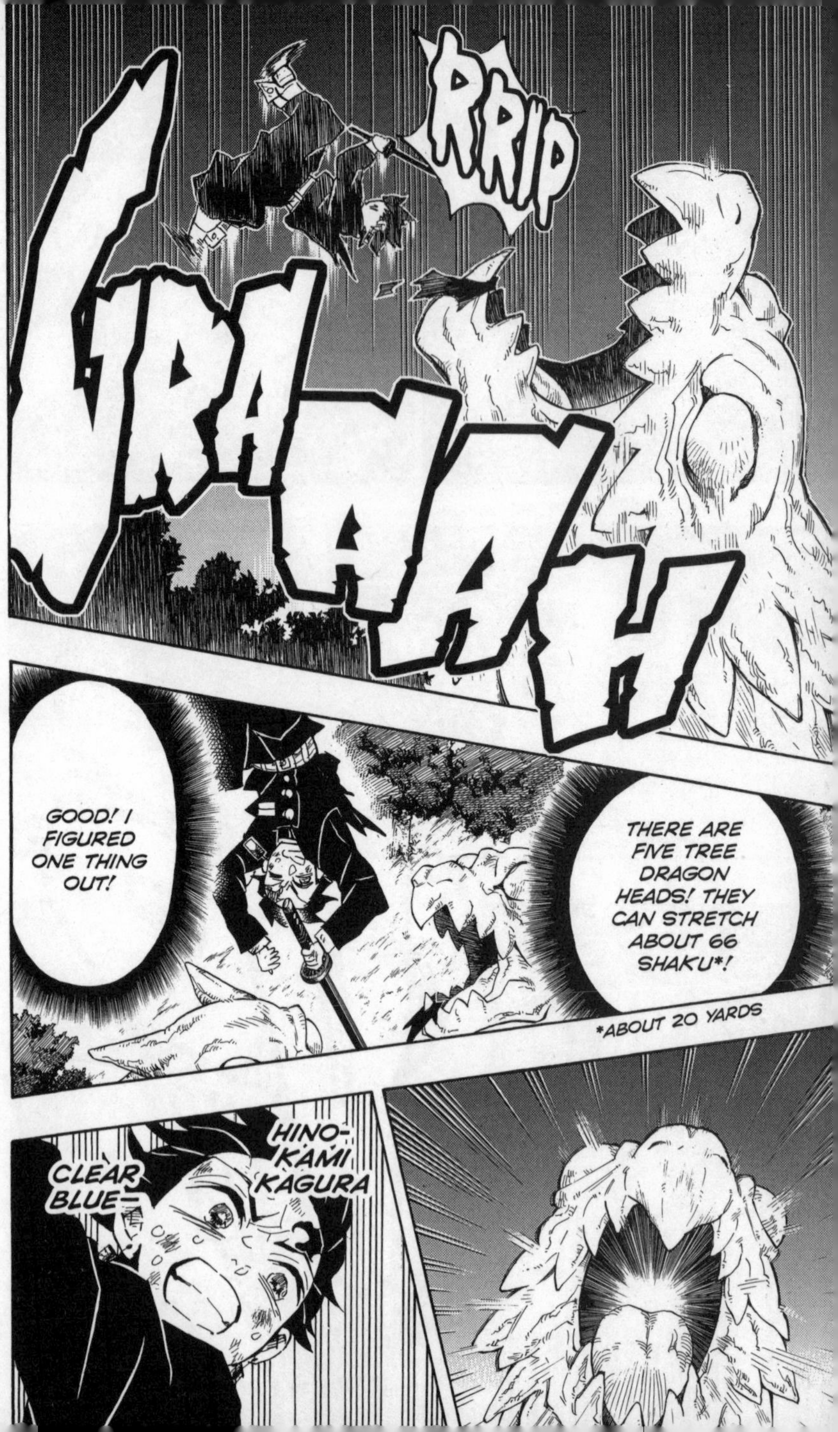
RRIP
URAAAH
THERE ARE FIVE TREE DRAGON HEADS! THEY CAN STRETCH ABOUT 66 SHAKU*!
*ABOUT 20 YARDS
GOOD! I FIGURED ONE THING OUT!
HINO-KAMI KAGURA
CLEAR BLUE—

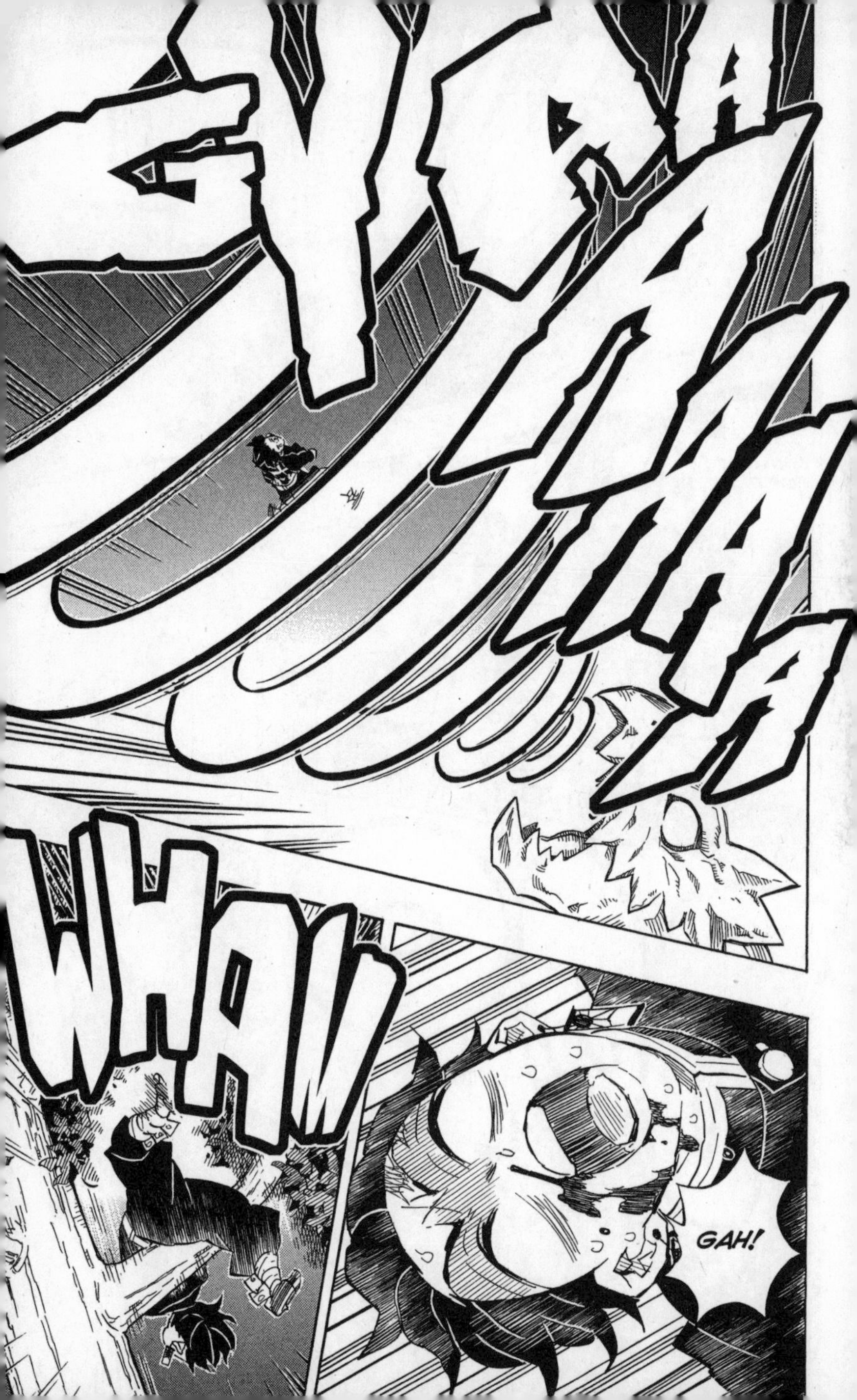
WHAM
GAH!

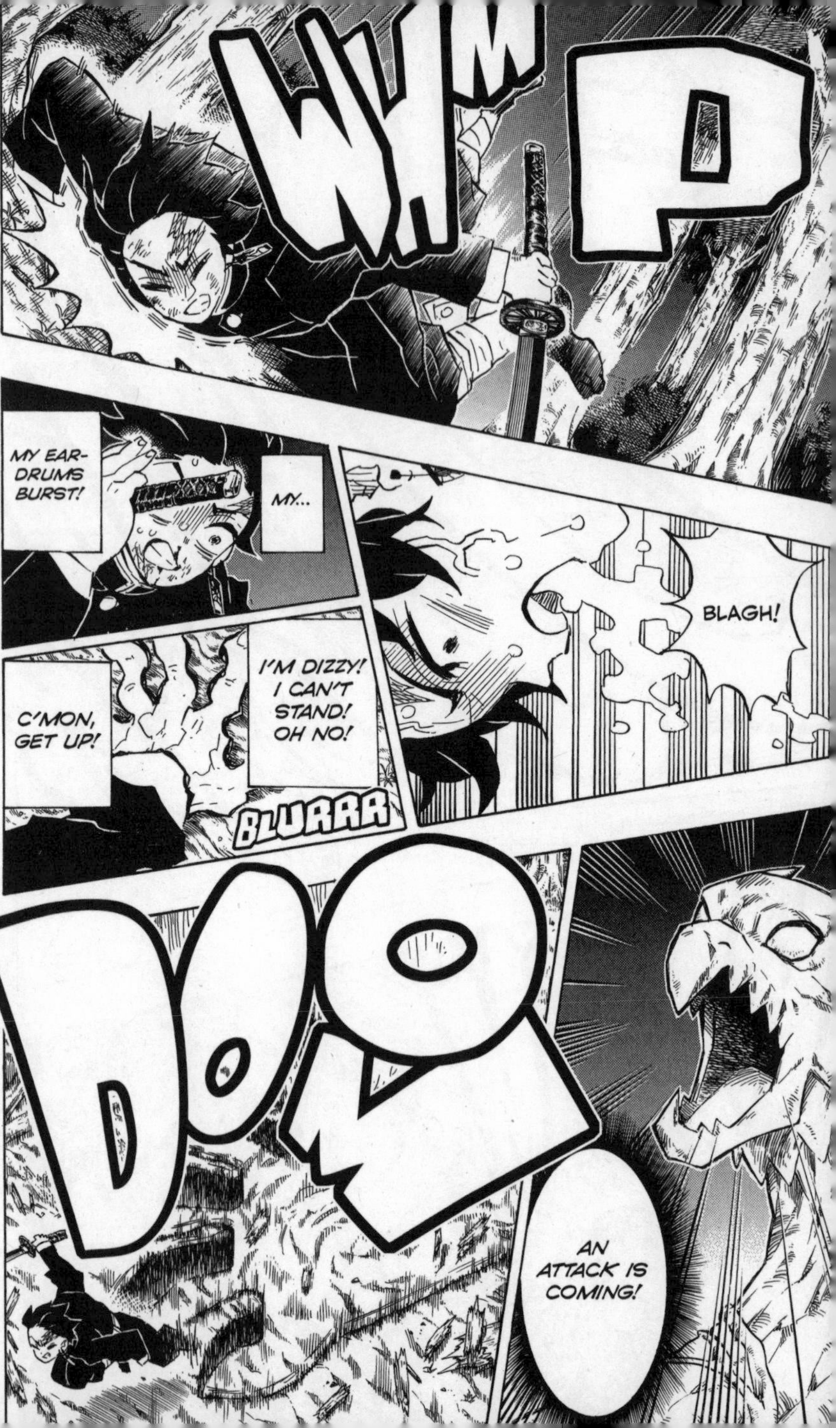
WHMP
BLAGH!
MY...
MY EAR-DRUMS BURST!
I'M DIZZY! I CAN'T STAND! OH NO!
C'MON, GET UP!
BLURRR
AN ATTACK IS COMING!
DOOM

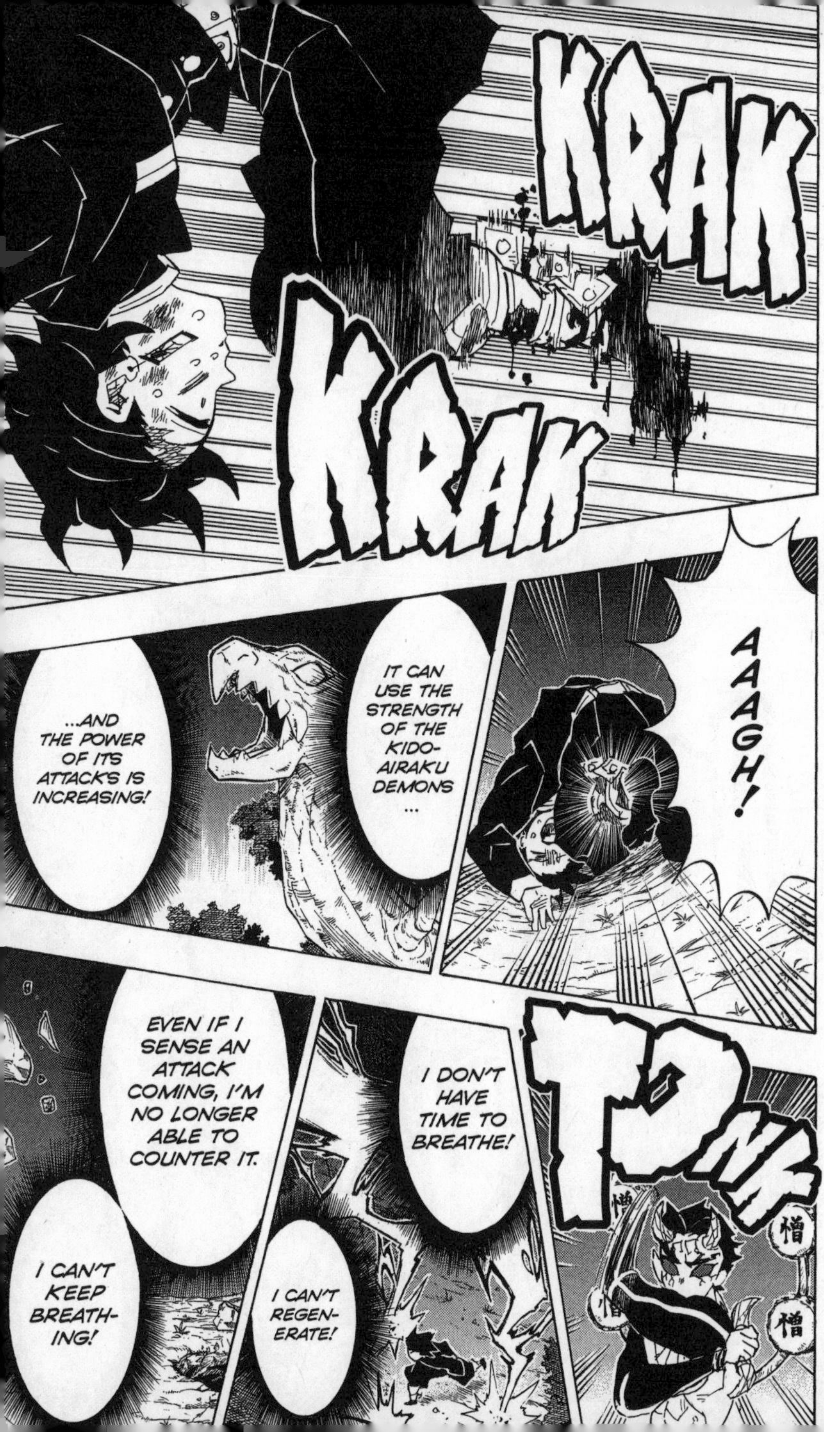
KRAK
KRAK
AAAAGH!
IT CAN USE THE STRENGTH OF THE KIDO-AIRAKU DEMONS ...
...AND THE POWER OF ITS ATTACK'S IS INCREASING!
T'ZNK
憎
憎
憎
I DON'T HAVE TIME TO BREATHE!
I CAN'T REGENERATE!
EVEN IF I SENSE AN ATTACK COMING, I'M NO LONGER ABLE TO COUNTER IT.
I CAN'T KEEP BREATHING!

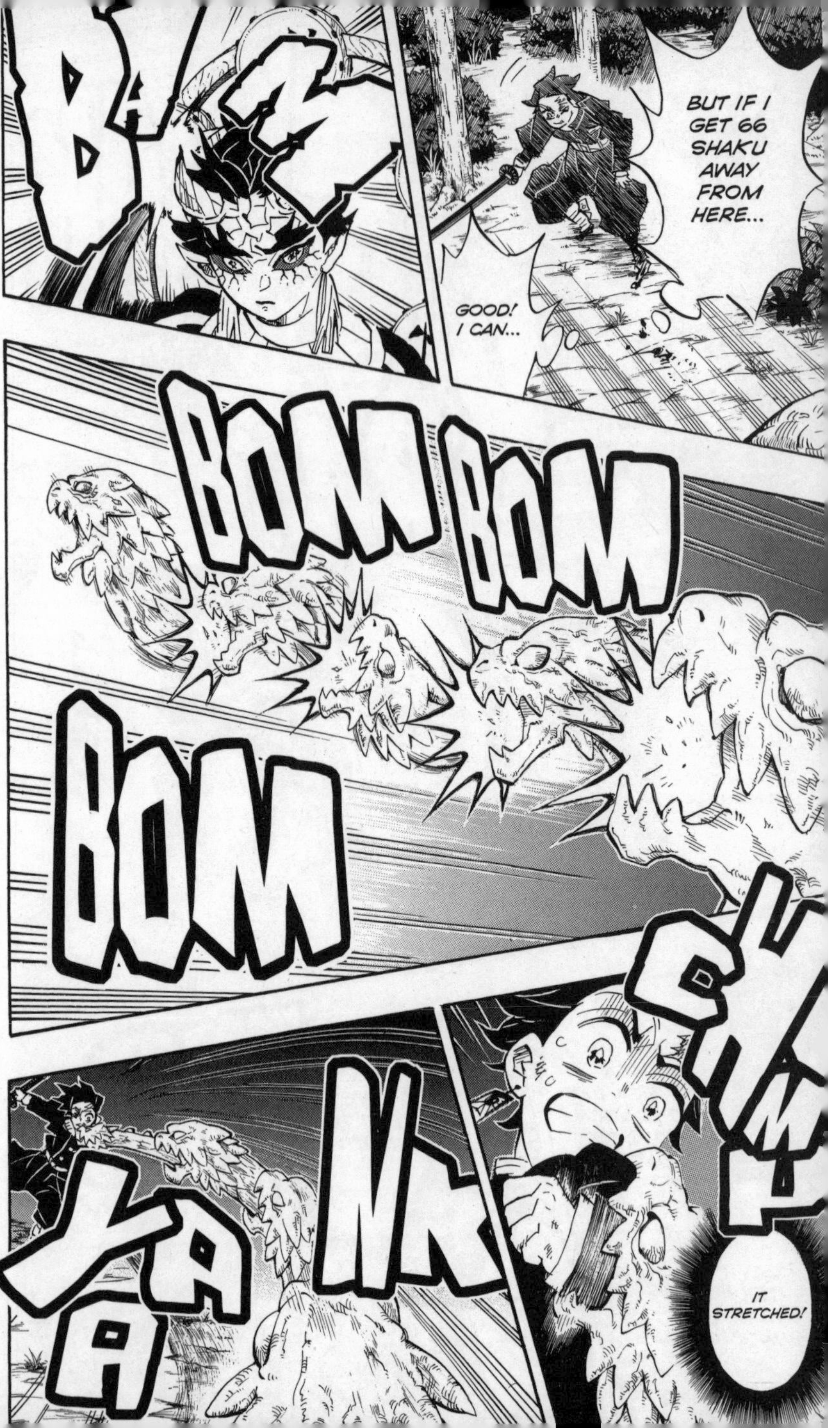
BUT IF I GET 66 SHAKU AWAY FROM HERE...
GOOD! I CAN...
BOM BOM
BOM
IT STRETCHED!

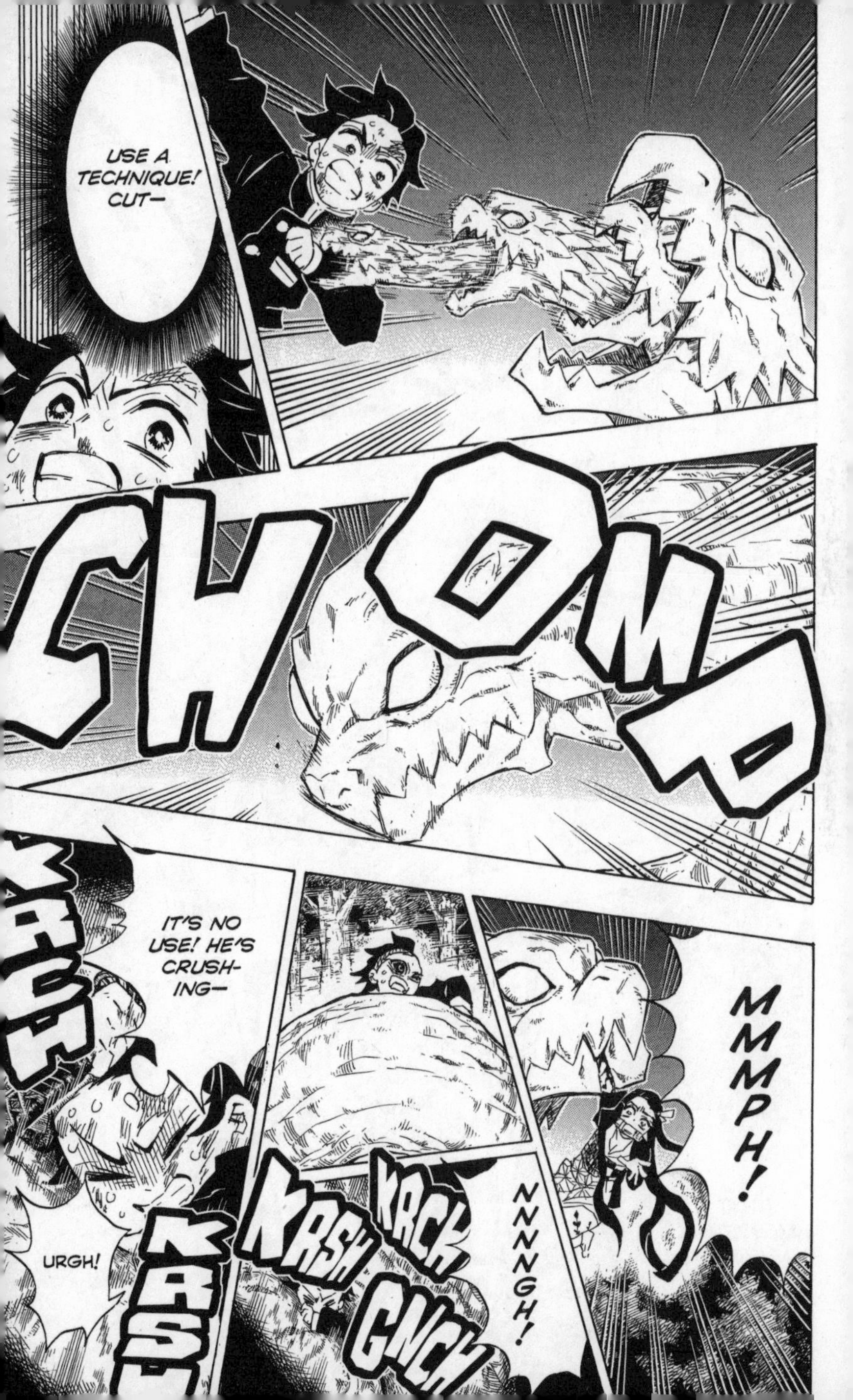
USE A TECHNIQUE! CUT—
CHOMP
MMMPH!
NNNNGH!
KRCH
KRSH
GNCH
IT'S NO USE! HE'S CRUSHING—
URGH!

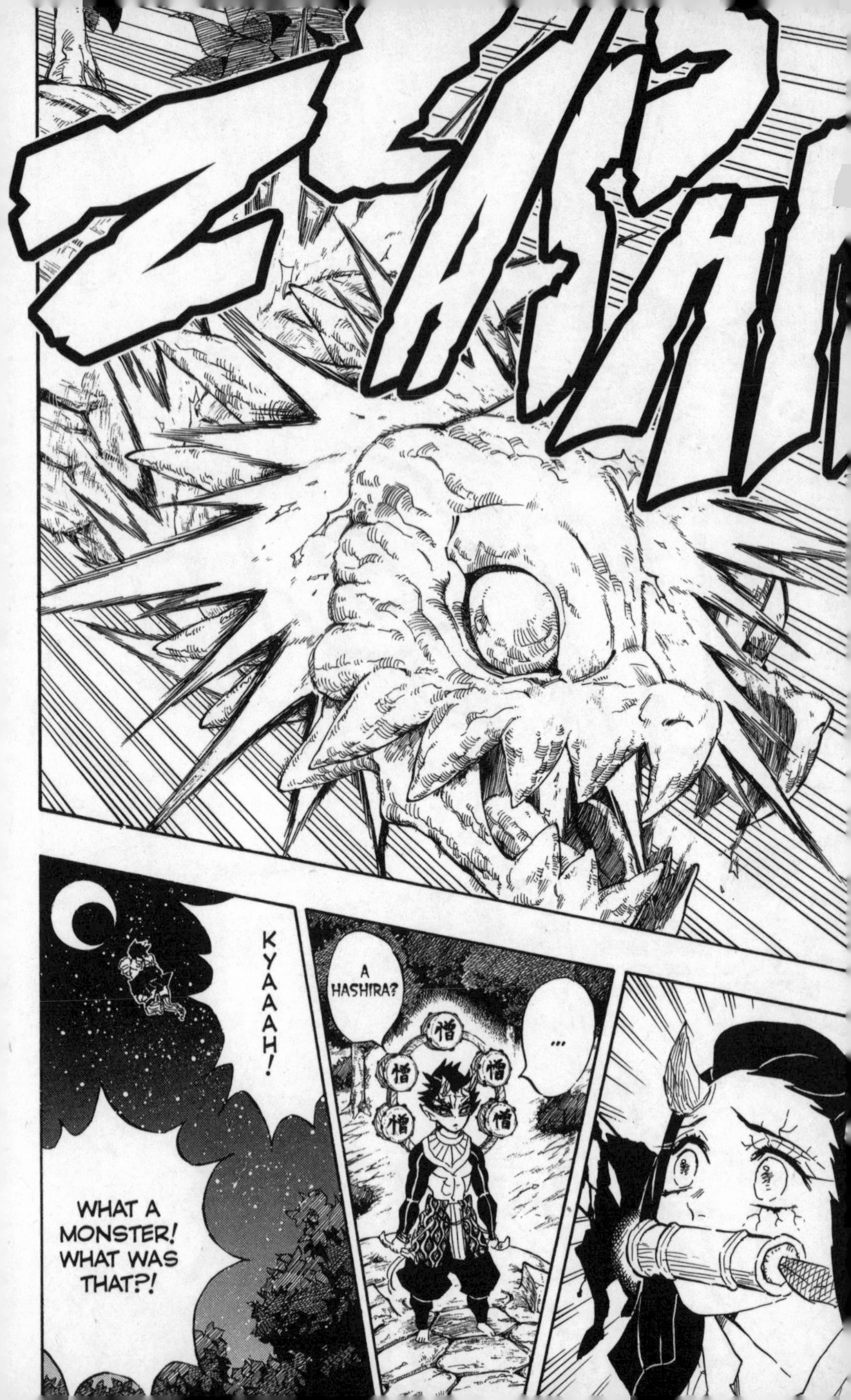
A HASHIRA?
...
KYAAAAH!
WHAT A MONSTER! WHAT WAS THAT?!

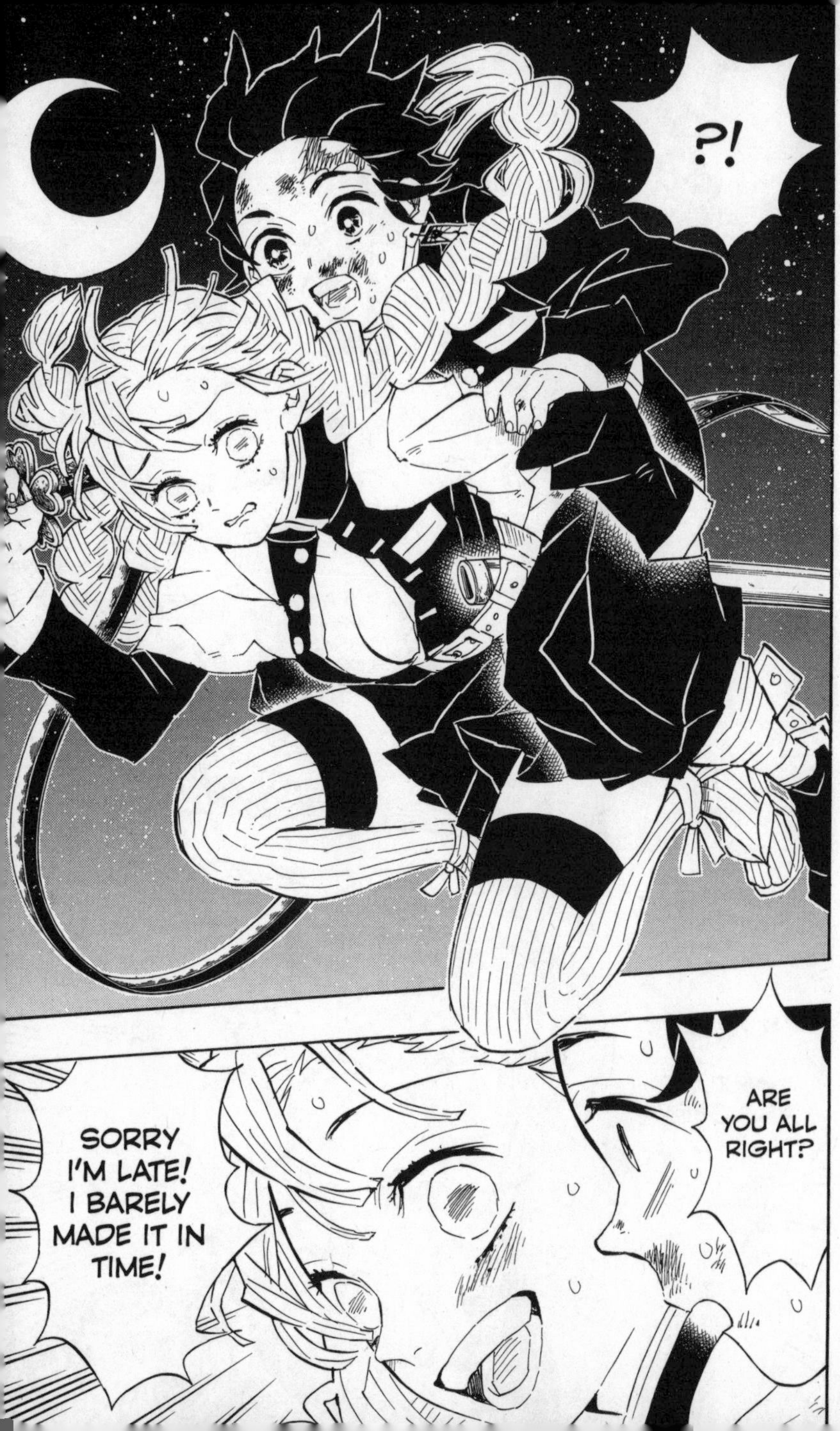
?!
ARE YOU ALL RIGHT?
SORRY I'M LATE! I BARELY MADE IT IN TIME!

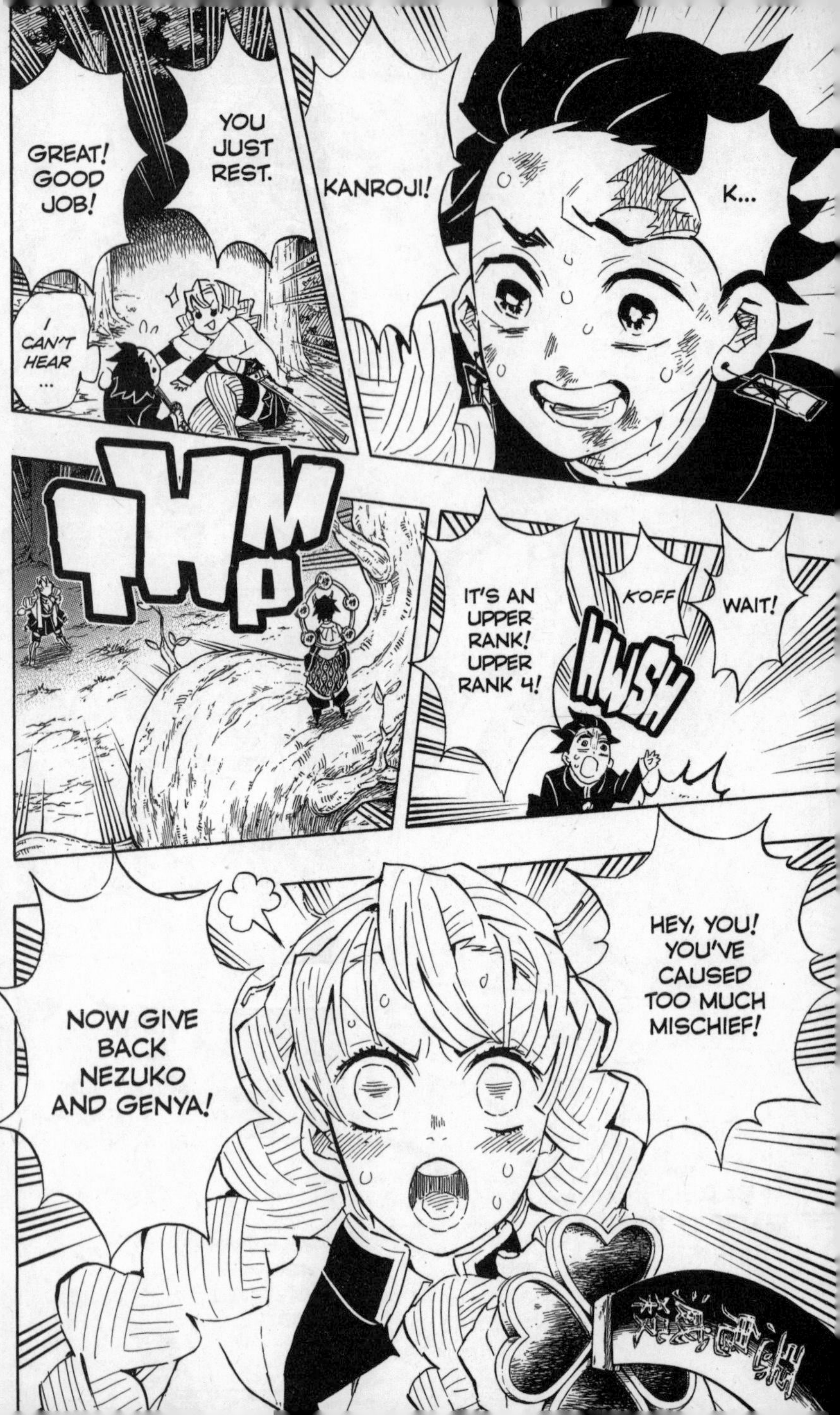
K...
KANROJI!
YOU JUST REST.
GREAT! GOOD JOB!
I CAN'T HEAR ...
WAIT!
KOFF
HWSH
IT'S AN UPPER RANK! UPPER RANK 4!
THMP
HEY, YOU! YOU'VE CAUSED TOO MUCH MISCHIEF!
NOW GIVE BACK NEZUKO AND GENYA!

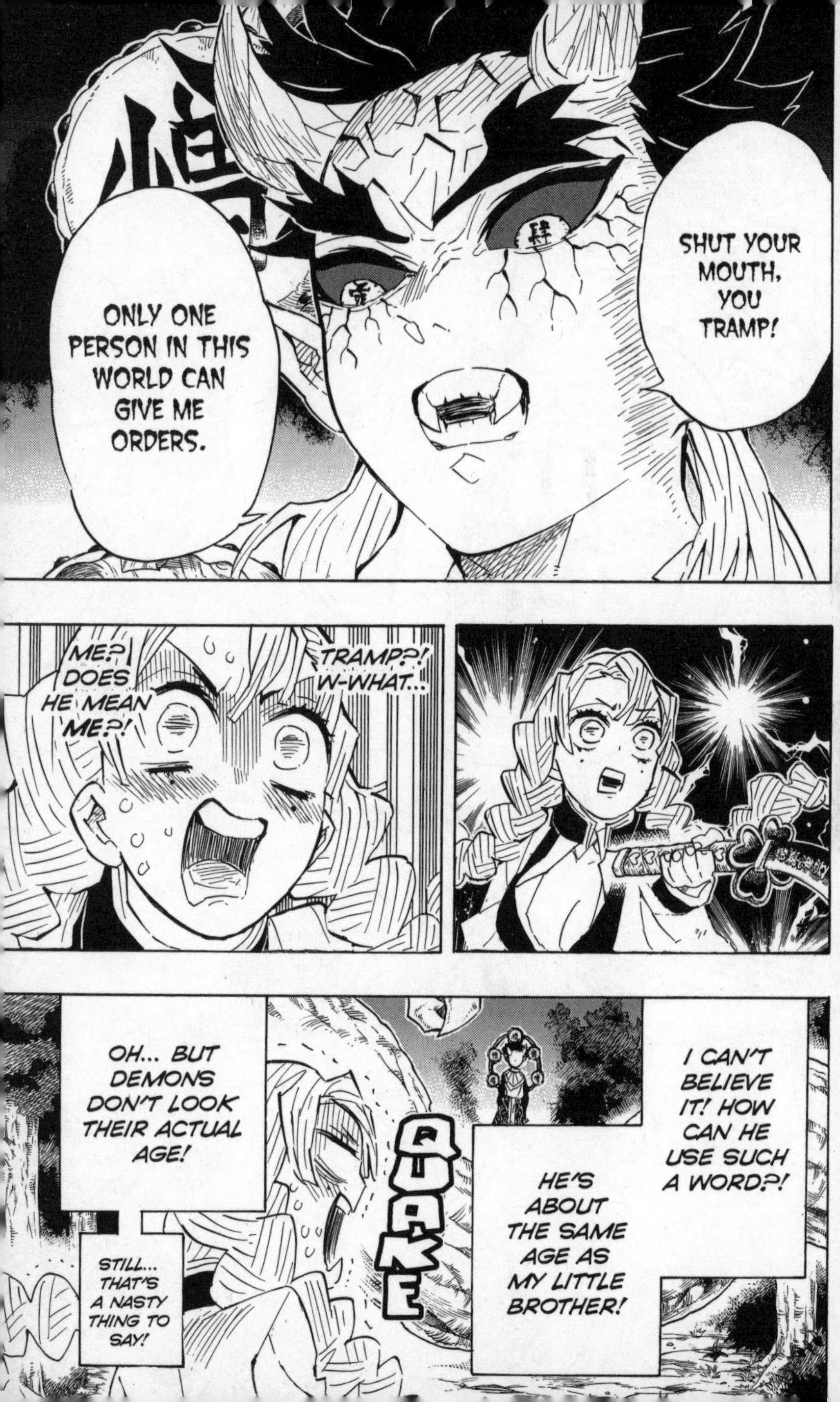
SHUT YOUR MOUTH, YOU TRAMP!
ONLY ONE PERSON IN THIS WORLD CAN GIVE ME ORDERS.
TRAMP?! W-WHAT...
ME?! DOES HE MEAN ME?!
I CAN'T BELIEVE IT! HOW CAN HE USE SUCH A WORD?!
HE'S ABOUT THE SAME AGE AS MY LITTLE BROTHER!
QUAKE
OH... BUT DEMONS DON'T LOOK THEIR ACTUAL AGE!
STILL... THAT'S A NASTY THING TO SAY!

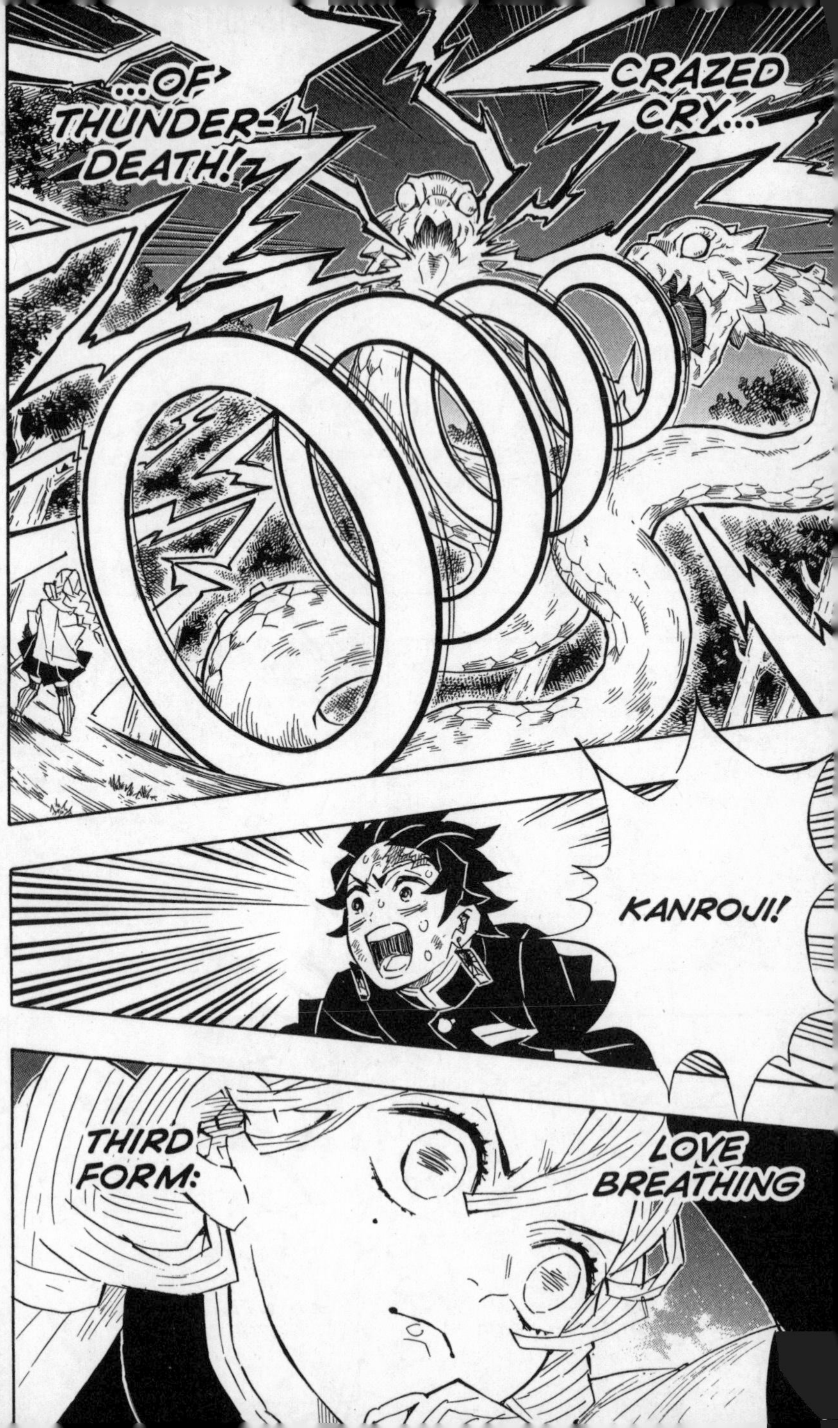
CRAZED CRY...
...OF THUNDER-DEATH!
KANROJI!
LOVE BREATHING
THIRD FORM:

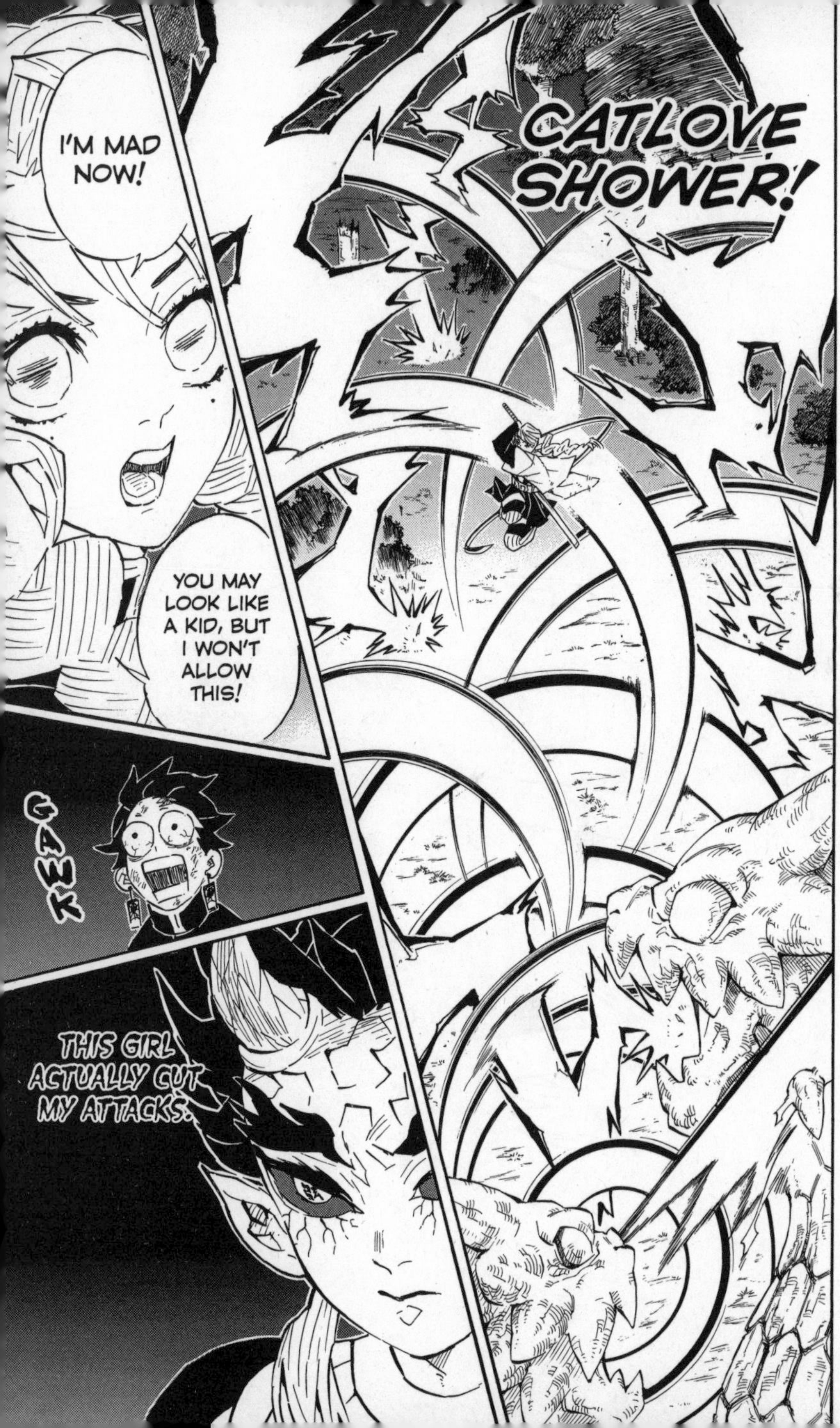
CATLOVE SHOWER!
I'M MAD NOW!
YOU MAY LOOK LIKE A KID, BUT I WON'T ALLOW THIS!
GAWK
THIS GIRL ACTUALLY CUT MY ATTACKS.

Five years ago they were
such a close couple that
they started resembling
each other. A happily
married couple.

Love
at
first
sight

Flexible
neck

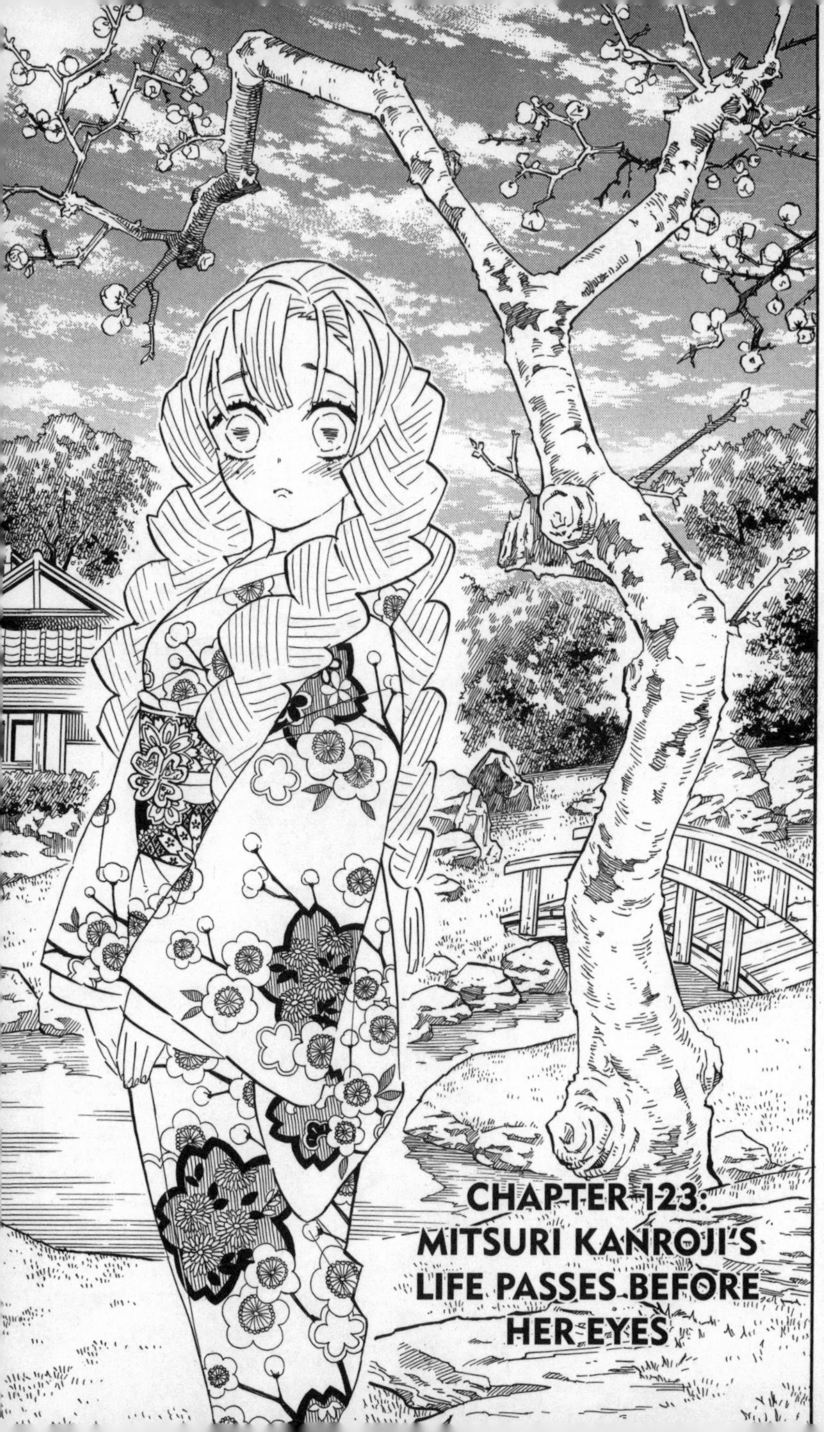
CHAPTER 123:
MITSURI KANROJI'S
LIFE PASSES BEFORE
HER EYES

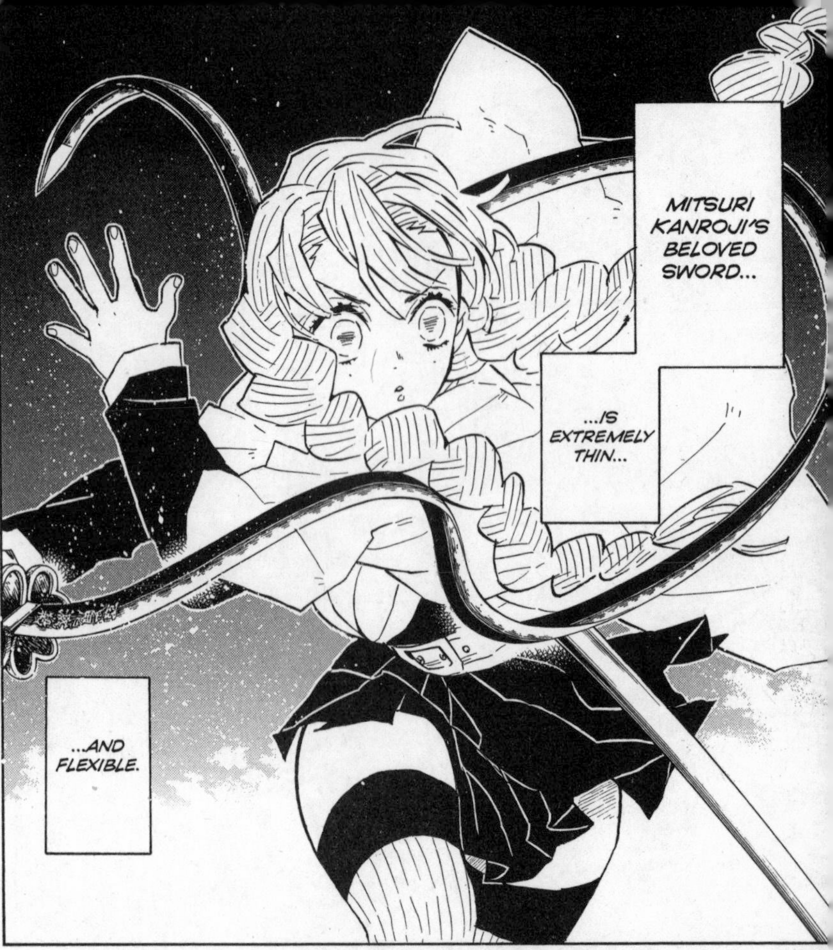
MITSURI KANROJI'S BELOVED SWORD...
...IS EXTREMELY THIN...
...AND FLEXIBLE.

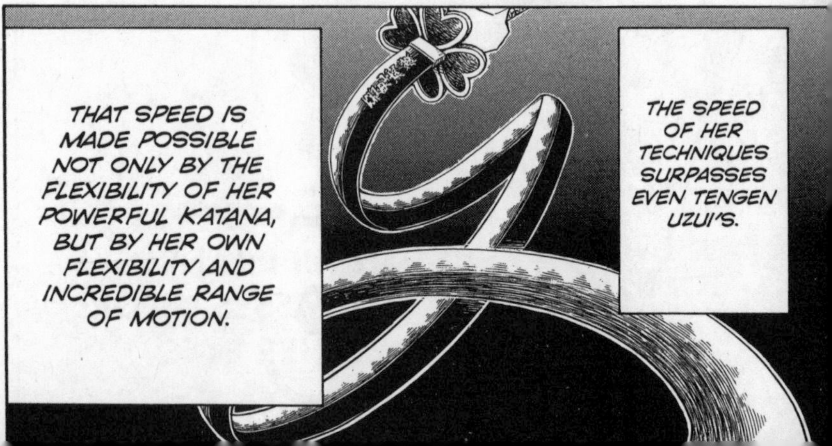
THE SPEED OF HER TECHNIQUES SURPASSES EVEN TENGEN UZUI'S.
THAT SPEED IS MADE POSSIBLE NOT ONLY BY THE FLEXIBILITY OF HER POWERFUL KATANA, BUT BY HER OWN FLEXIBILITY AND INCREDIBLE RANGE OF MOTION.

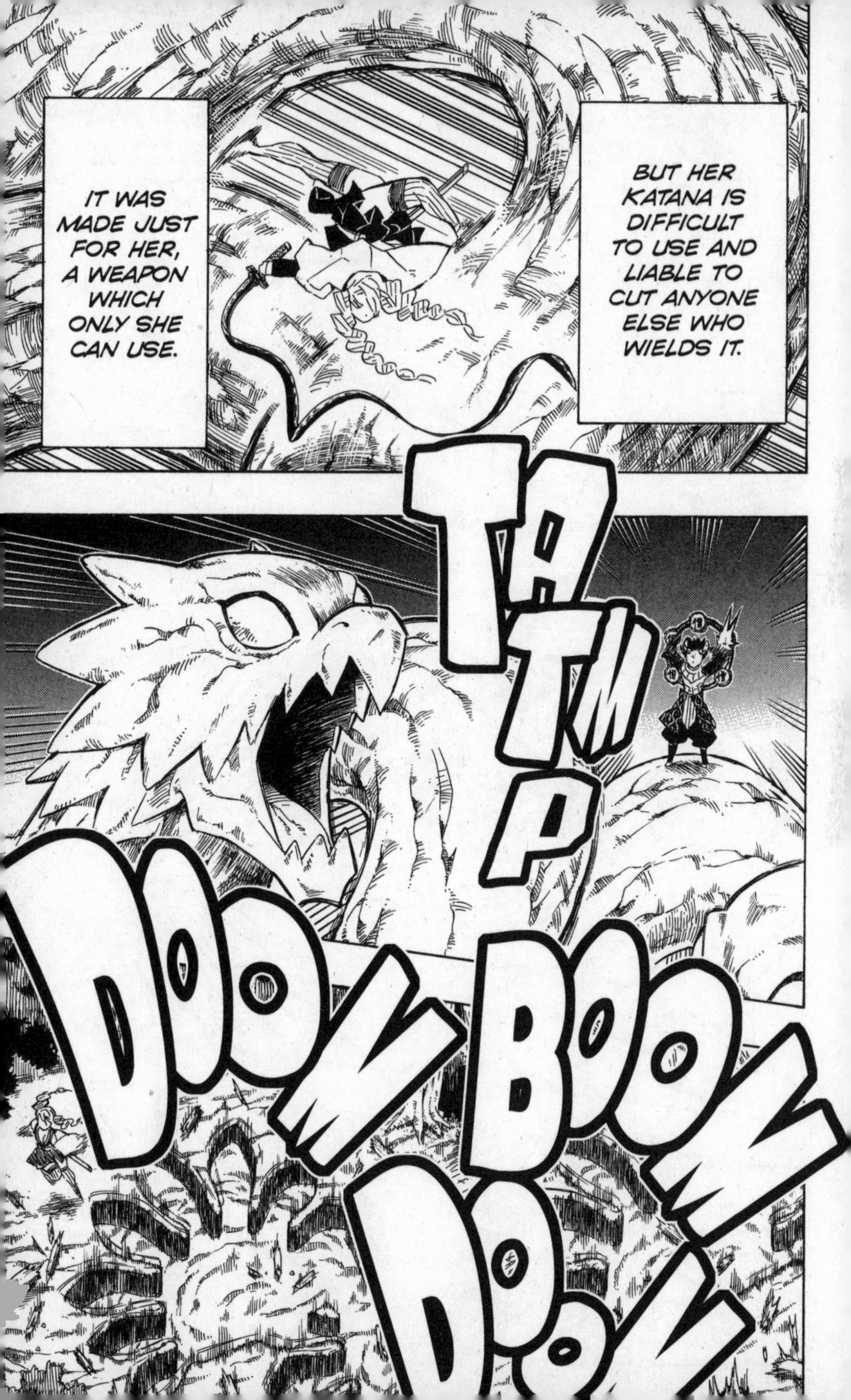
BUT HER KATANA IS DIFFICULT TO USE AND LIABLE TO CUT ANYONE ELSE WHO WIELDS IT.
IT WAS MADE JUST FOR HER, A WEAPON WHICH ONLY SHE CAN USE.
TATAP
BOOM
DOOM
DOOM

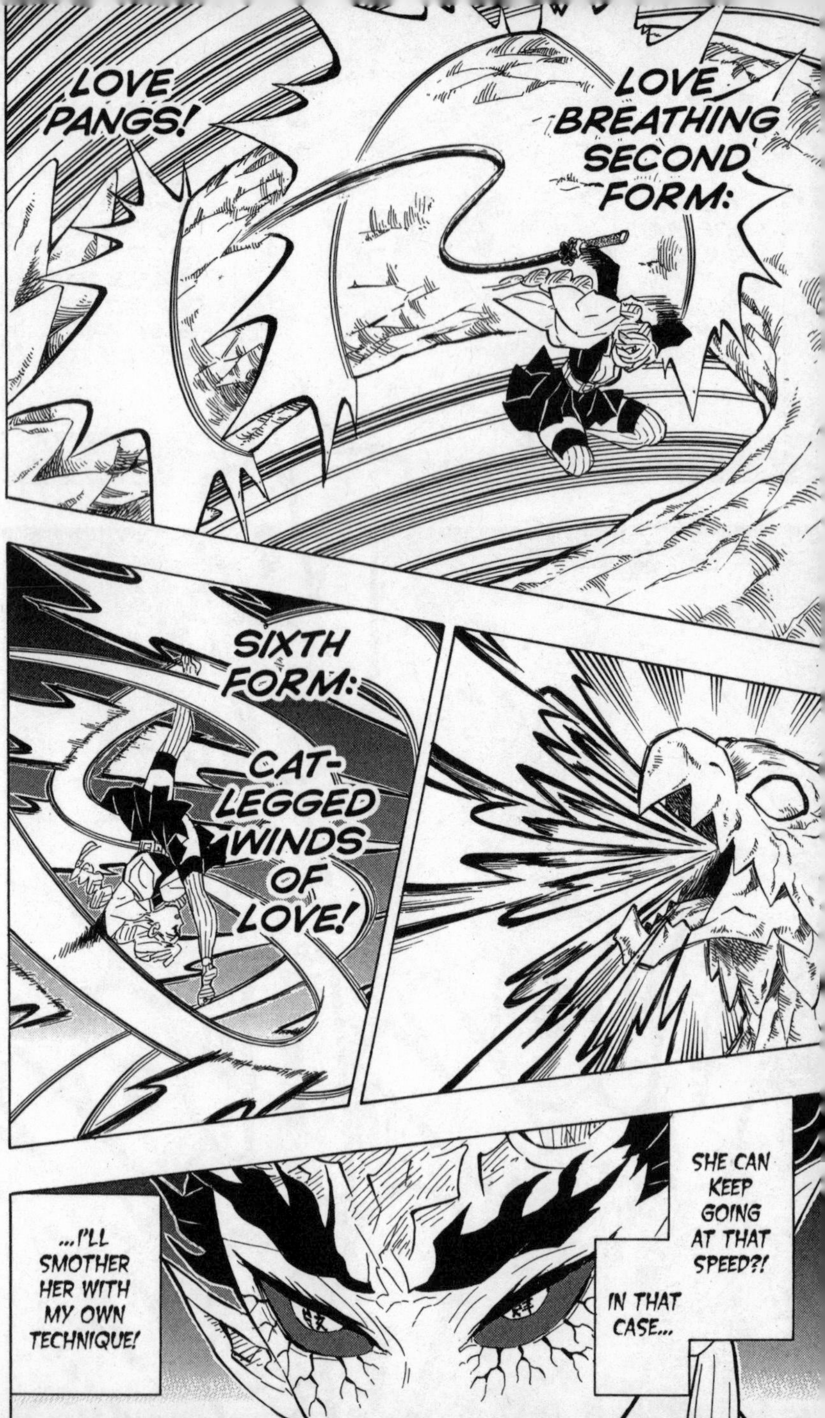
LOVE BREATHING SECOND FORM:
LOVE PANGS!
SIXTH FORM:
CAT-LEGGED WINDS OF LOVE!
SHE CAN KEEP GOING AT THAT SPEED?!
IN THAT CASE...
...I'LL SMOTHER HER WITH MY OWN TECHNIQUE!

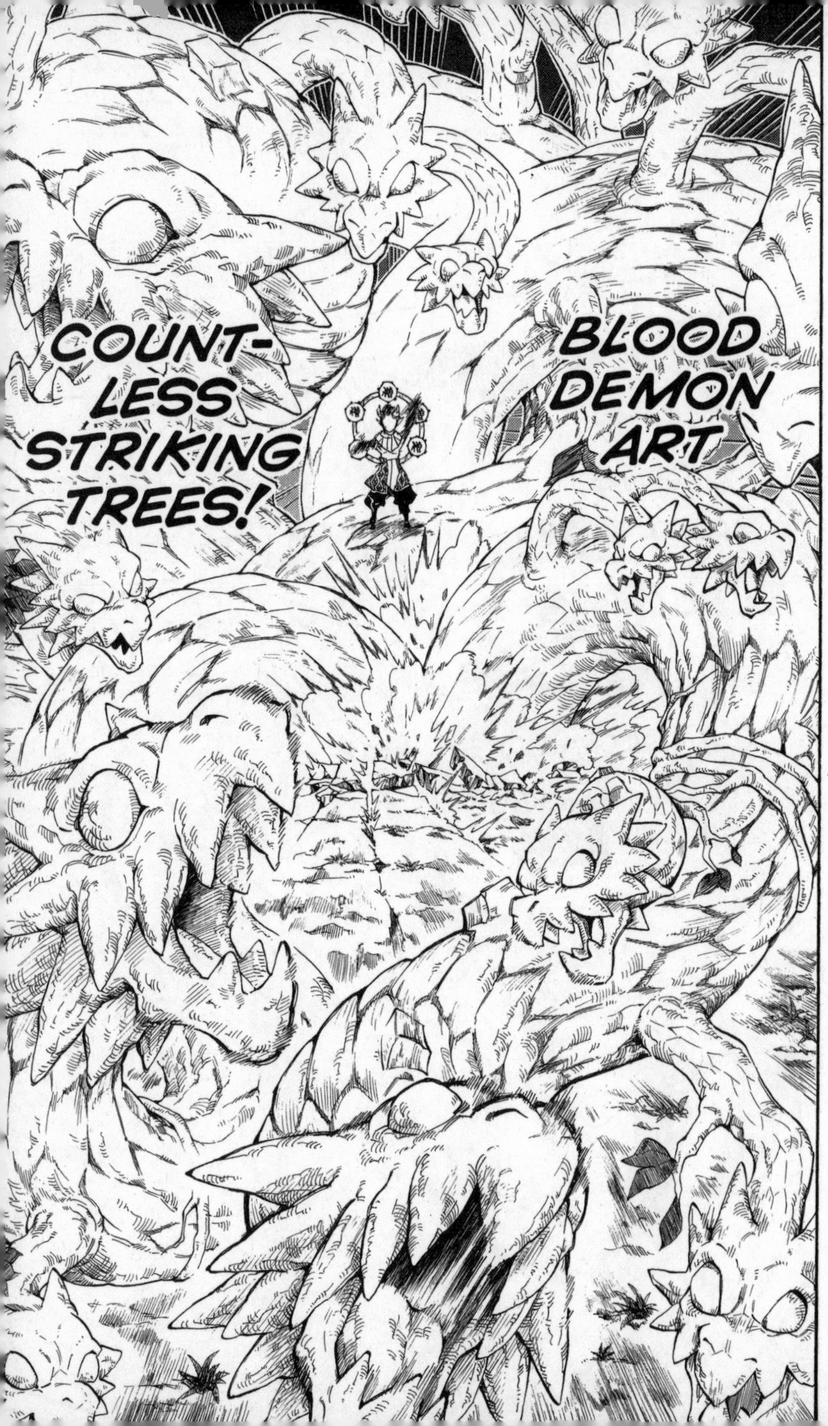
BLOOD DEMON ART
COUNT-LESS STRIKING TREES!

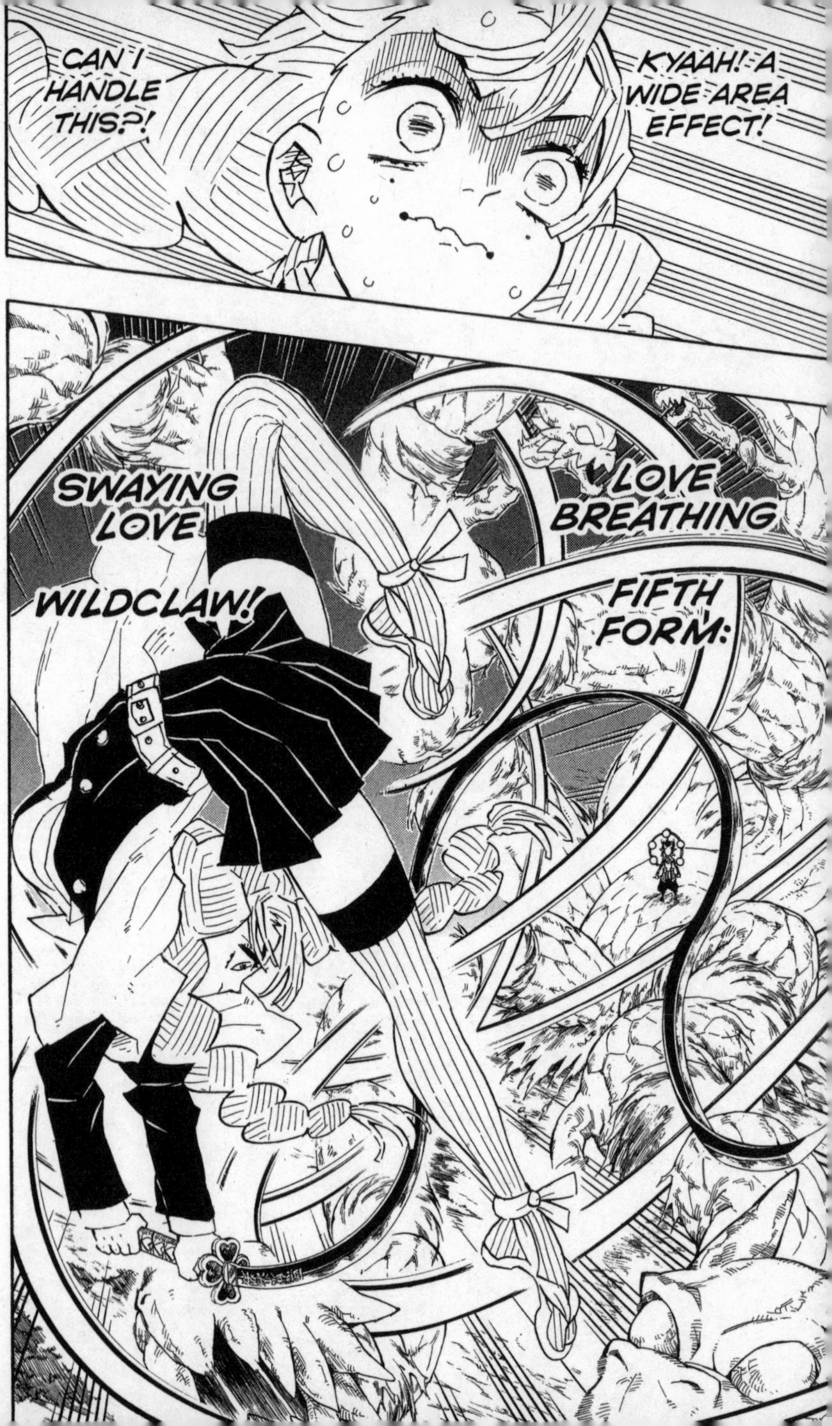
KYAAH! A WIDE AREA EFFECT!
CAN I HANDLE THIS?!
LOVE BREATHING
FIFTH FORM:
SWAYING LOVE
WILDCLAW!

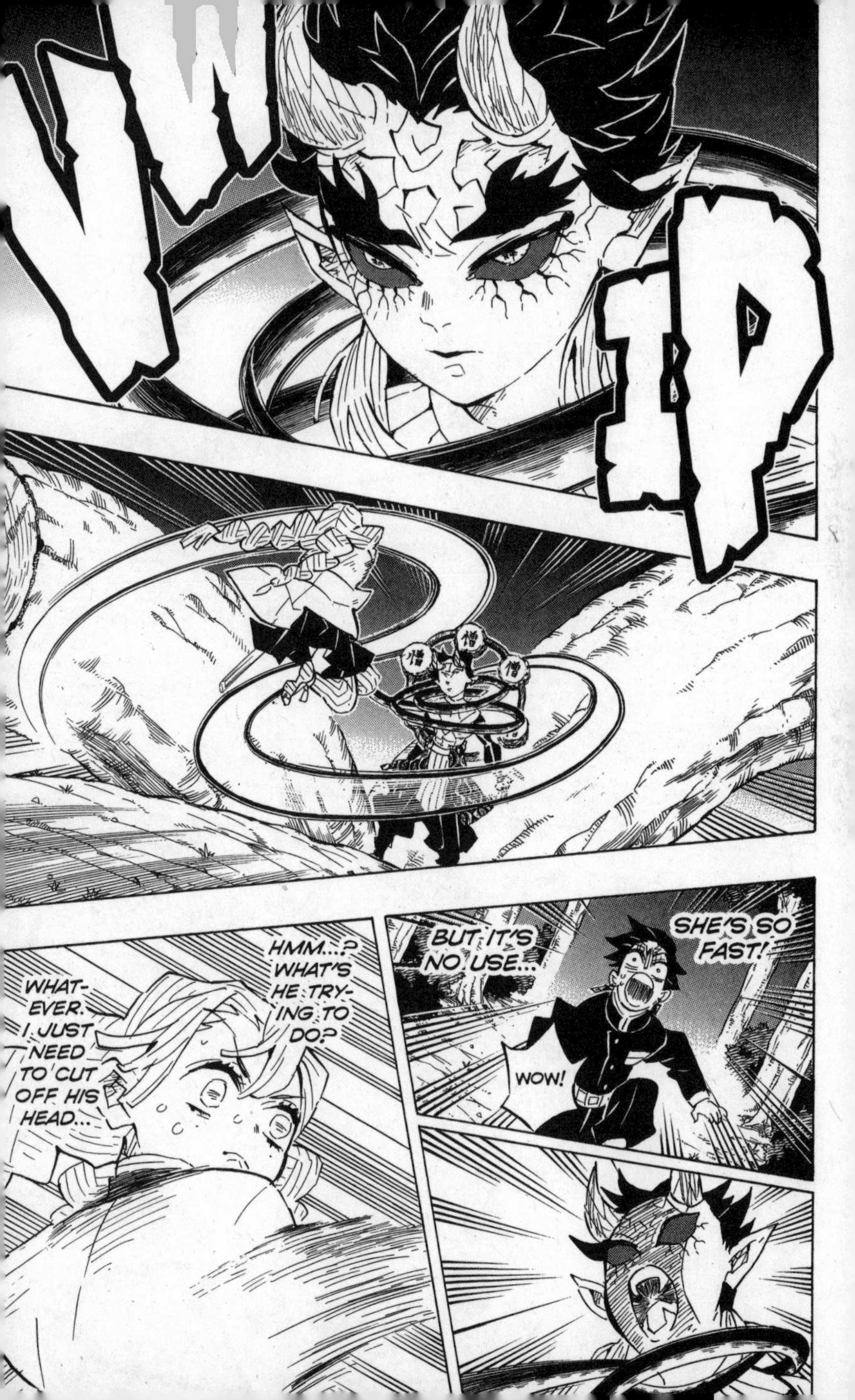
WHIP
SHE'S SO FAST!
BUT IT'S NO USE...
WOW!
HMM...? WHAT'S HE TRYING TO DO?
WHAT-EVER. I JUST NEED TO CUT OFF HIS HEAD...

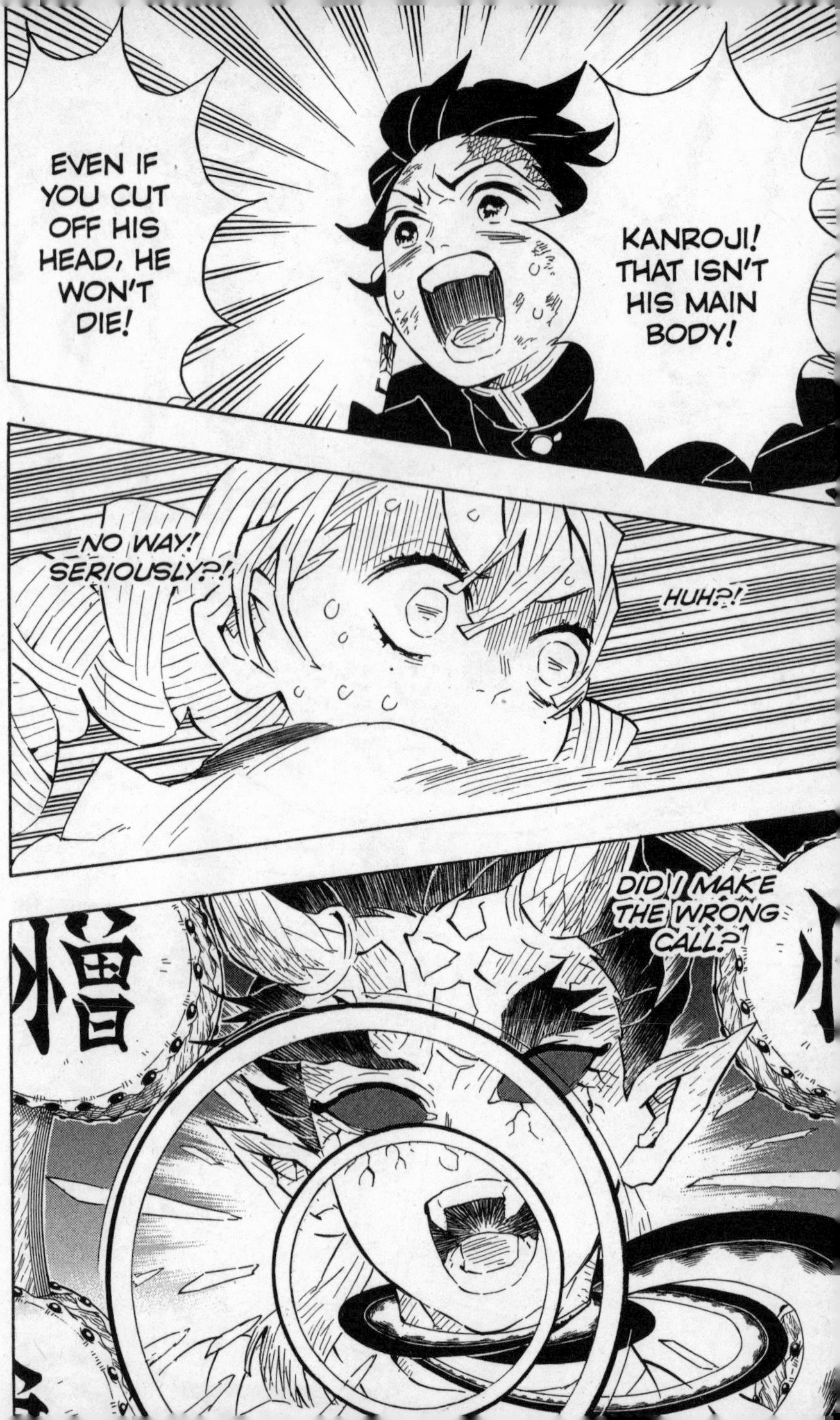
KANROJI! THAT ISN'T HIS MAIN BODY!
EVEN IF YOU CUT OFF HIS HEAD, HE WON'T DIE!
HUH?!
NO WAY! SERIOUSLY?!
DID I MAKE THE WRONG CALL?
憎

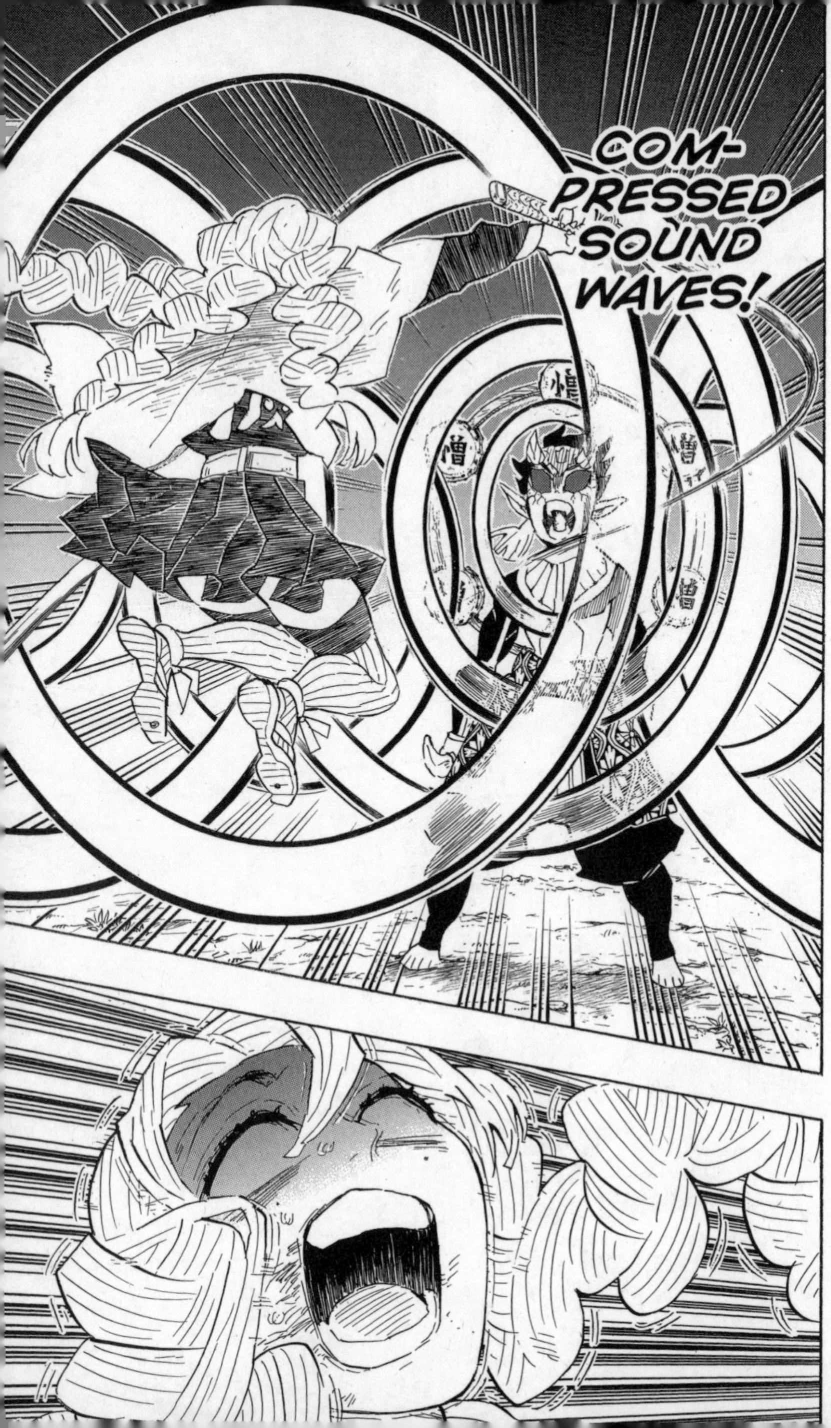
COM-PRESSED SOUND WAVES!

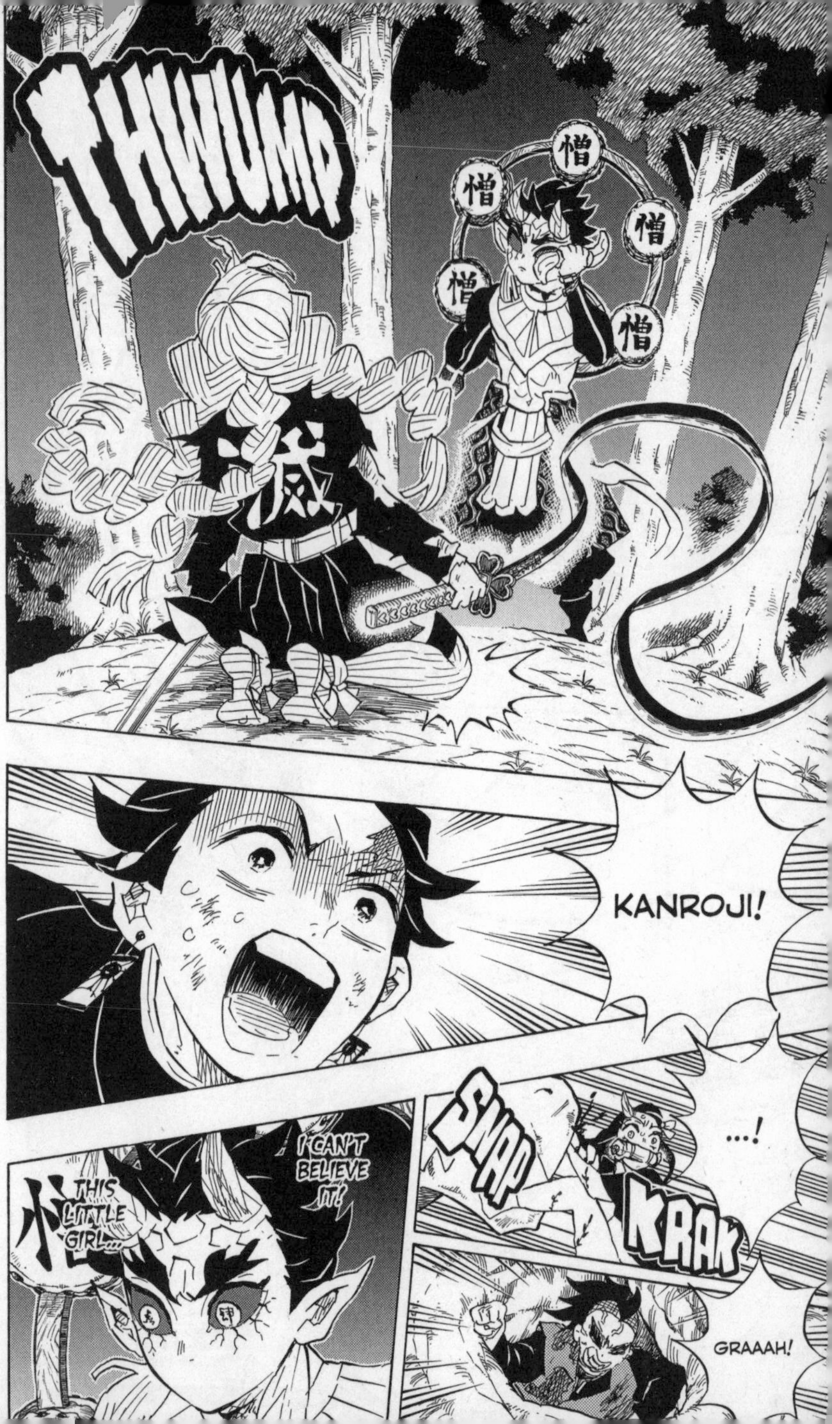
THWUMP
憎
憎
憎
憎
憎
KANROJI!
SNAP
...!
KRAK
GRAAAH!
I CAN'T BELIEVE IT!
THIS LITTLE GIRL...

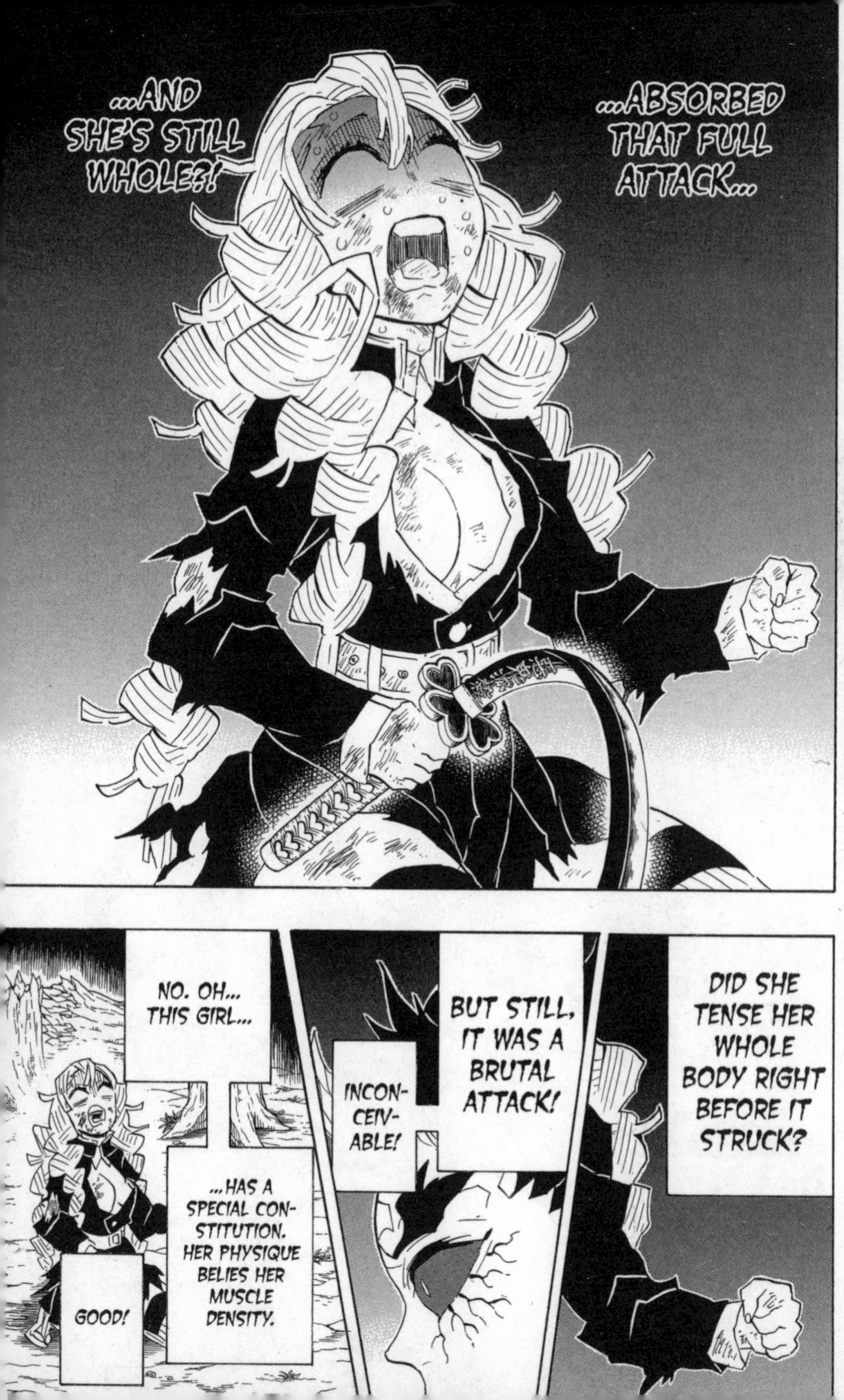
...ABSORBED THAT FULL ATTACK...
...AND SHE'S STILL WHOLE?!
DID SHE TENSE HER WHOLE BODY RIGHT BEFORE IT STRUCK?
BUT STILL, IT WAS A BRUTAL ATTACK!
INCON-CEIV-ABLE!
NO. OH... THIS GIRL...
...HAS A SPECIAL CON-STITUTION. HER PHYSIQUE BELIES HER MUSCLE DENSITY.
GOOD!

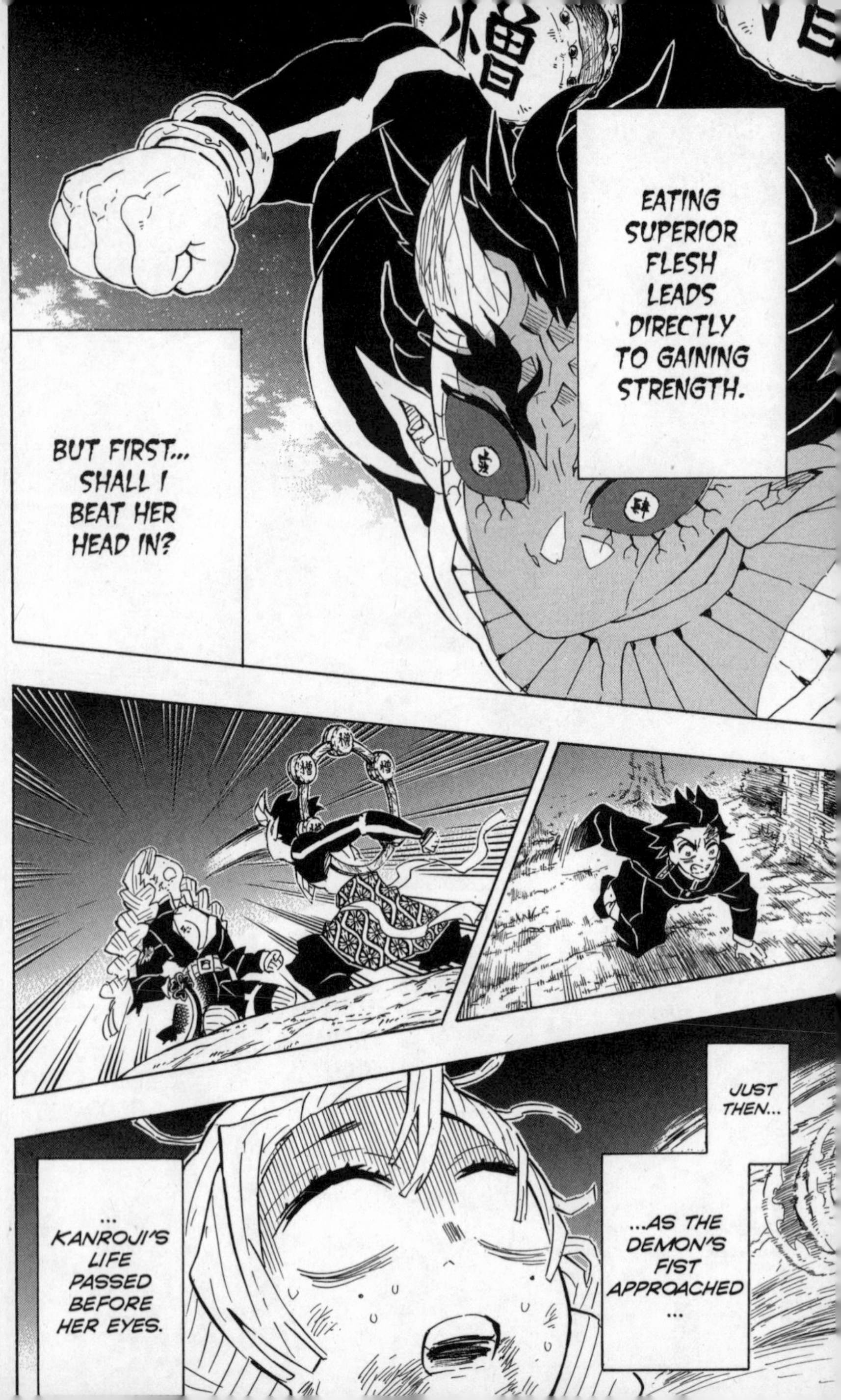
憎
EATING SUPERIOR FLESH LEADS DIRECTLY TO GAINING STRENGTH.
BUT FIRST... SHALL I BEAT HER HEAD IN?
JUST THEN...
...AS THE DEMON'S FIST APPROACHED...
...KANROJI'S LIFE PASSED BEFORE HER EYES.

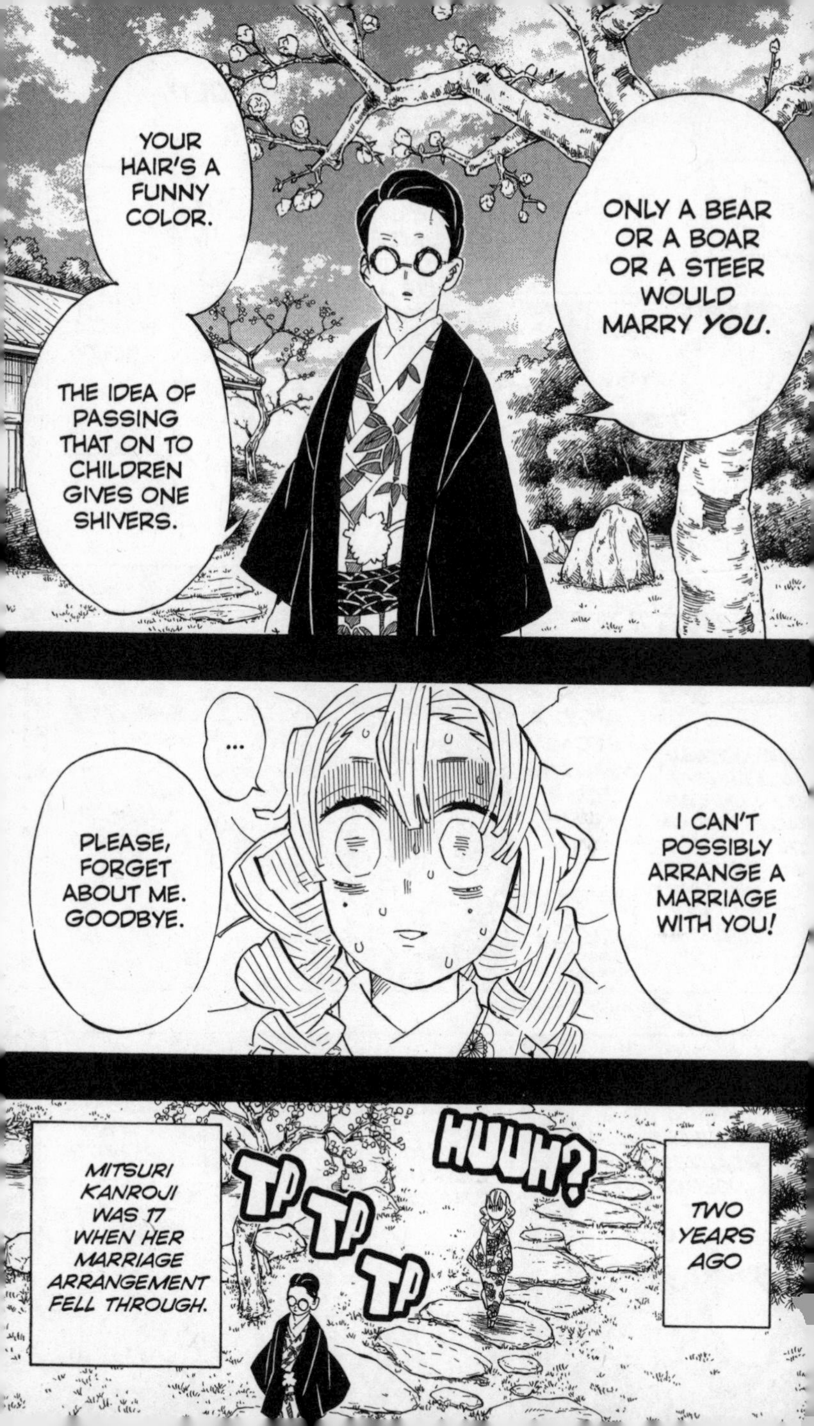
ONLY A BEAR OR A BOAR OR A STEER WOULD MARRY *YOU*.
YOUR HAIR'S A FUNNY COLOR.
THE IDEA OF PASSING THAT ON TO CHILDREN GIVES ONE SHIVERS.
I CAN'T POSSIBLY ARRANGE A MARRIAGE WITH YOU!
...
PLEASE, FORGET ABOUT ME. GOODBYE.
TWO YEARS AGO
HUUH?
TP TP TP
MITSURI KANROJI WAS 17 WHEN HER MARRIAGE ARRANGEMENT FELL THROUGH.

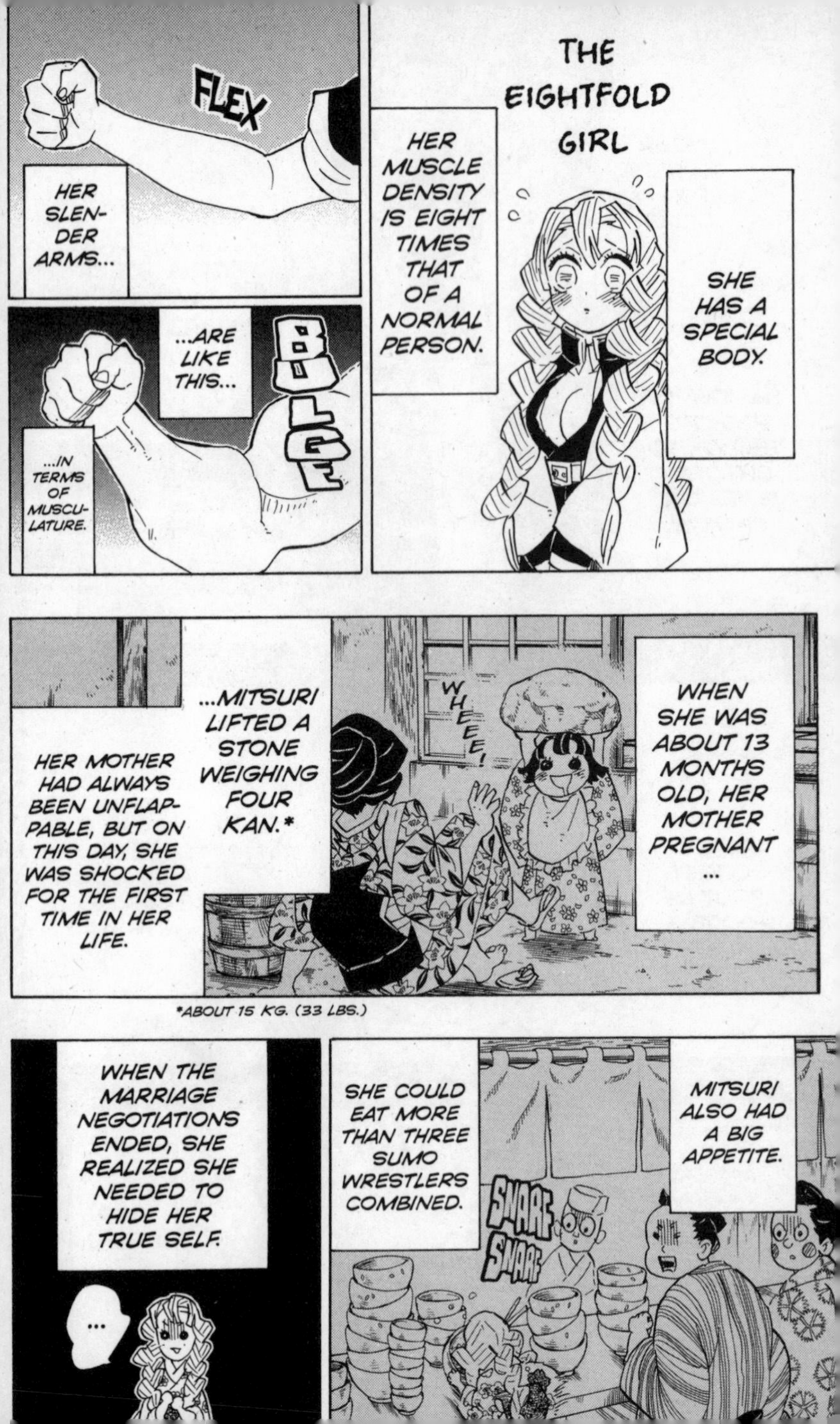
THE EIGHTFOLD GIRL
SHE HAS A SPECIAL BODY.
HER MUSCLE DENSITY IS EIGHT TIMES THAT OF A NORMAL PERSON.
FLEX
HER SLENDER ARMS...
...ARE LIKE THIS...
BULGE
...IN TERMS OF MUSCULATURE.
WHEN SHE WAS ABOUT 13 MONTHS OLD, HER MOTHER PREGNANT ...
WHEEEE!
...MITSURI LIFTED A STONE WEIGHING FOUR KAN.*
HER MOTHER HAD ALWAYS BEEN UNFLAPPABLE, BUT ON THIS DAY, SHE WAS SHOCKED FOR THE FIRST TIME IN HER LIFE.
MITSURI ALSO HAD A BIG APPETITE.
SHE COULD EAT MORE THAN THREE SUMO WRESTLERS COMBINED.
SNARF
SNARF
WHEN THE MARRIAGE NEGOTIATIONS ENDED, SHE REALIZED SHE NEEDED TO HIDE HER TRUE SELF.
...

*ABOUT 15 KG. (33 LBS.)

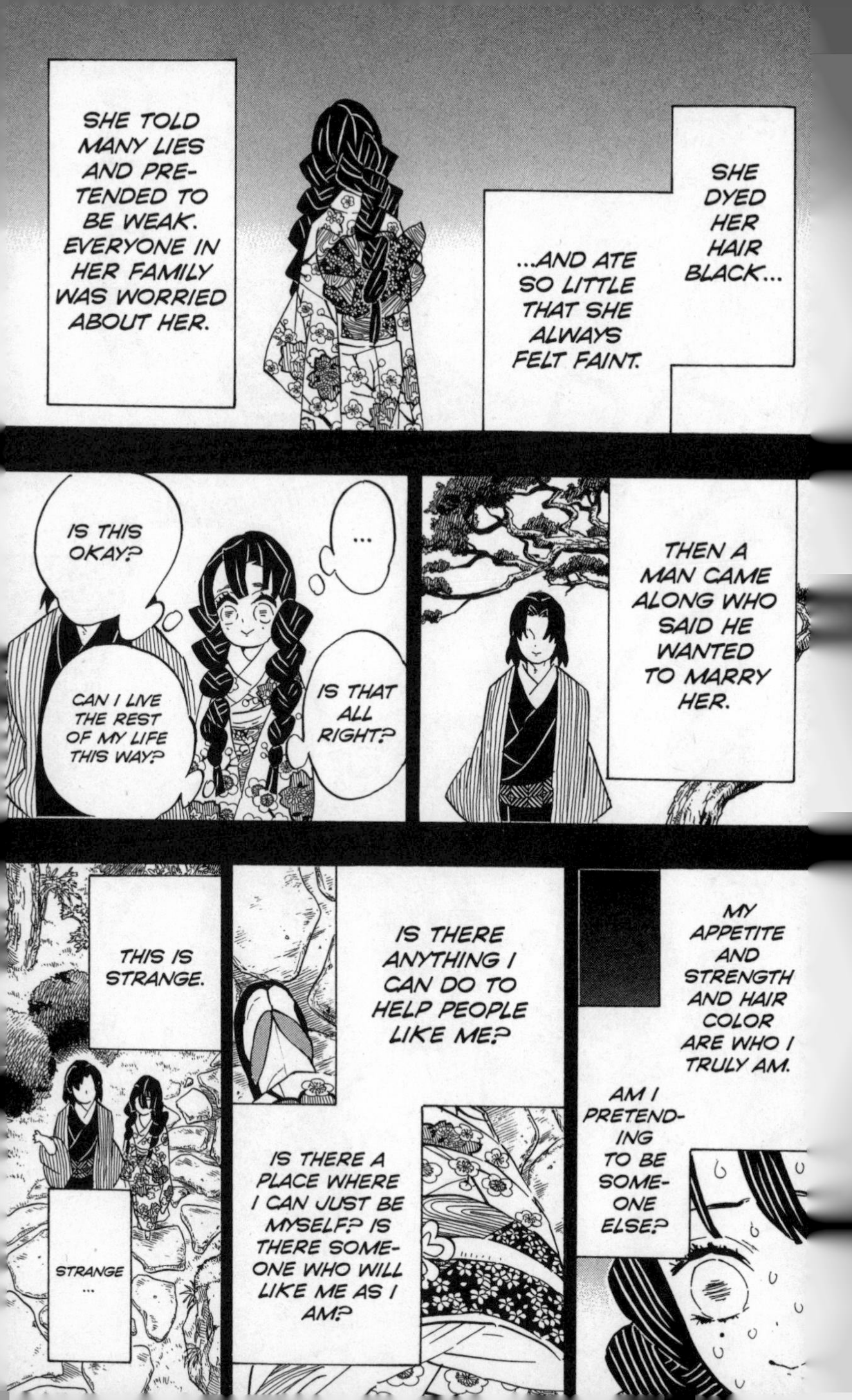

SHE DYED HER HAIR BLACK...
...AND ATE SO LITTLE THAT SHE ALWAYS FELT FAINT.
SHE TOLD MANY LIES AND PRE-TENDED TO BE WEAK. EVERYONE IN HER FAMILY WAS WORRIED ABOUT HER.
THEN A MAN CAME ALONG WHO SAID HE WANTED TO MARRY HER.
...
IS THIS OKAY?
IS THAT ALL RIGHT?
CAN I LIVE THE REST OF MY LIFE THIS WAY?
MY APPETITE AND STRENGTH AND HAIR COLOR ARE WHO I TRULY AM.
AM I PRETEND-ING TO BE SOME-ONE ELSE?
IS THERE ANYTHING I CAN DO TO HELP PEOPLE LIKE ME?
IS THERE A PLACE WHERE I CAN JUST BE MYSELF? IS THERE SOME-ONE WHO WILL LIKE ME AS I AM?
THIS IS STRANGE.
STRANGE...

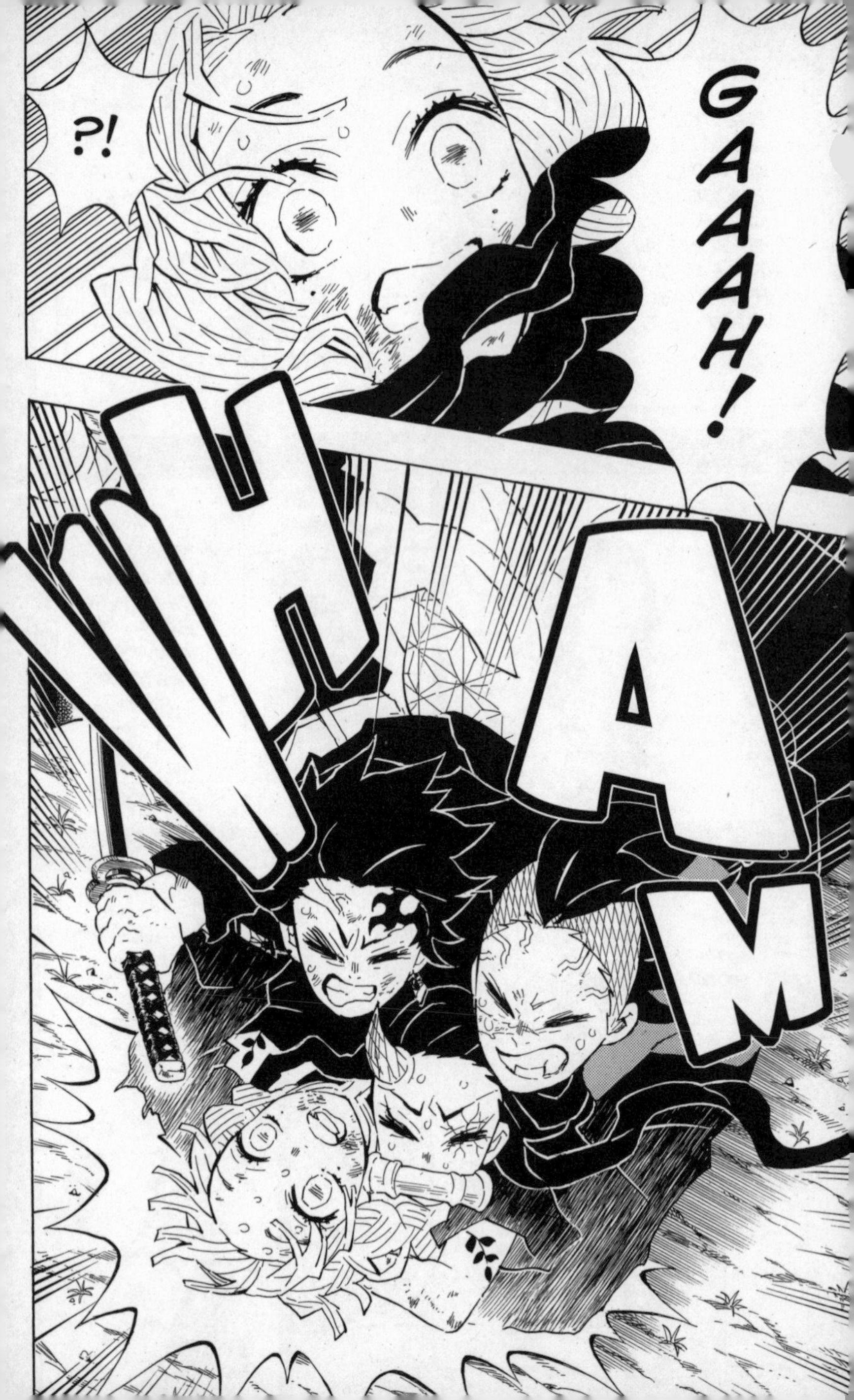
GAAAH!
?!
WHAM

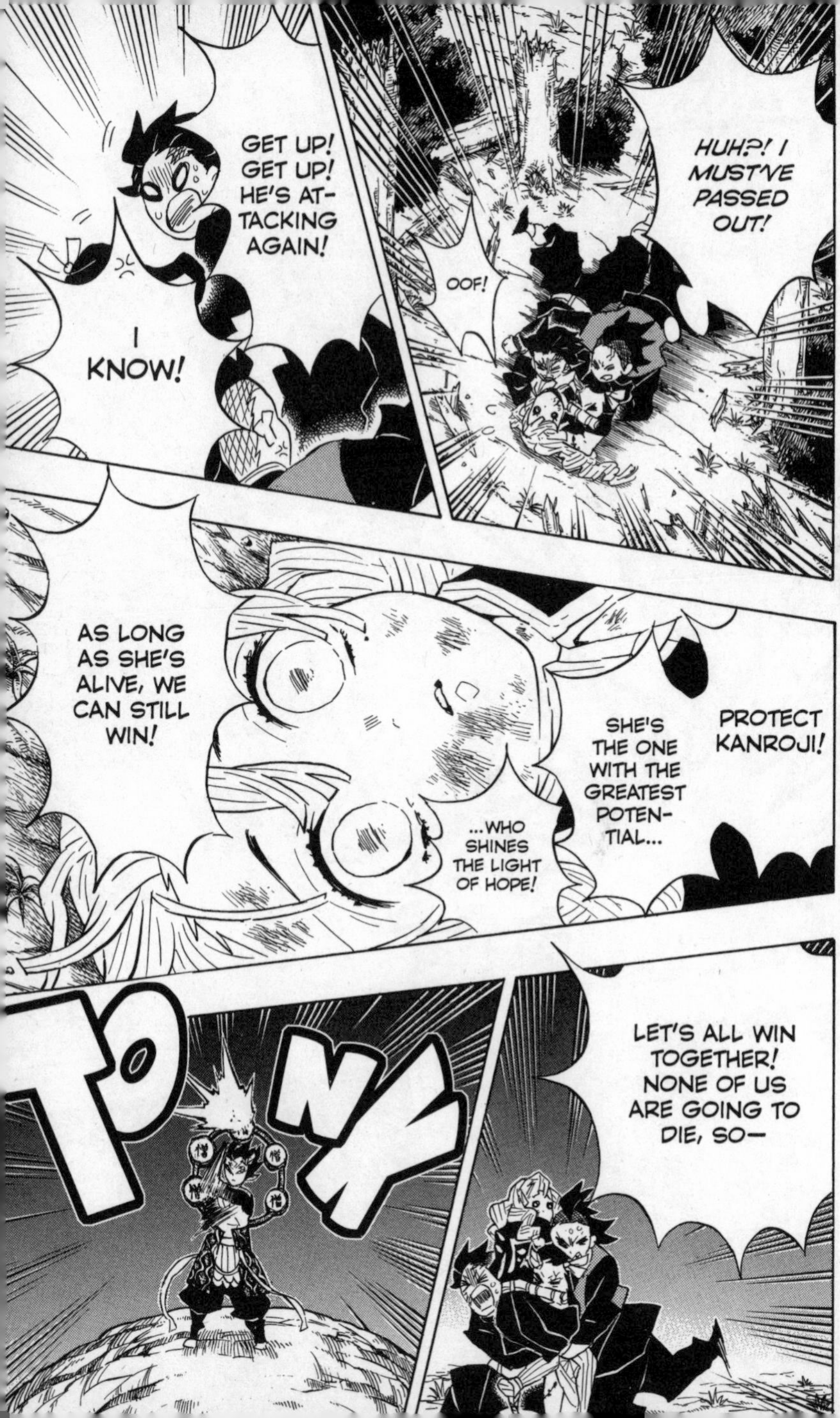
HUH?! I MUST'VE PASSED OUT!
OOF!
GET UP! GET UP! HE'S AT-TACKING AGAIN!
I KNOW!
PROTECT KANROJI!
SHE'S THE ONE WITH THE GREATEST POTEN-TIAL...
...WHO SHINES THE LIGHT OF HOPE!
AS LONG AS SHE'S ALIVE, WE CAN STILL WIN!
LET'S ALL WIN TOGETHER! NONE OF US ARE GOING TO DIE, SO—
TONK

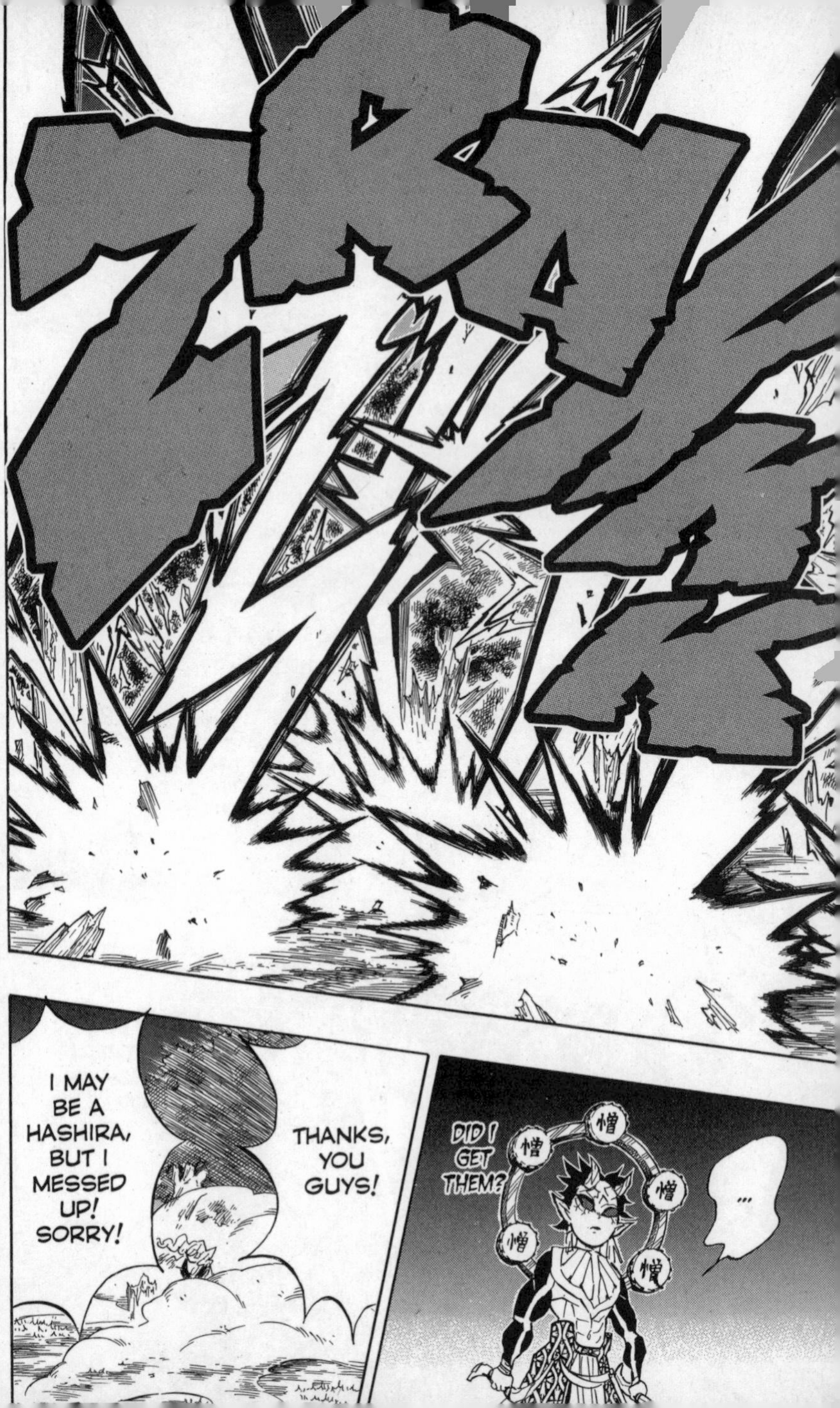
DID I GET THEM?
...
I MAY BE A HASHIRA, BUT I MESSED UP! SORRY!
THANKS, YOU GUYS!

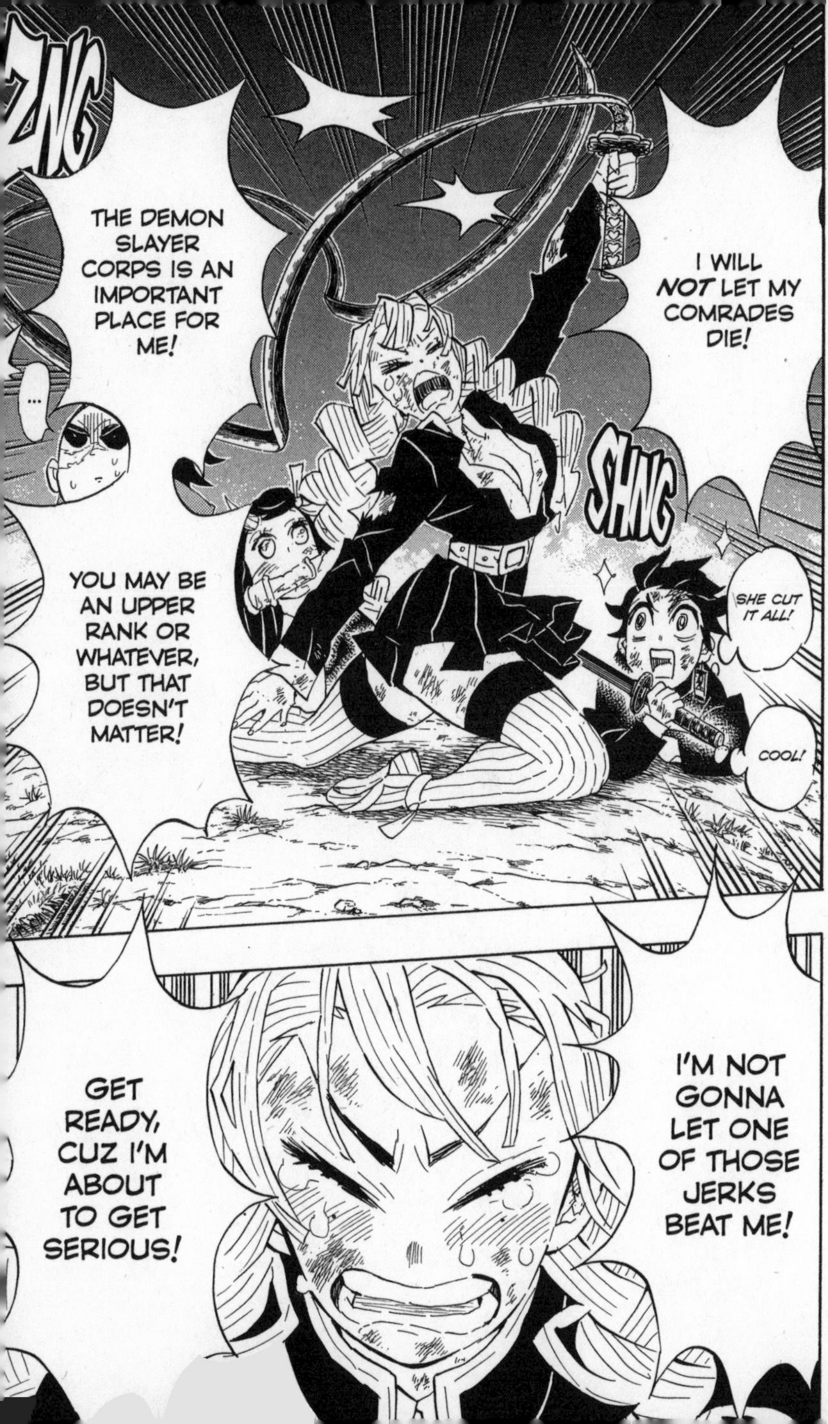
I WILL NOT LET MY COMRADES DIE!
ZNG
THE DEMON SLAYER CORPS IS AN IMPORTANT PLACE FOR ME!
...
SHNG
SHE CUT IT ALL!
COOL!
YOU MAY BE AN UPPER RANK OR WHATEVER, BUT THAT DOESN'T MATTER!
I'M NOT GONNA LET ONE OF THOSE JERKS BEAT ME!
GET READY, CUZ I'M ABOUT TO GET SERIOUS!

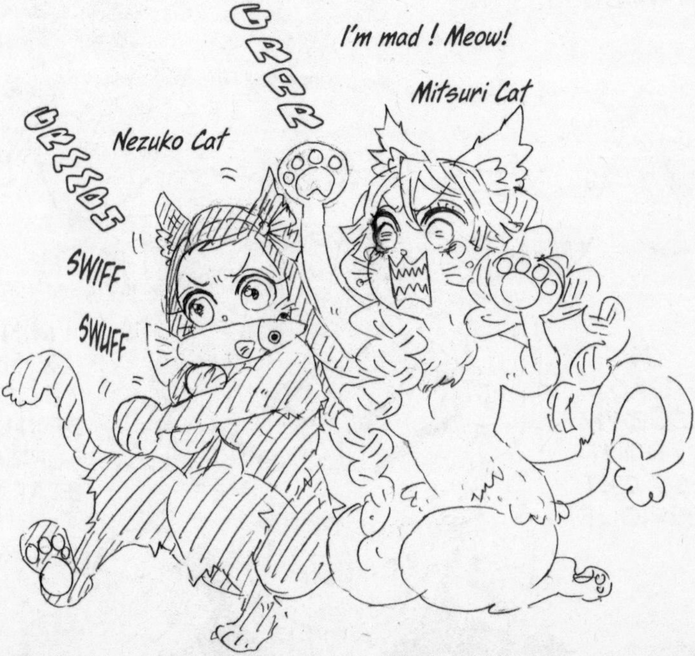
I'm mad ! Meow!
Mitsuri Cat
GRAR
Nezuko Cat
SWIFF
SWUFF

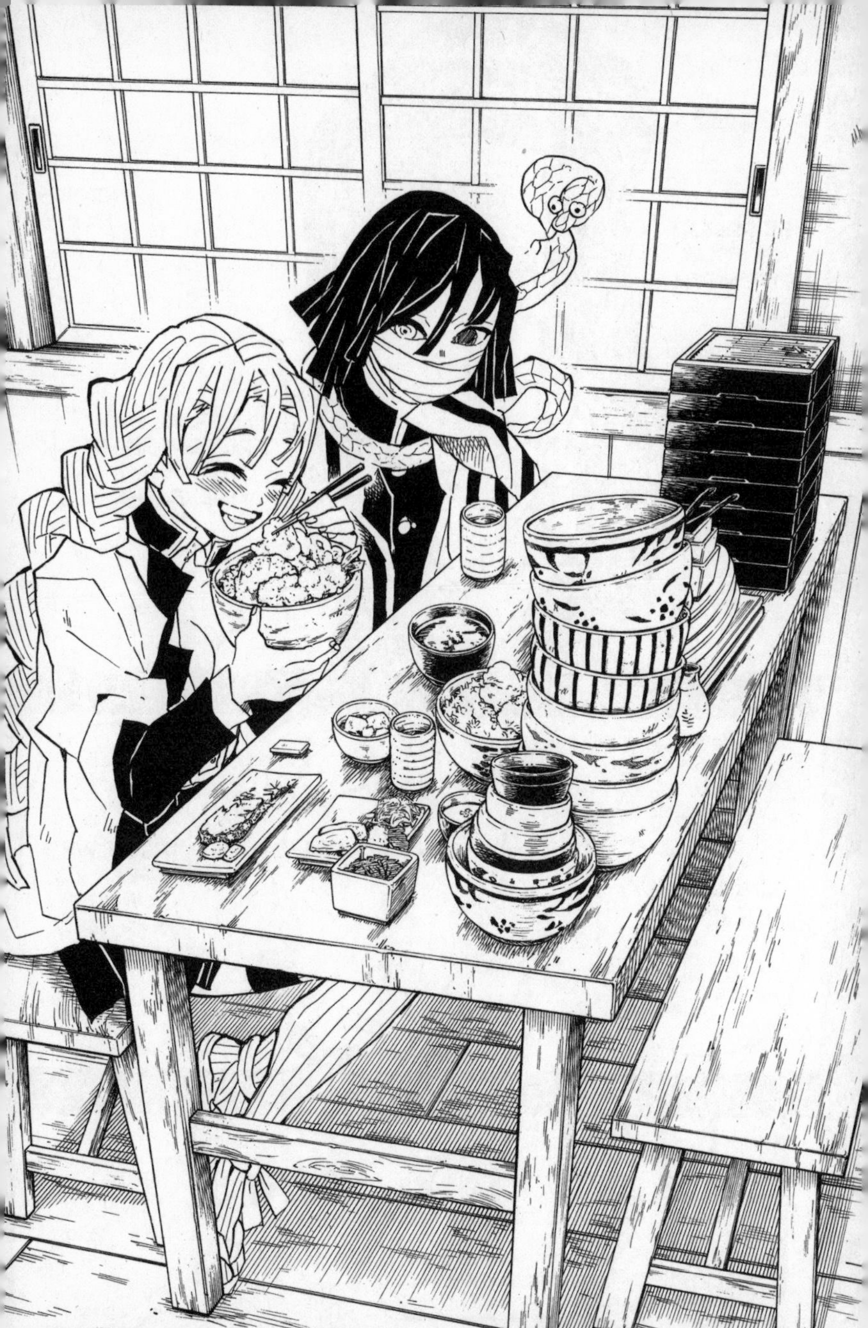

CHAPTER 124: GET IT TOGETHER, MORON!

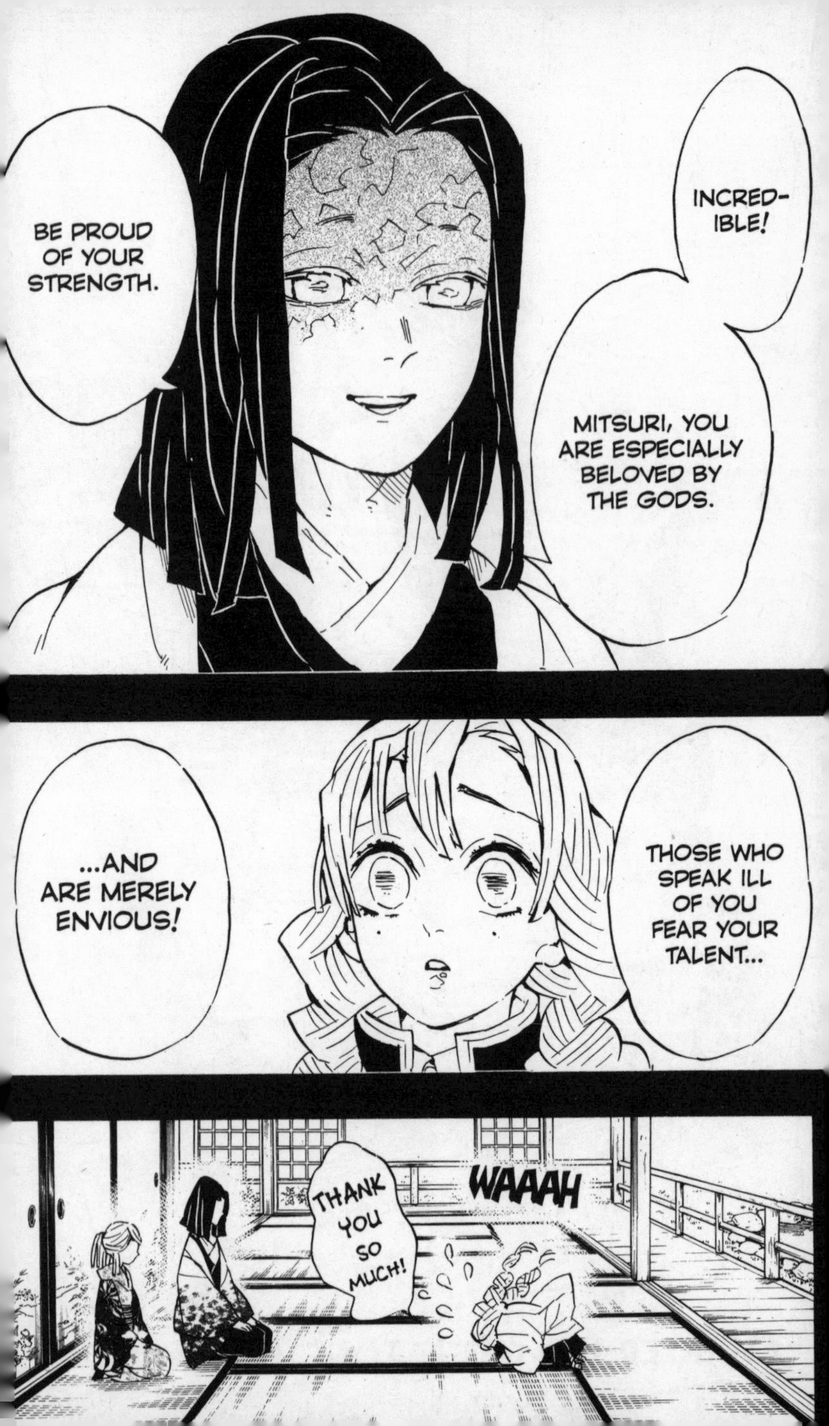
INCRED-IBLE!
MITSURI, YOU ARE ESPECIALLY BELOVED BY THE GODS.
BE PROUD OF YOUR STRENGTH.
THOSE WHO SPEAK ILL OF YOU FEAR YOUR TALENT...
...AND ARE MERELY ENVIOUS!
WAAAH
THANK YOU SO MUCH!

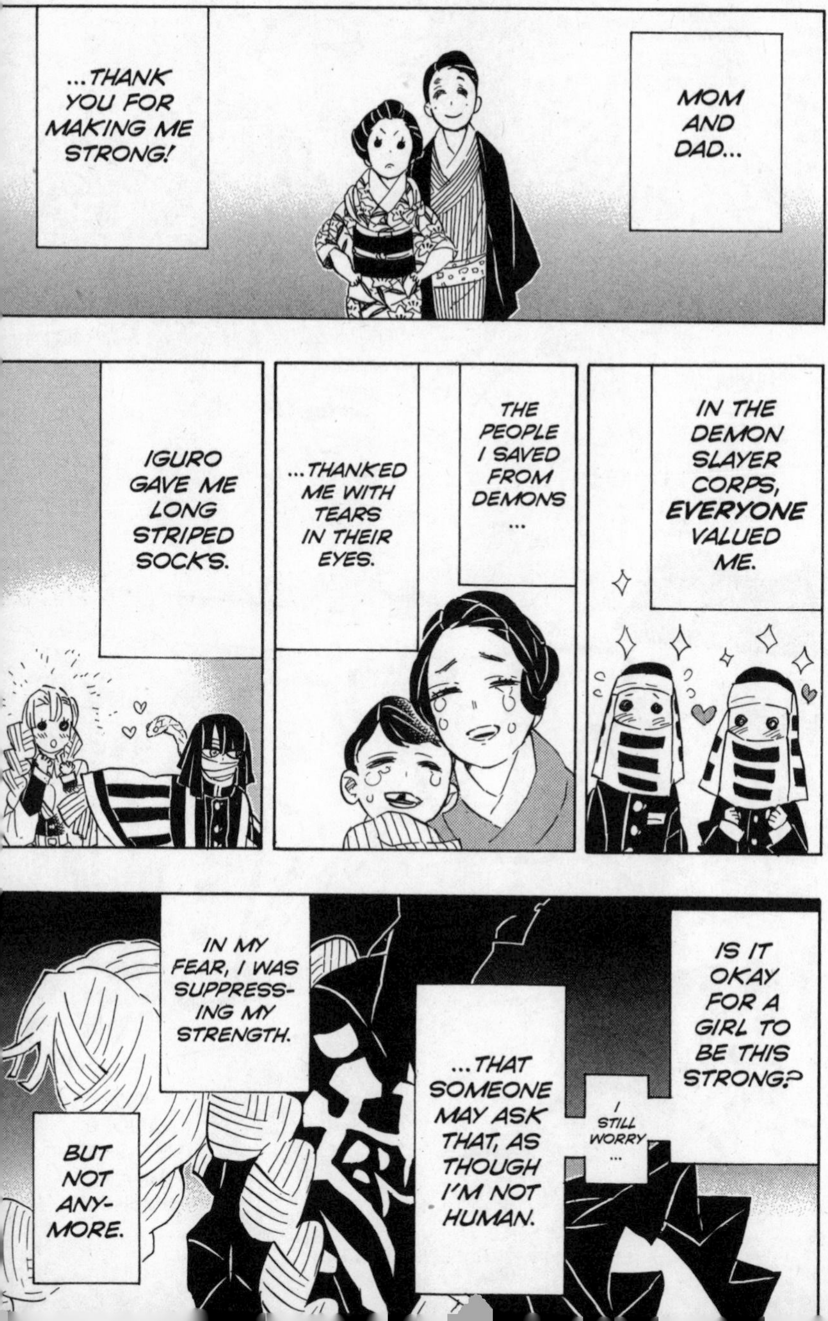
MOM AND DAD...
...THANK YOU FOR MAKING ME STRONG!
IN THE DEMON SLAYER CORPS, EVERYONE VALUED ME.
THE PEOPLE I SAVED FROM DEMONS ...
...THANKED ME WITH TEARS IN THEIR EYES.
IGURO GAVE ME LONG STRIPED SOCKS.
IS IT OKAY FOR A GIRL TO BE THIS STRONG?
I STILL WORRY ...
...THAT SOMEONE MAY ASK THAT, AS THOUGH I'M NOT HUMAN.
IN MY FEAR, I WAS SUPPRESS-ING MY STRENGTH.
BUT NOT ANY-MORE.

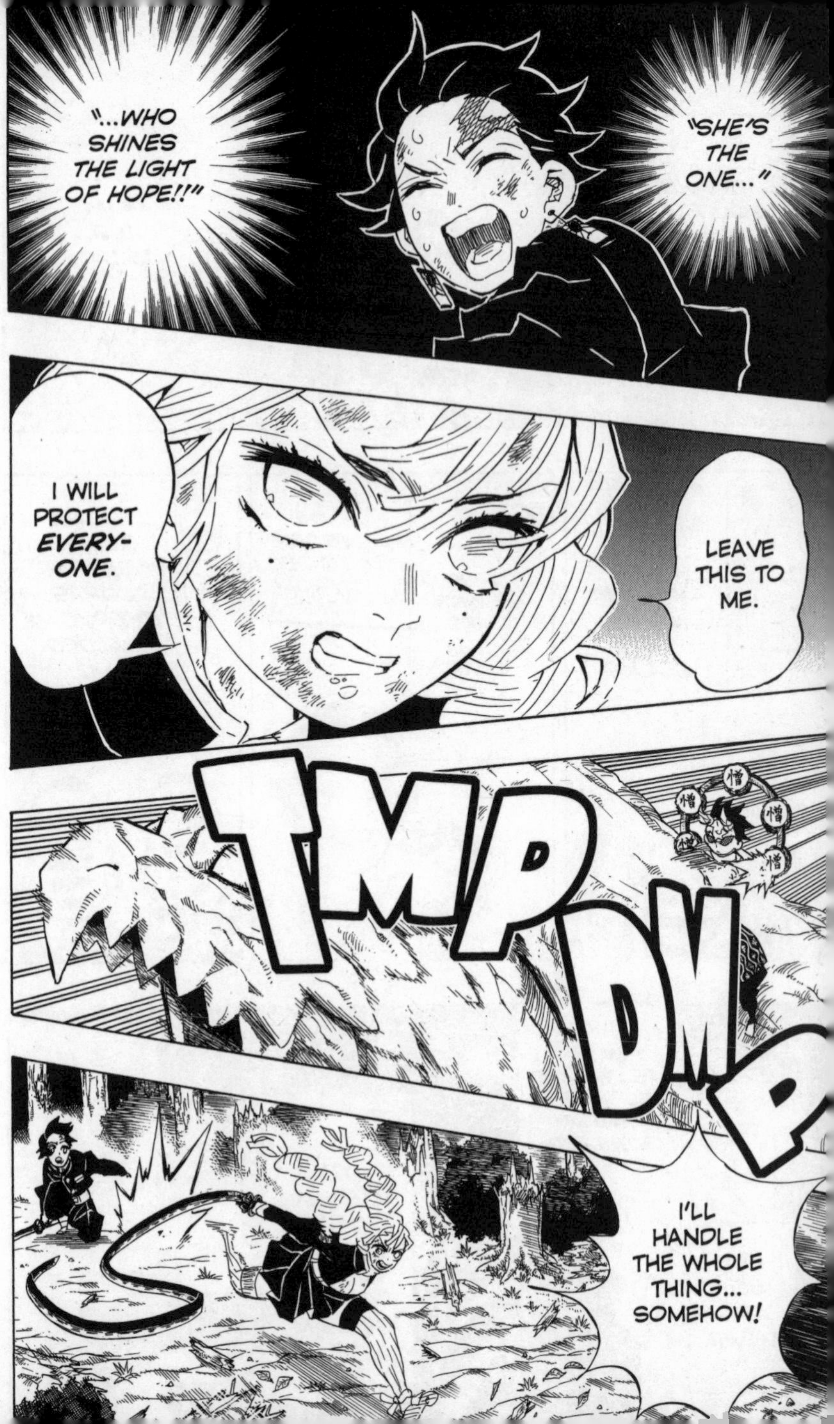
"SHE'S THE ONE..."
"...WHO SHINES THE LIGHT OF HOPE!!"
LEAVE THIS TO ME.
I WILL PROTECT *EVERY-ONE.*
TMP
DMP
I'LL HANDLE THE WHOLE THING... SOMEHOW!

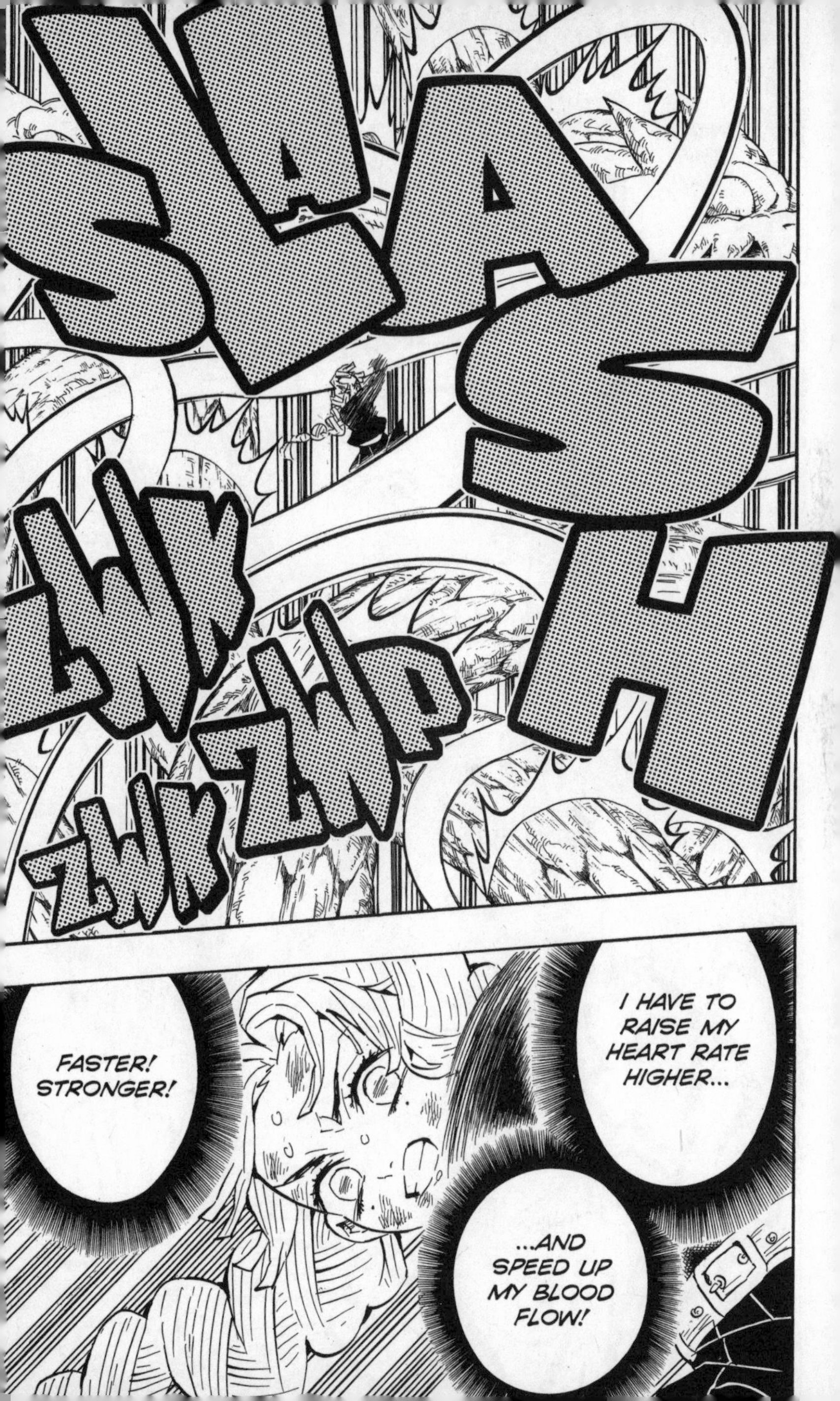
SLASH
ZWIP
ZWIK
ZWIK
I HAVE TO RAISE MY HEART RATE HIGHER...
...AND SPEED UP MY BLOOD FLOW!
FASTER! STRONGER!

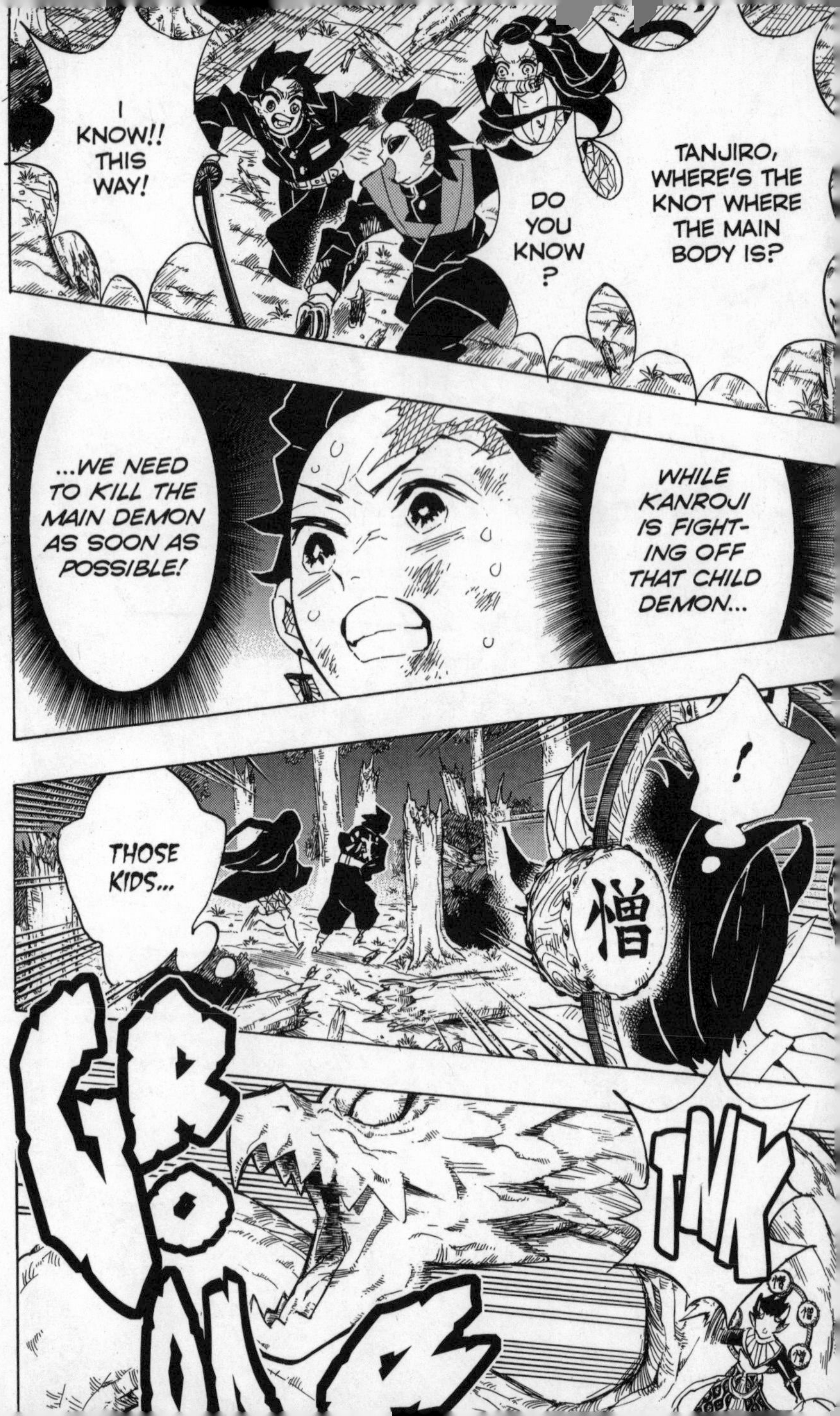
TANJIRO, WHERE'S THE KNOT WHERE THE MAIN BODY IS?
DO YOU KNOW?
I KNOW!! THIS WAY!
WHILE KANROJI IS FIGHTING OFF THAT CHILD DEMON...
...WE NEED TO KILL THE MAIN DEMON AS SOON AS POSSIBLE!
!
THOSE KIDS...
TNK

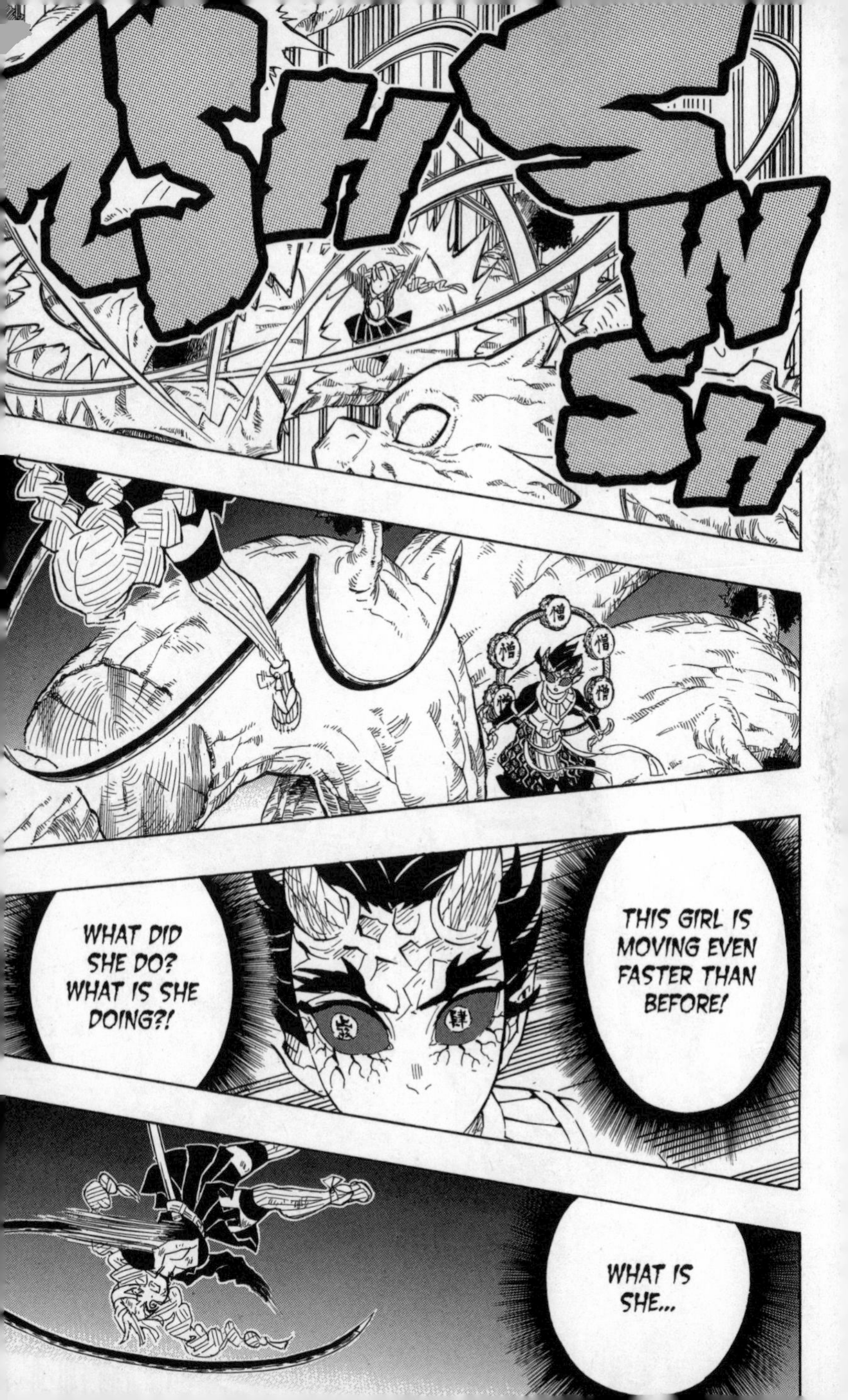
SH
SWSH
THIS GIRL IS MOVING EVEN FASTER THAN BEFORE!
WHAT DID SHE DO? WHAT IS SHE DOING?!
WHAT IS SHE...

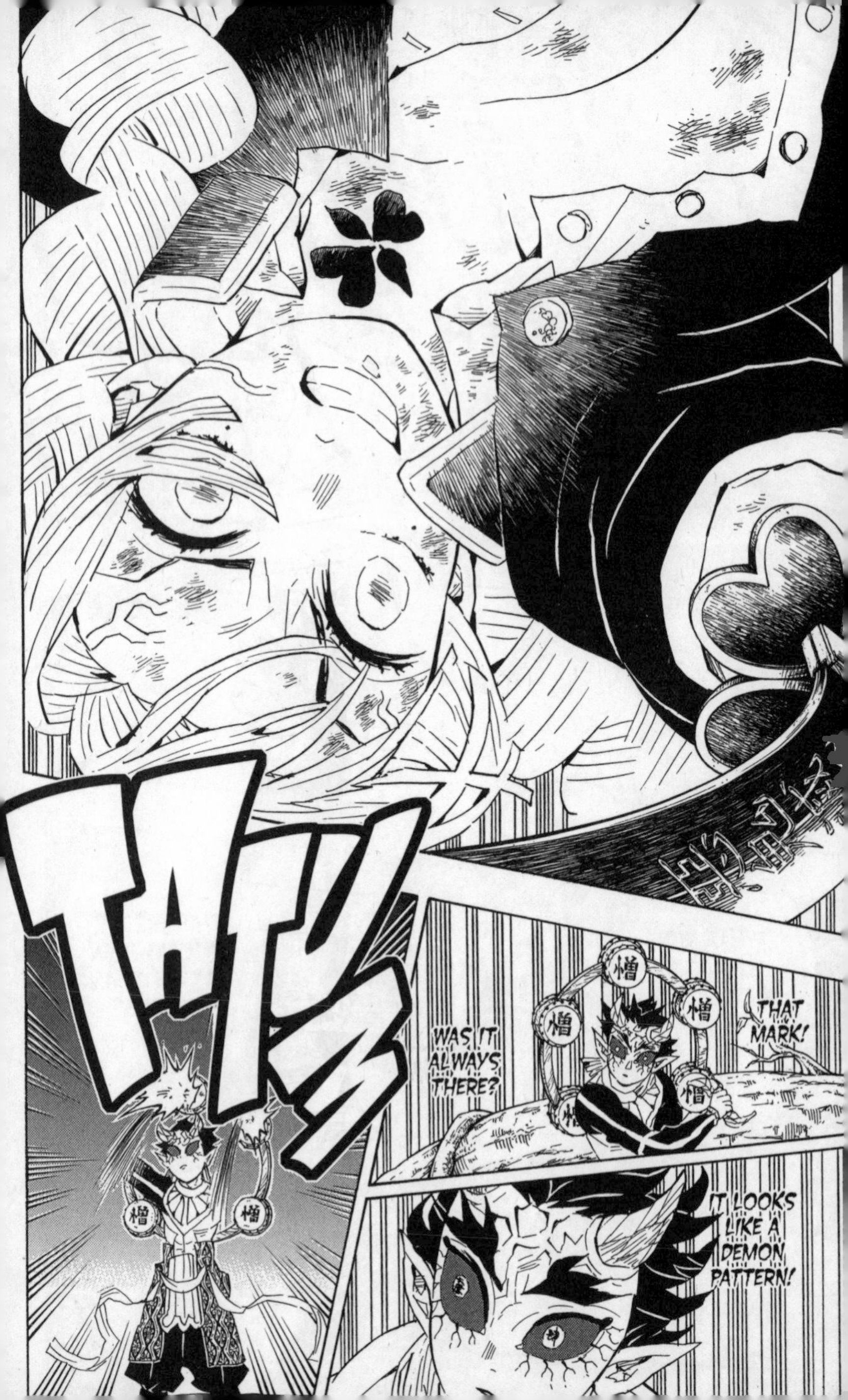
THAT MARK!
WAS IT ALWAYS THERE?
IT LOOKS LIKE A DEMON PATTERN!

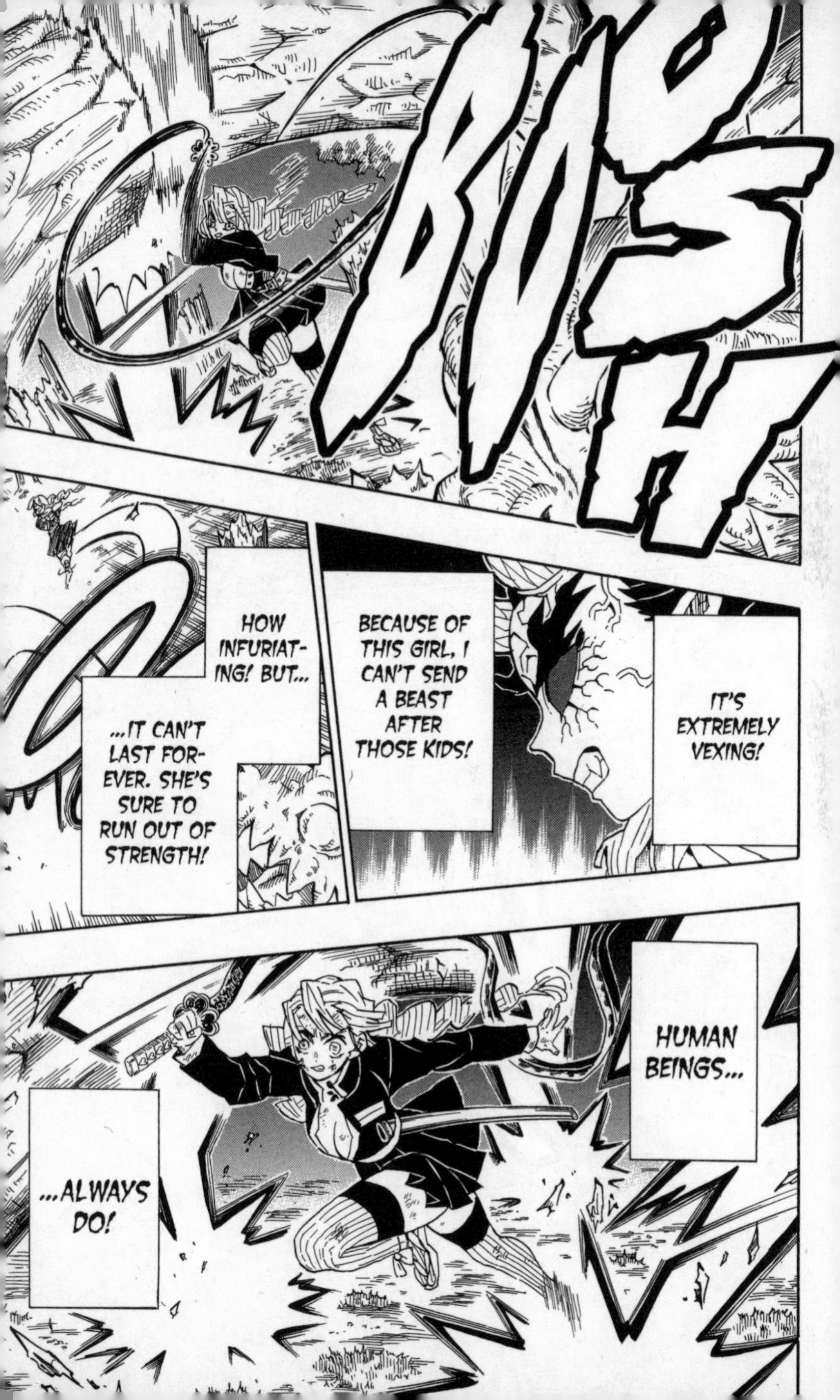

IT'S EXTREMELY VEXING!
BECAUSE OF THIS GIRL, I CAN'T SEND A BEAST AFTER THOSE KIDS!
HOW INFURIAT-ING! BUT...
...IT CAN'T LAST FOR-EVER. SHE'S SURE TO RUN OUT OF STRENGTH!
HUMAN BEINGS...
...ALWAYS DO!

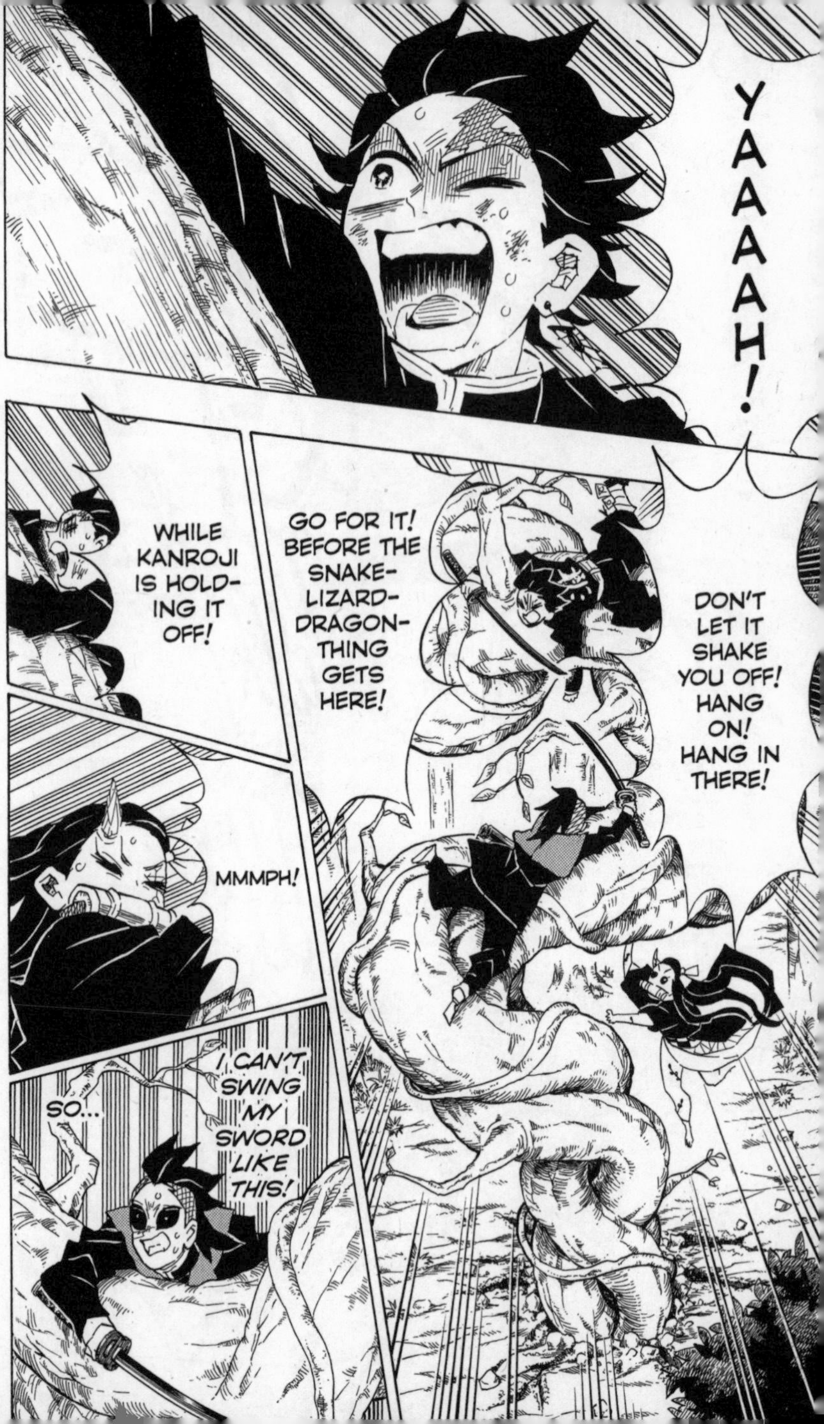
YAAAAH!
DON'T LET IT SHAKE YOU OFF! HANG ON! HANG IN THERE!
GO FOR IT! BEFORE THE SNAKE-LIZARD-DRAGON-THING GETS HERE!
WHILE KANROJI IS HOLDING IT OFF!
MMMPH!
I CAN'T SWING MY SWORD LIKE THIS!
SO...

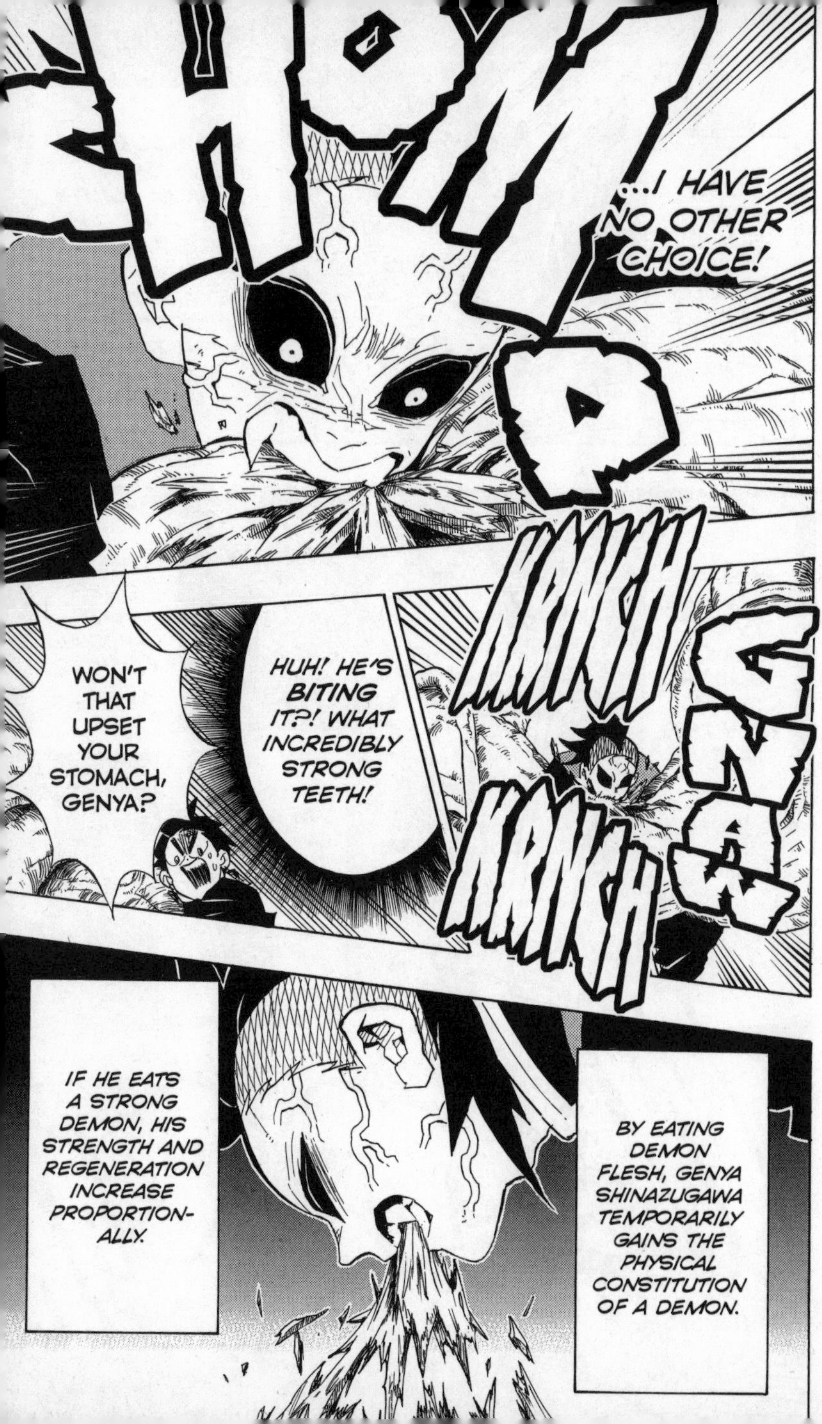

...I HAVE NO OTHER CHOICE!
KRNCH
KRNCH
HUH! HE'S BITING IT?! WHAT INCREDIBLY STRONG TEETH!
WON'T THAT UPSET YOUR STOMACH, GENYA?
BY EATING DEMON FLESH, GENYA SHINAZUGAWA TEMPORARILY GAINS THE PHYSICAL CONSTITUTION OF A DEMON.
IF HE EATS A STRONG DEMON, HIS STRENGTH AND REGENERATION INCREASE PROPORTIONALLY.

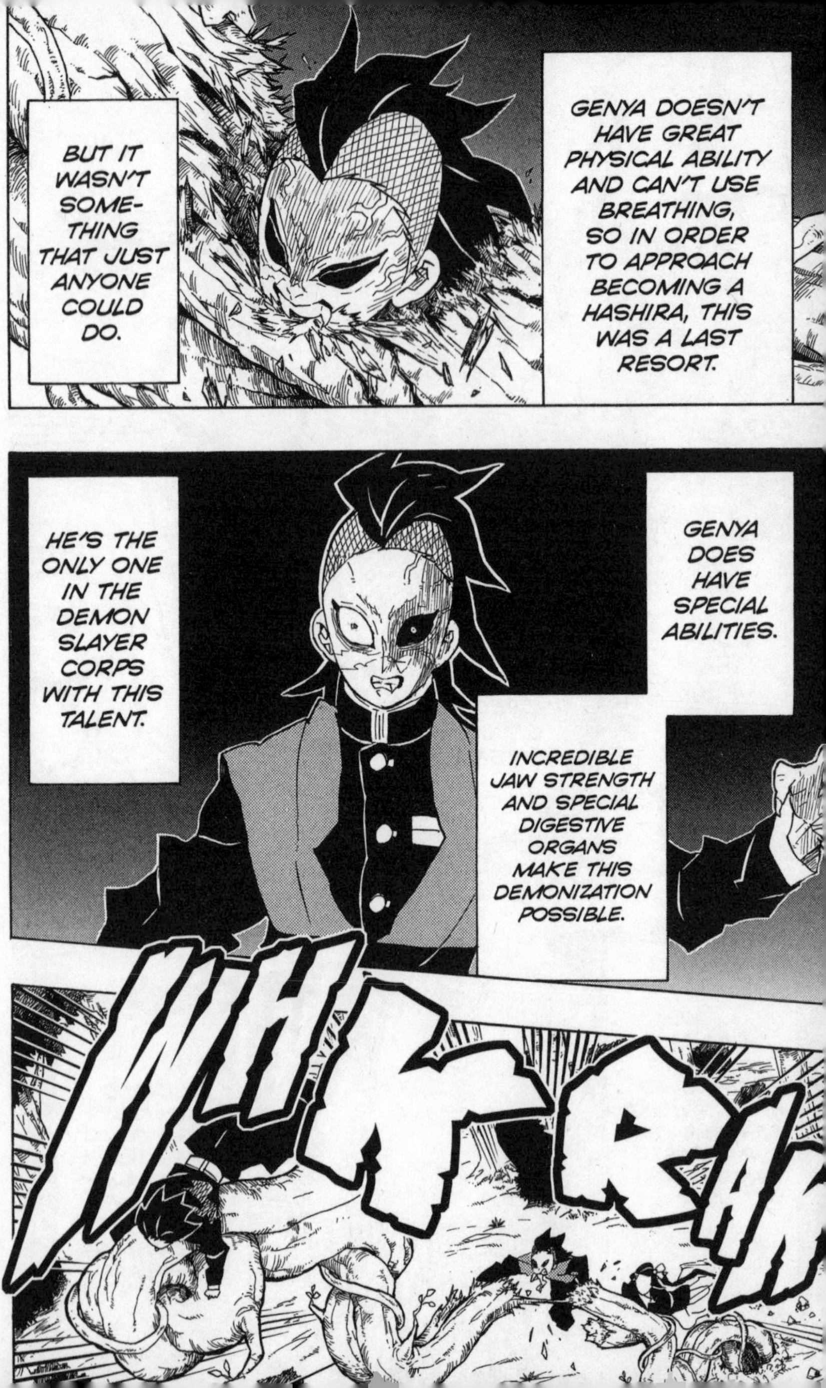
GENYA DOESN'T HAVE GREAT PHYSICAL ABILITY AND CAN'T USE BREATHING, SO IN ORDER TO APPROACH BECOMING A HASHIRA, THIS WAS A LAST RESORT.
BUT IT WASN'T SOME-THING THAT JUST ANYONE COULD DO.
GENYA DOES HAVE SPECIAL ABILITIES.
INCREDIBLE JAW STRENGTH AND SPECIAL DIGESTIVE ORGANS MAKE THIS DEMONIZATION POSSIBLE.
HE'S THE ONLY ONE IN THE DEMON SLAYER CORPS WITH THIS TALENT.

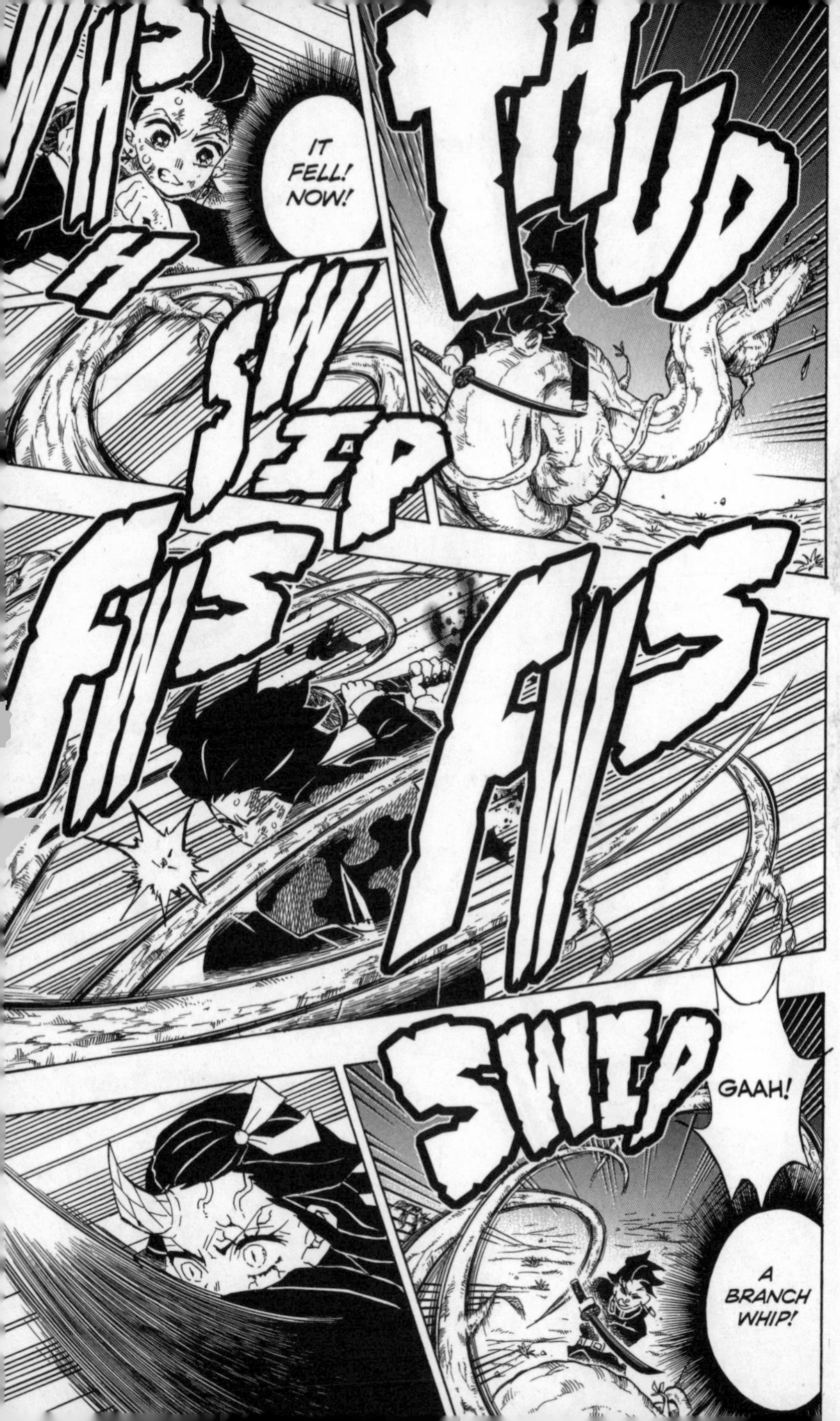
THUD
IT FELL! NOW!
SWIP
GAAH!
A BRANCH WHIP!

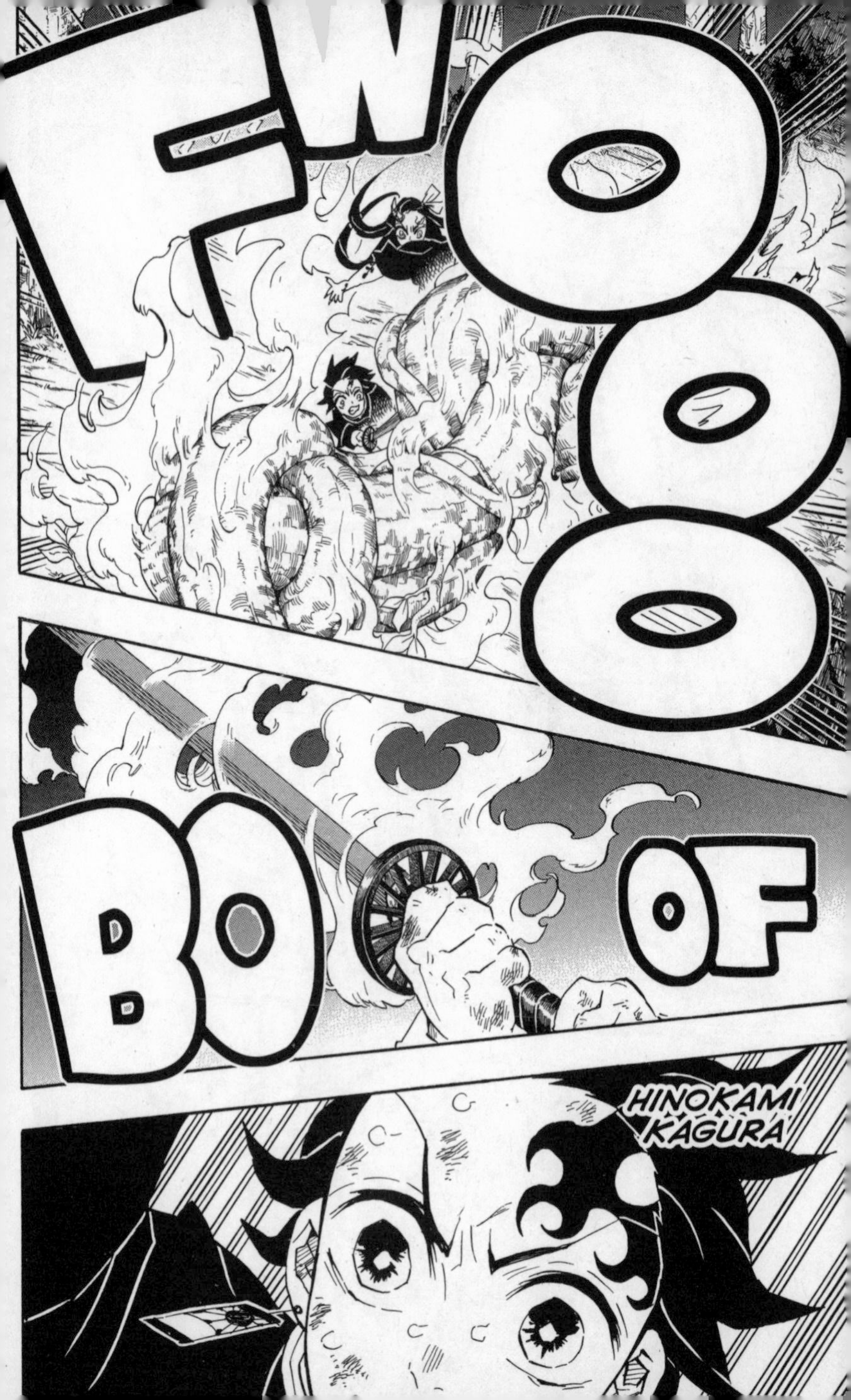
FWOOOO
BOOF
HINOKAMI KAGURA

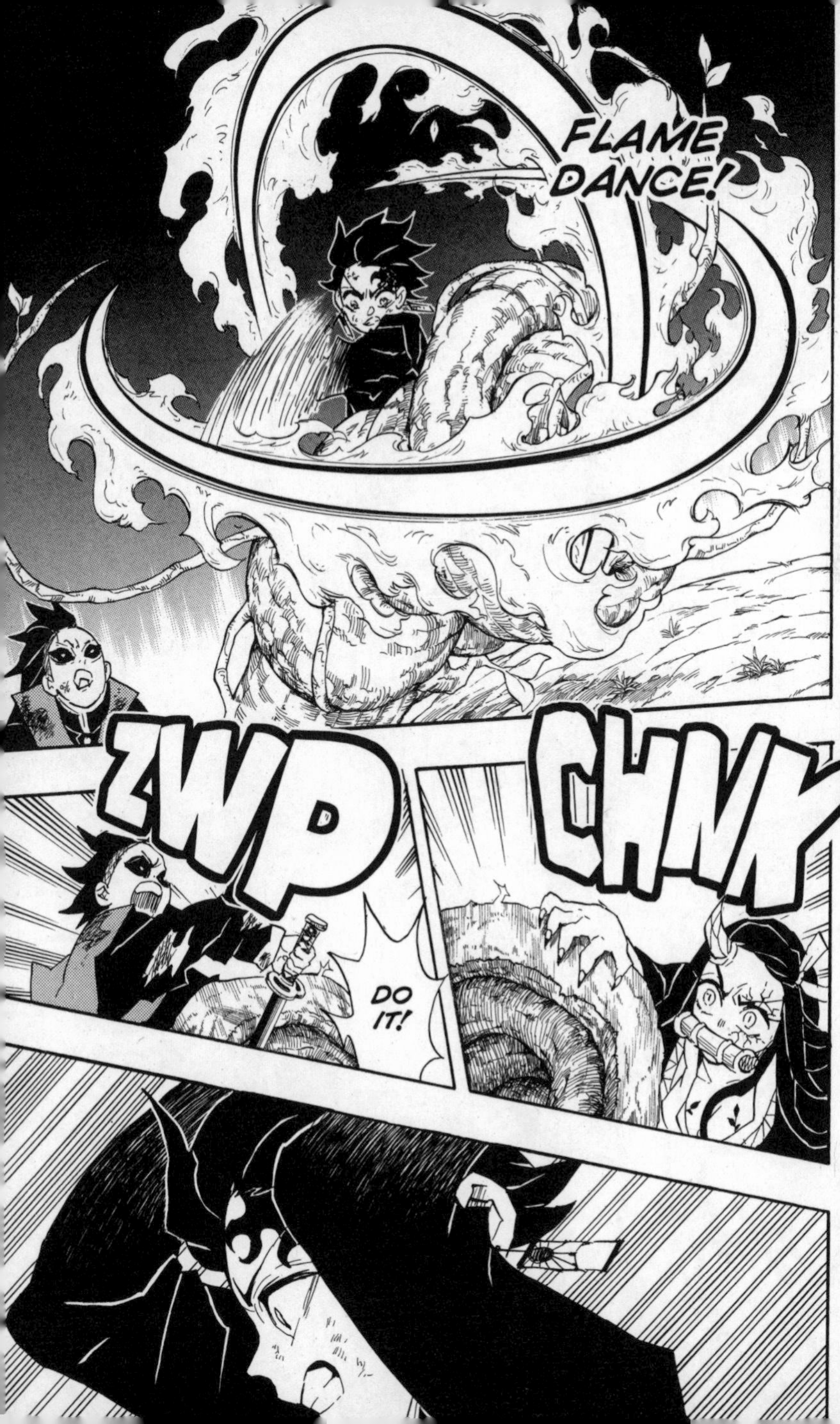
FLAME DANCE!
CHNK
ZWP
DO IT!

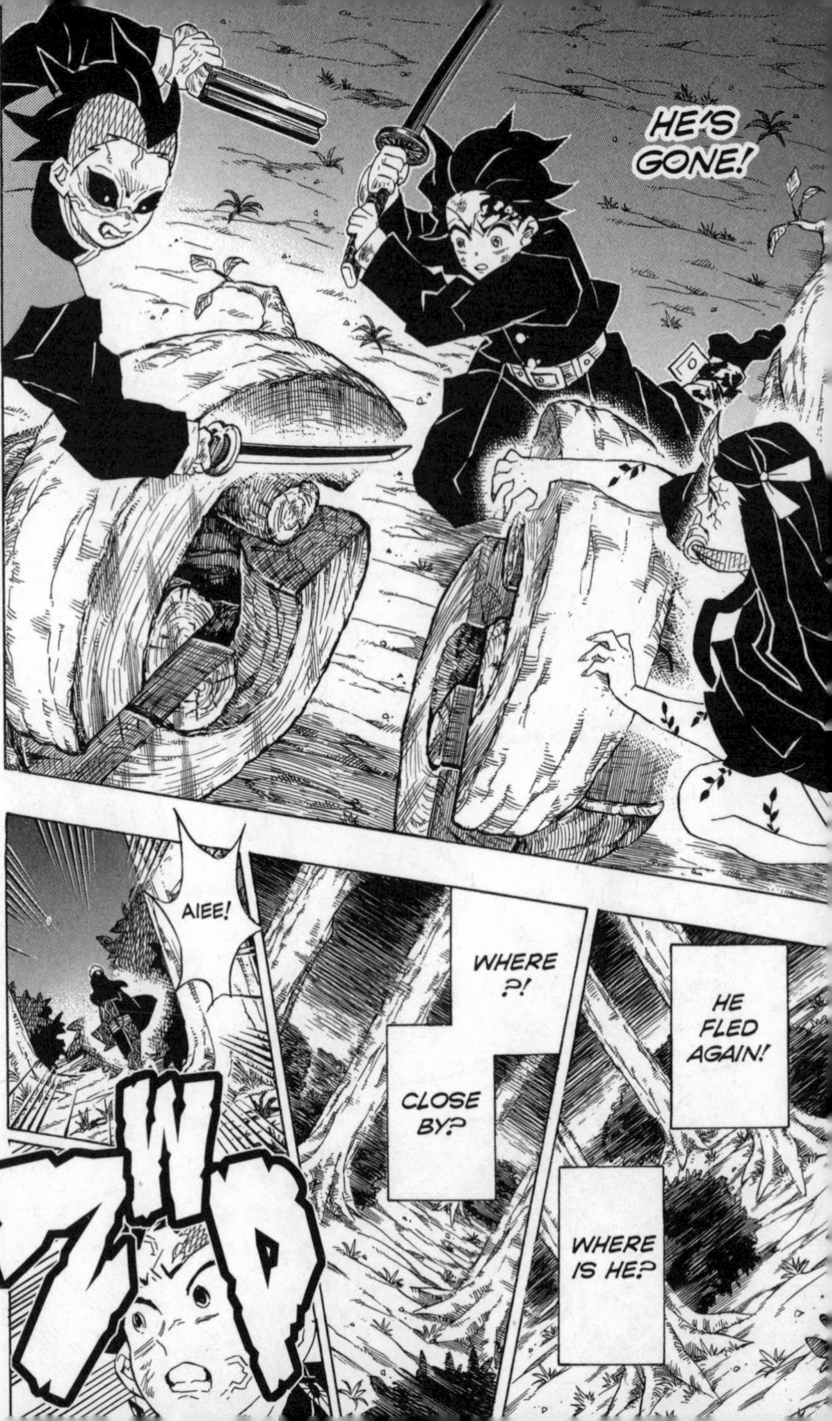
HE'S GONE!
HE FLED AGAIN!
WHERE IS HE?
WHERE ?!
CLOSE BY?
AIEE!

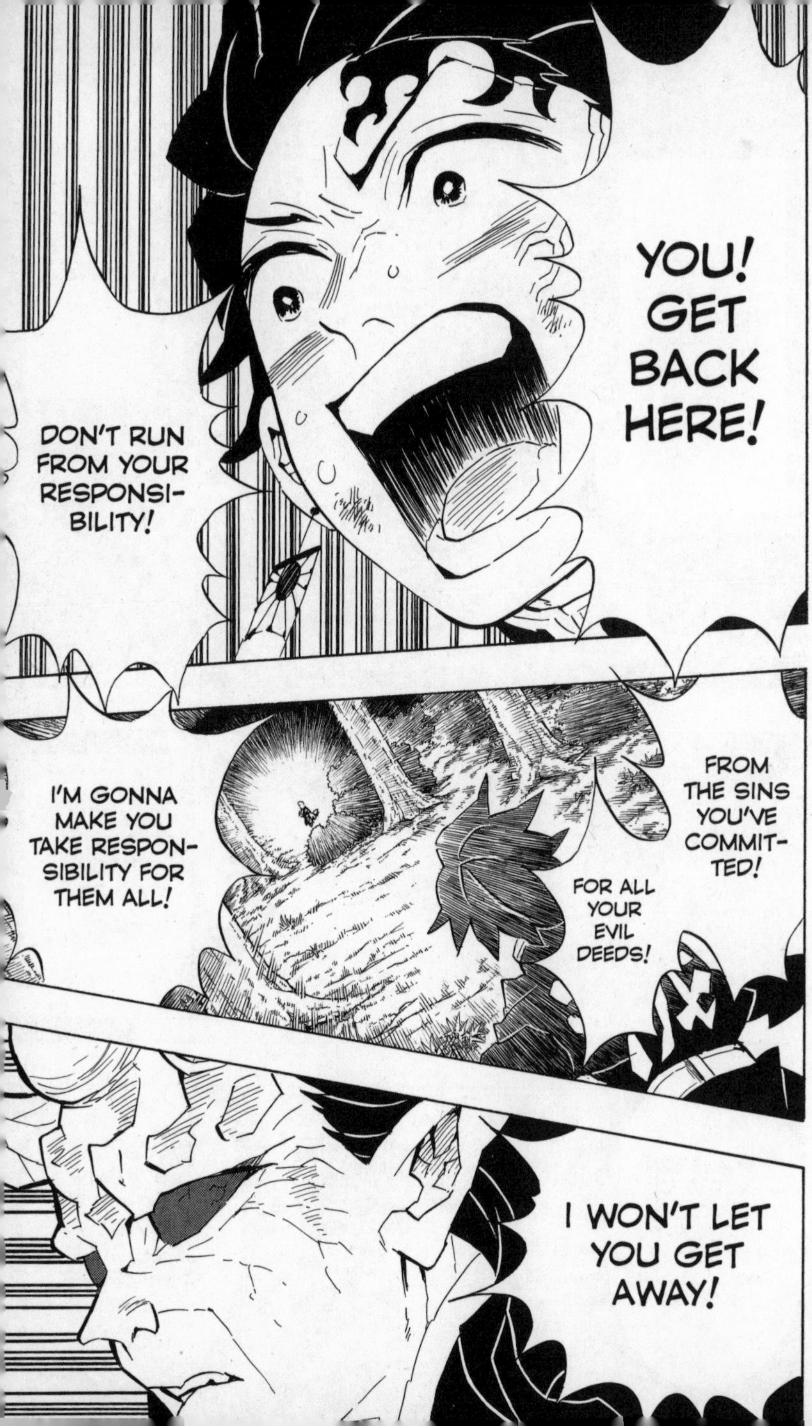
YOU! GET BACK HERE!
DON'T RUN FROM YOUR RESPONSI-BILITY!
FROM THE SINS YOU'VE COMMIT-TED!
FOR ALL YOUR EVIL DEEDS!
I'M GONNA MAKE YOU TAKE RESPON-SIBILITY FOR THEM ALL!
I WON'T LET YOU GET AWAY!

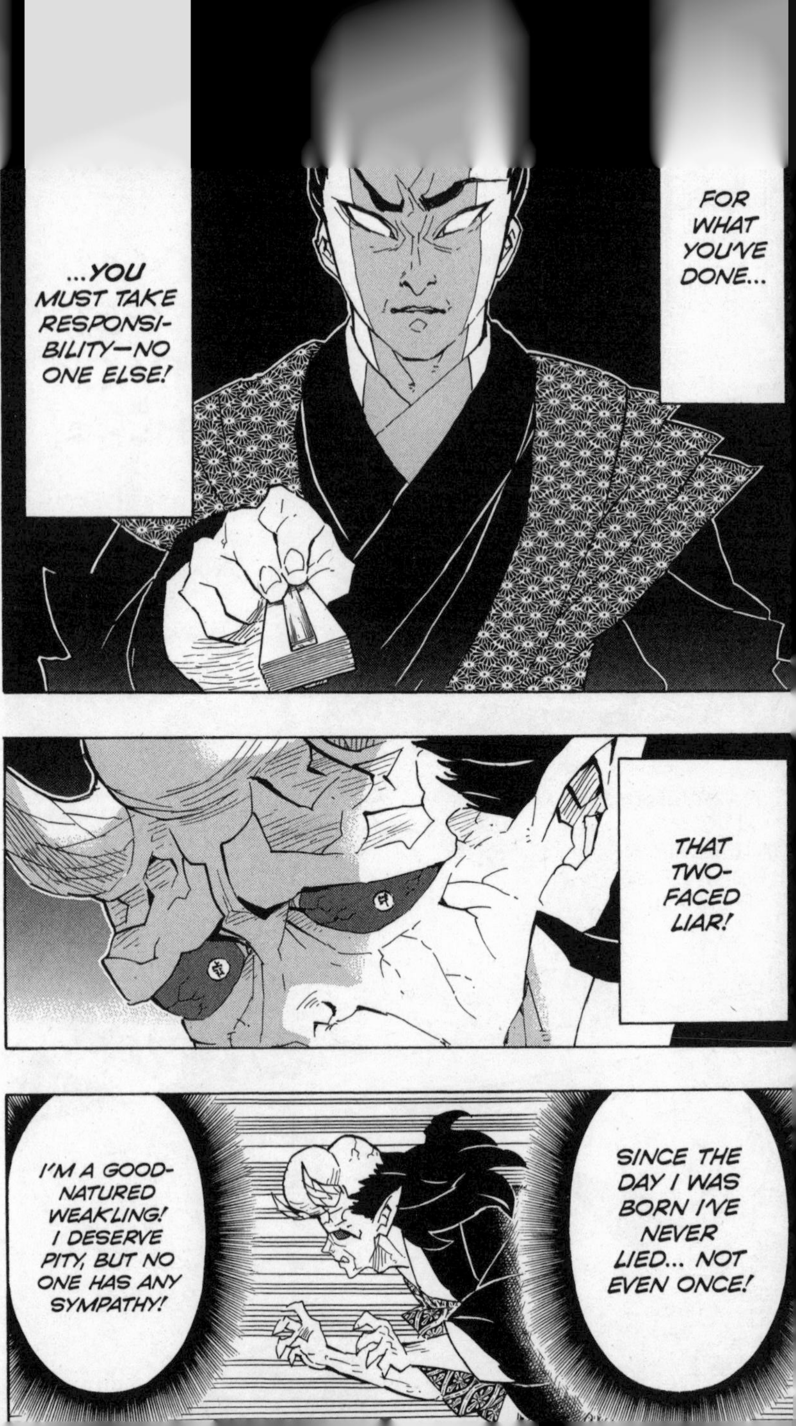
FOR WHAT YOU'VE DONE...
...YOU MUST TAKE RESPONSI-BILITY—NO ONE ELSE!
THAT TWO-FACED LIAR!
SINCE THE DAY I WAS BORN I'VE NEVER LIED... NOT EVEN ONCE!
I'M A GOOD-NATURED WEAKLING! I DESERVE PITY, BUT NO ONE HAS ANY SYMPATHY!

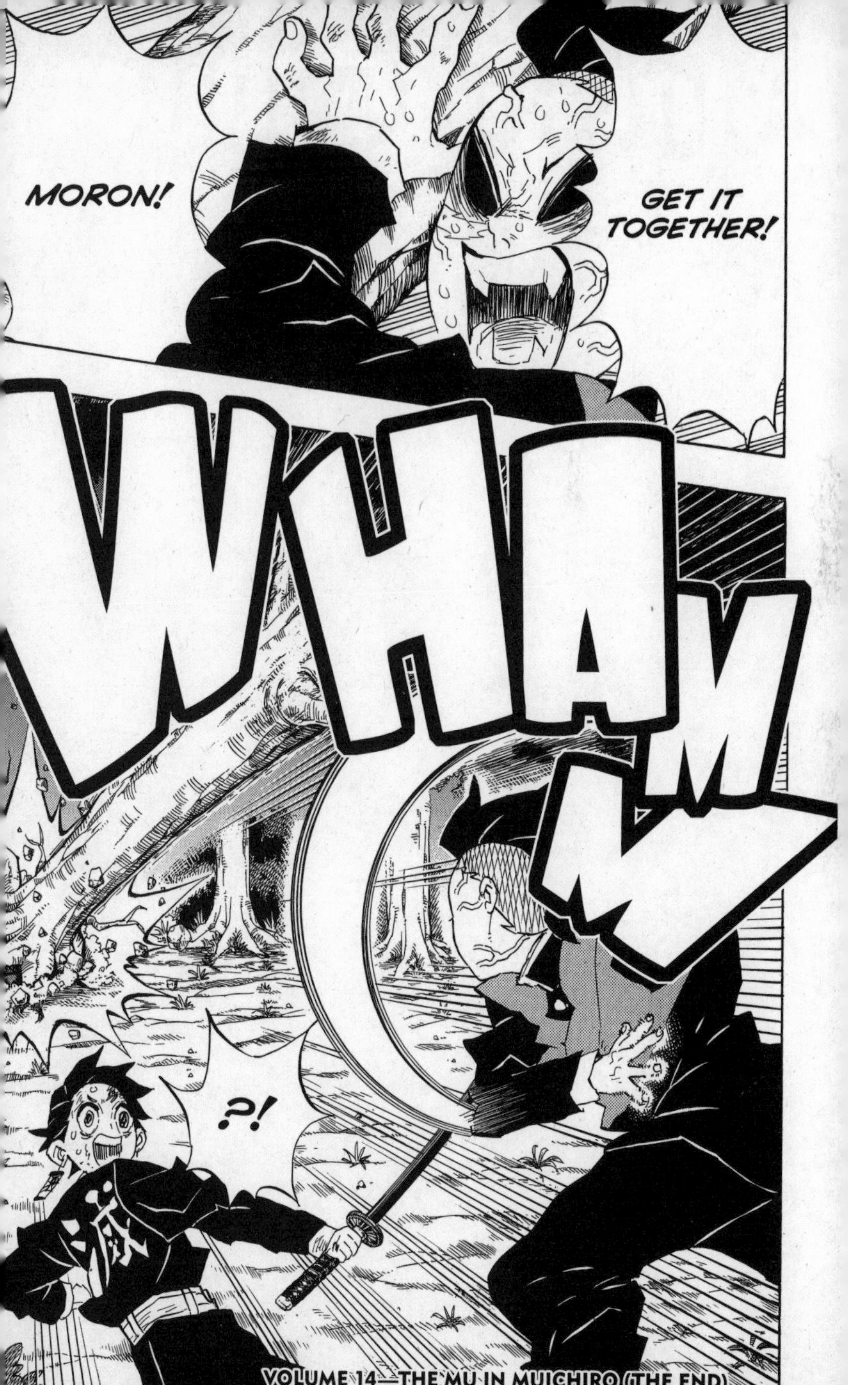
GET IT TOGETHER!
MORON!
WHAM
?!

VOLUME 14—THE MU IN MUICHIRO (THE END)

Ruby, Weiss, Blake and Yang are students at Beacon Academy, learning to protect the world of Remnant from the fearsome Grimm!

RWBY

MANGA BY **Shirow Miwa**

BASED ON THE ROOSTER TEETH SERIES
CREATED BY **Monty Oum**

RATED
T
TEEN

VIZ
viz.com

YOU'RE READING THE
WRONG WAY!

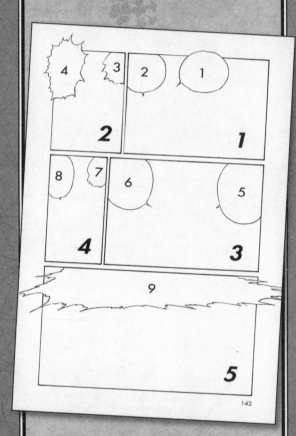

DEMON SLAYER: KIMETSU NO YAIBA
reads from right to left, starting in the
upper-right corner. Japanese is read from
right to left, meaning that action, sound
effects and word-balloon order are completely reversed from English order.